THE STRANGE CAREERS OF THE JIM CROW NORTH

The Strange Careers of the Jim Crow North

Segregation and Struggle outside of the South

Edited by
Brian Purnell *and* Jeanne Theoharis,
with Komozi Woodard

NEW YORK UNIVERSITY PRESS
New York

NEW YORK UNIVERSITY PRESS
New York
www.nyupress.org
© 2019 by New York University

References to Internet websites (URLs) were accurate at the time of writing. Neither the author nor New York University Press is responsible for URLs that may have expired or changed since the manuscript was prepared.

Library of Congress Cataloging-in-Publication Data
Names: Purnell, Brian, 1978– editor. | Theoharis, Jeanne, editor. | Woodard, Komozi, editor.
Title: The strange careers of the Jim Crow North : segregation and struggle outside of the South / edited by Brian Purnell and Jeanne Theoharis, with Komozi Woodard.
Description: New York : New York University Press, [2019] | Includes bibliographical references and index.
Identifiers: LCCN 2018037657| ISBN 9781479801312 (cl : alk. paper) | ISBN 9781479820337 (pb : alk. paper)
Subjects: LCSH: African Americans—Civil rights—History—20th century. | Civil rights movements—United States—History—20th century. | African Americans—Segregation—History—20th century. | Racism—United States—History—20th century. | United States—Race relations—History—20th century. | Northeastern States—Race relations—History—20th century. | Middle West—Race relations—History—20th century. | West (U.S.)—Race relations—History—20th century.
Classification: LCC E185.61 .S9143 2019 | DDC 323.1196/0730904—dc23
LC record available at https://urldefense.proofpoint.com/v2/url?u=https-3A__lccn.loc.gov_2018037657&d=DwIFAg&c=slrrB7dE8n7gBJbeOog-IQ&r=gT953V3c8BdcJV4pugGaWue Y1IXCnXKbUfEC8Smo3jI8m=OM6f_RGB6AFJbX7ZQnlKZG-viPbauFZSSFMX8oxJF_k&s=1_CPUgRHQfc_lwTdHSq9NQfCfj7TRZdbfxoBevJEW8M&e=

New York University Press books are printed on acid-free paper, and their binding materials are chosen for strength and durability. We strive to use environmentally responsible suppliers and materials to the greatest extent possible in publishing our books.
Manufactured in the United States of America
10 9 8 7 6 5 4 3 2
Also available as an ebook

CONTENTS

Introduction

Histories of Racism and Resistance, Seen and Unseen: How and Why to Think about the Jim Crow North

BRIAN PURNELL AND JEANNE THEOHARIS

In my travels in the North I was increasingly becoming disillusioned with the power structures there. . . . Many of them sat on platforms with all their imposing regalia of office to welcome me to their cities and showered praise on the heroism of Southern Negroes. Yet when the issues were joined concerning local conditions only the language was polite; the rejection was firm and unequivocal.[1]
—Martin Luther King Jr., November 1965

The concentration upon the South . . . should not lead to the inference that the attitudes and policies described here were peculiar to the South. Indeed, if there were time and space, it would be a simple matter to point out the many parallel lines of prejudice and discrimination against the Negro in the North, prejudice that often worked as great a hardship upon the race as it did in the South.[2]
—C. Vann Woodward, 1955

Americans have been taught that Jim Crow's history lies in the South. The story begins in the 1880s and 1890s, when southern states, faced with interracial democracies that Reconstruction created, rewrote their constitutions to eliminate black people from civic life. "We came here to exclude the Negro," one Mississippi politician explained at the state's constitution convention in 1890. "Nothing short of this will answer."[3]

Racially segregated schools, voter registrar hours, buses, lunch counters, water fountains, hospitals, factories—even separate Bibles to swear upon, gallows to hang from, and, at least in Louisiana, asylums for blind people—followed.[4] By the turn of the century, these laws entrenched segregation across the South. The Supreme Court of the United States sanctioned these laws. Terrorist violence punished dissidents who opposed, or resisted, the new racial order.[5]

The North, as the story goes, frowned upon the South's peculiarities, but turned a blind eye to that region's Jim Crow injustices; while imperfect, its own systems were open to change and racial progress. Courageous opponents of southern Jim Crow began to rise up against racism and white supremacy in the 1930s and 1940s, but it was not until the 1950s and 1960s that an intrepid movement of black people across the South, with help from northern black people, reached a crescendo. Thus began the heroic civil rights movement history that many Americans learn about in school. Southern blacks, with the help of a sympathetic media and northern white liberals, challenged racial segregation through a mass struggle, and the nation overthrew Jim Crow segregation. Amid these victories, in the late 1960s, northern black people, frustrated by their own lack of progress and supposedly lacking the community values and institutions that had undergirded the southern struggle, erupted in riots across the urban North. Popular narratives, student textbooks, Hollywood dramas, and documentaries tell this moving history of a triumphant southern movement and its northern demise.[6]

The Strange Careers of the Jim Crow North tells different stories, seeking to reshape that dominant narrative. The essays in this volume shift our attention to histories of entrenched, endemic racism outside the South. In the liberal North, legal systems supported, and hid, practices of racial segregation. Robust fights against racism unfolded. People who dissented against the racial system were dismissed, disparaged, patronized, and punished. This anthology is part of a growing academic field that highlights the long history of northern racism and social movements that challenged northern racial discrimination and segregation.[7] Yet, in popular memory, in national celebration, and even within parts of the historical profession, the southern narrative dominates the way we remember the era. The legacies of the Jim Crow North continue to influence contemporary political and social arenas, such as policing, housing, education, and employment, but Americans know little about this history. The southern story continues to hold sway, in part because it makes racism a regional malady rather than a national cancer, expressed in violence and epithets rather than policy imperatives and political sway. A moving tale of good guys, bad guys, and successful endings, the popular story of Jim Crow and its defeat resounds as proof of the courage of individual Americans and the strength of U.S. democracy.

What we do know about the North, we do not associate with the term "Jim Crow." Northern black activists, however, used this terminology regularly, and they repeatedly made comparisons to the South to disrupt the national tendency to see systematized racism only as a regional issue. Extending into every region, state, and community, Jim Crow was a crucial feature of national life. Its "strange careers" outside of the South need fuller incorporation in histories of the United States during the twentieth century.[8]

Jim Crow began in the North, not the South. Long before the Civil War, northern states like New York, Massachusetts, Michigan, New Jersey, Ohio, and Pennsylvania had legal codes that promoted black people's racial segregation and political disenfranchisement. While these northern Jim Crow laws predated the South's, these racial systems never dominated or defined the region in a uniform way. Throughout the nineteenth century, black and white abolitionists and free black activists challenged the North's Jim Crow practices, won some victories, waged war against slavery in the South and the North, and even changed some of the North's racist laws in housing, voting, education, and marriage. Nonetheless, northerners wove Jim Crow racism into the fabric of their social, political, and economic life in ways that shaped the history of the region, and the entire nation. Jim Crow, outside of the South, coexisted, even thrived, alongside efforts to reform its worst manifestations in social and political life. This characteristic distinguished it from its southern version. A commonplace saying captured the two Jim Crows perfectly: in the South, black people could get close to white people, so long as they did not become too "uppity" by advocating for their social, political, or economic equality with whites. In the North, black people could get as "uppity" as they want—they could run successful businesses, consume luxury goods, and sit next to white people on the bus—so long as they did not try to get too close to whites, as their neighbors, sexual partners, classmates, or union brothers. This aphorism's wisdom recognizes that Jim Crow, whether in the North or in the South, demanded that black people remain in their "place." The essays in this volume reveal this history of northern systems of racial segregation, as well as the resistance people mounted against them.[9]

Northerners sowed the nation's social soil with seeds of modern racism during the seventeenth, eighteenth, nineteenth, and early twentieth centuries. But the Jim Crow North metastasized during the mid-twentieth century. Black migration to northern metropolises increased while the New Deal expanded new forms of racialized citizenship. Over the course of the twentieth century, laws and policies cemented Jim Crow in northern housing, employment, education, and law-enforcement systems.[10] Six million black people moved north and west between 1910 and 1970, seeking jobs, desiring education for their children, and fleeing racial terrorism. Some industrial jobs opened up for black workers. Everyday life in the North was different compared to the South. Blacks did not have to step off the sidewalk to let whites pass. Black citizens in the North in many places could vote. Public transportation was not, as a rule, segregated. We agree with other historians who have argued that "in some respects, the South did seem distinctive in privileging white supremacy," but we also argue that historical narratives of the Great Migration have tended to obscure the entrenched realities of northern racism.[11]

An ideology that dated to the years before the Civil War framed the North as a "promised land." Rather than their own Canaan, a more apt metaphor, to use historian Vincent Harding's framing, was that black migrants found Pharaoh on both sides of the river.[12] The millions of black people who fled to the North attest to their hopefulness that this region would serve them better than their homeland in the South, but they did not escape American racism. Instead, they found a different form of it. Rosa Parks, who was forced to leave Montgomery in 1957 and settled in Detroit, called it the "Northern promised land that wasn't."[13] Malcolm X, one of the greatest orator-theorists on the Jim Crow North, used the symbol of a predatory, straightforward wolf to represent southern racism and a sly, conniving fox to illustrate the trickiness of northern racism.[14]

New Deal policies, combined with white Americans' growing apprehension towards the migrants, created a raw deal for the country's black people. Despite the ability of northern African Americans—in Chicago and Detroit—to elect black people to local offices as early as the late nineteenth century, and to the U.S. Congress during the 1930s, and despite the temporary relief the New Deal brought to the catastrophes blacks suffered during the Great Depression, public policies, from the Wagner Act to the 1935 Social Security Act to the Home Owners' Loan Corporation, wrote racial inequity and segregation into policy.[15] And the black vote was often gerrymandered and diluted, making black political power in the North elusive.[16] Faced with these new realities, black people relentlessly and repeatedly challenged northern racism. A major theme of this anthology concerns the way Jim Crow racism in northern life produced longstanding, multifaceted social movements that theorized, unveiled, and opposed northern forms of racial discrimination at their most systematic institutional and cultural levels.

A close examination of the history of the Jim Crow North demonstrates how racial discrimination and segregation operated as a system, upheld by criminal and civil courts, police departments, public policies, and government bureaucracies. Judges, police officers, school board officials, PTAs, taxpayer groups, zoning board bureaucrats, urban realtors and housing developers, mortgage underwriters, and urban renewal policy makers created and maintained the Jim Crow North. There did not need to be a "no coloreds" sign for hotels, restaurants, pools, parks, housing complexes, schools, and jobs to be segregated across the North as well.

Northerners who resisted desegregation took many forms. From the Northeast to the West Coast, some northern whites screamed "nigger" and "monkey" and "Go Back to Africa." They posted signs reading "We want white tenants in our white community," threw bananas and bottles, and used violence against black people who attempted to move into "their" neighborhoods or schools. Nonviolent protests in the summer of 1963 urging White Castle in the Bronx to hire more black people were met with Confederate flags, KKK hoods, and racist epithets.[17] Following years of open housing advocacy in Milwaukee, a 1967 open housing march over the Sixteenth Street viaduct connecting the black North Side with white working-class Southside was attacked by a white mob spewing racial slurs; as historian Patrick Jones details, black and white Milwaukeeans then marched for two hundred consecutive nights and were consistently met with mobs of white people and regular appearances of the KKK and neo-Nazis, along with an intractable city leadership.[18] In Hartford, white activist Ned Coll and groups of schoolchildren attempting to desegregate Connecticut's beautiful beaches found "closed gates, slammed doors and threats of arrest," according to historian Andrew Kahrl.[19]

George Wallace, one of the most iconic figures of the Jim Crow South, found ample support in the North as well. When Wallace blocked the University of Alabama door in 1963, more than one hundred thousand letters streamed in from all over the country applauding his actions. "They all hate black people," Wallace realized. "All of them. They're all afraid, all of them. . . . The whole United States is Southern."[20] In 1968, when Wallace ran for president, he drew support in the Northeast and Midwest away from Hubert Humphrey and turned out overflow crowds from Boston to Madison Square Garden in what historian Dan Carter describes as "the largest political rally held in New York City since Franklin Roosevelt."[21]

But many northerners kept their distance from such tactics, deploring such hate-filled rhetoric and violence. At the same time, they employed the levers of policy, law, and bureaucracy to maintain segregation and racial privilege. Countless everyday actions, municipal, state, and federal policies, legal decisions, and byzantine bureaucracies created the scaffolding for a northern Jim Crow system that hid in plain sight. Northern Jim Crow practices often unfolded through so-called color-blind ideologies. The context of twentieth-century liberalism distinguished the Jim Crow North from the Jim Crow South. Northern Jim Crow evolved, in part, through New Deal and Great Society liberalism. Explanations for racial differences were rooted in arguments about culture and behavior, not biology. Claims to taxpayer rights, law and order, and anti-busing, not states' rights, became ideological rationales for hardening racial inequality within northern liberal societies. Black activists labored throughout the twentieth century to unmask and challenge these modes of Jim Crow ideology.

Defenders of the Jim Crow South often hid behind a brand of conservatism that they claimed reflected the rights of states to determine their own laws, and of individuals to choose their own social equals, because separation of the races, they believed, was good for individuals and society. Beyond the social order, defenders of southern Jim Crow sometimes argued that racial separation reflected the will of a Christian God who predetermined different social castes through biological distinctions. Many who believed in the rightness of Jim Crow in the South argued that criticisms of their ways of life only came from illegitimate, outside agitators—Communists, Jews, and uppity northern blacks—who riled up southern-born Negroes and sowed trouble where none existed. Still, other southerners who lacked overt racial animus felt afraid of racial integration, especially in public schools, or saw a need to balance the interests of emerging civil rights groups with those of White Citizens Councils. In truth, there was no single, unified way that American southerners thought about, or fought to protect, racial segregation.[22] The idea that all southerners were white, or that all whites in the South were inveterate racists, is as much of a myth as the idea that all whites in the North were liberal, or that all liberals in the North were not racist. Seeing clearly the history of Jim Crow in the North not only helps Americans think differently about the North but also helps them to reconsider one-dimensional understandings of the South and southerners.

Through its promotion of universal affluence and social stability through individuals' industry, market economies, and democratic political systems, northern liberalism rejected southern defenses of their Jim Crow societies, but these northern attacks against the South's racial system regularly ignored the racism that defined the North. Defenders of the Jim Crow North relied upon color-blind ideology and notions of the North as a meritocracy to explain how and why pervasive inequality in their society mapped, almost perfectly, onto patterns of race and class. The same ideas they used to take down the South's brand of Jim Crow became ones that masked and perpetuated the Jim Crow North. They created and maintained a system of racial inequality—all the while denying it was a system. The South learned from this. Many of the hallmarks of the Jim Crow North were taken up in the South in the late twentieth century.[23]

The New Deal and the Fair Deal opened some doors for black citizens, but they also embedded segregation in federal policy, and widened opportunity gaps. On top of that, expansions of putatively universal citizenship entitlements passed during this era made color-blind explanations for racial inequity a hallmark of mid-twentieth-century liberalism. Color-blindness blamed social inequality and lack of access on the motivations, choices, and culture of the individual, not on systems, institutions, or power structures. Northern liberals upheld the pretense of meritocracy while hording resources, power, and affluence in housing, schools, and city services. Defenders of the Jim Crow North turned the problem back onto black people: *What do you mean we are racist? Prove it. We don't see race. Our policies are color-blind. Why are you so angry? You're the racist because you obsess over race.* Such approaches made racism outside of the South harder to see.

Theories of a "culture of poverty" became the most effective way northerners justified their segregation. According to this theory, when faced with the structural inequities of northern cities and untethered from the religion, community institutions, and kinship that had characterized southern black life, northern black people developed a set of cultural behaviors and practices that impeded their economic and educational success.[24] Politically, they grew alienated and angry, unable to sustain movements and organizations like their southern brethren, and erupting in riots to express their disaffection. Such "cultural" arguments developed a powerful grip on northern journalists, scholars, and policy makers by affirming meritocracy, acknowledging structural inequality, and positing that the greatest barriers blacks now faced stemmed from their own behaviors, family structures, and cultural norms. Black behavior, not the social systems of racism, and racist northerners, became the focus for change. Thus black people bore the burden of fixing massive social inequities through their own individual efforts.

The national media, based largely in the North, maintained the mythologies that justified the Jim Crow North. By the 1960s, many national news sources had turned their attention to racism and struggle in the South. At the same time, they promoted ideologies of black people in the North as criminal and pathological and devoted much of their attention to in-depth stories plumbing life in the "ghetto." Newspapers refrained from sustained coverage of northern racism *as* racism and often treated black activism in the North as deviant, disruptive, and irrelevant. They undercovered local movements and overcovered uprisings. This journalism largely framed the nation's real racial problem, and noble struggle against it, as southern.

Given the centrality of "culture of poverty" justifications for masking and enabling northern inequality, black freedom movement activists and intellectuals attacked those analytical frameworks. Challenging the myth that they lived in a color-blind world based on merit, the activists described in this book rejected the widespread argument that racism and segregation in the Jim Crow North was an anomalous accident transplanted from the South or that black behaviors and values were primarily what held black people back. Too much evidence from their lives communicated otherwise. Black activism thus becomes the chief historical lens through which to see the complexity of the Jim Crow North.

Building on two decades of scholarship, the essays in this book make three related interventions in order to shift the historiography of racism in this country.[25] Despite two decades of robust scholarship on the North, national commemorations, most history textbooks, and even much of the best public history on African American life and struggle still picture systematized segregation and the civil rights movement as largely southern.[26] And so, one of the questions we, and the authors of these chapters, asked was: why? Why do Americans, even people who immerse themselves in scholarship on racism, continue to maintain a southern story of Jim Crow if so much new research reveals the structural and systemic nature of northern racism? Using a Jim Crow frame reveals how northern racism worked as *a racial system* with its own ideologies, rules, cultures, and practices, refuting the idea that racism outside the South was haphazard, transplanted, or resulting from private prejudices. But there has been a reluctance to understand it for what it is: a Jim Crow system. So we use that framing explicitly and directly—to show how northern racism worked as a racial system, to demonstrate the various ways in which northern officials maintained it all the while denying it as a system, and to underline the breadth of northern black activism and how deep and wide white opposition to it was.

Second, unmasking Jim Crow in the North reveals the ways in which northern liberals created ideologies to defend their system, and deflect black movements, with defensive assertions that their cities *were not* the South. Rather than deal with their own racism honestly, northerners pivoted constantly by calling attention to problems in the South while defending and maintaining their own status quo. Northern liberals, including the northern liberal media, played a pivotal role in maintaining racial discrimination throughout the twentieth century while proclaiming their own openness and lack of racial bias. Liberalism created opportunities for some racial minorities to advance socially and economically, but it also erected barriers against others, patronized and disparaged black activists, trumpeted examples of successful black people to justify no further intervention on matters related to racial inequity, and blamed those stuck in poverty or joblessness as individuals lacking the right character or cultural values to succeed.

Third, laying claim to a Jim Crow North takes seriously the ways generations of black writers and activists framed and theorized their own cities as places marred by "Jim Crow" policies. After years of study, investigation, and struggle, these activists mounted multiple resistance movements to challenge northern Jim Crow practices all the while being constantly asked to "prove" that there was even a problem. These essays return the history of activism against the Jim Crow North to a place of parity with the more well-known histories of racism and resistance in the American South.

In forwarding these three contentions, we recognize that Jim Crow operated differently from the East Coast to the Midwest to the West to the South. We do not argue that systems of racial segregation that developed in New York were mirror images of those that developed in Los Angeles, or that they were the same as those in Little Rock, Arkansas, or Jackson, Mississippi, for that matter. We also do not contend that uniform practices and ideologies defined the Jim Crow North. For example, the ideologies and practices that propped up New York City's racial system were not the same as those that developed four hours north of Gotham in a place like Rochester, New York. We use the plural, "strange careers," to foreground the ways Jim Crow took many forms, had many guises, and burrowed into the law in many ways. Journalists, politicians, policy makers, and citizens who denied the existence of Jim Crow in their own northern metropolises shared a common investment in a claim of racial innocence, in *not* being the South. They protected their own racial system through denying its existence and differentiating it from the South's.

Despite widespread patterns of racism in their housing, employment, police departments, and public schools that were supported, maintained, and defended through law and policy, whites living in the West, Midwest, and Northeast defended their society's race relations as more enlightened, open, and democratic than those that existed in the Jim Crow South. And so we use the term "North" in its historic sense to encompass all the places not the South and to take on this longstanding dichotomy northerners invested in between the "Jim Crow South" and the "liberal North." Doing so denies the protective cover that the idea of an exceptionally racist South long gave to practices and ideas that stretched deep into northern and western social, political, economic, and cultural history. Given the ways this historical reality and its contemporary effects still shape life throughout the nation, rooting out racial segregation from American life requires a more sober examination of Jim Crow's national scope and depth.

Such an examination is increasingly urgent today. Americans can see the effects of mid-twentieth-century racism—the racial ghettos, the incredibly disproportionate incarceration rates, the underfunded black public schools, the wealth gap, and the shorter average life span for American blacks regardless of their class or education—but the causes of this historic racism remain, largely, hidden in plain sight behind a veil of color-blind, meritocratic ideology. Americans like their racism, and their racists, southern and conservative, not northern and liberal. The idea that a system of segregation and inequality was propagated and maintained in the North—and largely survived despite a myriad of movements—demands a different reckoning from Americans today. To see the history that made the American ghetto, the prison industrial complex, the racial wealth gap, and the crisis in urban education today is to see how the Jim Crow North thrived through explanations that blamed the victims of racism for the causes *and* the effects of racism. Arcane bureaucracies, convoluted processes, and interminable, ineffective committees powered the social and political engines that produced northern Jim Crow systems—but proved easy to ignore and excuse amid the proclamations of fairness and color-blindness. Perhaps most important, we cannot, or do not, see the history of the Jim Crow North because our scholarship and policy makers have long dismissed the critiques and protests that northern black activists made about the origins, causes, effects of, and solutions for the social conditions in which they lived.

The Strange Careers of the Jim Crow North

To understand the Jim Crow North, we must look at its origins. Jim Crow segregation began in the North, then moved to the South. The early history of the Jim Crow North carries all of the hallmarks we associate with southern Jim Crow: segregation written into law, upheld by the court, and maintained by violence. It also contains distinctiveness: segregation constructed, and denied, through the bulwark of American liberal policy and thought, moments of social progress that morphed into new modes of racist prejudices and practices.

Most narrative histories of southern Jim Crow highlight how northern Republicans abandoned efforts to promote civil and economic equality for black citizens in the South after 1877 because, in the words of one popular textbook, the GOP "had other fish to fry."[27] By the last decade of the nineteenth century, when Jim Crow laws took hold in the South, the nation turned a blind eye to southern racism. For decades, Americans viewed Jim Crow and all its southern horrors as regional eccentricities. In deference to states' rights, national reconciliation, and the power of southerners in Congress, and because many white Americans were white supremacists, the federal government proved unable, or unwilling, to stop these peculiar practices. Failures to pass antilynching legislation in Congress, legislative reappropriation of Native American tribal lands into the hands of individual Indians, harsh restrictions against immigrants from China and Japan, and passive acceptance of the practical annulment of the Fourteenth and Fifteenth Amendments throughout Dixie led one historian to conclude that by about 1900, "[T]he Southern way had become the American way."[28]

Despite this commonly accepted narrative, a closer look at policies, attitudes—and even lynching—in the eighteenth and nineteenth centuries shows how the North led the nation in systemized racial injustice. Around the time of the American Revolution, as free blacks and fugitives from slavery populated northern cities, political and legal restrictions on black life increased. Racial segregation and public exclusion grew. In the late eighteenth century, for example, black citizens petitioned Boston's city government for redress because their skin color denied them access to state-sponsored schools. Whites and blacks in Boston paid taxes, but only whites could attend public schools. The Commonwealth ignored their plea.[29] In 1850, in Massachusetts, the Roberts family went to court so that five-year-old Sarah could attend a closer, whites-only school. The Massachusetts Supreme Court threw out the case, but the Supreme Court, in its 1896 case, *Plessy v. Ferguson*, cited the Roberts case as a legal precedent that justified separate facilities. Similarly, Pennsylvania passed a law in 1854 mandating segregated schools for blacks. On March 17, 1855, the Massachusetts legislature passed, and the governor signed, a bill that prohibited racial or religious distinctions in public school admissions, but the damage to American jurisprudence (and northern white expectations) had already been done.[30] Boston schools struggled with Jim Crow racism all the way through the twentieth century,[31] and Jim Crow moved from the North to the South, from northern state courts to the highest court in the nation.[32]

The Jim Crow North expanded with the nation. When states such as Vermont, New Hampshire, Massachusetts, and New York abolished slavery, northern legislatures often instituted gradual manumission laws that bound black people to service for a generation, privileged slave owners' rights to compensation and reparation, and simultaneously placed strict limitations on blacks' citizenship. New York rewrote its state constitution after 1827 to restrict black male suffrage and all but eliminated blacks' service on juries (only sixteen black men in the state qualified). Blacks could also not ride on city streetcars, and they were segregated on the ferries that ran between Brooklyn and Manhattan.[33] Racial segregation spread west into new territories and states. Ohio, Indiana, Illinois, Michigan, and Wisconsin outlawed slavery, but restricted black settlement and enshrined official discrimination against black people.[34]

As more blacks became free people in the North, and white northerners adjusted to sharing citizenship and public space with more black people, mechanisms of social distinction grew. When Alexis de Tocqueville toured the United States in 1831, he observed that "[t]he prejudice of race appears to be stronger in the states that have abolished slavery than in those where it still exists; and nowhere is it so intolerant as in those states where servitude has never been known."[35] The word "nigger" as a derogatory term for all black people first gained political, cultural, and social currency in the Jim Crow North, the historian Elizabeth Stordeur Pryor shows, "precisely at the moment when gradual abolition and emancipation began to free people of color in the North." In the 1820s and '30s, white northerners used the word "nigger" to describe all black people "as backward and beyond redemption . . . incapable of achieving real freedom and citizenship." Blacks in the antebellum North who entered interracial public spaces experienced the word "nigger" as an epithet that connoted violence, claimed space, and indicated that the northern public sphere belonged to whites only. Future generations of southern whites used the word "nigger" in similar ways.[36]

Beyond vile epithets and cultural entertainments such as minstrelsy, which found their greatest purchase in the urban North,[37] the Jim Crow North manifested in virulent policies and violent practices. Before the Civil War, many cities and towns in the Midwest passed measures to disenfranchise black people, restrict black settlement, and segregate schools and town services.[38] The tactics of racial violence and intimidation ran through the North. Before white southerners lynched more than four thousand people from the 1880s through the 1960s, nineteenth-century white northerners, especially Irish immigrants and American-born, ethnically Irish citizens, used lynching to protect racialized notions of citizenship, manhood, labor, community, and criminal justice against expanding notions of free labor ideology, and state bureaucracy. According to historian Michael Pfeifer, in New York and Wisconsin, "[N]orthern Irish Americans in the Civil War used strategies of racial violence that would also be employed by white Southerners in Reconstruction. Urban Irish Catholics were, then, innovators as they were among the first white Americans to lynch free blacks in a society organized around principles of free labor."[39] Just as using the term "nigger" as a way to keep black American citizens in their place and mark their subordinate position moved from the Jim Crow North to the Jim Crow South, and from the post-emancipation era of the 1820s and '30s to the postbellum era, so too did the promotion of racial terrorism through lynching practices.

Northerners adapted their Jim Crow practices to conform to the political, economic, and social changes that the end of slavery brought to national life. The North also had to adjust to a national Constitution that recognized black citizens' equality before the law. "Despite the rapid toppling of traditional racial barriers," Eric Foner argues, "the North's racial Reconstruction proved in many respects less far reaching than the South's."[40] During and after Reconstruction, northern unions barred blacks.[41] In language that would echo across the decades, northerners during Reconstruction argued that black citizens' behavior, not whites' racism, or even legal protection, did the most to effect black social advancement. Despite laws in many states declaring formal equality, white northerners used segregation practices to deny blacks equal chances at jobs and housing. They justified these practices with arguments that black people did not act right, and that their poor behavior caused their misfortune. According to 1867 editors of the pro-unionist liberal magazine *The Nation,* legislation could not reverse the "great burden" that weighed upon black people, a burden that came, not from white racism, but from black people's "want of all ordinary claims to social respectability."[42]

Midwestern states that had barred black settlement in their original constitutions also reacted to national protections for black citizenship with violence and intimidation. After the Civil War, sundown towns proliferated across the Midwest and West. Such towns kept African Americans out by law, force, or custom and were so named because some posted signs reading, "Nigger Don't Let the Sun Go Down on You in [name of municipality]." Many such towns had an early black population that was summarily removed. Five hundred and seven sundown towns existed in Illinois alone, where black people were banished, or forcibly evicted.[43]

The rejuvenation of the KKK during the early twentieth century—what historian Linda Gordon refers to as the "northern Klan"[44] —demonstrated the national appeal of white supremacy. Largely defunct for forty years, the KKK was reborn in 1915 in part due to the success of D. W. Griffith's film *Birth of a Nation*—the first film ever to be screened in the White House. By the 1920s, Klan membership had skyrocketed, not just in the old Confederacy but also in Indiana, Oregon, Kansas, Colorado, Pennsylvania, Washington, Ohio, and California, their ranks swollen with middle-class white women and men. Members claimed the mantel of patriotism and white Protestantism against immigrants, Catholics, Jews, and blacks, sought legislation and political office, controlled many churches and positions of law enforcement, and numbered five million. In 1925, more than fifty thousand Klansmen were cheered as they marched through the streets of Washington, DC.[45] In New York City, in 1927, one thousand Klansmen marched through Jamaica, Queens, and clashed with police officers. Fred C. Trump, father of future U.S. president Donald J. Trump, was one of seven "be-robed" people arrested at that parade for fighting against law enforcement or, in Trump's case, "refusing to disperse."[46]

Thus, Jim Crow was not an exceptional social, economic, legal, and cultural system that defined the South during the nineteenth and early twentieth centuries. Jim Crow had a national history and scope that originated in the North in the Revolutionary era, and grew there in even more powerful ways during the mid-twentieth century.

Revisiting Woodward

There is probably no historical scholarship more pivotal to cementing an understanding of the Jim Crow South than C. Vann Woodward's best-selling 1955 book, *The Strange Career of Jim Crow.*[47] Part of the book's power came from its argument that recent historical events, not time-less, inevitable, unchanging traditions, had created southern segregation. Woodward located the Jim Crow South's origins in the 1880s and 1890s. While powerful and important, his argument ended up reinforcing the notion that American segregation and disfranchisement were a regional problem. His cursory treatment of the North stemmed from his limited knowledge on the subject, as he made clear, and "not on the mistaken assumption that Jim Crow disappeared in the North after the Civil War."[48]

In the 1966 reprint, Woodward added a new first chapter, "Of Old Regimes and Reconstructions." "Segregation in complete and fully de-veloped form," Woodward argued, "did grow up contemporaneously with slavery, but not in its midst. One of the strangest things about the career of Jim Crow was that the system was born in the North and reached an advanced age before moving South in force."[49] By the 1830s, with slavery abolished in the North, and gradual manumission laws in place, thirty-five hundred black people remained in bondage through-out the region. Free black citizens in the North, however, had freedom of movement (in states that did not bar black settlement) and freedom to engage in contracts for work, and, perhaps most important, blacks' children were not bound to a state of slavery. "For all that," Woodward argued, "the Northern Negro was made painfully and constantly aware that he lived in a society dedicated to the doctrine of white supremacy and Negro inferiority."[50] Few, if any, northern politicians challenged this reality of American racism. Instead, the "system permeated all aspects of Negro life in the free states by 1860," Woodward wrote: from transpor-tation conveyances to theaters and lecture halls. In hotels, restaurants, and resorts, blacks were barred as customers, but not as servants; white Christian churches had "Negro pews"; and blacks who worshiped with whites had to receive Holy Communion separately from them. Blacks were "educated in segregated schools," Woodward wrote, "punished in segregated prisons, nursed in segregated hospitals, and buried in segregated cemeteries."[51]

Some of the most entrenched segregation in the North happened in urban residential patterns, as Woodward demonstrates. In 1847, "not a single colored family" lived in South Boston, Woodward noted. Boston had its "Nigger Hill" and "New Guinea" for black residents. Cincinnati had "New Africa," as did New York and Philadelphia, at a time, Woodward demonstrates, when Richmond, Virginia, Charleston, South Carolina, and New Orleans, Louisiana, lacked such blacks-only residential districts. Racial segregation was harsher in the West, Woodward argued. In the places where blacks could vote, only 6 percent of northern blacks lived. Custom or law also prevented blacks from serving on juries in the North.[52] As Woodward summarized, "It is clear when its victory was complete and the time came, the North was not in the best possible position to instruct the South, either by precedent and example, or by force of conviction, on the implementation of what eventually became one of the professed war aims of the Union cause: racial equality."[53] In the 1880s and 1890s, northern publications, such as the *Nation, Harper's Weekly,* the *North American Review,* and the *Atlantic Monthly,* regularly printed "the shibboleths of white supremacy regarding the Negro's innate inferiority, shiftlessness, and hopeless unfitness for full participation in the white man's civilization."[54]

Woodward's own work shows the importance of the research that produced the essays in this volume. Part of our goal in this anthology joins Woodward's mission from years ago: to show how Americans created and maintained a northern system of segregation and racial injustice through specific historical circumstances, policies, laws, and actions, not as byproducts of southern decisions, private practices, or chance events; and thus to show how such a system can be dismantled and democracy can rise in its place.

New Deal Jim Crow and the Katznelson Thesis

In many twentieth-century northern cities, as black migration surged, racial segregation hardened and worsened. In the expanded social citizenship it created, the New Deal also encoded a new kind of Jim Crow citizenship, as political historian Ira Katznelson's *When Affirmative Action Was White* shows.[55] In a similar way that C. Vann Woodward demystified the seemingly natural history of racism in the South, Ira Katznelson has also shown how histories of racial preferences, instituted by the government and embedded deeply within public policies, benefited white Americans by expanding their ranks in the middle class and protecting their wealth. In multiple ways—from Federal Housing Administration (FHA) policies that rated neighborhoods for residential and school racial homogeneity to the ways Aid to Dependent Children carved a requirement for "suitable homes" to arcane policies that blamed black "cultural deprivation" for social disparities—segregation and inequality worsened after the New Deal of the 1930s. But by laying it at the feet of southern congressmen, Katznelson's analysis misses the northern agency and investment in institutionalizing these racial hierarchies, as well as the modern roots of the Jim Crow North.

In his powerful interpretations of the New Deal's racial history, and its national effects, Katznelson argues that the expansion of social citizenship under the New Deal created "affirmative action for whites."[56] In perhaps the most far-reaching expansion of social citizenship since the end of the Civil War, federal New Deal policies provided loans for homes, underwrote racially exclusive suburban development, expanded higher education opportunities for veterans, granted Social Security entitlements, and protected unions for certain jobs. Katznelson shows how, by design, all of these social welfare policies benefited white citizens, stabilized and increased the ranks of the white middle class, distributed more wealth among white working- and middle-class citizens, and largely excluded blacks and Latinos.

Katznelson blames the racial discrimination baked into New Deal policies on the political machinations of racist southern Democrats. If the Woodward thesis contends that Jim Crow did not arise in the years that immediately followed the end of the Civil War, but instead waited until after Reconstruction, the Katznelson thesis argues that Jim Crow spread throughout government institutions, and created generational inequality through the actions of racist southern Democrats.[57] These southern congressmen held New Deal and Fair Deal legislation hostage through their tremendous power in Congress. "Without the South," Katznelson argued, "there could have been no New Deal."[58] Katznelson does not absolve Roosevelt, northern Democrats, or New Deal liberals from complicity and "pragmatic forgetfulness" in allowing the South to manipulate New Deal and Fair Deal social welfare policies at the expense of black citizens. But Katznelson concludes, "[I]t was the white South that acted as the key agent in Congress"[59]—ensuring the maintenance of racial segregation and job hierarchies, promoting the local control of federal social welfare policies, like Social Security, and blocking antidiscrimination statutes from infecting progressive programs and policies. "When southern members of Congress controlled the gateways to legislation," Katznelson wrote, "policy decisions dealing with welfare, work and war either excluded the vast majority of African Americans or treated them differently from others."[60]

Katznelson emphasizes that northern Democrats and Republicans complied with the white southern oligarchy to build Jim Crow into the fabric of New Deal liberalism. His analysis of northern liberals' corrupt bargain to pass New Deal legislation at the expense of racial equality, however, promotes an imbalanced view of the way New Deal liberalism enabled inequality that already existed in the Jim Crow North and the proactive investments of northern politicians in these racialized practices. Liberals did not just bite their tongues and wince while southern racists built Jim Crow through New Deal legislation. They too had a stake in local control and embraced their own forms of Jim Crow racism that had nothing to do with the South.

In her book *The Segregated Origins of Social Security*, Mary Poole demonstrates how a consortium of northern and southern interests, not merely southern congressmen, influenced the racialized shape of the 1935 Social Security Act. University of Wisconsin–trained researchers, who dominated the Committee on Economic Security, infused racially exclusionary practices into the legislation. "African Americans were not denied the benefits of Social Security because of the machinations of southern congressional leadership," Poole argues. "The Act was made discriminatory through a shifting web of alliances of white policymakers that crossed regional and political parties. The members of the group that wielded the greatest influence on these developments were not southerners in Congress but President Franklin D. Roosevelt's own people . . . who genuinely sought to build a fairer and better world, . . . but whose vision was steeped in racial privilege."[61]

Northerners too seized upon the local control to maintain their own racial prerogatives. Northern and western legislators built a weak structure around the state-level Fair Employment Practices Committees and antidiscrimination commissions that proliferated in the Northeast and Midwest during the 1940s.[62] They created structures of inequality and exclusion through the New Deal's protections of county-level administrators of federal welfare benefits. While the Katznelson thesis does a great deal to show how color consciousness, not color-blindness, defined the New Deal and the Fair Deal, his arguments do not account for the ways Jim Crow racism spread throughout states and counties where no southern Democrats held sway—why local control produced even more segregation in the North.[63] The Katznelson thesis also does little to explain why FHA and Home Owners' Loan Corporation surveyors used assumptions about the supposed primacy of white racial homogeneity to structure investment ratings systems throughout northern, midwestern, and western cities. By funneling the flow of investment capital and development dollars away from metropolitan communities where black people lived to suburbs and segregated housing developments from Levittown to Bensonhurst, those assessments provided the legalized underpinnings that created racial ghettos in mid-twentieth-century American cities.[64]

The thrust of this anthology thus differs from the arguments of scholars like Ira Katznelson and Jason Sokol who, while noting how northern liberalism coexisted with northern racism, do not emphasize its proactive racial politics. Jason Sokol's synthesis history of racial politics of the Northeast, *All Eyes Upon Us*, argues for the North's "conflicted soul" when he writes that "the Northeast has been, and remains, the most American of regions" not "because it is a glittering model of freedom and democracy" but "because the Northeast has long held genuine movements for racial democracy, and for racial segregation, within the same heart."[65] Yet, liberalism provided significant cover for northern forms of racial inequality by defending its racial prerogatives and aggressively demonizing black activism.[66] Like Katznelson, Sokol fails to deal with the Jim Crow North as a racial system that grew strong from perpetuating its own racism and its claims to racial innocence.

Sokol's argument places northern racism on a continuum of southern racism but without the same moral absolutes. "The North had few Bull Connors or Jim Clarks, few swaggering sheriffs who had built entire careers out of brutalizing black people," writes Sokol. "The dearth of such villains made for an absence of moral absolutes. There would be no Selmas of the North." We argue that the North *did* have its Selmas. Sokol's contention overlooks the ideologies of the time that liberals used to obscure their own racial wickedness. They rationalized their own racial inequities as venial when compared with the South's sins. They turned individual culture and behavior into explanatory causes of pervasive social inequities. They had become so adept at making excuses for their own racism that they often ignored, for decades, even the most blatant examples of Jim Crow in the North. As Martin Luther King Jr. observed in 1965, "As the nation, Negro and white, trembled with outrage at police brutality in the South, police misconduct in the North was rationalized, tolerated, and usually denied."[67] Northern liberals pointed to the beams and branches of racism that existed in southerners' eye, and in doing so, deflected attention—especially their own attention—away from the splinters, sticks, and boughs lodged in their own sockets.

The North had many Bull Connors: judges, prosecutors, entire police departments that committed countless instances of harassment, brutality, and kangaroo courts that overcriminalized black people while covering up police brutality throughout the Jim Crow North's ghettos. There were also many such dramatic confrontations: Milwaukee's open housing marches that drew mobs of angry whites; the killing of civil rights activist Bruce Klunder at a school protest in Cleveland; the growing confrontations between Boston's civil rights movement and its School Committee; the police killing of Nation of Islam secretary Ron Stokes outside his LA mosque in 1962 and the actions of LAPD Chief William H. Parker.[68] The key difference was not the injustice, nor the level of black struggle, nor the level of white resistance to change. The main difference between the regions was an unwillingness of the nation to understand its race problem as national and to see that those who would protect and defend racial injustice came in many different guises.

"[A]lthough the North had no terrible bridges to march across, and no mass protest that riveted the nation," Sokol continues, "it came to possess something almost as incredible: a black senator."[69] Part of Jim Crow North's staying power was also that liberals could point to "black firsts" like Edward Brooke as a senator of Massachusetts and say, "See? Progress." Meanwhile, in spite of these black firsts, the "not segregated" schools in Boston and Springfield stayed segregated for decades, and worsened in the ways they failed to educate black students and confined them to overcrowded, underresourced, and often decrepit schools. Through the ideology of liberal color-blindness, black students and their families became responsible for perpetuating their own underachievement through their insufficient motivation and their lack of value for education and deferred gratification.

Focusing on Jackie Robinson, Edward Brooke, Shirley Chisholm, David Dinkins, and Deval Patrick, Sokol only cursorily mentions grassroots activists like Ruth Batson, Ellen Jackson, Mae Mallory, and Ella Baker who labored for years to call out the Jim Crow North, faced down city officials who hamstrung their activism, became mired in studies and commissions to prove there was a problem, experienced disparagement by the media, and deflected red-baiting by many public officials. By giving short shrift to the perspectives of these activists and the ways they framed northern injustice and hypocrisy, both Katznelson and Sokol miss the proactiveness of northern racism, the extent of black struggle to challenge it, and the cunningly effective fictions of "color-blindness," "crime," and "culture" that provided the ideological rubrics to maintain it.

Indeed, modern liberal urban governance and the growth of northern cities in the early twentieth century were inseparable from race. In *Managing Inequality*, Karen Miller has documented how "color-blind" discourses originated in the early twentieth century among northern white political leaders eager to distinguish their municipal leadership as modern and progressive, maintained segregationist urban structures, and deflected black demands for change.[70] "Northern racial liberalism," Miller contends, "is the notion that all Americans, regardless of race, should be politically equal, but that the state cannot and indeed should not enforce racial equality by interfering with existing social or economic relations."[71] In early-twentieth-century Detroit, political leaders would claim this liberalism to simultaneously assert their administration's color-blindness and maintain practices that produced segregation, dismissing black people who pointed them out. Similarly, historian Khalil Muhammad outlines how crime statistics, migration patterns, and discourses of law and order "were woven together into a cautionary tale about the exceptional threat black people posed to modern society," fueling a regime of punishment that flourished in early-twentieth-century northern cities while providing the acceptable veneer for their "Jim Crow Justice."[72]

Increasingly in the post–World War II era, many northern liberal politicians, citizens, and news outlets would push for change in the South while endeavoring to protect segregation at home. Martin Luther King Jr.'s quotation, which begins this introduction, zeroes in on this double standard; King took to the pages of the *Saturday Review* a few months after the Watts uprising to highlight longstanding resistance to change in cities like LA, despite years of local black protests. Looking at New York City's school desegregation movement and how white resistance to it determined the shape and passage of the 1964 Civil Rights Act is instructive. In the decade after *Brown*, New York City had witnessed a growing movement in the city insisting that *Brown* must be upheld in New York, and demanding a comprehensive desegregation plan from the Board of Education. Over and over, in the decade after *Brown*, grassroots activists and local parents confronted school officials over the inequities in their children's schooling. They picketed, attended PTA meetings, took their kids out of school, and wrote letters but were deflected, dismissed, and denied. After a decade of struggle with little change, the city's black community was at its limit. On February 3, 1964, 460,000 students and teachers boycotted the city schools because of their refusal to even come up with a comprehensive desegregation plan. The *New York Times* called the February school boycott "unreasonable and unjustified" and "violent."[73] White parents were terrified—and so the next month, a much, much smaller group of white people, not even fifteen thousand, mostly white mothers, marched over the Brooklyn Bridge to protest the Board's exceedingly modest plan to desegregate just sixty schools through school pairings. Opposition to civil rights activism was fierce and widespread in New York. In a poll conducted by the *New York Times*, a majority of white New Yorkers in 1964 said the civil rights movement had gone too far. Respondents spoke of black people receiving "everything on a silver platter" and of "reverse discrimination" against whites. Nearly half said that picketing and demonstrations hurt black people's cause.[74]

Their congressmen heard their pleadings, as historian Matthew Delmont demonstrates; the coverage of the (white) mothers' march played as the backdrop of congressional debates around the Civil Rights Act.[75] In drafting the act, mindful of their white constituents back home, the bill's northern and western liberal sponsors like Brooklyn congressman Emanuel Celler okayed a loophole to keep federal civil rights enforcement of school desegregation away from the North (they wanted to keep federal education dollars and their racially imbalanced schools). They amended Title IV, section 401b to read, "'Desegregation' means the assignment of students to public schools and within such schools without regard to their race, color, religion, or national origin, but *'desegregation' shall not mean the assignment of students to public schools in order to overcome racial imbalance*" (emphasis added).[76]

The intentions of northern and western congressmen were clear at the time, even though this reality has largely been lost to history. Southern politicians noted the hypocrisy of the bill's supporters in carving out this loophole for their own schools. Praising New York's senators as "pretty good segregationists at heart," Mississippi Senator James O. Eastland noted, "I do not blame the two distinguished Senators from New York for their desire to protect New York City, as well as Chicago, Detroit, and similar areas. But why should they attempt to penalize our part of the country?"[77] And the loophole worked—providing cover from Chicago to Boston to maintain their segregated schools and their federal money. Contextualizing why many African American communities rioted the summer after the bill passed, civil rights organizer Bayard Rustin observed, "People have to understand that although the civil-rights bill was good and something for which I worked arduously, there was nothing in it that had any effect whatsoever on the three major problems Negroes face in the North: housing, jobs, and integrated schools. . . . [T]he civil-rights bill, because of this failure, has caused an even deeper frustration in the North."[78]

Returning Black Agency: How Recent Work on Northern Inequality Largely Misses Northern Black Activism

This anthology also insists that, alongside examining how the Jim Crow North worked as a system, we need to see the variety of ways black people theorized, unveiled, subverted, and challenged it at the time. Groundbreaking work from writers like Ta Nehisi Coates, Isabel Wilkerson, and Nikole Hannah-Jones has documented, for wide audiences, the northern practices and structures that entrenched housing segregation, exacerbated school segregation, and hardened Jim Crow in policing and criminal justice in northern cities.[79] These writers powerfully demonstrate the relentless and evolving nature of racism that shaped and influenced northern black life in the twentieth century. But a common and significant flaw in their work—and in many of the public commemorations of civil rights movement and the fiftieth anniversaries of the Detroit, Watts, and Newark uprisings as well—is a superficial examination of the deep and wide organizing and theorizing northern black people, and their allies, did to challenge such practices.[80]

Seeing the multitude of tactics northern black people employed, the many organizations they built, the numbers of rallies, sit-ins, and meetings they held shows how black writers and activists were theorizing and challenging these issues all the time. It also reveals how hard northern whites fought to maintain the status quo. By not centering the ways northern black intellectuals and activists have long formulated ways to highlight and oppose northern segregation and exclusion, these writers hew, however inadvertently, to the idea that black urban communities could not or did not recognize, articulate, and challenge what was happening because they possessed a weaker character and frailer community values than their southern brethren. Highlighting the structures and practices of the Jim Crow North without also highlighting northern black activism maintains a fiction that northern black people were too alienated and disorganized to build movements—a key misapprehension that has blinded us to northern movements for racial justice since their first days. By marginalizing this longstanding activism, these major public intellectuals also miss documenting how deep and wide white resistance was in the North (including by people who pushed for change in the South). When northern white people faced a host of local movements for racial justice, they labored just as hard to protect racial segregation and discrimination, albeit at times using different methods, as whites did in the South.

Similarly, the new Legacy Museum in Montgomery that accompanies the Equal Justice Initiative's searing lynching memorial, along with its reports on lynching and segregation, powerfully trace the lines from slavery to Jim Crow lynching and segregation to contemporary mass incarceration. As EJI president Bryan Stevenson eloquently explains, "I want to get to the point where we experience something more like freedom. . . . I don't think we are going to get there until we create a new consciousness about our history." Yet the museum and EJI's "Segregation in America" report glances over the northern movement. And, it fundamentally ignores opposition to the civil rights movement outside of the South. This oversight neglects a crucial portion of how racial inequality operated throughout the nation.[81] By not foregrounding this northern history of struggle, even some of the most hard-hitting analyses of American racism by Ta Nehisi Coates, Isabel Wilkerson, Nikole Hannah-Jones, and the Equal Justice Initiative miss crucial dimensions of American history that help show the present more clearly.

Michelle Alexander's groundbreaking book *The New Jim Crow* highlights what she terms "the new Jim Crow"— the ways criminalization and mass incarceration fueled by the War on Drugs have denied millions of black people rights in housing, voting, and jobs: "I came to see that mass incarceration in the United States had, in fact, emerged as a stunningly comprehensive and well-disguised system of racialized social control that functions in a manner strikingly similar to Jim Crow."[82] Following the successes of the civil rights movement, not only did racial discrimination infect law enforcement and the courts, Alexander explains, but a destructive *system* of criminalization and incarceration evolved to accelerate racial segregation and political and economic disfranchisement, in ways replicating the Jim Crow South. Alexander is correct, but this anthology reminds readers that creating a system of segregation and oppression through law and policy without explicit racial invocations is an age-old northern strategy. Justifications for a racial caste system "through the lens of popular social science" is far older than the War on Drugs; rather, it follows from culture-of-poverty theories that justified northern inequality by criminalizing and blaming black behavior across the twentieth century. Black northerners have spent the century highlighting and challenging this culture-of-poverty framing. This is not merely semantics: the new Jim Crow is merely the old Jim Crow. Understanding this racial system necessitates seeing its roots in modern American liberalism; it requires understanding how this system lay at the heart of the creation of the modern American metropolis, was fortified through liberals' defining their cities as *not-the-South*, gained steam after World War II made cultural explanations the necessary ways for liberals to talk about race, and was challenged by black people across the twentieth century.[83]

Expanded Jim Crow systems of northern racial segregation confined black citizens to American ghettos; criminalized the spaces where they lived and learned and played; denied them schooling that would make college possible, and then turned around and refused to hire them; imprisoned hundreds of thousands of people; extracted resources from their schools; plundered their property-based wealth; allowed a rapacious, lucrative drug economy to flourish; and supported victim-blaming ideologies that laid the burden for all of these social ills at the foot of urban black people's behavior and cultures.[84] Too often, when black activists, writers, and parents pointed this out, they were treated as crazy, dangerous, and potentially Communist. The difficulty of seeing the Jim Crow North and the disregarding of the long and varied movements that took place across the Northeast, Midwest, and West was a "structured blindness," to use philosopher Charles Mills's formulation, "in no way *accidental*, but *prescribed*."[85]

This blindness was a blindness of the time, corresponding not only to northerners' investments in deflecting scrutiny of their own racism but also to U.S. global interests. Hoping to win the allegiances of the Third World, the United States sought to cast racism as a regional anachronism rather than a national condition while portraying those who highlighted the systems of racial injustice outside the South (from Malcolm X to Mae Mallory to Milton Galamison) as dangerous and un-American. Increasingly the United States showcased the southern movement to highlight the power of American democracy to reform its own regional troublespots—holding up American liberalism as the country's identity. News of southern victories made international headlines.[86] Over time, the southern movement came to be celebrated across the political spectrum as proof of American exceptionalism.[87] The North complicates that story—and thus the added investment in holding up the openness of the liberal North and marginalizing those who pointed out otherwise.

Fitting with this Cold War paradigm, news organizations propped up the myth of northern racism as aberrant and accidental while intrepid journalists journeyed south to cover the movement and racism there, demonstrating the power of American democracy at work. Critics of northern, liberal institutions and practices were dismissed as reckless, extreme, unjustified, or Communist sympathizers.[88] Given these Cold War realities, culture became the chief analytical lens through which to talk about race, and ethnographers journeyed to ghettos from Chicago to Delhi to capture and expose these "cultural traditions," and "deprivations"[89] that trapped people in poverty. U.S. Cold War interests painted people of color at home and abroad as possessing cultural values and practices at odds with the successful modern life and in need of cultural remediation. Thus, part of the work these essays do is consider the investments, both historical and contemporary, in casting the black freedom struggle and American racism in certain ways.

Unveiling the Jim Crow North: What These Chapters Do

Analyzing the paradoxes and contradictions that veiled northern Jim Crow, especially those around arguments that reduce racial inequality to inherent cultural differences, these chapters chart the arduous, frustrating struggles black citizens waged against the Jim Crow North, and the historical memories surrounding it. These essays span a variety of locales—big cities like New York City, Los Angeles, Detroit, and San Francisco, and smaller industrial ones like Milwaukee and Rochester. They bring black freedom fighters well known in their time back to the fore: Say Burgin looks at Smith Act lawyer and Recorder Court judge George Crockett, while John Portlock examines the work of newspaper editor and candidate for the U.S. vice presidency Charlotta Bass. Other essays turn their attention on northern whites. Mary Barr examines the white people who sought to unveil the Jim Crow North, like the 1965 North Shore Summer Project, and their neighbors who refused. Laura Warren Hill zeroes in on the white people who defended their entitlements and racial prerogatives through a "Jim Crow discourse" that united North and South, like those who wrote Rochester's mayor after the 1964 uprising.

These essays unveil the racial underbellies of liberal institutions like the *New York Times* and the City University of New York, as Tahir Butt shows in the struggles around free tuition at CUNY in the 1960s. Others open up discussion of the Jim Crow North in American memory, literature, and film; essays by Balthazar Beckett and Ayesha Hardison demonstrate how much more there is to see about classic texts like *Brown Girl Brownstones* and *Raisin in the Sun* and independent films like *Night Catches Us* by examining how they center a critique of northern liberal racism. The chapters show how challenges to the Jim Crow North were sometimes embedded in global anticolonial struggles, and that the critique of northern racism often necessitated a challenge to Cold War liberalism, which brought down the full weight of American anticommunism and red-baiting tactics onto the heads of northern antiracist activists.

Moving chronologically, these essays are set in familiar places, such as courtrooms, schools, municipal offices, and metropolitan streets, where citizens in northern and western cities encountered racial segregation and discrimination in ways that were mundane, institutional, and structural. As Shannon King, Say Burgin, and Peter Levy demonstrate, they reveal the role of the law and law enforcement—and the collusion of police, prosecutors, judges, politicians, and the media—in maintaining this system of injustice. They show how northern black intellectuals like Ella Baker and Mae Mallory, as Kristopher Burrell outlines, theorized that system and fought against Jim Crow in New York City, and the ways in which black activists in Milwaukee came up with creative ways to use religious networks to press for hiring nondiscrimination, as Crystal Moten does in her chapter.

Fewer vigilantes populate these essays because many northerners preferred the civility of entrusting the task of racial management and control to police on the beat, and judges on the bench. Picking up gaps in the first generation of scholarship on the northern struggle, Aliyah Dunn Salahuddin looks at the role and context of the uprisings of the mid-1960s and the long history of organizing and grievances that preceded the 1966 uprising in the Bay View–Hunters Point neighborhood of San Francisco. Levy focuses on the coverage of SNCC chair H. Rap Brown and how the media laid the ideological groundwork for "law-and-order politics" that furthered imprisoning black people and criminalizing radical black activism. Several of these pieces—Peter Levy's and Shannon King's explicitly—demonstrate that the media was not so noble when it came to struggles in the North and the West.

The work in this volume is both a product of fifteen years of scholarship on the North and a response to certain gaps in that scholarship. Several themes about the history of the Jim Crow North emerge in these essays. The first is a critique of language, practices, and ideologies of northern liberalism and an attention to the ways black activists, artists, and intellectuals developed theories about the limits of the North as "promised land." Color-blind liberalism allowed northern Jim Crow to hide in plain sight. To do this, as these pieces detail, a lexicon of the Jim Crow North developed: "de facto segregation," "racial imbalance," "separation," "cultural deprivation," "underprivileged," "neighborhood schools," "busing," "crime," "juvenile delinquency," "law and order"—all were framings developed to assuage and explain northern segregation in the era of *Brown*. Part of the challenge that black citizens encountered—as many of these chapters demonstrate—was how to make the Jim Crow North visible, and hold officials accountable amid these slippery ideological framings.

With years of protests and petitions falling on deaf ears, or producing token changes, as a number of essays show, the "Great Uprisings" of the mid-to-late 1960s occurred.[90] Blacks in the North and West no longer waited for change to happen through "acceptable" means of political process. As these essays argue, after years of frustrated struggle had produced little change and much silence from the very liberals decrying southern racism, the uprisings of the mid-to-late 1960s disrupted and unmasked the oft-ignored and overlooked systematic nature of the Jim Crow North. They revealed the injustices of violence in the North—violence that was "legalized" because it came from the police and from the structures that ghettoized black people into decrepit housing and underserved neighborhoods, with little access to decent jobs or health care. And so a second strategic intervention the volume makes is to more explicitly intertwine the northern black freedom movement with the uprisings of the 1960s: the latter occurred because, for decades, northerners ignored, or paid lip service to, the former.[91]

Third is a critique of culture-of-poverty framings of northern black life that rendered northern black people as alienated and different from southern black people, and of the assumption that they did not produce the kinds of movements southerners did. The North experienced a long activist, intellectual movement, and witnessed decades of citizens' use of "proper channels" to express grievances with school segregation, housing segregation, job exclusion, and police brutality—whose push for reform largely fell on deaf ears before the uprisings in many cities. While Bill Cosby's 2004 poundcake speech alleged that black behaviors and cultures were now what held the black community back and President Obama's My Brother's Keeper initiative similarly proffered cultural solutions, these essays remind us of the extended and foul history of "cultural" explanations to deflect calls for desegregation—and how long black community activists have been fighting such explanations.

The essays in this volume also force us to reexamine the role of the media and civil rights. Built through books like the Pulitzer Prize–winning *The Race Beat*, there is an assumption that the media was a champion of movement.[92] But the national media, based largely in the North, covered northern inequality and struggle in its own backyard very differently from its intrepid coverage, by the early 1960s, of the Jim Crow South. At home, it dismissed black protest, treating it as episodic, deviant, and violent (even when no destruction of people or property occurred). It overlooked and undercovered racism outside of the South and replicated the frame of surprise over the uprisings of the mid-1960s, forgetting the years of black protest and helping to further a law-and-order politics.

The Strange Careers of the Jim Crow North helps us to reconsider and reject the idea of northern racism as episodic and transplanted, rather than state-sponsored and indigenous. It forces us to question the idea of urban disorders and uprisings as products of culture, not reflections of political resistance and outgrowths of longstanding struggle met with fierce white resistance. These essays demonstrate the ways in which the Jim Crow North proved much harder to unveil and destroy and how hard people would fight to preserve these racially inequitable systems, all the while taking umbrage at being called racist. They disrupt culture and behavior as explanatory, analytical frameworks for black urban problems associated with poverty, crime, and educational disparities—that too often framed northern blacks as angry, alienated, and unable to build movements like their southern counterparts. And they insist on examining the variety of ways black people wrote, organized, and agitated to reveal this Jim Crow system. Taken together, these chapters show how misapprehensions of northern virtue and innocence have worked to obfuscate the structural violence and racial inequality that continues to assail black communities today.

The essays in this anthology argue that it is impossible to avoid the Jim Crow North as a central concept for understanding the United States in the twenty-first century. The history of its strange careers and the black freedom movements that challenged it deserve more attention, especially if we, as a nation, want to have any hope of addressing their manifestations in contemporary political, economic, social, and cultural life. These northern stories provide a missing link that can ground current analyses of American racism within broader, deeper histories of American racial inequality. This history helps us to make sense of the recent findings that the most segregated school systems are largely outside the South,[93] that the most segregated cities are largely outside the South,[94] that most of the police killings that have galvanized a growing Black Lives Matter movement have taken place outside the South. Tracing the history of the long black freedom struggle in the Jim Crow North provides important historical antecedents of #BlackLivesMatter and where we must go today.

The sooner Americans recognize this aspect of our history, the sooner we can devise real solutions for real historical and contemporary social problems connected to racism. With Donald Trump—whose racist discourses and practices were homegrown in the Jim Crow North[95]— as president, understanding this history has become even more urgent. The United States in 2018 is paying dearly for failing to recognize this history of northern segregation and struggle. The ideologies, bureaucratic structures, and practices of the Jim Crow North are still with us today. The black activism documented in these essays provides lessons on how we can imagine a different society and chart an alternative, just future.

NOTES

1 Martin Luther King Jr., "Beyond the Los Angeles Riots: Next Step, the North," *Saturday Review* (November 13, 1965), 33–35, 105.

2 C. Vann Woodward, *The Strange Career of Jim Crow* (New York: Oxford University Press, 1955), 99–100.

3 Neil R. McMillan, *Dark Journey: Black Mississippians in the Age of Jim Crow* (Urbana: University of Illinois Press, 1989), 41.

4 Leon Litwack, *Trouble in Mind: Black Southerners in the Age of Jim Crow* (New York: Vintage, 1998), passim, 236; *Garner v. Louisiana*, 368 U.S. 157 (1961), 181.

5 *Plessy v. Ferguson*, 163 U.S. 537 (1896); Litwack, *Trouble in Mind*, 280–325.

6 Examples of popular narrative histories include David Halberstam, *The Children* (New York: Random House, 1998); Taylor Branch, *Parting the Waters: America in the King Years, 1954–1963* (New York: Random House, 1988); Howell Raines, *My Soul Is Rested: The Story of the Civil Rights Movement in the Deep South* (New York: Putnam, 1977); Richard Kluger, *Simple Justice: The History of* Brown v.

Board of Education *and Black America's Struggle for Equality* (New York: Knopf, 1976); Alan Brinkley, *The Unfinished Nation*, 4th ed. (New York: McGraw Hill, 2004), chapters 30–31. Perhaps even more powerfully, documentaries like *Eyes on the Prize* (1987–1990), and feature films like *Selma* (2014), *Mississippi Burning* (1988), *The Help* (2011), and *The Butler* (2013) have engraved this idea of southern exceptionalism into common sense.

7   Overviews of this field include Brian Purnell, "Freedom North Studies, the Long Civil Rights Movement, and Twentieth-Century Liberalism in American Cities," *Journal of Urban History*, 42:3, 634–40; Patrick Jones, ed., "Beyond Dixie: The Black Freedom Struggle outside of the South," special issue, *Organization of American Historians Magazine of History*, 26:1 (January 2012). An early example of civil rights movement history that paid equal attention to the North, South, and West was August Meier and Elliot Rudwick, *CORE: A Study in the Civil Rights Movement, 1942–1968* (New York: Oxford University Press, 1973). A key essay that called for civil rights movement historians to broaden their geographic scope is Steven Lawson, "Freedom Then, Freedom Now: The Historiography of the Civil Rights Movement," *American Historical Review*, 96:2 (April 1991), 456–71. Later historians who focused specifically on the North include James Ralph, *Northern Protest: Martin Luther King, Jr., Chicago, and the Civil Rights Movement* (Cambridge, MA: Harvard University Press, 1993); Thomas Sugrue, *The Origins of the Urban Crisis: Race and Inequality in Postwar Detroit* (Princeton, NJ: Princeton University Press, 1996); Thomas J. Sugrue, "Crabgrass-Roots Politics: Race, Rights, and the Reaction against Liberalism in the Urban North, 1940-1964," *Journal of American History*, 82:2 (September 1995), 551–78; Arnold R. Hirsch, "Massive Resistance in the Urban North: Trumbull Park, Chicago, 1953-1966," *Journal of American History*, 82:2 (September 1995), 522–50; Clarence Taylor, *Knocking at Our Own Door: Milton A. Galamison and the Fight for School Integration in New York City* (New York: Columbia University Press, 1997); Martha Biondi, *To Stand and Fight: The Struggle for Civil Rights in Postwar New York City* (Cambridge, MA: Harvard University Press, 2003); Komozi Woodard, *A Nation within a Nation: Amiri Baraka (LeRoi Jones) and Black Power Politics* (Chapel Hill: University of North Carolina Press, 1999), and Jeanne Theoharis and Komozi Woodard, eds., *Freedom North: Black Freedom Struggles outside the South, 1940–1980* (New York: Palgrave Macmillan, 2003). This scholarship of activism against racial discrimination in the North grew, in part, from a historiography that examined the Old Left, especially in northern black communities. See, for example, Mark Naison, *Communists in Harlem during the Great Depression* (Champaign: University of Illinois Press, 1983).

8   On how histories of racism and racial segregation influence contemporary American life see Michael B. Katz, Mark J. Stern, and Jamie J. Fader, "The New African American Inequality," *Journal of American History*, 92:1 (June 2005), 75–108. On how histories of the black freedom movement overlook the North, see Jeanne Theoharis and Komozi Woodard (eds.), *Freedom North*; and Jeanne Theoharis, *A*

More Beautiful and Terrible History: The Uses and Misuses of Civil Rights History (Boston: Beacon, 2018).

9 One of the first studies to address these questions was Leon Litwack, *North of Slavery: The Negro in the Free States, 1790–1860* (Chicago: University of Chicago Press, 1961). See more recent scholarship by Richard Archer, *Jim Crow North: The Struggle for Equal Rights in Antebellum New England* (New York: Oxford University Press, 2017); Eric Foner, *Gateway to Freedom: The Hidden History of the Underground Railroad* (New York: Norton, 2015); Stephen Kantrowitz, *More Than Freedom: Fighting for Black Citizenship in a White Republic, 1829–1889* (New York: Penguin, 2012); Desmond S. King and Stephen G. N. Tuck, "De-centering the South: America's Nationwide White Supremacist Order after Reconstruction," *Past and Present*, 194 (February 2007), 213–54. Patrick Rael's scholarship is indispensable; see Patrick Rael, *Black Protest and Black Identity in the Antebellum North* (Chapel Hill: University of North Carolina Press, 2003); *African American Activism before the Civil War: The Freedom Struggle in the Antebellum North* (New York: Routledge, 2008); *Eighty-Eight Years: The Long Death of Slavery, 1777–1865* (Athens: University of Georgia Press, 2015); as is David Gellman and David Quigley, *Jim Crow New York: A Documentary History of Race and Citizenship* (New York: NYU Press, 2003). An exciting examination of early histories of race, racism, black, white, and indigenous people is Tiya Miles, *The Dawn of Detroit: A Chronicle of Slavery and Freedom in the City of Straits* (New York: New Press, 2018).

10 For a synthesis of this history, see Tom Sugrue, *Sweet Land of Liberty: The Forgotten Struggle for Civil Rights in the North* (New York: Random House, 2008). On housing, see Richard Rothstein, *The Color of Law: A Forgotten History of How Our Government Segregated America* (New York: Norton, 2017); Destin Jenkins, "Who Segregated America," *Public Books*, Dec. 21, 2017, http://www.publicbooks. org; Beryl Satter, *Family Properties: How the Struggle over Race and Real Estate Transformed Chicago and Urban America* (New York: Metropolitan, 2009); Ta-Nehisi Coates, "The Case for Reparations," *Atlantic* (June 2014), 54–71; "America's Federally Financed Ghettos," *New York Times*, editorial (April 7, 2018) "Blacks Still Face a Red Line on Housing," *New York Times*, editorial (April 14, 2018) and N. D. B. Connolly, *A World More Concrete: Real Estate and the Remaking of the Jim Crow South* (Chicago: University of Chicago Press, 2014). On employment, see Katz et al., "The New African American Inequality," 85–92, 95–108; William Sites and Virginia Parks, "What Do We Really Know about Racial Inequality? Labor Market, Politics, and the Historical Basis of Black Economic Fortunes," *Politics and Society*, 39:1, 40–73. On education, see Katz et al., "The New African American Inequality," 92–95; Nikole Hannah-Jones, "Choosing a School for My Daughter in a Segregated City," *New York Times Magazine* (June 9, 2016.) On the carceral state, see Heather Thompson, "Why Mass Incarceration Matters: Rethinking Crisis, Decline, and Transformation in Postwar American History," *Journal of American History*, 97:3 (December 2010), 703–34; James Foreman Jr., *Locking Up Our Own: Crime and Punishment in Black America* (New York: Farrar, Straus, Giroux, 2017); Michelle

Alexander, *The New Jim Crow: Mass Incarceration in the Age of Colorblindness* (New York: New Press, 2012); and Devah Pager, *Marked: Race, Crime, and Finding Work in an Era of Mass Incarceration* (Chicago: University of Chicago Press, 2007).

11 King and Tuck, "De-centering the South," 215. Histories of the great migration include James R. Grossman, *Land of Hope: Chicago, Black Southerners, and the Great Migration* (Chicago: University of Chicago Press, 1989); Nicolas Lemann, *The Promised Land: The Great Black Migration and How It Changed America* (New York: Knopf, 1991); James N. Gregory, *The Southern Diaspora: How the Great Migration of Black and White Southerners Transformed America* (Chapel Hill: University of North Carolina Press, 2005); Isabel Wilkerson, *The Warmth of Other Suns: The Epic Story of America's Great Migration* (New York: Random House, 2011).

12 Vincent Harding, *There Is a River: The Black Struggle for Freedom in America* (New York: Harcourt, Brace, 1981), 254. Harding had borrowed his image from Henry Highland Garnet, who once warned, "[T]he Pharaohs are on both sides of the blood-red waters." See Henry Highland Garnet, *An Address to the Slaves of the United States*, 1843. Available at http://www.blackpast.org.

13 David Brinkley, *Rosa Parks: A Life* (New York: Penguin, 2000), 67.

14 See Malcolm X interviewed by Professor John Leggett and Herman Blake (graduate student) (Dept. of Sociology) at the University of California–Berkeley, October 11, 1963 (0:19:43–0:25:07), available for viewing at www.lib.berkeley.edu.

15 On the history of black elected officials in Detroit, see Roosevelt Ruffin, *Black Presence in Saginaw* (Saginaw, MI: Roosevelt Ruffin, 1978) for information on William Q. Atwood, an influential late-nineteenth-century lumber businessman and political organizer. See also information on the life of Samuel C. Watson (1832–1892), who served on the Detroit City Council, 1883–1886. On Chicago's black congressman, who served from 1929 to 1935, see Elliott M. Rudwick, "Oscar De Priest and the Jim Crow Restaurant in the U.S. House of Representatives," *Journal of Negro Education*, 35 (Winter 1966): 77–82. On the New Deal, see the thirtieth anniversary edition of Harvard Sitkoff, *A New Deal for Blacks: The Emergence of Civil Rights as a National Issue; The Depression Decade* (New York: Oxford University Press, 2008). On the "raw deal" aspects of the New Deal, see Joe William Trotter Jr., "From a Raw Deal to a New Deal, 1929–1945," in Robin D. G. Kelley and Earl Lewis (eds.), *To Make Our World Anew: A History of African Americans* (New York: Oxford University Press, 2000), 409–44; Ira Katznelson, *When Affirmative Action Was White: An Untold History of Racial Inequality in Twentieth-Century America* (New York: Norton, 2005); and "New Deal, Raw Deal," *Washington Post* (September 27, 2005); Richard Rothstein, *The Color of Law: A Forgotten History of How Our Government Segregated America* (New York: Norton, 2017); and Charles Lane, "The New Deal as Raw Deal for Blacks in Segregated Communities," *Washington Post* (May 25, 2017).

16 *Baker v Carr* (1962) was a landmark case for black urban voting, giving federal courts the ability to intervene in redistricting to address urban

underapportionment—Earl Warren would call it the most important in his tenure as chief justice. But it gathers barely a mention in the popular story of the struggle for voting rights. See "More Perfect" podcast (June 10, 2016) at https://www.wnycstudios.org.

17 Brian Purnell, "Confederate Flags in the Jim Crow North," *Black Perspectives* (July 1, 2015). Available at https://www.aaihs.org.

18 See Patrick Jones, *The Selma of the North: The Civil Rights Insurgency in Milwaukee* (Cambridge, MA: Harvard University Press, 2009). See also Thomas Sugrue, *The Origins of the Urban Crisis*, on similar confrontations in Detroit and Arnold Hirsch, *Making the Second Ghetto: Race and Housing in Chicago, 1940–1960* (Chicago: University of Chicago Press, 1998), for Chicago.

19 Andrew Kahrl, *Free the Beaches: The Story of Ned Coll and the Battle for America's Most Exclusive Shoreline* (New Haven, CT: Yale University Press, 2018).

20 Ian Haney Lopez, *Dog Whistle Politics: How Coded Racial Appeals Have Reinvented Racism and Wrecked the Middle Class* (New York: Oxford University Press, 2014), 16.

21 Dan Carter, *The Politics of Rage: George Wallace, the New Conservatism, and the Transformation of American Politics* (New York: Simon & Schuster, 1995), 365–66.

22 An excellent, thorough overview of the diversity of southern responses to calls to end Jim Crow in the South is Jason Sokol, *There Goes My Everything: White Southerners in the Age of Civil Rights, 1945–1975* (New York: Knopf, 2006). On southerners who opposed racial segregation and discrimination, see Glenda Gilmore, *Defying Dixie: The Radical Roots of Civil Rights, 1919–1950* (New York: Norton, 2006).

23 See Matthew Lassiter and Joseph Crespino, *The Myth of Southern Exceptionalism* (New York: Oxford University Press, 2009); Matthew Lassiter, *The Silent Majority: Suburban Politics in the Sunbelt South* (Princeton, NJ: Princeton University Press, 2006).

24 E. Franklin Frazier, Gunnar Myrdal, and Oscar Lewis were early proponents of such cultural explanations.

25 Scholars have produced multiple studies on the Black Freedom Movement outside the South. See Theoharis and Woodard (eds.), *Freedom North*, and *Groundwork: Local Black Freedom Movements in America* (New York: NYU Press, 2005); James Ralph, *Northern Protest*; Martha Biondi, *To Stand and Fight: The Struggle for Civil Rights in Postwar New York City* (Cambridge, MA: Harvard University Press, 2003); Thomas Sugrue, *Sweet Land of Liberty: The Forgotten Struggle for Civil Rights in the North* (New York: Random House, 2008); Brian Purnell, *Fighting Jim Crow in the County of Kings: The Congress of Racial Equality in Brooklyn* (Lexington: University Press of Kentucky, 2013); Robert O. Self, *American Babylon: Race and the Struggle for Postwar Oakland* (Princeton, NJ: Princeton University Press, 2003); Josh Sides, *LA City Limits: African American Los Angeles from the Great Depression to the Present* (Berkeley: University of California Press, 2003); Matthew Countryman, *Up South: Civil Rights and*

Black Power in Philadelphia (Philadelphia: University of Pennsylvania Press, 2006); Angela Dillard, *Faith in the City: Preaching Radical Social Change in Detroit* (Ann Arbor: University of Michigan Press, 2007); Yohuru Williams, *Black Politics/White Power: Civil Rights, Black Power, and the Black Panthers in New Haven* (Malden, MA: Blackwell, 2008); Clarence Lang, *Grassroots at the Gateway: Class Politics and Black Freedom Struggles in St. Louis, 1936–1975* (Ann Arbor: University of Michigan Press, 2009); Donna Murch, *Living for the City: Migration, Education, and the Rise of the Black Panther Party in Oakland, California* (Chapel Hill: University of North Carolina Press, 2010); Joan Singler, Jean Durning, Bettylou Valentine, and Maid Adams, *Seattle in Black and White: The Congress of Racial Equality and the Fight for Equal Opportunity* (Seattle: University of Washington Press, 2011); Jacobi Williams, *From the Bullet to the Ballot: The Illinois Chapter of the Black Panther Party and Racial Coalition Politics in Chicago* (Chapel Hill: University of North Carolina Press, 2013); Rhonda Y. Williams, *The Politics of Public Housing: Black Women's Struggle against Urban Inequality* (New York: Oxford University Press, 2003); Premilla Nadasen, *Welfare Warriors: The Welfare Rights Movement in the United States* (New York: Routledge, 2004); Annelise Orleck, *Storming Caesar's Palace: How Black Mothers Fought Their Own War on Poverty* (Boston: Beacon, 2005); Felicia Kornbluh, *The Battle for Welfare Rights: Politics and Poverty in Modern America* (Philadelphia: University Press of Pennsylvania, 2007); Lisa Levenstein, *A Movement without Marches: African American Women and the Politics of Poverty in Postwar Philadelphia* (Chapel Hill: University of North Carolina Press, 2009); Matthew F. Delmont, *Why Busing Failed: Race, Media, and the National Resistance to School Desegregation* (Berkeley: University of California Press, 2016); and Mark Speltz, *North of Dixie: Civil Rights Photography beyond the South* (Los Angeles: J. Paul Getty Museum, 2016).

26 Textbooks like Alan Brinkley's *Unfinished Nation* have not substantially incorporated these two decades of scholarship on the North into the way they tell the story of race in the twentieth century. Here we also refer to important public history syntheses like Henry Louis Gates's PBS series *The African Americans: Many Rivers to Cross* and *Black America: And Still I Rise*, the section on post–WWII black life and the civil rights movement at the National Museum of African American History and Culture, and the Equal Justice Initiative's Legacy Museum and "Segregation in America" report (2018) found at https://segregationinamerica.eji.org.

27 This phrase comes from the 1992 edition of George B. Tindall and David E. Shi, *America: A Narrative History* (New York: Norton, 1992), 469–70. See Thomas C. Holt, "Reconstruction in United States History Textbooks," *Journal of American History*, 81:4 (March 1995), 1641–51, esp. 1650.

28 Harvard Sitkoff, *A New Deal for Blacks*, 6.

29 See Rev. Prince Hall et al., "1787 Petition for Equal Education Facilities," in Jonathan Birnbaum and Clarence Taylor (eds.), *Civil Rights since 1787: A Reader on the*

Black Struggle (New York: NYU Press, 2000), 35. See also, Tony Hill, "Class and Inequality, Ethnicity and Education: The Politics of Black Education, 1780–1980," *Boston Review* (Oct. 1981), available at http://bostonreview.net.

30 Leon Litwack, *North of Slavery: The Negro in the Free States, 1790–1860* (Chicago: University of Chicago Press, 1961), 113–52, esp. 147–49.

31 Matthew Delmont and Jeanne Theoharis (eds.), special issue, "Rethinking the Boston 'Busing Crisis,'" *Journal of Urban History* (March 2017). See also, Lily Geismer, *Don't Blame Us: Suburban Liberals and the Transformation of the Democratic Party* (Princeton, NJ: Princeton University Press, 2015), 71–96; 199–226.

32 In 1956, in an effort to defend their "massive resistance" to the Supreme Court's *Brown* decision, which overturned *Plessy*, southern members of the House of Representatives issued what they called the "Southern Manifesto." These pro-segregationists reminded their liberal colleagues, and the nation, that the type of Jim Crow they wanted to protect had its origins in the North. "This constitutional doctrine" of separate but equal "began in the North—not in the South," the Southern Manifesto stated, "and it was followed not only in Massachusetts, but in Connecticut, New York, Illinois, Indiana, Michigan, Minnesota, New Jersey, Ohio, Pennsylvania and other northern states until they, exercising their rights as states through the constitutional processes of local self-government, changed their school systems." See John Kyle Day, *The Southern Manifesto: Massive Resistance and the Fight to Preserve Segregation* (Jackson: University Press of Mississippi, 2014).

33 On New York, see Leslie M. Harris, *In the Shadow of Slavery: African Americans in New York City, 1626–1863* (Chicago: University of Chicago Press, 2003); and Eric Foner, *Gateway to Freedom*.

34 On restrictions against black settlement in other northern states, see Leon Litwack, *North of Slavery*.

35 Leon Litwack, *North of Slavery*, passim; Tocqueville quoted on 65.

36 Elizabeth Stordeur Pryor, "The Etymology of Nigger: Resistance, Language, and the Politics of Freedom in the Antebellum North," *Journal of the Early Republic*, 36:2 (Summer 2016), 203–45, esp., 210–11, 213–14, 216–18, 224–25.

37 Eric Lott, *Love and Theft: Blackface Minstrelsy and the American Working Class* (New York: Oxford University Press, 1993).

38 Hugh Davis, "*We Will Be Satisfied with Nothing Less*": *The African American Struggle for Equal Rights in the North during Reconstruction* (Ithaca, NY: Cornell University Press, 2011).

39 Michael J. Pfeifer, "The Northern United States and the Genesis of Racial Lynching: The Lynching of African Americans in the Civil War Era," *Journal of American History* (Dec. 2010), 621–35, quoted from 623–24. See also, Pfeifer (ed.), *Lynching beyond Dixie: American Mob Violence outside the South* (Urbana: University of Illinois Press, 2013); Pfeifer, *The Roots of Rough Justice: The Origins of Lynching in the U.S.* (Urbana: University of Illinois Press, 2011); Pfeifer, *Rough Justice: Lynching and American Society, 1874–1947* (Urbana: University of Illinois Press, 2004).

40 Eric Foner, *Reconstruction: America's Unfinished Revolution, 1863–1877* (New York: Harper and Row, 1988), 460–71, quotation on 471.

41 The National Labor Congress wanted either to create racially segregated locals for blacks and whites or to drop the issue.

42 Eric Foner, *Reconstruction*, 479, 496, 498, 499.

43 James Loewen, *Sundown Towns: A Hidden Dimension of American Racism* (New York: New Press, 2005).

44 See Start Making Sense podcast of *The Nation* with Linda Gordon, "Fred Trump and the Making of the Ku Klux Klan" (January 4, 2018) at https://www.thenation.com; Linda Gordon, *The Second Coming of the KKK: The Ku Klux Klan of the 1920s and the American Political Tradition* (New York: Norton, 2017).

45 Joshua Rothman, "When Bigotry Paraded through the Streets," *Atlantic*, December 4, 2016. See also, Linda Gordon, *The Second Coming of the KKK.*

46 Mike Pearl, "All the Evidence We Could Find about Fred Trump's Alleged Involvement with the KKK," *Vice* (March 10, 2016); Adam Hothschild, "Ku Klux Klambakes," *New York Review of Books* (December 7, 2017).

47 According to Oxford University Press, the book sold nearly a million copies (https://global.oup.com).

48 C. Vann Woodward, *The Strange Career of Jim Crow* (New York: Oxford University Press, 1966), preface, ix.

49 Ibid., 17.

50 Ibid., 18.

51 Ibid., 18–21, esp. 19.

52 Ibid, passim.

53 Ibid., 21.

54 Ibid., 70.

55 Ira Katznelson, *When Affirmative Action Was White.*

56 Ibid.

57 Sean Farhang and Ira Katznelson, "The Southern Imposition: Congress and Labor in the New Deal and Fair Deal," *Studies in American Political Development*, 19 (Spring 2005), 1–30; Ira Katznelson and Quinn Mulroy, "Was the South Pivotal? Situated Partisanship and Policy Coalitions during the New Deal and Fair Deal," *Journal of Politics*, 74:2 (March 2012), 604–20; for a fascinating debate on whether or not the GI Bill exacerbated racial inequality or reduced it, see Ira Katznelson and Suzanne Mettler, "On Race and Policy History: A Dialogue about the G.I. Bill," *Perspectives on Politics*, 6:3 (September 2008), 519–37; Ira Katznelson, Kim Geiger, and Daniel Kryder, "Limiting Liberalism: The Southern Veto in Congress, 1933–1950," *Political Science Quarterly*, 108:2 (Summer 1993), 283–306.

58 Ira Katznelson, *Fear Itself: The New Deal and the Origins of Our Times* (New York: Norton, 2013), 21.

59 Ibid., 22.

60 Ira Katznelson, "New Deal, Raw Deal." Other noteworthy scholarship that advances this argument includes Anthony S. Chen, *The Fifth Freedom: Jobs, Politics, and Civil Rights in the United States, 1941–1972* (Princeton, NJ: Princeton University Press, 2009); and Eric Schickler, *Racial Realignment: The Transformation of American Liberalism, 1932–1965* (Princeton, NJ: Princeton University Press, 2016).

61 Mary Poole, *The Segregated Origins of Social Security: African Americans and the Welfare State* (Chapel Hill: University of North Carolina Press, 2006), 6.

62 Anthony Chen, "The Party of Lincoln and the Politics of State Fair Employment Practices Legislation in the North, 1945–1964," *American Journal of Sociology*, 112:6 (May 2007), 1713–74.

63 Craig Wilder, *A Covenant with Color* (New York: Columbia University Press, 2001); Jackson, *Crabgrass Frontier: The Suburbanization of the United States* New York: Oxford University Press, 1987; Rothstein, *The Color of Law*.

64 Rothstein, *The Color of Law*.

65 Jason Sokol, *All Eyes Are upon Us: Race and Politics from Boston to Brooklyn* (New York: Basic Books, 2016), xi.

66 When black activists first took their case of Boston's segregated schools to the Massachusetts Commission Against Discrimination, MCAD pronounced them "not segregated." That was how the Jim Crow North worked; at times the very bodies convened to monitor discrimination became barriers. Ruth Batson, A Chronology of the Educational Movement in Boston, manuscript in Ruth Batson's papers, 2001-M194, Schlesinger Library, Radcliffe Institute.

67 Martin Luther King Jr., "Beyond the Los Angeles Riots."

68 See Jones's *Selma of the North*; Frazier's *Harambee City: The Congress of Racial Equality in Cleveland and the Rise of Black Power Populism* (Fayetteville: University of Arkansas Press, 2017); and Theoharis's *More Beautiful and Terrible History* for fuller descriptions of these events.

69 Sokol, *All Eyes*.

70 Karen Miller, *Managing Inequality: Northern Racial Liberalism in Interwar Detroit* (New York: NYU Press, 2014).

71 Ibid., 4.

72 Khalil Muhammad, *The Condemnation of Blackness: Race, Crime, and the Making of Modern Urban America* (Cambridge, MA: Harvard University Press, 2010), 7, 226.

73 "A Boycott Solves Nothing," editorial, *New York Times* (January 31, 1964) "No More School Boycotts," editorial, *New York Times* (February 3, 1964).

74 "Poll Shows Whites in City Resent Civil Rights Drive," *New York Times*, September 21, 1964.

75 See chapter 1 of Matthew Delmont's *Why Busing Failed*.

76 "Racial imbalance" became the preferred northern euphemism for northern segregation—and even more curiously, all-white or nearly all-white schools, per Massachusetts law, were not considered "racially imbalanced." Matthew Delmont, "The Origins of Anti-Busing Politics", *Gotham* blog, found at: www.gothamcenter.org.

77 As cited by Matthew Delmont, *Why Busing Failed*, 50.

78 Matthew Delmont, "When Black Voters Exited Left," *Atlantic* (March 31, 2016).

79 Isabel Wilkerson, *The Warmth of Other Suns: The Epic Story of America's Great Migration* (New York: Random House, 2010); Ta Nehisi Coates, "The Case for Reparations," *Atlantic* (June 2014); Nikole Hannah-Jones, "Choosing a School for My Daughter in a Segregated City," *New York Times Magazine* (June 9, 2016); Nikole Hannah-Jones, "The Continuing Reality of Segregated Schools" *New York Times* (July 31, 2015); Nikole Hannah-Jones "School Segregation, the Continuing Tragedy of Ferguson," *Pro Publica* (December 19, 2014).

80 Kathryn Bigelow's feature film *Detroit* and much of the commentary surrounding it was a particularly egregious example of the erasure of black perspectives. See Jeanne Theoharis, Say Burgin, and Mary Phillips, "*Detroit* Is the Most Irresponsible and Dangerous Movie of the Year," *Huffington Post* (September 8, 2017).

81 Equal Justice Initiative, "Segregation in America" (2018). For a contemporary report that centers the history of northern Jim Crow, see the Brennan Center, "Jim Crow in New York" (2009) at https://www.brennancenter.org.

82 Michelle Alexander, *The New Jim Crow: Mass Incarceration in the Age of Colorblindness* (New York: New Press, 2010), 4.

83 Recent work by Naomi Murakawa, *The First Civil Right: How Liberals Built Prison America* (New York: Oxford University Press, 2014), and Elizabeth Hinton, *From the War on Poverty to the War on Drugs: The Making of Mass Incarceration* (Cambridge, MA: Harvard University Press, 2016) has moved our understandings of the rise of mass incarceration and criminalization as a hallmark of the new Right's ascendancy in American politics to seeing its earlier liberal roots.

84 Loïc Wacquant, "From Slavery to Mass Incarceration: Rethinking the Race Question in the U.S.," *New Left Review*, 13 (Jan.–Feb. 2002), 41–60; Craig Wilder, *A Covenant with Color* (New York: Columbia University Press, 2001); Khalil Muhammad, *Condemnation of Blackness*.

85 Charles Mills, *The Racial Contract* (Ithaca, NY: Cornell University Press, 1998), 18–19.

86 Mary Dudziak, *Cold War Civil Rights: Race and the Image of American Democracy* (Princeton, NJ: Princeton University Press, 2000).

87 See the preface and chapter 1 of *A More Beautiful and Terrible History* for further exposition of contemporary uses of civil rights history to further narratives of American exceptionalism.

88 The *New York Times* covered desegregation struggles in Birmingham, Alabama, in 1962 and 1963 in strikingly different ways to the way it covered school desegregation struggles in New York City at this time.

89 Alice O'Connor, *Poverty Knowledge: Social Science, Social Policy, and the Poor in Twentieth-Century U.S. History* (Princeton, NJ: Princeton University Press, 2002).

90 Peter Levy, *The Great Uprising* (New York: Cambridge University Press, 2018).

91 Early works on the black freedom struggle outside the South—like Theoharis and Woodard's *Freedom North* and *Groundwork*—sought to expand the conversa-

tion on what aspects of black life and struggle in the North were even seen and understood—and gave limited attention to northern uprisings, given how much attention had focused on them in the preceding decades and in textbooks.

92 Gene Roberts and Hank Klibanoff, *The Race Beat: The Press, the Civil Rights Struggle, and the Awakening of the Nation* (New York: Knopf, 2006).

93 "UCLA Report Finds Changing US Demographics Transform School Segregation Landscape 60 Years after Brown," press release (May 15, 2014). Downloaded from www.civilrightsproject.ucla.edu.

94 "Top Ten Most Segregated Cities in the US," *Atlanta Black Star* (March 24, 2014.)

95 Fred C. Trump, Donald Trump's father, built his racially discriminatory housing empire and wealth largely through public subsidy. He ran afoul of the government in the 1950s for profiteering off public contracts, admitting he had dramatically overinflated costs to get larger FHA mortgages. The New York Commission for Human Rights investigated the Trump Organization for racial discrimination in the 1960s and 1970s, finding Trump Village in South Brooklyn had only seven black families out of thirty-seven hundred units. In 1973, the U.S. Justice Department sued Trump Management for housing discrimination, naming both Fred and Donald as defendants. The Trumps countersued, with Donald claiming that the government was trying to force him to rent to "welfare recipients." Records released suggest evidence of black applicants being steered away and applications being tossed in drawers or marked with "No. 9" or "C" for colored. The suit ended in a 1975 consent decree with new antidiscriminatory practices in place (the government claimed in 1978 that the Trump Organization had violated the consent decree but no action resulted). In May 1989, before the criminal trials had concluded, and in ways reminiscent of post-Reconstruction-era newspaper calls for lynchings of black men accused, but not convicted, of crimes, Donald Trump took out ads in four New York newspapers calling for reinstituting the death penalty for the "Central Park 5." He told TV interviewer Larry King, "[M]aybe hate is what we need if we're going to get something done." Peter Dreier, "Trump's Housing Hypocrisy," *Prospect* (April 7, 2017); Michael Kranish and Robert O'Harrow, "Inside the Government's Racial Bias Case against Donald Trump and How He Fought It," *Washington Post* (January 23, 2016).

1

A Murder in Central Park

Racial Violence and the Crime Wave in New York during the 1930s and 1940s

SHANNON KING

"I had never before been so aware of policemen, on foot, on horseback, on corners, everywhere," remembered James Baldwin, Harlem native, describing his arrival home in early June of 1943. Police presence had increased since the winter of 1941 after a series of robberies and assaults by blacks upon whites inspired white newspapers to define the illegal acts a "crime wave." White New Yorkers sent a flood of angry letters to Mayor Fiorello H. La Guardia and Police Commissioner Lewis J. Valentine. Thus, during the spring of 1942, the confluence of the crime-scare stories and whites' demands for safety had transformed Harlem into a zone of police violence.

Home to attend his father's funeral, Baldwin could not have known that less than ten years after the Harlem Riot of 1935, the area would explode again. But that happened in August 1943 when Harlem experienced its second racial uprising. This outpouring of anger occurred on August 1 and 2 after a white police officer, James Collins, shot and wounded Robert Bandy, a soldier on leave. Even twenty years later, after Harlem experienced yet another paroxysm of racial violence, Baldwin bore witness to the community's unrelenting occurrences of police brutality. His argument in 1943 proved even truer in 1966: "Harlem is policed like occupied territory."[1]

This chapter explores black New Yorkers' encounters with violence between the Harlem riots of 1935 and 1943, and their demands for equitable policing. Black people's criticisms of their experiences of underprotection and overpolicing at the hands of law enforcement brings to light their efforts to challenge Jim Crow practices that defined the New

York Police Department (NYPD), but often remained hidden in plain sight. Race riots have preoccupied historians who focus on this period of the Jim Crow North's history, but attention on those subjects, I argue, has blinded us to blacks who demanded safety as a pivotal aspect of their citizenship and community rights.[2]

The NYPD, as law enforcement and therefore agents of the state, both overpoliced *and* underprotected black New Yorkers. Black citizens understood policing as a civil right. By centering Harlemites' demands for safety, this chapter illuminates blacks' vulnerabilities to state-sponsored violence as conditions of Jim Crow policing in New York City. The story of police underprotection of black New Yorkers likely echoes across the entire Jim Crow North.

In the aftermath of the Harlem rebellion of March 19, 1935, triggered by the rumor that Lino Rivera, an Afro–Puerto Rican Harlemite, had been killed by the police, La Guardia commissioned an investigation into the uprising's causes. The investigation's controversial report evidenced a pattern of institutionalized racism in five areas: relief, housing, youth services (education and recreation), health care (and hospital services), and criminal justice (crime and police). The mayor concealed the report from the public because he feared it would damage his administration's reputation. On matters of racial equality, convenience and expedience, more than justice and democracy, motivated even the most liberal northerners.

La Guardia was not alone among northern liberals in prioritizing his own political or personal interests at the expense of black people's civil rights. Newspapers in New York City provided sensational portrayals of black criminality, but buried mundane stories about blacks who demanded safety from crime and police brutality. Thus, as black New Yorkers initiated their own anticrime drives to make up for police underprotection, they checked white dailies' stories of "crime waves" and "Negro thugs," and they argued that La Guardia's failure to remedy Jim Crow conditions outlined in the report perpetuated inequities.

White dailies' racist narratives during the 1930s and 1940s served as ideological forebears of the "culture of poverty" thesis.[3] They interpreted crimes committed by blacks as social problems associated with poverty, not inveterate conditions of the Negro race. White dailies' crime-laden narratives about blacks and white citizens' fears drove the NYPD's

Jim Crow policies of overpolicing through brutality and underpolicing through neglect. The way liberals policed black neighborhoods in Harlem and Bedford-Stuyvesant revealed less about black criminal behavior and more about the methods, and failures, of white liberal governance. White New Yorkers and the white dailies constructed blacks as criminals and leveraged their political power to punish black citizens as threats to white security. Whether blacks were actual criminals or their criminality was just a figment of white imaginations, newspaper stories about crime and blackness contributed to a widespread NYPD practice that rendered black citizens unworthy of protection and subject to suppression.

Words became black people's weapons against these malpractices. In the late 1930s, black New Yorkers initiated a letter-writing campaign, and the black press published a series of editorials, urging Mayor La Guardia and Commissioner Valentine to protect black people from rape, petty theft, and burglary. Black New Yorkers expressed fear of, and anger against, intraracial crimes, especially against black women and children. They argued that racism explained the NYPD's underprotection of black citizens. Framing safety and police protection as a civil right, they criticized the police for "Jim Crow policing." These policies and practices promoted unequal protection and punishment of black citizens for no other reasons than the neighborhoods where they lived and the color of their skin.[4]

As blacks spotlighted police negligence, crimes against whites precipitated a law-and-order campaign. To halt the movement of blacks to Bedford-Stuyvesant, Brooklyn, in the late 1930s, the Midtown Civic League (MCL) claimed that black crime constituted a "crime wave." Black Brooklynites condemned MCL's racist allegations. After three blacks killed a white youth in Central Park in 1941, white dailies apprised readers of the outbreak of "muggings." By singling out and publicizing crimes committed by blacks on whites, and dubbing them "crime waves," white news media manufactured racial panic. Such stories rendered invisible black citizens who required adequate police protection. They crowded out the black press's standing demands for adequate police protection. These exaggerated media-driven narratives, depicting black areas as crime zones, triggered a letter-writing campaign by white New Yorkers, who demanded that La Guardia protect them from "negro thugs." Others insisted that La Guardia favored blacks because of their political support in the 1941 mayoral election, and that the mayor failed to punish black criminals. Motivated by white dailies and white complaints, Police Commissioner Valentine assigned more patrolmen to target areas to protect white people. Police violence and harassment against blacks increased.[5]

Aghast at the mayor's instant protection of white citizens, the black community mobilized to expose the color-conscious policing practices of the NYPD, the media-manufactured "crime wave," and police neglect and brutality. Black New Yorkers explained juvenile delinquency as a symptom of poverty and unequal access to municipal sources. They framed Valentine's law-and-order campaign as a proxy for La Guardia's failure to enact recommendations detailed in the earlier report on the causes of the Harlem race riot. They demanded protection and experienced punishment. This pattern became a defining characteristic of policing practices and politics in the Jim Crow North.

* * *

In New York City, racism became manifest through police brutality, especially during Prohibition and the Great Depression, when political and cultural discussions of urban crime served as coded language for the class and race differences that blackness connoted.[6] Harlem, once the cultural hub of black America, became ground zero for two race riots. After the first riot in 1935, Mayor La Guardia commissioned a group of white and black leaders and social scientists, such as labor leader A. Philip Randolph, poet Countee Cullen, and Howard University's E. Franklin Frazier, to investigate the cause of the riot. While they researched, the number of police officers in Harlem increased. The NYPD detailed five hundred policemen to guard the district.[7]

The report, Mayor La Guardia's *Commission on the Harlem Riot* of March 19, 1935, not only pinpointed racism among white civilians, but in each of the five areas, it also argued that the general neglect to serve black citizens caused the uprising. The Pittsburgh black daily, the *Courier*, noted that "the report . . . holds Mayor La Guardia personally responsible for the jim crow conditions in the city." Wary about exposing the culpability of his administration, La Guardia never released the report. Yet in July 1936, the *New York Amsterdam News*, a black weekly, secured a copy and printed sections.[8] Thereafter, a committee of twenty-seven leaders of the community, including the Reverend William Lloyd Imes of St. James Presbyterian Church, Mrs. Mabel K. Staupers of the National Association of Colored Graduate Nurses, and Mr. James E. Allen of the NAACP (National Association for the Advancement of Colored People), met the mayor on July 22 and, making a reference to the increased police presence since the riot, asked for the "withdrawal of the 'police army of occupation in Harlem.'"[9] While La Guardia claimed he "would not tolerate police brutality in Harlem nor in any other section of Manhattan," he also claimed no power over the police force, and that Police Commissioner Valentine was "a responsible commissioner." The mayor offered Harlem's leadership little in the way of implementing the report's recommendations. He acknowledged the economic plight of Harlemites, but explained there was nothing he could do about it.[10]

After the initial meeting, La Guardia requested the committee to form a delegation of five that would meet periodically with him to discuss the report's recommendations. Throughout the remainder of the 1930s, Harlemites complained about police brutality. In 1937, the *New York Amsterdam News* charged, "Police terror in New York City must go." The newspaper stated that police brutality should not happen in "'a land of the free and the home of the brave.' But it can, and does, happen here, even two years after the Harlem rioting and the more recent revelations of the Mayor's Commission on Conditions in Harlem."[11] Mayor La Guardia proved more capable of meeting to discuss social problems in Harlem than of doing anything substantive to alleviate those problems.

"The Spirit of Fascism" and the 1930s Crime Waves

During the late 1930s, southern black migrants and Afro-Caribbean immigrants, as well as black New Yorkers, moved to Brooklyn. Affordable housing and less congested living spaces drew them to the Bedford-Stuyvesant section. Between 1930 and the 1950s, Brooklyn's black population tripled; Bedford-Stuyvesant became, according to the *New York Times*, "Brooklyn's Harlem."[12] In July of 1937, the Bethel African Methodist Episcopal Church endeavored to purchase the "white debt-ridden" Grace Congregational Church, at Stuyvesant and Jefferson Avenues in Bedford-Stuyvesant. Sumner Sirtl, the leader of the Midtown

Civic League (MCL), protested black settlement in that section, and especially Bethel AME's attempts to purchase the white-owned church. According to Sirtl, "[C]ertain white realtors have the habit of renting houses to colored people without making any repairs thereby depreciating the value of property." Denying racial discrimination, he charged that blacks neglected to request repairs to their homes. "Now, white people demand repairs on the houses they rent from realtors. As a rule, colored families don't. Therefore, the houses run down. Slum conditions start. Whites move out. All because the colored people don't demand their repairs. They should!"[13]

Throughout the remainder of the year and the decade, Sirtl and the MCL tried to incite fear among white Brooklynites to thwart black settlement in Bedford-Stuyvesant. Besides claiming that blacks depreciated property values, in November 1937 Sirtl and the MCL argued that a "crime wave" existed in the neighborhood. More specifically, he claimed that black youths had harassed, robbed, and physically assaulted white women and children. Sirtl, along with heads of four police precincts, assigned a patrol of fifty black and white police officers to the area. The MCL also threatened to organize a vigilante committee, which, by December, had begun practicing at a shooting range at the 106th Armory.[14] The *Amsterdam News* claimed that Sirtl's alleged "crime wave" was a sinister attempt to thwart efforts of blacks to rent and purchase property. More significantly, the black weekly compared the Midtown Civic League's tactics to those of white supremacist organizations, such as the Ku Klux Klan. Comparing Sirtl and his league to the Axis powers, in January the *Amsterdam News* asserted that "the spirit of fascism [had] reared its ugly head in Brooklyn, in the guise of the Midtown Civic Association in the Bedford-Stuyvesant section."[15]

Blacks in Brooklyn and Harlem also complained about crimes against blacks, especially intraracial crime against black women. Thus, while black Brooklynites and the *Amsterdam News* framed Sirtl's clarion calls for crime prevention as machinations of racism, they never denied the occurrence of crime. They asserted that both black and white youth were responsible for crime, and demanded that the police department assign more police officers, particularly black patrolmen, to problem areas.[16]

By 1939, the *Amsterdam News* and the black community, especially in Harlem, had begun to challenge black ministers, civic leaders, educators, and parents to halt crime among black youth. As Archie Seale, a columnist for the *Amsterdam News*, asserted, "[S]o many of our leading citizens will throw the blame on our present economic problem, which in reality is just an 'OUT' for them. . . . The youth of Harlem have too much freedom."[17] Although crime was a concern for all Harlemites, the campaign also reflected intraracial class tensions within Harlem, particularly the Sugar Hill section of the neighborhood. As Enos Coyle of the *Amsterdam News* described in July 1939, "[T]he once most-exclusive residential section of Harlem . . . today is plagued with evils of a most virulent sort—evils which, unless soon taken in hand and removed, threaten to wipe out the last vestiges of respectability in which the section once basked."[18]

Harlemites and Brooklynites were also disturbed by crimes committed against black women. In early March 1939, an anonymous person wrote to the *New York Amsterdam News*, "[T]he streets of Harlem are getting more and more unsafe for our women." Highlighting the contradiction between overpolicing and underpolicing in Harlem, the writer lamented, "This is a terrible state of affairs when you consider that we have so many police and they cannot protect us." Only a week later, the *Amsterdam News* reported a similar story that exposed the vulnerability of black women to intraracial crime.

* * *

"I ought to kill you!" spewed Mrs. John Miller's assailant, a tall, thin black man, marked "with a scar on his right cheek." According to the *Amsterdam News*, Mrs. Miller, forty-one years old, of 531 Madison Street, lived "in the heart of the respectable section where 200 extra police are patrolling the streets." Arthur Holmes, arrested in April, violated Mrs. Miller on the first of March 1939. The imposing and scarred perpetrator, armed with a switchblade, broke into her apartment, robbed her of some money, forced her to the roof of the building, and made her cross several rooftops. The "maniac," described the black weekly, tied her up and brutally raped her on the rooftop of the building at 525 Madison Street. Noting both Mrs. Miller's beauty and her vulnerability, the newspaper chastised the New York Police Department for failing to protect black women, and all black people, from criminals.[19] The black weekly, along with neighborhood residents, wanted to know the status of the police's investigation, but police "told Mrs. Miller's family that they could 'work better' if no mention of the case reached the press." Thus, rather than pursuing the culprit, the *Amsterdam News* criticized, "[T]he police have been doing all in their power to keep the affair quiet."[20]

Mrs. Miller and her concerned black neighbors complained about police inaction. They described what might be called "Jim Crow policing," the unequal protection of black citizens, signaling the color-conscious policing of the NYPD. Many of the residents, noted the black weekly, asserted "that had a white woman been raped by a Negro every man answering the general description of the rapist would have been placed under arrest within 24 hours. But they felt, since it was a case which concerned Negroes only, police were indifferent." Throughout the remainder of March and April, the *Amsterdam News*, the Millers, and "incensed" black Brooklynites persistently pinpointed the contradiction between the expansion of the police presence in Bedford-Stuyvesant, induced by Sumner Sirtl and the MCL, and the lackluster efforts of the police to find the rapist. They demanded "adequate policing," they protested against police malfeasance, and they spotlighted intraracial crime and violence that rendered black women invisible in the enforcement of the law.[21]

Under Jim Crow policing, black citizens experienced overpolicing, which subjected them to constant suspicion of being criminals, brutal treatment when in police custody, and the presence of police officers as an occupying force in black neighborhoods that abutted white ones. They also received underpolicing when the NYPD did not investigate crimes against black citizens with professionalism or zealousness. This paradox revealed the racist nature of law enforcement throughout the Jim Crow North: black people were perpetrators of crime, but not victims of it. Police gave blacks attention as suspects standing on one side of a knife or a gun, but rarely as citizens confronting assailants standing on the other side and thus deserving police protection. In the minds and practices of a Jim Crow police force in New York City, black individuals became lumped together into a singular, dangerous, criminal entity— the gang, the thug, the animal, the nigger—always dangerous, always demanding surveillance, never worthy of respect, service, or protection.

"Gangs of Nigger Thugs Who Molest White People"

On November 1, 1941, one of three black youths near Central Park fatally stabbed James O'Connell, a white fifteen-year-old, who lived at 1518 Madison Avenue. Two days later, the *New York Times* ran a headline that read "Hoodlums Hunted in Fatal Stabbing." Four days thereafter the headline read, "Crime Outbreak in Harlem Spurs Drive by Police."[22] Following the killing of O'Connell, on November 6, Joseph Keelan, a thirty-two-year-old laundry worker, was found on a footpath in Morningside Park. According to the police, Keelan was probably "mugged." A mugging occurred when "one member of a gang 'mugs' the victim by stealing up behind him, throwing an arm around his neck and holding a knee in his back. . . . [while] other members of the gang turn his pockets inside out and sometimes steal his clothing as well." The *Times* added that muggings were a "favorite way of throttling a victim in Harlem."[23] Both Morningside Park and Central Park bordered Harlem's predominantly black neighborhood. These areas, therefore, were locally understood and policed as racially distinct and contested spaces. As various newspapers, both black and white, noted, the stabbing of O'Connell occurred only ten blocks from the La Guardias' home, on Central Park East. Juvenile crime had begun to incite fear among businesses in the black district. As the *Times* explained, "[M]ilk and insurance companies have curtailed their business in Harlem because of the repeated robberies of their collectors."[24]

La Guardia and Commissioner Valentine responded to the news of the killings, stating that they had been aware of the crime around Central Park. Unlike the blatant racist motivations of the Midtown Civic League in Bedford-Stuyvesant, the killing of a white youth (and the incident's proximity to where La Guardia himself lived) ensured that the story would make mainstream white media, and that La Guardia would have to respond. The mayor explained, "[T]he matter has received attention for some time. The fact that arrests were made indicates that. The situation is indeed a bad one. What makes it all the more difficult is that the crimes are committed by young hoodlums in their teens, from 12 to 16 years." By acknowledging the assailants' youth, noting that they were "mere youngsters," La Guardia suggested that the allegation of a "crime wave" was exaggerated and that he had control over the situation. He claimed that he "personally took charge of one case," ordering "strong reinforcements of police in that locality," and was positive that the problem would be resolved. Valentine claimed that the police were on the job, and that they had augmented the police presence in Central Park. Yet unlike La Guardia's color-blind description of juvenile crime, Valentine mentioned the race of the perpetrators and described violent crimes by adults. Highlighting the work already done, he revealed, "[O]nly last week two men were arrested for raping and assaulting a white woman in Central Park, and, as you know three Negro boys were apprehended in the murder of the O'Connell boy."[25]

In response to the white dailies' and citizens' outcries, Police Commissioner Valentine assigned 250 more police in Harlem "to Stamp out Crime Wave," and doubled patrols near Central Park. Valentine described policing in Harlem as if NYPD patrolled a war zone. According to the commissioner, "[U]p in Harlem even my own men are not safe. You remember some time ago two policemen were attacked by two hold-up men in Harlem and one of the policemen had his clothing slashed, although they finally shot and killed the men who attacked them."[26] The police department, Mayor La Guardia, and white dailies directed their attention, resources, and police patrols to Harlem—though only to "protect and serve" white neighborhoods bordering black-occupied areas. As the white dailies published more and more stories of crimes committed by blacks against whites, manufacturing this public transcript of a black "crime wave," as well as La Guardia's alleged neglect of whites' safety, white New Yorkers demanded police protection, and the punishment of black criminals.

The *New York Times'* and other white-owned dailies' editorials sparked a "moral panic" and spun a powerful narrative of black criminality among many white New Yorkers in the early 1940s.[27] Outraged by the murder of a white youth, but also by what seemed like a torrent of crime committed by blacks against whites, white New Yorkers initiated a letter-writing campaign demanding that La Guardia protect white people from black thugs. The so-called 1941 crime wave in Harlem, however, was framed differently than those in the late 1930s. Then, the *Amsterdam News*, Bedford-Stuyvesant's mobilized black community, and black activists from various organizations across the city framed the rhetoric and actions of MCL and Sirtl as those of segregationists and white supremacists. The crime wave of 1941, however, focused on white innocence and defense of white neighborhoods. The white press tethered stories of white victimization to the act of "mugging" and the epithet "hoodlum" to black offenders, portraying crime as a problem of governance and blackness. By insinuating that La Guardia prevented the police from doing their jobs to win black support, the white press convinced many white New Yorkers that no white person was safe.[28]

For many letter writers, the O'Connell killing provided an opportunity to share their own personal encounters with juvenile crime, as well as their children's, friends', and neighbors', with an official with greater authority than their local police precinct. Anne Kolodney, a woman from the Bronx, explained that a gang of "hoodlums" robbed her nine-year-old nephew "of a brand new football." Kolodney had even interviewed some of the kids in the neighborhood, who told her the name of the gang, and that they "take delight in frightening the children and have been known to threaten them with an open penknife." She informed the mayor that she had made complaints to her local precinct, but they had done nothing; disappointed, she queried, "[M]ust we wait until a child is killed before the police will take action?" Similarly, another letter writer, George Belmont from Yonkers, explained to the mayor that he was assaulted in August in Harlem, on 117th Street near Seventh Avenue. Belmont believed that "the technique employed by my assailants was exactly the same as that used on the late John Keelan except that they probably were scared away before [they] finish[ed] me up by the presence a hundred yards away of two unsuspecting police officers." Belmont, unlike Kolodney, identified the race of the assailants, noting that he was "the victim on the part of a gang of young Negroes." Without using the word "mugging," as defined by the New York Times, he used its description to conclude that "Keelan's murderer may also be responsible for my hold-up." But despite reporting his assault in August and again in October, he "received no reply."[29]

Beyond reporting their experiences of crime and the negligence of their police precinct, other letter writers made more explicit connections among juvenile crime, race, blackness, and punishment. In a letter to Mayor La Guardia dated November 7, Thomas Curtin, a white New Yorker, claimed that "life among the Negroes [wa]s cheap." Consequently, the perpetuation of crime—regardless of the kind—was likely to result in violence, because "whether or not the potential victim's life has to be taken in order to obtain the loot, is not considered." They also believed that crimes committed by blacks against whites was a city-wide problem. As Curtin noted, "[N]ot only has Harlem been affected by these hoodlums, but also colored sections in Brooklyn and Queens. The negroes travel in cliques of three or four and pounce on their prey who is usually alone."[30] Many of the letter writers, like Curtin, described blacks not as individuals but as part of a violent mob. This discourse reflected white New Yorkers', and arguably northern whites', encounters with crime committed by blacks as well as their internalization of stereotypes of blacks as inherently criminal—ideas perpetuated in both southern and northern news outlets, popular culture, and social science scholarship.[31]

Despite La Guardia's tepid response to blacks' demands for more and better jobs, and his shelving of the report on the riot of 1935, he still secured the black vote with a record voting turnout of 90 percent in the mayoral election in which he had edged out a victory against O'Dwyer only days before. The temper of whites' ire about the murder of O'Connell in Central Park, therefore, was also, in part, a reflection of the perceived political power that Harlemites and black New Yorkers had gained in the aftermath of the election. In a letter to the mayor dated November 10, an anonymous letter writer claimed, "On the eve before election you went up to Harlem to tell the niggers what fine people they are and that you of course expected them to vote for you for favors received, such as relief etc. All of this has made the niggers unmeasureably bold."[32] Other letter writers agreed. Because he won the election with the support of the black vote, according to this logic, La Guardia somehow sanctioned their criminal activity. As one letter writer, with the pseudonym "The Real American," wrote, "[E]very nigger in Harlem has the Mayors telephone in case the Police interferes in any way with this business whether lawful or otherwise, a nice state of affairs, in my humble opinion this should be brought to the attention of the Grand Jury."[33]

For many letter writers, La Guardia prevented the police from fighting crime and, more importantly, protecting white citizens. As one wrote, "[T]he present crime wave in Harlem would never have arisen if you had let the police take the measures which were necessary long ago. But you asked the police to go easy for fear there might be another riot."

Some police officers, noted the *Times*, expressed similar sentiments: "Individual policemen assigned to Harlem have often complained to newspaper men in a district that they were hampered in doing their work by Mayor La Guardia's repeated invitations to the population to report any instances of police oppression directly to City Hall."[34] Questioning the mayor's, and especially the police department's manhood, the writer described the police's behavior as "cowardly," adding, "If the niggers cannot behave and leave the white people alone they will have to be treated as they are down south."[35] Similarly, another letter writer warned La Guardia and black leaders in Harlem that "their race . . . will have to reform or take the consequences."[36] Thus, as crime bled into white areas, the crime scare overshadowed the paradox of overpolicing and underpolicing of black neighborhoods. As white dailies' race-laden stories interlaced with white New Yorkers' tales of black crime, whites rendered themselves as victims, and represented La Guardia as both negligent and corrupt. Altogether, the preponderance of whites' narratives of fear and insecurity secured what blacks' clarion calls for safety could not—mayoral accountability and police protection.

"Blitzkrieg on Harlem"

Black Harlem was infuriated by the news of the "crime wave." While blacks expressed a variety of opinions on the significance of O'Connell's death, Harlem was united in denouncing the allegation that there was, in fact, a "crime wave." Many believed that white dailies, particularly the *New York Times*, misnamed the unfortunate recent killings and unfairly targeted Harlem as a war zone. One editorial in the *New York Amsterdam News* described white reportage of the so-called crime wave as a "Blitzkrieg on Harlem."[37] As the editorial explained, continuing with World War II metaphors, "[T]his isn't the first time the daily press has let loose its big guns, firing adverse publicity at Harlem and its people. But this time some of them, the *Times* particularly, have opened up both barrels, which has set many alert persons in this community to thinking about the motive behind their action."[38] The NAACP, like the *Amsterdam News*, both criticized the *Times* and called for a conference to explore what triggered the recent string of crimes. The NAACP warned New Yorkers not to jump "to hasty conclusions" about the juvenile crime around Central Park, and argued that the white dailies' reportage constituted "shameless racial slander and incitement to hatred and distrust between the races." The *Amsterdam News* and the NAACP were especially troubled since both had for years zealously requested not only more police to stop crime in Harlem and Bedford-Stuyvesant but also more resources—such as better jobs, juvenile recreations, and welfare facilities—in the district.[39]

Not all of Harlem, or black New York for that matter, agreed that greater resources would adequately halt juvenile crime. Ebenezer Ray and Ludlow W. Werner, columnists at the *New York Age*, directed their attention at the black community. Werner, in his column, "Across the Desk," agreed that the black community needed better-paying jobs, but he believed that black parents were negligent. He even went so far as to assert that corporal punishment was necessary to discipline children.[40] In his column, "About People and Things," Ray stated plainly that crime among blacks in Harlem was a major problem. He wrote, "[W]e might as well be frank about it. Lawlessness in Harlem is reaching an unbearable point and nobody is doing anything about it." Ray directed his criticisms at adult and juvenile crime; he especially censured the offensive language that black men and boys used around women and girls in public, protesting that a man "can rarely take his wife, his mother, his sister, or his daughter on the streets of Harlem without a volley of indecent language offending her ears." Arguably, Ray's mention of black women became a way to focus on black men, for he seemed particularly concerned about how the usage of "indecent language" around black women reinforced disreputable masculinity; consequently, Ray reframed black men's and black youth's use of indecent language as a criminal act, encouraging "Commissioner Valentine . . . [to] add more police officers to Harlem armed with their night sticks, to crack the skulls of these older men with their foul tongues." So, while he sincerely wanted to halt criminal activity in Harlem, especially against black people, crime fighting for Ray was an act of erasing problematic public representations of black manhood.[41]

Black New Yorkers' letters to La Guardia reflected the complaints of black leadership. Adele Wist wrote to the mayor, "I read, with much disgust and humiliation, that statement Commissioner Valentine made in *The News* to reporters, that colored boys are found to be perpetrators of all the crime thus far com[mi]tted in that section. I think the statement to be unjust and would like very much to have him retract it." Another concerned black citizen, H. Widgen, described the New York Times' reportage as "hysterical" and like Mrs. Wist argued that "there is no crime wave in Harlem and [there] never was."[42]

Yet Harlem's collective denunciation of the white dailies' smear campaign and the police department's criminalization of black youth did not silence the community's critique of crime committed by blacks in Harlem. The black community—citizens, news outlets, civil rights organizations, and black leaders—consistently requested the New York Police Department to both hire more black police officers and augment police presence in their neighborhood. So, the murder of O'Connell was no surprise to Harlemites. As recently as February 1941, nine months before the O'Connell incident in Central Park, the New York Amsterdam News had "urg[ed] some kind of New Deal at the 30th police precinct, located on Amsterdam Avenue near 150th Street, and responsible for policing practically all the so-called Sugar Hill district. The immediate cause of our campaign was the mysterious death of two women in one week, both having been killed by falling from windows."[43] Thus, Harlemites knew that they had a crime problem, but they described it as a problem of crime, child delinquency, economic inequality, and policing—not their blackness.

Both Mrs. Wist and Mr. Wigden criticized the mayor and the police for not fighting crime and protecting black citizens in Harlem. As Wigden, recalling a conversation with a friend, explained, "[A] man I know at 2434 Eighth Avenue went out to report to the police suspicious actions indicating one of the roof-top robberies that are prevalent in Harlem, and could not find one, of course. That is my contention—the police are paid, but they don't care what happens to the colored people." For many Harlemites, police negligence was the problem, not black people. Yet like white New Yorkers, black citizens also viewed police behavior as a reflection of the NYPD's racial politics.[44]

So when Wigden claimed that the police "don't care what happens to the colored people," he spoke to his own and many Harlemites' conviction that the NYPD only valued and protected the lives of white people. As Mrs. Wist indignantly interrogated, "[D]o you think that because the white people of the 99th Street section and thereabouts have received protection ample enough for their needs that since colored boys are doing all the killing, robbing, etc., that the colored people of Harlem condone it and need no protection?" Wist and the Dunbar Housewives League (DHL), a black women–led civic association that had been instrumental in the Don't Buy Where You Can't Work campaign during the mid-1930s, were especially concerned about the welfare of black women. As Wist noted, "[W]e need protection from these groups of boys, who grab pocketbooks, waylay and molest women (colored women), brandish and use their knives all too freely!!!" By stressing "colored women," Mrs. Wist suggested, as the black community in Bedford-Stuyvesant had in 1939, that black women were ignored, unlike white women, whom the police protected. Anna L. Moore, the president of the DHL, bluntly stated, "[A]ttacks have been made upon our women; assaults and robberies, against our men. Our boys and girls have been forced to use roundabout ways to and from school, in order to avoid the possibilities of these criminal attacks." Mrs. Wist and Moore zeroed in on not only the occurrence of crime but also, and more significantly, the consequences of crime and Jim Crow policing. Both centered the impact crime had on the black community—the children, adults, and especially women. Thus their invocation of black women and girls, unlike Ebenezer Ray's, had less to do with respectable masculinity and femininity. The consequence of Jim Crow policing meant that black people, especially the most vulnerable and often invisible, were oftentimes targets of crime. For the black letter writers, this policy of the NYPD's color-conscious protection of white-occupied areas brought into high relief the observation that Commissioner Valentine and Mayor La Guardia were primarily concerned about the welfare and protection of their white citizens.[45]

"This Report Is Still Unpublished"

Describing white dailies' characterization of crime and policing in the *Amsterdam News*, L. D. Reddick, historian and then curator of the Schomburg Collection of Negro Literature at the New York Public Library, wrote that they "confuse 'adequate policing' with 'police brutality.'" Reddick believed "the majority of residents in Harlem, as elsewhere, insist upon law and order," but they were "equally insistent" that this situation should not be taken advantage of as a reason to instigate "a reign of terror by the clubs and firearms of the police." By conflating adequate policing with police brutality, the white dailies, La Guardia, and Valentine sanctioned police brutality. According to Reddick, the lack of municipal resources to improve the economic situation of the black community was the relevant issue. He asked, "[W]hat are the conditions which produce these mostly teen age 'muggers,' purse-snatchers and pilferers? Many of the answers to this question are found to be in the report of the Mayor's Commission on the 'Harlem Riot' of 1935. This report still is unpublished."[46] White New Yorkers' impression was that the mayor "asked the police to go easy for fear there might be another riot."

Black New Yorkers continued to endure police violence across the city as blacks migrated to the city and branched out to outer boroughs. In February 1941, police officers shot Lindsey Weaver, a black man working as a junkyard helper, in Brooklyn. As Weaver walked home carrying three tires, officers Barney Shannon and William Long asked Weaver where he got the tires. He explained that a garage man had left them on the street. Officers Shannon and Long took him to the garage man, who verified his story, but nonetheless they "dragged Weaver away . . . whereupon . . . they began beating him mercilessly with their nightsticks." When Weaver tried to escape, the police shot him twice, in the right shoulder and right thigh. Once he fell to the ground, the "officers lunged upon him and beat him severely."[47] The Brooklyn branch of the National Negro Congress held several meetings at the Mount Carmel Baptist Church to support Weaver and discuss police brutality in the borough. At the meeting, the predominant message was "Free Lindsey Weaver," prosecute, and "bring to justice and convict" officers who assaulted Weaver and other "Negro young men." By mid-April, Weaver was convicted of simple assault.[48]

From November 1941, when O' Connell was killed in Central Park, to the spring of 1942, black New Yorkers continued to demand protection from crime and police brutality. During May 1942, several cases of police misconduct involving black women and girls in Brooklyn and Queens rekindled the grassroots movement against police brutality. At the Brooklyn Regent Theater, the manager asked two black women, Mamie Cephos and Laura Brown, to leave the movie theater because they were "making unnecessary noise." When they refused to, Patrolman Dooley escorted them out of the theater and refunded them their money. Another officer, Patrolman Leo Murphy, "lambasted" Brown "to such an extent that she was unable to appear in the Pennsylvania Ave. Court on Monday morning."[49] Weeks later in Queens, a committee of the United Negro League held a special hearing at Ozone Park to protest the way "detectives swooped upon a beauty parlor at 109–03 Union Hall Street, Jamaica and manhandled the proprietress, Mrs. India Stepp." Police officer Oscar Wiesner, who led the raid, apparently was given incorrect information. A concerned resident, Mr. Benowitz, had given the police the address of the beauty parlor because he worried that gambling, "crap" games, would jeopardize the businesses in the neighborhood, though no one was gambling. Indeed, Mrs. Stepp complained that "the raid affected her business."[50]

On May 9, Assemblyman Hulan E. Jack wrote a letter to Mayor La Guardia requesting that he provide more municipal resources to remedy the economic plight of the black community. While acknowledging Police Commissioner Valentine's efforts to rid Harlem of "vice and crime," describing the arrests as "sensational," Jack questioned the efficacy of this approach, explaining flatly that while he supported "law and order," he was "unalterably opposed to any attempt to indict all of the citizens of Harlem and newspapers printing columns of articles that are degrading. Crime prevails in every underprivileged and poverty stricken community." Crime, in other words, was mainly a symptom of the deeper problem of poverty and racism in the city, and punishing the black community was no way to remedy the situation. The "vicious claws of discrimination in employment lashing out against Negroes and Puerto Ricans," he asserted, caused poverty. Schools provided inadequate facilities and were overcrowded and understaffed. Jack also believed that La Guardia had not gone far enough to provide blacks with adequate services. He reminded La Guardia of the "shelving of the 1936 report of the Mayor's Commission of Harlem on the riot of 1935" as evidence that he had the opportunity to get at the root of the problem but La Guardia had not "dared to." Harlem was "impatient." Now was the time for the mayor to act. Yet if he neglected to, Jack warned, "the oppression of the exploiters" would destroy the morals of the community.[51]

* * *

Just three days after the assemblyman's letter to the mayor, police officer Harold Reidman fatally shot Wallace Armstrong, a mentally ill black man. According to the *Amsterdam News*, "2000 angry Harlemites swarm[ed] around Harlem Hospital." The killing of Armstrong reignited the movement against police brutality. Although short-lived, the justice campaign for Wallace Armstrong symbolized the dilemma black New Yorkers encountered as they fought for safety from criminal activity and police brutality in their neighborhoods. The so-called crime wave in the fall of 1941 set in motion and sanctioned the formal aggressive policing of black neighborhoods, especially those bordering white communities. Once the white dailies began to broadcast stories of crime-ridden black neighborhoods that threatened the safety of white citizens, white New Yorkers furiously demanded police protection and doubted La Guardia's commitment to white people. Although whites' concern for their safety initiated the letter-writing campaign, the letters also reflected whites' insecurity around the perceived political power of the black electorate, as well as blacks' presence in formerly all-white neighborhood and public places. The confluence of angry letters, incidents of crime, and the white dailies' crime-wave narrative pressured La Guardia and Valentine to send more police officers to black neighborhoods. Because of the mayor's efforts to establish law and order, the NYPD operated as an occupying force in black neighborhoods across the city.

Throughout 1942 and the spring of 1943, black New Yorkers' battles around criminal justice had expanded from challenging the double bind of overpolicing and underpolicing to defending the reputation of the black community. La Guardia's promise in 1936 that he would not "tolerate police brutality in Harlem" was never fulfilled. Yet this promise manufactured a narrative that the mayor was soft on crime and ignored black criminal activity. The truth was that police violence against black New Yorkers was uninterrupted, contradicting some whites' impression of La Guardia's newfound preference for and protection of the black electorate. What was different, however, was that now La Guardia, Valentine, and white citizens authorized the NYPD to punish black New Yorkers. Unsurprisingly, the killing of Armstrong was followed by other cases of police violence. In early April 1943, only four months from the August uprising, employing language analogous to Baldwin's "occupied territory," Frank Griffin, writing to the *New York Amsterdam News*, asserted that blacks must write letters and telegrams and organize against "the colonialistic policing of our neighborhoods." Reverend Ethelred

Brown, of the Harlem Unitarian Church, branded police misconduct as an act of criminality. Recalling the catalogue of police aggression, Brown averred that "all these violators of law are policemen and not one was arrested or even suspended. Herein is their license to continue to insult, to beat and to kill."[52]

During the next three decades, as black and Latinx populations grew and spread across the city, they collided against white people who used city officials and the "culture of poverty" thesis to entrench Jim Crow barriers in education, jobs, and housing. Police violence remained a staple of the city's Jim Crow system. "Stop and Frisk" and "No Knock" laws, signed by New York governor Nelson Rockefeller, precipitated uprisings in Harlem in 1964 and East Harlem in 1967. Black and Latinx activists, such as the Young Lords, never trusted this legislation as true anticrime reform. Rather, they interpreted Rockefeller's anticrime bills for what they were—policies that represented an unbroken line of Jim Crow policing that sanctioned police brutality and abrogated the protection of communities of color in Gotham City.[53]

NOTES

1 James Baldwin, "Me and My House," *Harper's Magazine* (November 1955), 58, and "A Report from Occupied Territory," *Nation* (July 11, 1966); Dominic J. Capeci Jr., "Fiorello H. La Guardia and the Harlem 'Crime Wave' of 1941," *New York Historical Society* 64, no. 1 (January 1980): 7–29; *The Complete Report of Mayor La Guardia's Commission on the Harlem Riot of March 19, 1935* (New York: Arno Press and New York Times, 1969). For the 1935 and 1943 Harlem rebellions, see Dominic Capeci's *Harlem Riot of 1943* (Philadelphia: Temple University Press, 1977); Cheryl Greenberg's *Or Does It Explode? Black Harlem in the Great Depression* (New York: Oxford University Press, 1991); Nathan Brandt, *Harlem at War: The Black Experience in WWII* (New York: Syracuse University Press, 1996); and Marilynn Johnson's *Street Justice: A History of Police Violence in New York City* (New York: Beacon, 2004).

2 Some of this scholarship includes, William M. Tuttle, *Race Riot: Chicago in the Red Summer of 1919* (Urbana: University of Illinois Press, 1970); Capeci, *The Harlem Riot of 1943*; Janet L. Abu-Lughod, *Race, Space, and Riots in Chicago, New York, and Los Angeles* (New York: Oxford University Press, 2007). Some exceptions include Victoria W. Wolcott, *Race, Riots, and Roller Coasters: The Struggle over Segregated Recreation in America* (Philadelphia: University of Pennsylvania Press, 2014) and David F. Krugler, *1919, The Year of Racial Violence: How African Americans Fought Back* (New York: Cambridge University Press, 2015).

3 As historian Jeanne Theoharis writes, black northerners often had to "'prove' segregation and contend with theories that blamed them for their children's

and community's inadequacies." Jeanne Theoharis, "Black Freedom Studies: Re-imagining and Redefining the Fundamentals," *History Compass* 4, no. 2 (2006): 357.

4   For police violence in black New York before the Great Depression, see Marcy Sacks, *Before Harlem: The Black Experience in New York City before World War I* (Philadelphia: University of Pennsylvania Press, 2006); and Shannon King, *Whose Harlem Is This, Anyway? Community Politics and Grassroots Activism during the New Negro Era* (New York: NYU Press, 2015); for post–World War II New York, see Marth Biondi, *To Stand and Fight: The Struggle for Civil Rights in Postwar New York City* (Cambridge, MA: Harvard University Press, 2003) and Clarence Taylor, "Race, Class, and Police Brutality in New York City," *Journal of African American History* 98, no. 2 (Spring 2013): 205–28. For scholarship on intraracial crime before World War II, see Kali N. Gross, *Colored Amazons: Crime, Violence, and Black Women in the City of Brotherly Love, 1880–1910* (Durham, NC: Duke University Press, 2006); Khalil Gibran Muhammad, *The Condemnation of Blackness: Race, Crime, and the Making of Modern Urban America* (Cambridge, MA: Harvard University Press, 2010); Cheryl Hicks, *Talk with You like a Woman: African American Women, Justice, and Reform in New York, 1890–1935* (Chapel Hill: University of North Carolina Press, 2010); and LaShawn D. Harris, *Sex Workers, Psychics, and Numbers Runners: Black Women in New York's Underground Economy* (Urbana: University of Illinois Press, 2016); and post-1945, see Michael Fortner, *Black Silent Majority: The Rockefeller Drug Laws and the Politics of Punishment* (Cambridge, MA: Harvard University Press, 2015); James Forman Jr., *Locking Up Our Own: Crime and Punishment in Black America* (New York: Farrar, Straus, Giroux, 2017), and Noel K. Wolfe, "Battling Crack: A Study of the Northwest Bronx Community and Clergy Coalition's Tactics," *Journal of Urban History* 43, no. 1 (April 2015): 18–32.

5   Michael W. Flamm, *Law and Order: Street Crime, Civil Unrest, and the Crisis of Liberalism in the 1960s* (New York: Columbia University Press, 2005).

6   Khalil Gibran Muhammad, "Where Did All the White Criminals Go? Reconfiguring Race and Crime on the Road to Mass Incarceration," *Souls: A Critical Journal of Black Politics, Culture, and Society* 13, no. 1 (2011): 74.

7   "Police End Harlem Riot," *New York Times*, March 21, 1935, 1; "Police Still on Riot Duty," *New York Amsterdam News*, March 30, 1935, 1.

8   *The Complete Report of Mayor La Guardia's Commission*; "Discrimination Caused Harlem Riot, Report," *Pittsburgh Courier*, April 18, 1936, A3; Capeci, *The Harlem Riot of 1943*.

9   Police occupation in Harlem was on account of the uprising in 1935, the anti-Italian protests, and multiple cases of police misconduct. "Harlem Youth Shot While at Play by Police," *Chicago Defender*, May 16, 1936, 1; "Thousands in Protest Here against Italy," *New York Amsterdam News*, May 16, 1936, 1; "Cops to Stay, Is Valentine's Terse Decree," *New York Amsterdam News*, May 30, 1936, 1; "Harlem Sets Up Group to Press Demands on City," *Chicago Defender*, August 15, 1936, 20.

10   "The Mayor Promises to Confer Often on Harlem Situation," *New York Amsterdam News*, July 25, 1936, 11.

11 "Police Brutality Must Go," *New York Amsterdam News*, March 27, 1937, 14.

12 Demographics and quotation from the *New York Times* from Craig S. Wilder, *A Covenant with Color* (New York: Columbia University Press, 2001), 178, 195.

13 "Presbytery Approves Bethel Purchase," *New York Amsterdam News*, July 17 1937, 11.

14 "50 Policemen Map Drive to Halt Beatings," *New York Amsterdam News*, November 27, 1937, 11; and "League Starts Terror War to Combat 'Crime,'" *New York Amsterdam News*, December 11, 1937, 11.

15 Marvel Cooke, "Brooklyn," *New York Amsterdam News*, January 29, 1938, 11. For more on Sirtl, see Wilder, *A Covenant with Color*, 195–98; Clarence Taylor, *Reds at the Blackboard: Communism, Civil Rights, and the New York City Teachers Union* (New York: Columbia University Press, 2013), 80.

16 "They Can Learn Plenty," *New York Amsterdam News*, March 18, 1939, 10.

17 Archie Seale, "Around Harlem," *New York Amsterdam News*, January 7, 1939, 13.

18 Enos Coyle, "See Once Exclusive 'Sugar Hill' Fading," *New York Amsterdam News*, July 22, 1939, 4; Harris, *Sex Workers, Psychics, and Numbers Runners*.

19 Hicks, *Talk with You like a Woman;* and Farah J. Griffin's "'Ironies of the Saint': Malcolm X, Black Women, and the Price of Protection," in *Sisters in the Struggle: African American Women in the Civil Rights–Black Power Movement*, eds. Bettye Collier-Thomas and V. P. Franklin (New York: NYU Press, 2001), 214–29.

20 "B'klyn Police Try to Dodge Rape Probe in Vicious Attack," *New York Amsterdam News*, March 11, 1939, 1.

21 "They Can Learn Plenty," 10; "Police Trail Alleged Rape Case Suspect," *New York Amsterdam News*, March 25, 1939, 2; and "Police Seize Alleged Rapist," *New York Amsterdam News*, April 22, 1939, 13. In April, the police apprehended and arrested Arthur Holmes in the Flatbush area of Brooklyn.

22 "Hoodlums Hunted in Fatal Stabbing," *New York Times*, November 3, 1941, and "Crime Outbreak in Harlem Spurs Drive by Police," *New York Times*, November 7, 1941, 1.

23 "Crime Outbreak in Harlem Spurs Drive by Police," 1.

24 Ibid.

25 Ibid.

26 "250 More Police in Harlem to Stamp Out Crime Wave," *New York Times*, November 8, 1941, 1.

27 See Stuart Hall, Chas Critcher, Tony Jefferson, John Clake, and Brian Roberts's *Policing the Crisis: Mugging, the State, and Law and Order* (London: Macmillan, 1978).

28 "Hoodlums Hunted in Fatal Stabbing," *New York Times*, November 3, 1941, 21, and "Crime Outbreak in Harlem Spurs Drive by Police," 1; Thomas Sugrue, "Crabgrass-roots Politics: Race, Rights, and the Reaction against Liberalism in the Urban North, 1940–1964," *Journal of American History* 82, no. 2 (September 1995): 551–78.

29 Anne E. Kolodney to Mayor F. H. La Guardia, November 8, 1941, reel 76, Papers of Fiorello H. La Guardia, New York City Municipal Archives, hereafter La Guardia Papers; and George Belmont to The Honorable Fiorello H. La Guardia, November 8, 1941, reel 76, La Guardia Papers.

30 Thomas Curtin to the Honorable Fiorello H. La Guardia, November 7, 1941, reel 76, La Guardia Papers.

31 Muhammad, *Condemnation of Blackness*.

32 "O'Dwyer Vote High: Mayor Retains Office by Thin Margin in Closest Contest since 1905," *New York Times*, November 5, 1941, 1; "Harlem Swings to La Guardia," *New York Amsterdam News*, November 8, 1941, 1; From LT to Hon. Fiorello H. La Guardia, Mayor, November 10, 1941, reel 76, La Guardia Papers.

33 From "The Real American" to Mayor La Guardia, December 2, 1941, reel 76, La Guardia Papers.

34 "Crime Outbreak in Harlem Spurs Drive by Police," 1.

35 To Hon. Fiorello H. La Guardia, November 10, 1941, reel 76, La Guardia Papers.

36 Unnamed, undated, reel 76, La Guardia Papers.

37 "Blitzkrieg on Harlem," *New York Amsterdam News*, November 15, 1941, 8.

38 Ibid.

39 "Statement by the NAACP Board of Directors," NAACP Records, Box II. A298, folder 4, Harlem, Crime Conferences.

40 Ludlow W. Werner, "Across the Desk," *New York Age*, November 22, 1941, 6.

41 Ebenezer Ray, "About People and Things," *New York Age*, November 15, 1941, 6.

42 Adele Wist to Mayor La Guardia, November 10, 1941, Reel 76, La Guardia Papers.

43 "The Thirtieth Precinct," *New York Amsterdam News*, February 15, 1941, 16. The *Amsterdam News* had made a similar complaint about the inaction of the 30th precinct in 1938. "Police in New Crime Campaign on Sugar Hill," *New York Amsterdam News*, November 19, 1938.

44 H. Wigden to Hon. Lewis J. Valentine, November 22, 1941, Reel 76, LaGuardia Papers.

45 Adele Wist to Mayor La Guardia, November 10, 1941, Reel 76, La Guardia Papers; H. Wigden to Hon. Lewis J. Valentine, November 22, 1941; and Anna L. Moore President of Dunbar Housewives League to Honorable Fiorello H. La Guardia, November 19, 1941, reel 76, La Guardia Papers.

46 L. D. Reddick, "In Harlem," *New York Amsterdam News*, November 22, 1941, 8.

47 "Brooklynites Assail 'Police Brutality' at Rally," *New York Amsterdam News*, March 15, 1941, 10; "Civic Groups Rally against 'Police Brutality,'" *New York Amsterdam Star-News*, February 22, 1941, 10.

48 "Convict 110 Lb. Man for Assault on 2 Hefty Cops," *Chicago Defender*, April 19, 1941, 3.

49 "400 Boroughites Watch Near-Riot," *New York Amsterdam News*, May 2, 1942, 18.

50 "Hearing Held for Cops Facing Brutality Charges during Raid," *New York Amsterdam News*, May 16, 1942, 18.

51 Hulan E. Jack to His Honor Fiorello H. La Guardia, May 9, 1942, reel 76, La Guardia Papers.

52 Frank D Griffin, "Press on the New Rampage in Its Smear," and Ethelred Brown, "Minister Assails Police Brutality," *New York Amsterdam News*, April 3, 1943, 10.

53 Biondi, *To Stand and Fight*; Adina Back, "Exposing the 'Whole Segregation Myth': The Harlem Nine and New York City's School Desegregation Battles," in *Freedom North: Black Freedom Struggles outside the South, 1940–1980*, eds. Jeanne F. Theoharis and Komozi Woodard (New York: Palgrave Macmillan, 2003); and Johanna Fernandez, "The Young Lords and the Social and Structural Roots of Late Sixties Urban Radicalism," in *Civil Rights in New York City: From World War II to the Giuliani Era*, ed. Clarence Taylor (New York: Fordham University Press, 2011).

2

In the "Fabled Land of Make-Believe"

Charlotta Bass and Jim Crow Los Angeles

JOHN S. PORTLOCK

For four decades, in the heart of South Central Los Angeles, a woman few now remember helped to lead the fight against California's version of Jim Crow. She was a newswoman—an editor and publisher, to be precise—and she ran the "oldest Negro newspaper in the West," the *California Eagle*.[1] From her bully pulpit she waged, as she put it later in life, "bloodless [and] fearless war against segregation and discrimination."[2] It was a war for which she won praise, numerous supporters, and even a measure of renown. Indeed, in 1952, this dedicated champion of civil rights became the first African American woman to garner the vice-presidential nomination from a major political party.

That the story of Charlotta Bass is a scant-told tale in the annals of twentieth-century African American history is due to a number of factors. The first most certainly regards geography. For almost the entirety of her activist career, Bass resided in Los Angeles, thousands of miles removed from the better-known and better-populated black metropolises to the east. Then and since, this fact—that she waged her civil rights fights in a faraway land long synonymous with dreams, not discrimination—has cost her visibility. Second, she was a woman, and although certainly as prolific as any of her male contemporaries, she did not at the time garner their level of attention nor has she since. And third, Bass was a political radical—"[s]hocking pink" was how *Time* magazine thought to describe her in 1952—and it has only been of late that black female leftists of the early Cold War era have begun to receive their scholarly due.[3]

Though lesser known, Bass's story remains an important one on a number of counts. For starters, it reminds that California—that "fabled land of make-believe," as some blacks were wont to call it—was no racial utopia, that the so-called race problem that plagued New York and Alabama, Texas and Michigan, also plagued the Land of Milk and Honey.[4] Bass herself remained clear-eyed about this, writing in 1949, "[T]he lot of the Negro in California is not as rosy as some would have you believe."[5] Her story too offers an important reminder that the Cold War, which opened in the mid-1940s, did not completely snuff out black radical activity. Her politics certainly cost her readers, and organizations she supported were red-baited out of existence, but she was never silenced. In fact, one could argue that Charlotta Bass's star never shone brighter than during the postwar Red Scare.

Finally, Charlotta Bass's civil rights story offers a window on the myriad strategies a uniquely positioned individual such as herself thought to employ in order to loosen Jim Crow's grip on a community and on a nation. Unquestionably, her preferred bludgeon was the press; her *Eagle* offered unique means to cajole, shame, and convince politicians, city leaders, and everyday Angelenos of the need for race equity. But, Bass's strategies for change extended far beyond her printing offices. This was a woman who founded a plethora of organizations, initiated letter-writing campaigns, led pickets, gave lectures, waylaid city officials, confronted the Ku Klux Klan, led throngs to courtrooms, took leading roles in two political parties, championed a third, and ran three times for political office, all to forward her civil rights agenda. That she employed so many varied strategies to topple Jim Crow remains the most powerful reason to know her story. Hers was without question a remarkable career of activism, one that began in earnest the day she stepped from a Southern Pacific railcar that had ferried her from back east.

When Bass, then an unmarried Charlotta Spears, arrived in Los Angeles in 1910, her plan was to remain only two years. She came on sojourn, hoping warmer climes might remedy what a doctor back in Providence, Rhode Island, diagnosed as exhaustion.[6] As it turned out, she did not return east for another forty-one years. That she stayed was due to a number of factors, not least of which was the fact that in 1912 Spears became the proud owner of the longest-running black weekly west of the Mississippi River, California's *Eagle*. After two years' work at the paper, Spears chose to purchase the *Eagle* following the untimely death of her boss, the paper's founder, John Neimore. The "talk of the town" when she did, Spears set out on a publishing life to defend, as she put it, "liberty and equality for all Americans."[7]

The defense of liberty in the City of Angels was to be a tall task, as tall certainly as other black editors faced nationwide. Given statehood in 1850, California had proven a decidedly mixed bag for African Americans from the beginning. It was a free state but one that had abided the Fugitive Slave Act (1850) and disallowed blacks from testifying in court. The state's public schools were ostensibly integrated, and had been since the mid-1870s, but segregation schemes constantly lurked. In Los Angeles itself, blacks relished the highest home ownership rate of any other major American city (above 36 percent), as well as relative residential freedom, but as in New York City, Detroit, and Chicago, a "black belt" would take shape in L.A. by the mid-1910s. Los Angeles was a multiethnic city—with Mexicans, Japanese, Chinese, and Native Americans, as well as blacks and whites—and it was said that blacks felt the tinge of racism far less, here than elsewhere, as white animus fixed far more "upon the Oriental."[8] And yet clear indications abounded that any buffer was paper-thin. For example, the accepted shorthand for L.A.'s Chinese neighborhood was "Nigger Alley."

A mixed bag L.A. remained when Charlotta Spears took over at the *Eagle*. Black male employment, thanks to the "open shop," was healthy. So was black education, with literacy rates in the city an astounding 95 percent.[9] Signs, however, abounded that black fortunes were trending not upwards but downwards in the city. These included but were not limited to a rise in police brutality, creeping housing discrimination, and a growing number of incidences of segregation. That this new reality showed itself when it did hardly surprises given demographic shifts taking place at the time. Where in 1900 the total black population of L.A. stood at 1,817, the number in 1912 topped 9,000 and was well on its way to over 15,000 by 1920.[10] At the same time, those claiming Japanese and Chinese descent were shrinking as a share of the total population. Over 4 percent in 1900, by 1910 those of Asian descent made up less than 2 percent of L.A.'s total population. And finally, the number of those identifying as white ballooned in 1910 to well over 480,000 from less than 100,000 a decade before. What all of this amounted to was a city in which Asians were becoming less visible, blacks if anything a bit more so, and whites, many of whom notably hailed from the Jim Crow South, increasingly powerful.

The new editor had big shoes to fill when she assembled her staff and set out on her quest to cover what she dubbed the "more important issues" of the day.[11] By the time of his death, John Neimore was an icon and his paper "the pride of the Negro people."[12] The *Eagle* was a veritable institution in the city and Neimore himself a giant. Many then and since credited him with drawing black southerners out of Dixie and to the Promised Land of the West. In addition to his boosterism, Neimore also worked tirelessly to keep Jim Crow out of Los Angeles, his efforts culminating in the passage of an antidiscrimination bill—the Dribble Bill—he helped usher through the California state house.

Bent on further blazing the trail her mentor had begun, Charlotta Bass, who in 1914 married her co-editor and midwestern newsman, Joseph Bass, got right to it. An early chance for *California Eagle* readers to glimpse the style and substance of their new editor came in winter 1914–15 as Hollywood's D. W. Griffith readied the release of his much-anticipated film, *The Birth of a Nation*. (In 1914, the newly married Joe and Charlotta Bass also added the state name to the paper's title.) Like the rest of black America who thought the racist and incendiary motion picture a frontal assault on the "moral dignity of six million" blacks, Bass protested. In the *Eagle*, she called on theaters to pull the film, for civic organizations to condemn it, and for black actors to refuse roles, arguing that Griffith's cinematic manifesto of Reconstruction could only serve to "stir up race hatred."[13] The film, of course, went ahead, becoming a blockbuster and winning high praise from none other than President Woodrow Wilson. For her part, though Bass did not succeed in preventing the release of *The Birth of a Nation*, she could lay claim— and did in her memoirs—to having effected a modicum of change as regards the film. Recalled the editor in 1960, "We did not succeed in stopping production, but we did achieve some small progress by forcing Griffith to cut some of the most vicious attacks against the morals of the Negro people which had been in the early rushes, in the early reels, of the production."[14]

Three years later Bass was at it again, this time turning her ire on L.A. County Hospital, where she found not a single tax-paying black Angeleno in the employ of this publicly-funded institution. Irate, she covered the issue, but also sought a meeting with the local Board of Supervisors to discuss among other things the possibility of black women being brought on as nurses. Here Bass spotted a golden opportunity to improve black female employment in Los Angeles, which was almost wholly limited to domestic work. A meeting eventually happened, and the supervisors in the end proved amenable to two courses of action, the first being the hiring of black female custodians so long as Bass was willing to vet applicants first, and the second being assurances that some of these very same pre-vetted candidates would be considered for nurse training and employment "at some future date."[15] While certainly not an unqualified success, the meeting did bear fruit, and also demonstrated, as had her protest against Griffith's film, that the *Eagle* editor was more than willing to use her bully pulpit as a battle axe against employment discrimination. Of her work to pry open County Hospital, Bass recalled that it stood as a high watermark in early efforts to "establish a healthy climate industrially, socially, and politically for Negroes in Los Angeles."[16]

Ten years in, then, the *Eagle's* nearly sixty thousand readers nationwide knew who they had in Charlotta Bass—a fearless crusader for justice who welcomed conversation if not conflict with Los Angeles power brokers to secure justice and opportunity for the city's black residents.[17] Readers also knew what they had in their *Eagle*. Headquartered and published on L.A.'s Southside along Central Avenue, the *Eagle* was an eight-page journal (until the mid-1920s when it went to twenty pages) that teemed with story and protest. Each week subscribers, who paid yearly dues of two dollars, could expect a front page dedicated to local and national topics of interest and import to the race. Representative was the front page from September 13, 1919, where articles on the recent Red Summer race riots shared space with stories on local performance and speaking engagements. Inside, sections included "Social Intelligence," which offered a rundown of club, group, and individual meetings taking place in and around Los Angeles; the "San Diego Department," which reported on news from down state; and the always hard-hitting and political editorial page. It was race coverage black Angelenos had come to expect from the oldest black weekly in the state, and it was coverage they knew they could not get anywhere else. They certainly could not get *Eagle*-quality coverage in the white press, of which the *Los An-*

geles Times and the *Los Angeles Herald-Examiner* loomed largest. Both papers rarely ever covered blacks—less than 1 percent of total coverage, according to one study. And when they did, black portrayals were more often than not stereotypic and degrading.[18] As concerned other black newspapers in the city, readers in truth had limited options. The *Liberator*, which had been an L.A. mainstay since its founding in 1900, was no longer publishing, having been forced to shutter following the death of its founder, Jefferson Edmonds, in 1914. Indeed, the only viable alternative to the *Eagle* was the *New Age*. But an ownership change in 1915 saw this once-serious paper—Bass's early criticism notwithstanding—turn to "fluff," as one historian tells it. The title of "leading Race paper in the city," then, belonged to the *Eagle*, a reputation the paper would solidify in the 1920s.[19]

If segregation and discrimination inside Los Angeles crept during the 1910s, both rose to a gallop in the 1920s. This was due in no small measure to the resurgence of the Ku Klux Klan, whose emergence after decades of seeming dormancy shook the entire country, L.A. included. Black residents were harassed and some injured. Bass, as usual, kept her readers abreast of it all. Also as usual, Bass prodded her readers to action. In two separate columns in 1921, readers were met with the following queries: "Shall We Entertain the Ku Klux Klan?" and "Can We Exterminate the Ku Klux Klan?"[20] The tactic was textbook Bass, who was continually trying to inspire fellow foot soldiers in her fight to topple Jim Crow in Los Angeles. The fight came to one of its many heads in 1925 when the editor lucked into a way to shame, if not exterminate, the California KKK. In spring that year, Bass obtained a "secret letter" penned by the Klan's Imperial Representative of California, G. W. Price. In it, Price detailed just how the Klan, ahead of the May municipal elections in Los Angeles, planned to muzzle and discredit black leaders who sought to steer voters away from Klan-favored candidates. "We could plant a bottle of booze in an enemy's car," wrote Price, "[or] fall back on the old method of 'a woman.'" Whatever the means, Price concluded that the "Negro vote" had to be "corralled."[21] On April 10, Bass published the letter in its entirety on her front page. Reaction was immediate. The *Eagle* reported a "furor" in Watts and "a grand rush . . . for copies" of the paper, which quickly sold out.[22] Within days, Price himself contacted *Eagle* offices to deny authorship of the letter and demand a retraction. When one was not forthcoming, Price sued both Charlotta and Joe Bass for libel. Two months later, the editors, whose legal fees were paid by donation, were acquitted on all charges. This experience reinforced for the Basses and their readers the power of the press. Wrote the editors, "[I]f they [the KKK] succeed in throttling the press, you take away from [black Angelenos] one of their greatest weapons for defense and offense."[23]

To win elections there were secret letters; to segregate L.A. neighborhoods there was a far less discreet and far more effective method: the restrictive covenant. For years—from the 1880s through 1910—black Angelenos had been able, for the most part, to live where they pleased. That all started to change as the Great Migration—that steady march of black souls out of the South from the 1890s through the mid-1970s—brought blacks in greater and greater numbers to the city. By the 1910s, blacks began, as Bass told it, to be moved "out of every desirable section of the city."[24] (This was longhand for the city's Westside.) To do this, white homeowners—Klan members and not—relied on restrictive covenants, i.e., deeds on homes that stipulated to whom an owner could sell. Unsurprisingly, blacks challenged these in court, bringing suit as early as 1915. One of the earliest cases Bass and the *Eagle* covered came in 1919 when the Los Angeles Investment Company brought a case against black homeowner Homer Garrott, claiming he had no right to his Los Angeles property because it had a covenant on it. Though multiple courts ruled in favor of Garrott, the practice of covering properties with covenants only grew. In 1925, restrictive covenants received California State Supreme Court sanction, and by the late 1920s they proliferated, with a newly organized White Homeowners Association established in L.A. to lobby local and state authorities for the enforcement of these "invisible walls of steel," as one black Angeleno described them.[25]

Aside from her vice-presidential run in 1952, it is Charlotta Bass's fight against these restrictive covenants for which she is best known, a fight whose intensity ratcheted up in the 1920s. As she had with the KKK, Bass protested, and she prodded. In 1925, the same year California declared covenants constitutional, she wrote state attorney general Willis O. Tyler to make clear her opposition to them.[26] One year later the editor began to prod, chiding black Angelenos for their inaction and lack of unity on the issue. A February 1926 *Eagle* article read, "Some of black

Los Angeles is still sleeping . . . while white Los Angeles is working to keep [their neighborhoods] for white citizens."[27] Bass, who in the early 1940s minted her own homeowners improvement association, went in for hyperbole here. Blacks were certainly not sleeping or unaware of the toll restrictive covenants and the later practice of "redlining" had on their neighborhoods. The number of court challenges to the former made this abundantly clear. Indeed, black Angelenos—Bass included—would not rest until the United States Supreme Court deemed restrictive covenants unconstitutional in 1948.

Rounding out her triad of major civil rights efforts during the 1920s was Bass's work to integrate youth recreation in L.A. Indeed, one of the most important biographical details about Bass is that she never had children. This fact helps to explain her devastation over the death of her nephew in 1945, a loss many believed decisive in moving her politics leftwards. It also goes a long way in explaining the attention she gave throughout her life to young activists. Declared the editor in 1948, "It is the job of the youth to correct the evils that are sorely affecting our democracy."[28] It is little surprise, then, that Bass spent so much time and energy fighting race discrimination against children. One of her first efforts in this regard began in the mid-1920s when she and her paper took a leading role in attempts to provide equal access to city pools for black children, whose use of these municipal facilities was limited to a single day a week. In 1925, Bass instructed readers to fill the courtroom where one of the first cases against the practice was being adjudicated. "It will be well worth while [to] attend this hearing," read an *Eagle* front page from October 1925, "and see whether or not the courts will uphold these sinister emissaries of the Ku Klux Klan by denying its very own citizens the rights guaranteed them under the constitution."[29] Integration of the pools took six years and the spearheading work of both black and white women. When, in 1931, the pools were thrown open to black youth, the *Eagle* called the victory a win of "gigantic proportions."[30]

It was not all wins for black Angelenos in the interwar period—far from it. As mentioned, restrictive covenants could not be stopped. Indeed, by the 1930s covenants had "severely circumscribed black residential mobility," limiting blacks mainly to the "South Central" corridor of the city.[31] Too, while city schools were on their face integrated, segregation and discrimination had a way of seeping into L.A.'s halls of learning.

Throughout the 1920s, the *Eagle* reported on "segregation scheme[s]" being planned by the city, and in the 1930s and early 1940s a slew of incidents of discrimination occurred, capped off by the mock lynching of six black students at Fremont High School in South L.A.[32] The chilling and heinous act had Bass asking whether the racial mores of Alabama had made their way to Avalon Boulevard—Fremont High School's address. And though Bass would open an investigation "to fight tooth and nail to make the educational authorities of this city conduct a penetrating probe into this whole affair," city schools only grew more segregated in the coming decades.[33]

And then there was police brutality, a reality in the 1910s when Bass arrived, and an issue more than fifty years later that would ignite the Watts riots. The *Eagle* reported constantly on police misconduct and abuse. And not only this, but in 1945 when Bass made her first go at electoral politics, entering the race for city council, the editor campaigned on the issue. Neither was Bass shy about going straight to Chief of Police R. Lee Heath. She did just this in 1924 after two black youths came to her with allegations of mistreatment by law enforcement. Accosting the chief outside his office, Bass wanted to know if "Mississippi and Georgia methods" of policing were to be used in Los Angeles.[34] Heath's rebuff of Bass that day suggested the answer.

"Wins" and "losses" aside, what is clear about the first two decades of Bass's tenure is that the *Eagle* proved not only the community's best news source but also its strongest advocate. What has to strike any chronicler of Bass or the *Eagle* are the number of times a victim of police misconduct, race discrimination, and the like came to her offices to tell his or her story, figuring that if anyone could do something—print the story, open an investigation, etc.—Charlotta Bass could. This is what happened in October of 1924 when the two aforementioned boys met prejudicial treatment at a local drug store and then at the hands of L.A. police.[35] This is how in 1933 Bass was made aware of segregation at the new County Hospital building.[36] And it was how, during the Second World War, she got hard evidence that the KKK was recruiting in the Los Angeles shipyards.[37] Informants and victims alike came to Bass for at least two reasons. First, she could give a story legs, thanks to her more than 17,500 subscribers citywide.[38] Second, aggrieved and concerned Angelenos knew that, of all people, Bass might be able to right their wrongs. She did after all have a seat at so many of the "high tables" inside the city—as well as quite a few outside L.A. In her lifetime, Bass served as lady president of the Los Angeles branch of Marcus Garvey's Universal Negro Improvement Association, sat on the executive board of the Los Angeles branch of the NAACP, presided over the Los Angeles arm of the National Negro Congress, and was a national board member of Paul Robeson's and W. E. B. Du Bois's Council on African Affairs. Maybe most importantly, though, for black Angelenos, Bass had the ear of numerous Los Angeles city officials, including Republican mayor Frank Shaw, whom she counted a close ally in the 1930s.

Bass's influence, however, did not go unchallenged. Never was this more apparent than in 1933 when one of her own protégés, a young man from Kansas City, Missouri, began his own race paper. From its inception, Leon Washington's *Los Angeles Sentinel* fashioned itself the antithesis of the *Eagle*. Where the former went in for brash and bold, the latter, as it had for decades, prided itself on being a practitioner of respectability politics. Case in point: during the throes of the Depression, as black Angelenos struggled to win a livable wage, the *Sentinel* endorsed aggressive labor tactics and enthused at the efforts of the Congress of Industrial Organizations to organize blacks. Bass, for her part, classed the CIO "high powered, well-paid Communistic agitators," and advised blacks to do as she had long done: meet, negotiate, letter write, even make pledges not to "Buy Where You Can't Work"—a campaign she helped to bring to the city in the early 1930s.[39] All were tactics that had borne fruit for Bass over the years, including the successful integration of the workforces at County Hospital and the Southern Telephone Company in 1936. But past successes were not all that motivated her to throw cold water on the *Sentinel* playbook; fear did as well. Rightly, Bass was concerned over the influence communism was having on blacks at the time. "[T]he masses," she wrote in 1932, "are slowly but surely turning their faces and their political hope of independence toward the Communist party."[40] For a devout woman, a capitalist, and a champion of what she termed "Americanism," this was anathema; hence the Washington program had to be challenged.[41]

The two papers also sparred over politics, with the *Sentinel* swinging Democratic and the *Eagle* leaning Republican. (Though she did not always vote Republican, Bass registered Republican until April 1948.) During President Roosevelt's first term, Bass had little patience for the New Deal, regarding the legislation as shot through with racism. Republicanism, however, was falling increasingly out of favor among black voters inside and outside L.A. When Bass failed to support victorious state and local Democrats, as in 1934 when she opposed the popular California assembly candidate from her district, Augustus Hawkins, she appeared out of touch. Competitors though they were, both editors respected each other. In 1936, Washington even found occasion to admit that while he and Bass had not "always seen eye to eye . . . on matters of policy," he never doubted that his competition "fought to the best of its ability for the ideals which its editors believed."[42]

Politics and much else changed for Bass during the Second World War, a conflict that transformed her city as well. For L.A. the war brought a new flood of migrants, blacks among them, all come to taste of the opportunities war industry was making possible. The *Eagle*, in its time-honored role as community advocate, did its mightiest to make sure all—newcomers and not—had equal access to jobs in the shipyards and the aviation plants, and that the unions represented black interests as determinedly as they represented white interests. This commitment had the paper fighting union segregation, as it did in 1943 inside the Boilermaker's Union. It had the *Eagle* supporting federal efforts under the newly passed Fair Employment Practices Committee (FEPC) to stamp out racial discrimination inside war industries. It had Charlotta Bass in particular working with local partners to open war industries not only to black men but also to black women, a victory she won in 1942. And finally it had the editor engaged in multiethnic coalition building to secure for black, Mexican, and Asian Angelenos the milk and honey L.A. ostensibly promised. "The Negro people in Los Angeles, and other California minorities," Bass recalled of the war years, "knew what they were fighting for, and they continued in battle against the forces in and out of government which kept them second class citizens."[43]

The change the war worked on Bass showed in her politics. Never blind to the importance politics, national and local, played in the realm of civil rights, she followed her nose, and in six years—from 1942 to 1948—went from the Republican fold to the newly minted Progressive Party. Everyone seemingly had an explanation for her transformation, some seeing rank opportunism, others pie-in-the-sky idealism, and still others a clear-eyed effort to advance black civil rights. Bass certainly claimed the latter. What we do know for certain is that the transformation began when she could no longer ignore Republican harboring of racists.[44] Abandoned, as she saw it, by the party of Lincoln, she fell in among the Democrats, heartened by the fact that their standard-bearer, President Franklin Roosevelt, appeared at least a sometime friend of the race, and that his New Deal continued to do such good for blacks. Bass was also won to the Democratic Party because she believed—as she had for some time—that an end to Jim Crow at home necessitated freedom for the oppressed abroad. Wrote the editor in October 1942, "[W]e see the struggles of the Negro people of America inextricably bound to the struggles for freedom of the people of the world."[45] For a woman of such mind, FDR, co-author of the 1941 Atlantic Charter, appeared to be an obvious political ally.

Then came the Cold War. As the Democratic Party baton passed from FDR to Harry Truman, Charlotta Bass again grew wary, this time not only of racists—long a powerful constituency inside the Democratic Party—but also of anticommunists. As Bass saw it, the Red Scare that swept the country in the wake of the Second World War, fanned by both Democrats and Republicans alike, augured poorly for blacks. Indeed, as early as 1945, black Angelenos felt the effects of anticommunist zeal. That year two racially progressive initiatives, a proposed interracial relations council and a California version of the federal FEPC, went down to defeat after both were pilloried in the white press as communist plots meant to incite a race war.[46] And while California State Democrats supported these measures, Democrats nationally—President Truman included—were doing little to calm anticommunist feeling, a feeling that all too often labeled that which was racially progressive "red." And so, when the opportunity presented itself to join herself to a new party, one claiming the mantle of FDR liberalism, as well as civil rights and peace, Bass jumped, becoming a Progressive in 1948.

Bass's advent into the Henry Wallace–led Progressive Party in 1948 marked the beginning of her most potent period of activism. Under the Progressive flag, whose black adherents included W. E. B. Du Bois, Paul Robeson, Shirley Graham, and a young Coretta Scott, she ran for Congress in 1950. Under it once again in 1952 she ran for the vice presidency.

It was during this period as well that Bass won for herself not only a national but an international platform. That the *Eagle* editor pledged herself to the Progressive cause, one that championed an end to war, an end to racism, and an end to colonialism—as well as a universal income and health insurance for all—should surprise no more than her earlier decision to join the Democratic fold. As regarded war, Bass had reported on two, and though she gave her and her paper's support to both First and Second World Wars, she knew their horrors. She knew the toll war took on families, having lost her own nephew, American GI John Kinloch, at the Battle of the Bulge in 1945. She also knew the increased domestic racial tensions that attended these wars. During the First World War—and in its immediate wake—she covered the torrent of race riots that swept the country, and two decades later, during World War II, she again covered similarly heinous rioting in Detroit, Michigan, and Harlem, New York. That Bass would cast "the fight for peace [as] one and indivisible with the fight for Negro equality," as she did in her vice-presidential run in 1952, makes sense.[47] With regard to Progressives' antiracism, this was what had many blacks, not only Bass, willing to give the party a hearing. And finally, as concerned the party's anticolonialism—a policy priority Progressives shared with FDR—Bass had long advocated self-determination for those under the thumb of imperialism. In 1921, she arranged to travel to the Second Pan-African Congress but was unable to attend on account of funding. And throughout the 1920s and 1930s, Bass lobbed criticism at multiple presidential administrations for inaction in the face of European imperial excess. As Bass saw it, black American freedom could not be decoupled from colonial freedom; the two were, in the time-honored assessments of black radicals—Bass included—indivisible.

As Bass's politics went, so went her *Eagle*. The content of the paper began to shift, as the editor and her ideologically compatible staff gave more and more attention to the Cold War, to happenings in Europe, to nuclear proliferation, and to the winning of peace, which Bass believed required dialogue with and conciliation to the Russians. The fact that their paper was changing frustrated, even angered and dismayed, some readers. (Some quit their subscriptions over what they felt was Bass's too-soft approach to communism.) In May 1947, Bass heard from one of this number—a friend in fact—who demanded to know why the editor continued to opine week after week about war and peace and not Jim

Crow and racial injustice. In response, the editor in her weekly "Side-walk" column explained, "We would send guns and tanks to China to defeat the Communists [but] would not make laws that would [end] discrimination in education and industry in our own country." "We use tax money," Bass continued, "to run down spies, to establish loyalty test committees [but] we do nothing at all about building homes for those who cannot afford to pay the high rents."[48] Bass's point, a time-honored one among black antiwar activists, was that American belligerence abroad had the potential to drain the nation of the money, motivation, and manpower necessary to wage an effective and winning war against Jim Crow at home.

Those who remained readers of the *Eagle* during the 1948 election year heard more of the same from their editor, who served as co-chairwoman of the Women for Wallace campaign. The election—which pitted former FDR vice president and Progressive standard-bearer Henry Wallace against incumbent Harry Truman and New York governor, Republican Thomas Dewey—proved a crucial one for blacks, and not only because their vote, according to Truman campaign advisors Clark Clifford and James Rowe, had the chance to prove decisive in November. The election would help clarify how blacks would orient themselves inside the new Cold War. It is key to recall that early in the campaign season, before the Democrats made heady pronouncements about "human rights" and added a civil rights plank of some heft to their platform, many thought, including many in the black press, that the race might very well swing to Wallace despite his bucking of anticommunist orthodoxy. Those at the *Sentinel*, no lovers of the Progressive candidate and instead supporters of the Republican Dewey, echoed the assessments of others—including the *Chicago Defender* and *Pittsburgh Courier*—when it ran a piece claiming that the Wallace "candidacy has an emotional pull for the majority of Negro voters."[49] Indeed, that pull was no better articulated than by a Chicago cabbie in the spring of 1948. "Maybe I don't stand for a lot of things Wallace does," the driver told the *Defender*'s Horace Cayton, "but I'm gonna let both the Republicans and the Democrats know that I's gonna vote for Wallace and I don't care who knows it. They can call me whatever they want. Lots of other colored folks feel just the way I do."[50]

As spring gave way to summer and summer to fall, however, and as Wallace continually refused to disavow communist endorsement of his campaign, black support fell away, save from his core supporters, of whom Bass was certainly one. In the end, two out of every three black votes went for Truman, and the race hooked their hopes to a Cold War liberalism bent on outgunning Communists abroad and, at least ostensibly, securing progressive gains at home.

Unconvinced civil rights gains could ever be made with a Cold War raging, Bass exited the 1948 election committed still to the Wallace program of peace and civil rights. In the waning days of 1949, Bass told her readership that she planned to "dedicate" the year 1950 to peace, and lest any of her faithful believe she was jettisoning civil rights, she also declared three months later that she intended to fight Jim Crow in California "to a finish" as well.[51] This included among other things an effort to desegregate San Quentin prison as well as lobbying the L.A. City Council "to adopt an ordinance that would forbid segregation and discrimination."[52] An ambitious one, Bass's program hit a serious roadblock when in late June war broke out on the Korean peninsula. Here again, Bass argued, was war shunting aside civil rights.

The Korean War, which her own NAACP supported, as did her crosstown rival the *Sentinel*, allowed Bass the opportunity to point out the contradiction for her readers that was a war to export democracy abroad while blacks still waited on the same at home. In June she wrote, "American leaders are applauding President Truman for taking such quick decisive action in the case of Korea. But what about the Civil Rights promised the Negro in [the President's] platform back in 1948?"[53] The next month, as the impending execution of Willie McGee, a black man wrongly accused and awaiting execution in Mississippi, came closer, she implored readers to understand that "[i]f we win the fight in Korea and lose the battle for justice and democracy in Mississippi, we will not have gained any territory in the struggle for democracy in a free world."[54] And in August, as the FEPC went down to a Senate filibuster, Bass named this the "First American Casualty in Korean War."[55]

Bass was quick to pin the blame for this and other civil rights setbacks not only on Washington but also on anticommunist, pro-war black leaders. "Perhaps," Bass mused in August, "if those [black leaders] had waxed as warm in their fight against the Mississippi lynch law, the Ku Klux Klan, [the] share-crop system [and] the fight for a Fair Employment Practice law . . . as they do now against those other men of darker hue in Korea, they perhaps would have gained the respect of even [white racists] . . . [a]nd [we] would have attained our goal."[56] Instead, groups like the NAACP were passing resolutions to out suspected Communists from their ranks, moves the *Eagle* editorial board deemed "stupid."[57]

In August, confident in the connection she saw between civil rights and peace, Bass left southern California on a mission overseas to "broaden," as she put it, "her scope [and] awaken a new understanding on international affairs."[58] Her primary destination was Prague, Czechoslovakia, where the World Committee of the Defenders of Peace conference was taking place. The event, to which she had received invitation and which drew the likes of W. E. B. Du Bois, proved a three-day brainstorming session on how to bring peace to Korea. The conference complete, an interested Charlotta Bass decided to continue east to Moscow and the Caucasus on a fact-finding mission to gauge just how menacing the "communist menace" in fact was. In the end, she came away unconvinced of its threat to world peace, claiming to have heard no "talk of war-making" during her visit, and also to have observed "no racial discrimination."[59]

When Bass returned to Los Angeles in the fall, she did so as a candidate for Congress. Progressives had nominated her while she was in Paris, thinking her star shone bright enough in California's Fourteenth District to make her candidacy a serious thing. And so it turned out to be. On a platform of "world peace, world-wide neighborliness, jobs for all, civil liberties, and security," Bass ran a vigorous and impressive campaign in the racially mixed district.[60] It was described as "a tremendous 4 weeks [sic] campaign for peace and Negro representation" by party regulars, who lauded the candidate for not only turning out the black vote but for drawing "people from various walks of life" to the party.[61] That she lost proved a decided afterthought.

Bass, then, was a sound choice for the second spot on the Progressive ticket when she received the nod two years later, and not only for her ability to woo Los Angeles voters. (As her running mate, Progressives chose California lawyer Vincent Hallinan.) In fact, in 1952 Bass no longer lived in the state. In 1951, she sold her *Eagle* and moved to Harlem, New York, where she fell in among a cadre of black female leftists, including Communist Louise Thompson Patterson and poet Beulah

Richardson, both longtime friends. As she had in L.A., Bass fast became a leader in her new milieu. When in 1951 Patterson and Richardson approached Bass to preside over a newly formed all-black, all-female organ known ever after as the Sojourners for Truth and Justice (SJT), Bass jumped, and in late September the group's national chairwoman found herself in Washington, D.C., leading a march on Washington of 117 black American women. The "sojourn," as organizers Patterson and Richardson called the rally, was a revelation for those who went, and another instance that catapulted Charlotta Bass's political star even higher. Of the SJT, which was red-baited out of existence the following year, historian Erik McDuffie argues that it was "the most important [organization of] black left feminism" during the early Cold War era.[62]

Well-chosen though she was for the Progressives' VP slot, Bass faced clear obstacles to turning blacks onto her candidacy, and this despite Republicans' and Democrats' determination in 1952—in contrast to 1948— to chart a "middle ground" on the race issue.[63] The *Pittsburgh Courier* put third-party chances plainly: "[The] 'save the world' Communist-dominated Progressive party will not be the tantalizing opposition to Republican and Democratic Presidential candidates this year."[64] It would not be on a number of counts. First, the Hallinan/Bass ticket lacked the star power Progressives enjoyed under Henry Wallace in 1948. Second, the nation was at war, a cold *and* a hot one, and few could countenance a vote for a party that was among other things calling for a friendship offering to the Soviet Union in order to ease global tension. And thirdly, the Progressives this time around had no monopoly on peace through deescalation. Both Republican and Democratic presidential nominees, Dwight Eisenhower and Adlai Stevenson, respectively, vied for the mantle of peace candidate, Eisenhower going so far as to say late in the campaign that he was willing to go to Korea to secure an end to the war. (Many thought this won him the race.)

With few giving her a chance, least of all it seemed her old rivals at the *Sentinel*, who lampooned Bass's qualifications as "debatable" and her chances as nil, the candidate got right to it, addressing crowds from New York to California.[65] (Importantly, Bass was without running mate Vincent Hallinan until August, when the labor lawyer won release from prison for an earlier contempt of court conviction slapped on him by a judge who did not take kindly to the lawyer's unapologetic defense of noted labor leader and suspected Communist Harry Bridges.) At an early campaign stop in Brooklyn, New York, she made clear the themes of her run: an end to the warring in East Asia, American demilitarization in Europe, decolonization in Africa and Asia, and an end to racism at home. With regard to the latter, she assured her audience of northerners that race hate and terror were far from just southern phenomena, but rather were national crises. "Terror [does] not abide in the South alone," read her speech notes from the evening. Racial terror was in Cicero, Illinois, the candidate averred, where a white mob the year before had set upon a black family for daring to reside across the city's color line. It was, she added, also in California, where they "are burning crosses in Negro and Jewish communities." And, according to the candidate, terror was "here in Brooklyn," as evidenced by "case after case of police brutality."[66]

On this night, as with so many others throughout the campaign, talk of race merged with talk of injustice abroad. In the same breath with which Bass chided Democrats and Republicans alike for inaction in the wake of the heinous murders of two civil rights workers—Harry and Harriette Moore—in Florida the year before, she also lambasted the ostensibly liberal foreign policy of the Truman administration for subverting the freedom dreams of the "colored peoples of the world." Despite four years of the Point Four Program—Truman's foreign assistance program—"the burning cry of the African and Tunisian people for justice" had not been heeded, according to Bass, and a war in Korea still raged. So long as this was the case—that American leaders turned a blind eye and deaf ear to cries of self-determination of black and brown folk abroad—Bass remained none too convinced that black and brown Americans would ever know justice. For this reason, Progressives were pushing for "freedom—peace—and justice—for all . . . peoples."[67]

On through the months, Bass continued to deliver this heartfelt if quixotic message. In July at the convention she stepped before thousands and, according to Michael Singer of the *Daily Worker*, delivered a "masterful" and "moving" speech that reached the "heights of oratory." In it, she declared she was running "because I could not leave our land to those who profit from jim crow slums and segregation and war."[68] The linkage was telling and anticipated a similar observation Dr. Martin

Luther King Jr. made some fifteen years later—that what undergirded war and racism was an out-of-control profit motive that took resources from one population and gave them to another. Two months later, in September, Bass repeated this theme to a national television and radio audience, which according to Progressive Party leadership was "the largest audience any Negro woman has ever had."[69]

Inevitably, the Hallinan/Bass ticket, which appeared on just over thirty state ballots, went down to sound defeat in November. General Eisenhower took the election in a landslide, beating out Democrat Adlai Stevenson, to whom black Americans had given a majority of their vote. Within three years the Progressive Party collapsed, drained of both funding and morale. For Charlotta Bass, however, the election only ended one chapter and began another. To live out the remainder of her days, she returned to California, settling this time in the lakefront town of Elsinore. Elderly, but still bent on political and social activism, Bass joined herself to the struggle against South African apartheid; she went in for criticism of the Space Race—which she considered provocative and unnecessary—and she opposed the war in Vietnam. Ever the gifted orator, Bass also continued to speak, accepting invitation from her local church to opine on black history and other topics.

Charlotta Bass, who had come to California in 1910 suffering from exhaustion, lived until 1969, making her by some estimates ninety-five at her death. (An exact birthdate is not known for Bass.) That she left behind a sparkling legacy is undoubted. To be sure, much of that rested on her transformational and effectual tenure at the *Eagle*. In 1948 she wrote, "The newspaper is the greatest force for good in the community," adding that the "Negro Press" in particular had a unique responsibility to "eliminate [the] evils that hamper the people's progress [and] lead in building a highway to world peace."[70] The paper Bass put out did these things, simple as that. Ably and repeatedly, Bass proved the adage that the black press is the "fighting press." Her legacy, though, extends far beyond her editorship. In addition to owning her own paper, the grand dame of early- and mid-twentieth-century black journalism also ran three times for elective office, led a march on Washington, and even founded her very own cosmetics line—Charlotta, Inc. And this is to say nothing of all the editorials written, meetings convened, injustices exposed, organizations founded, and trips taken, all in her struggle against injustice. The losses, too, are part of her legacy—the political ones as well as others. In this way, she is no different from many a civil rights leader, who championed but rarely triumphed. As Bass told audiences on the campaign trail in 1952, "WIN OR LOSE, WE WIN."[71] So she did, this civil rights giant of the Jim Crow West.

NOTES

1 Charlotta Bass, "I Accept This Call," in *Black Women in White America: A Documentary History*, ed. Gerda Lerner (New York: Vintage, 1972), 343.

2 Charlotta Bass, *Forty Years* (Los Angeles: Charlotta A. Bass, 1960), 33.

3 "Shocking Pink," *Time*, March 17, 1952, 22. On black women leftists, see Erik McDuffie, *Sojourning for Freedom: Black Women, American Communism, and the Making of Black Left Feminism* (Durham, NC: Duke University Press, 2011); and Dayo F. Gore, *Radicalism at the Crossroads: African American Women Activists in the Cold War* (New York: NYU Press, 2011).

4 Bass, *Forty*, 28.

5 "The Sidewalk," *California Eagle* (hereafter: *CE*), August 25, 1949, 2.

6 Bass, *Forty*, 27.

7 Ibid., 31, 29.

8 Scott Kurashige, *The Shifting Grounds of Race: Black and Japanese Americans in the Making of Multiethnic Los Angeles* (Princeton, NJ: Princeton University Press, 2008), 20.

9 James Jeter, "Rough Flying: The California Eagle (1879–1965)," American Journalism Historians Association (presentation, Salt Lake City, Utah, October 7, 1993).

10 Mame L. Campbell, *Making Black Los Angeles: Class, Gender, and Community, 1850–1917* (Chapel Hill: University of North Carolina Press, 2016), 37; Josh Sides, *L.A. City Limits: African American Los Angeles from the Great Depression to the Present* (Berkeley: University of California Press, 2003), 15.

11 Bass, *Forty*, 31.

12 Ibid.

13 "Thomas Dickson's Idea of American Liberality," *CE*, January 30, 1915, 4.

14 Bass, *Forty*, 35.

15 Ibid., 51.

16 Ibid., 50.

17 Rodger Streitmatter, *Raising Her Voice: African-American Women Journalists Who Changed History* (Lexington: University Press of Kentucky, 1994), 100.

18 Paula B. Johnson et al., "Black Invisibility, the Press, and the Los Angeles Riot," *American Journal of Sociology* 76 (January 1971), 706, 710.

19 Douglas Flamming, *Bound for Freedom: Black Los Angeles in Jim Crow America* (Berkeley: University of California Press, 2005), 108.

20 "Shall We Entertain the Ku Klux Klan?" *CE*, October 1, 1921, 1; "Can We Exterminate the Ku Klux Klan?" *CE*, October 8, 1921, 1.

21 "Ku Klux Monopolizes Watts," *CE*, April 10, 1925, 1.

22 "Editor Visits Klan Chief in His Lair," *CE*, April 17, 1925, 1.

23 "*Eagle* Editors on Trial," *CE*, June 19, 1925, 1.

24 Bass, *Forty*, 98.

25 Sides, *L.A. City Limits*, 17.

26 "Atty. Tyler Answers Editor," *CE*, March 20, 1925, 1.

27 "Are You Sleeping," *CE*, February 12, 1926, 1.

28 "*Eagle* Editor Speaks," *CE*, March 18, 1948, 5.

29 "Swimming Pool Case Up Monday," *CE*, October 30, 1925, 1.

30 "Swimming Pool Case Victory," *CE*, February 27, 1931, 1.

31 Sides, *L.A. City Limits*, 34.

32 "Editorial Fore and After Thought," *CE*, September 3, 1926, 1.

33 "Negroes Not Wanted in School," *CE*, February 20, 1941, 1.

34 Bass, *Forty*, 55.

35 "In Mississippi or Georgia—Which?" *CE*, October 3, 1924, 1.

36 "Segregation Looms at New Hospital," *CE*, August 4, 1933, 1.

37 "Klan at Work in Shipyards Here," *CE*, October 21, 1943, 1.

38 Regina Freer, "L.A. Race Woman: Charlotta Bass and the Complexities of Black Political Development in Los Angeles," *American Quarterly* 56 (2004), 609.

39 "The Strikes," *CE*, May 14, 1937, 2B.

40 Quoted in Freer, "L.A. Race Woman," 625.

41 Bass, "On the Sidewalk," *CE*, May 2, 1946, 20.

42 "Editorial," *Los Angeles Sentinel* (hereafter: *LAS*), June 11, 1936, 1.

43 Bass, *Forty*, 73.

44 "Biographical Notes on Mrs. Charlotta Bass," Box 1, Folder: "Bass, C.A.—Speeches 1940s," Charlotta Bass Collection, Additions, Southern California Library.

45 "People's Victory Demands People's Paper," *CE*, October 1, 1942, 8B.

46 Kevin Leonard, *The Battle for Los Angeles: Racial Ideology and World War II* (Albuquerque: University of New Mexico Press, 2006), 259–64, 283–93.

47 Bass, "I Accept This Call," 344.

48 "The Sidewalk," *CE*, May 5, 1947, 2.

49 "1948 Bargain Counter," *LAS*, January 8, 1945, 5.

50 Horace R. Cayton, "Two-Part Moral," *Pittsburgh Courier* (hereafter: *PC*), June 19, 1948, 19.

51 "We Re-dedicated . . ." *CE*, December 22, 1949, 1.

52 "NAACP Urges Anti-Discrimination Law," *CE*, June 30, 1950, 30.

53 "The Sidewalk," *CE*, June 30, 1950, 2.

54 "Koreans vs. Willie McGee," *CE*, July 28, 1950, 6.

55 "First American Casualty in Korean War," *CE*, August 4, 1950, 6.

56 "'Uncle Tom' Not Dead, Rears Ugly Head in Present Korean War," *CE*, July 14, 1950, 4.

57 "Has the National Association Changed Its Position?" *CE*, June 30, 1950, 6.

58 "Editor's Statement," *CE*, October 5, 1950, 6.

59 "Negro Woman Publisher Saw USSR Building Peace," *Daily Worker*, September 28, 1950, 3.

60 "Mrs. Bass' Candidacy Built on Years of Tireless Leadership," *CE*, October 26, 1950, 1.

61 Letter, Horace Alexander to Members of the Campaign Committee, October 27, 1950, Box 9, Folder 35, Progressive Party Records, University of Iowa Special Collection and University Archives.

62 Erik S. McDuffie, *Sojourning for Freedom*, 173.

63 Clayton Knowles, "Civil Rights Is an Issue for Both Major Parties," *New York Times*, May 4, 1952, E10.

64 John L. Clark, "'Mac,' Russell in 'Unholy Alliance,'" *PC*, April 5, 1952, 29.

65 "'Eagle' Spreads Her Wings: An Editorial," *LAS*, March 13, 1952, A1; Bass, "I Accept," 342.

66 "Draft of Mrs. Bass Speech for Brooklyn Dinner, April 18, 1952," Additions—Box 1, Mss. 002, Charlotta A. Bass Collection, Southern California Library for Social Studies and Research.

67 Ibid.

68 "Mrs. Bass Fights . . ." *Daily Worker*, July 14, 1952, 2.

69 "Acceptance Speech of Mrs. Charlotta Bass," July 5, 1950, Box 12, Folder 50, Progressive Party Records, University of Iowa Special Collection and University Archives.

70 Bass, "The Sidewalk," *CE*, December 16, 1948, 1.

71 "News Release," October 26, 1952, Box 12, Folder 50, Progressive Party Records, University of Iowa Special Collection and University Archives.

3

Black Women as Activist Intellectuals

Ella Baker and Mae Mallory Combat Northern Jim Crow
in New York City's Public Schools during the 1950s

KRISTOPHER BRYAN BURRELL

Introduction

The year is 1955. Imagine a city where, in 70 percent of public schools, over 85 percent of the students belonged to one racial group.[1] Zoning policies funneled children from racially homogenous neighborhoods into racially homogenous public schools. Residential patterns, brought on by racial segregation in housing, created a system whereby an overwhelming majority of underutilized public schools were in predominantly white areas, and the most overcrowded, overutilized schools were in predominantly black areas. The city's racial and ethnic minorities lived concentrated and clustered in a handful of neighborhoods. Thus, the demographics of public schools in those areas exhibited high levels of racial and ethnic concentrations clustered into specific schools. Imagine that this racial isolation, concentration, and clustering occurred outside of the city's central commercial, manufacturing, and industrial districts. Such an urban school system would, by definition, exhibit elements of what the sociologists Nancy Denton and Douglas Massey called "hyper-segregation."[2] One year prior, the Supreme Court had unanimously declared that such a public school system was unconstitutional, and that it must racially desegregate.

The above scenario of hyper-segregation described public schools not in the Deep South but in ground zero of the Jim Crow North: liberal, cosmopolitan New York City. In 1954, despite laws that forbade racially segregated schools, New York City had racially hyper-segregated public schools to the same degree as Atlanta, New Orleans, Memphis, Tallahassee, St. Louis, and cities in the seventeen states that legally mandated Jim Crow public schools. As Tahir Butt shows in his essay in this book, racial segregation in Jim Crow New York's education system followed African Americans all the way up through the public university.[3]

In Jim Crow New York, hyper-segregated black public schools were housed in old buildings, had staffs with fewer licensed and full-time teachers, and had larger class sizes. Overcrowding mandated that students typically only attended school on half-day schedules to accommodate two differnet cohorts. As a result of all these inequities, black students usually scored lower on standardized tests.[4] In fact, at the conclusion of their high school careers, less than 0.2 percent of black graduates were prepared to attend college.[5]

Activist-intellectuals in New York knew these facts. Through an array of organizations and social movements, they worked to ameliorate the disparities produced by the city's history of Jim Crow racism. During the decade after *Brown*, the Reverend Milton A. Galamison waged a decade-long struggle for racial integration in New York City's public schools. For years, the radical activist Annie Stein worked with Galamison's Parents Workshop for Equality and the Public Education Association, and investigated how hyper–racial segregation of New York's neighborhoods caused gross inequities in predominantly black public schools. During the early 1960s, the Brooklyn chapter of the Congress of Racial Equality staged a one-family sit-in at a predominantly white school to highlight the racial inequalities in all-black and Puerto Rican schools throughout the borough. During a city-wide school boycott in 1964, over four hundred thousand students were absent to protest the city's Jim Crow education system. During the mid- to late 1960s, city-wide movements for community control advanced earlier movements for equity and justice in New York's Jim Crow education system. These were movements initiated and led by, for the most part, unsung "local" people.[6] "Grassroots activists not only acted," Jeanne Theoharis and Komozi Woodard argue, but they also "theorized for themselves and tailored global ideas to suit their local circumstances."[7] Black women were central to this struggle to desegregate New York City's Jim Crow education system as theorists, organizers, advocates, and mothers.[8]

During the 1950s, Ella Baker and Mae Mallory, two black women activist-intellectuals, crossed paths around education inequity. Baker, who later helped form the Student Nonviolent Coordinating Committee, emerged as a key activist and theorist in New York City's battles against Jim Crow in schools. She organized conferences, served on city committees, and led key organizations.[9] Mallory exercised a more direct-action form of protest. She sued the New York City Board of Education (BOE) for maintaining a Jim Crow education system. Both women wrote letters, made public statements, and marched. Like other black women activist-intellectuals in the black freedom struggle, they compelled city leaders to acknowledge the existence of the Jim Crow North. As black women, they understood that this work required an intellectual agility born of wide reading, organizational and personal experience, and ideological pragmatism. As needed, Baker and Mallory altered their strategies, organizational affiliations, and partnerships. They merged revolutionary activity with adaptable praxis to combat Jim Crow in a region where political leaders claimed that systemic racial segregation did not exist.[10]

Baker and Mallory's work as activist-intellectuals was especially important given the particular nature of northern Jim Crow racism. White leaders and city institutions in the North attempted to hide their de jure segregation in plain sight. Rather than acknowledge how racism pervaded policies and institutions, like public education, they argued that racial inequality emerged from black people's poor behavior and culture. They used the South's laws as the exemplar of racism in America, and pointed to the Jim Crow North's antidiscrimination laws as evidence of progress. Mallory and Baker laid bare the lies that segregation did not exist in New York, that city leaders had nothing to do with it, and that nothing could be done to fix the Jim Crow North.

Just like in the South, northern cities and states relegated blacks to a second-class status through an effective combination of laws, policies, and customs. An ethos of "color-blindness," became ensconced in northern law, language, policy, ideology, and custom through the formulation of "de facto" segregation, a rhetorical invention that emerged after the *Brown v. Board* decision,[11] and absolved northern cities of responsibility to eradicate racial segregation because whatever separation existed happened accidentally and unintentionally. In the Jim Crow North, supposedly "color-blind" postal zones determined school districting. Restrictive covenants, redlining, and violence caused housing segregation, but "color-blindness" became a masking agent that made Jim Crow in the North more elusive, although not less insidious and destructive, than southern Jim Crow.

The ethos of "color-blindness" helped New York's politicians and bureaucrats feign ignorance about the unequal effects of their policies on black citizens.[12] New York's Democratic mayor, Robert Wagner, for example, characterized his city at midcentury as a democracy where all nationalities could thrive.[13] City officials also refuted charges of "segregation," blaming "separation"[14] on impersonal market forces. News media often downplayed, or ignored, widespread discriminatory practices.[15] Mae Mallory and Ella Baker had to develop ways to think about racism in the Jim Crow North, and activist practices for fighting against it. They rejected the premise of de facto segregation, and called the city's public school system a Jim Crow system. In doing so, Baker and Mallory argued that Jim Crow was national in scope.

At least four themes shaped Mallory's and Baker's intellectual activism against educational inequality in the Jim Crow North. The first was personal. Mallory had two children attending public schools during the 1950s. Because of the inferior public schools in Harlem, Baker chose a private school for the niece she raised.[16] Second, communal connections and relationships fueled their intellectual-activist work. Mallory credited female family members and teachers with fostering her agile, action-oriented philosophy. Ella Baker's mother, Georgianna, was an abiding influence on her sense of self and duty. As a young woman in Harlem, Baker also developed relationships with black women activists, such as Pauli Murray, Marvel Cooke, Anna Arnold Hedgeman, and Dorothy Height, that sustained her and helped her grow intellectually.[17] Third was their education. After high school, Mallory taught herself about communism, black nationalism, and racial liberalism,[18] tailoring these "global ideas" to her "local circumstances" of New York City. Baker graduated valedictorian from Shaw University. Later, she studied labor history and social movements. Baker and Mallory, both broad learners, became strategic activist-thinkers. Last was their pasts as political organizers. Baker had been codirector of the Young Negroes' Cooperative League (YNCL) during the 1930s, national field organizer for the National Association for the Advancement of Colored People (NAACP) during the 1940s, and president and Education Chair of the New York NAACP during the 1950s. Mallory connected with Ella Baker in the battle to desegregate schools, but possessed much less formal institutional experience, and learned most about how to mobilize people through her activism.

Ella Baker and Mae Mallory are part of a tradition of black women's activism and theorizing.[19] Their work in New York during the 1950s was part of an important era in the history of the city and the nation that challenged the notion that Jim Crow did not exist outside the South, and that black women could not be out front leading an effort for racial equality. Mallory and Baker helped build a movement to improve the quality of public education for black and Puerto Rican children by holding city leaders accountable for the Jim Crow school system in New York City.

The Need to "Move from Debate to Direct Action"

Twenty years before *Brown*, Ella Baker fought for school desegregation in New York City. During the 1930s, she collaborated with the journalist George Schuyler to build the Young Negroes' Cooperative League. Here, she honed her skills in the "mechanics of movement-building," and molded the YNCL's commitments to gender equality.[20] During the 1940s, she became national field organizer for the NAACP and traveled throughout the country. All that time, she maintained a connection with New York City, and in the early 1950s, Baker became the first female president of the Manhattan NAACP. She even ran, unsuccessfully, for a seat on the City Council as a Liberal Party candidate. Throughout her career as an activist and organizer, Baker built trust and friendships. She needed both during the 1950s, when she turned her attention to the thorny issue of school segregation in New York City.[21]

By the 1950s, the struggle for quality education for black and Puerto Rican children had been underway for two decades. Parent groups in Harlem, Bedford-Stuyvesant, and Williamsburg had protested against the city's Board of Education (BOE) during the 1930s and 1940s. They marshalled evidence that proved the inferiority of their children's schools. In comparison with white schools, black parents uncovered, black school buildings were old and in disrepair, poorly equipped, and lacking in books and supplies. Black students went without hot lunches, or school nurses. Their classrooms were overcrowded. Schools lacked yards and gyms. The Bedford-Stuyvesant-Williamsburg Schools Council found that school overcrowding led to half-day schedules, and that their schools lacked sufficient full-time teachers with proper certification. Parents' investigations also revealed that some teachers exhibited bigoted and racist behavior towards students.[22]

In 1954, Ella Baker immersed herself in organizations committed to fighting Jim Crow in New York City's public schools, which connected her to a broad network of activists and intellectuals. She chaired the Manhattan NAACP's Education Committee, and, along with Dr. Kenneth Clark, the prominent child psychologist, she served as a member of the Intergroup Committee on New York's Public Schools (IC). Baker's involvement in established institutions, and her diverse connections to activists who may have disagreed in their political philosophies (some were Marxists, others were liberals, others were black nationalists) but remained united on the need to break the power of New York's racially segregated education system, signaled her ability to facilitate pragmatic political solutions. To become an effective activist in the fight against Jim Crow schools in New York City, Baker needed to possess strong but nimble ideals, and deep appreciation for practical outcomes.

The IC, an umbrella organization representing groups concerned for the welfare of New York City's children, became an important laboratory for Baker's idealism and pragmatism.[23] In April, she and Clark organized a conference entitled "Children Apart: The Effects of Segregation on the Educational Future of Young People in New York's Public Schools." Clark delivered the conference's keynote address, which outlined the existence of racially segregated schools in the city. Clark argued, "There is strong suggestive evidence that the educational standards and achievement of Negro children in the New York City Public Schools are declining [compared to the 1930s]."[24] Baker helped organize the conference's events, and drafted some of the literature distributed to the nearly two hundred activists, social workers, educators, and parents in attendance.[25] The information illustrated the BOE's willful neglect of black students, as "some Negro children [had] been illegally placed in classes for the mentally retarded."[26] A few weeks later, the Supreme Court handed down *Brown I*.

The *Brown* decision signaled to Ella Baker that the time had come to "move from debate to direct action."[27] Conferences and debates among her NAACP colleagues had value, but not at the expense of tangible on-the-ground activity. For Ella Baker, the purpose of the "Children Apart" conference was not just to expose the Board of Education's intentional disregard of black and Puerto Rican youth but also to prime the participants to act on the Supreme Court's ruling.[28]

Baker was certainly ready to move, even if the national NAACP was more hesitant in "liberal," "color-blind" New York. The national NAACP's litigation had focused on the South, and national leaders wanted to maintain amicable relations with city leaders.[29] Baker pushed for changes to public education that included much more than desegregation. Her idealism connected an end to Jim Crow in New York City's public schools with better child-welfare policies and community involvement in improving public education for black and Puerto Rican children.[30]

In her battle against Jim Crow in New York, Ella Baker worked hard to get close to the levers of political power without compromising her activist idealism. To improve the quality of education for black youth, Baker accepted a position on the BOE's Commission on Integration. Baker and Kenneth Clark were two of the thirty-seven people tasked with examining all aspects of the public school system and providing recommendations to improve the schools. Baker was not so naïve as to believe that she had been appointed for altruistic reasons. She understood that she had been chosen, in part, to blunt her criticisms of the BOE. Baker accepted the appointment, nevertheless, and worked on reports for the subcommissions on zoning and teacher placement.

In the next year, the Public Education Association (PEA), and the BOE's own Commission in Integration (CI), issued statements that highlighted unequal conditions throughout New York City's schools.[31] While the reports were controversial, it was impossible to deny what black activists had pointed out for years: the BOE systematically harmed black and Puerto Rican children by perpetuating a Jim Crow public education system.

Black and Puerto Rican children, in addition to encountering dilapidated facilities and less qualified teachers, suffered from a less rigorous curriculum. There were fewer classes for "gifted" children, black children were more likely to be put into "retarded" classes, and teacher expectations of intellectual capacity were often much lower of black and Puerto Rican children than of white children.[32] While white children circumvented zoning restrictions to avoid attending predominantly black schools on the borders of their districts, black and Puerto Rican students remained virtually locked into inferior schools with few means of escape.[33]

When it came to turning any of the CI's recommendations into BOE policy, such as redrawing school zones to encourage integration or moving teachers to correct imbalances in teacher staffing, the BOE balked.[34] For example, although the Board of Education established a Central Zoning Unit in July 1957 at the CI's suggestion, Superintendent Jansen gave it no authority to implement the recommendations of Baker's subcommission. Zoning decisions remained in the hands of district superintendents, and permissive zoning for the purposes of integration was not permitted. The "neighborhood school" policy remained in effect. Rose Shapiro, the chair of the zoning subcommission, asserted that the zoning report was "altered substantially after the public hearing." Other commission recommendations were also ignored.[35]

So, Baker pursued educational and child-welfare policies through the NAACP, and as a member of the Commission on Integration, but also as the head of Parents in Action Against Educational Discrimination (PAAED), a grassroots organization of black and Puerto Rican parents that she would mobilize in Harlem. Her involvement on the CI and the NAACP honed her skills and intellect as a pragmatist, and her leadership within the PAAED readied her for direct action in a more confrontational fight against Jim Crow New York. The direct-action protest involved different types of activists from the ones, like Clark, whom Baker worked with to craft policy proposals and study the nature of New York's Jim Crow public school system. Direct protest against racial segregation in New York City's schools relied on countless "local people": civic agitators who insisted that racism in schools hurt black children and that black children deserved better treatment and opportunities. Perhaps the most important example of such an activist in New York City during the 1950s was Mae Mallory.[36]

Becoming a "Troublemaker"

Mallory spent the early years of her life in Macon, Georgia, where she dealt with racism and white supremacy, but people encouraged her to stand up for herself, and to believe she was as good as any white person. When she was three years old, a white female store owner tried to feed her and other black neighborhood children cheese crawling with maggots. Mallory slapped the tray out of the woman's hand. The store owner then slapped Mallory, who ran home to her adult cousin. Mallory told her she was crying because the store owner's daughter and Mallory's cousin commanded the little girl not to return home until she had hit the white girl back. When Mallory complied, fifteen police officers showed up at her cousin's home. Instead of backing down, Mallory's cousin protected her. She told off the police for responding in such an absurd way to the actions of a toddler. The experience taught Mallory, at a very young age, that black people deserved respect.[37]

Mae Mallory's first elementary school principal also made sure that her pupils possessed self-esteem. "[T]his woman said to us that we had to stand tall," Mallory remembered. "She said that the children that came from her school would face the world with their heads high, their shoulders thrown back and they would walk to the tune of 'The World Is Mine, The World Is Mine.'" The gravity of what this black woman instilled in her charges sunk in as Mallory matured. Mallory came to realize that a person's environment, especially his or her communities and schools, shaped what kind of person he or she became.[38]

Mallory developed her defiance and sense of self-worth after her mother moved the family to Brooklyn in 1939. In Brooklyn, Mallory dealt with racial stereotypes in school. On her first day, because she came from Georgia, Mallory's white teacher assumed she had picked cotton. When Mallory told the teacher she had never picked cotton, and that her assumptions about southern blacks were incorrect, the teacher dismissed Mallory and refused to readmit her without her mother.[39] In high school a teacher told Mallory to sit in the last row because of her race, and Mallory refused.[40] These instances of self-advocacy predisposed Mallory to stand up for her own children when they experienced racial inequality in school.

Mallory's activism fit into her life as a working-class, single mother of two children. During the early 1950s, Mallory saw that Communists in New York fought for workers' rights and against racial discrimination. Her affiliation with the Communist Party in New York was brief, but it expanded upon the knowledge she gained from family and community, and strengthened the intellectual basis upon which she thought about activism against structural discrimination. She dabbled in organizing with black nationalists, but found their inactivity and politics around gender unsatisfying.[41]

Mallory moved between and within different groups. While she never settled on one ideology or approach as the only way to combat northern racism, her children's experiences made Mallory focus her activist energies on the city's Jim Crow school system. One day Mallory's children came home from school and said their friend had been run over and killed outside the school. When Mallory investigated the incident, the principal speculated that the bereaved mother was better off. The dead child meant one less mouth to feed. The principal made sure to mention to Mallory, however, that the school's "Sunshine Club" had taken the mother of the dead child groceries.

The meeting incensed Mallory. How dare this man compare a bag of groceries to a black child's life! The principal's callousness opened her eyes to the school's dilapidated conditions and terrible smell. She learned that the building had two broken toilets for 1,650 students. Janitors irregularly used water to wash away the urine and excrement.[42] Why did children attend a school like this? Mallory asked the principal. What was the principal doing about student safety and the building's condition?

His answers failed to satisfy her, so Mallory took matters into her own hands. Mallory traveled to Albany to see Harlem's state assemblyman, James C. Thomas, and she told the entire assembly about conditions in her children's school. Her making noise in Albany inspired the principal to fix the bathrooms. He then assailed Mallory as a Communist and a "troublemaker." The principal wanted other parents to ostracize Mallory. "I hadn't related communism to the schools," Mallory said in 1970. "I had only related communism to jobs." But in New York during the 1950s, in the eyes of people who defended racial inequalities, Mallory's advocacy for black children's rights, or her work to ameliorate racist practices within an institution, like her child's school, was tantamount to advocacy of communism. Mallory was not cowed and did not cave in to these intimidation tactics. They emboldened her.[43]

Tired of empty talk, and desirous of substantive changes beyond two repaired toilets, in 1956 Mallory and twelve other Harlem mothers formed the Parents Committee for Better Education (PC). The group demanded the improvement of conditions in Harlem's schools. The PC quickly grew to four hundred members. It documented deteriorating conditions in public schools and secured other forms of evidence that showed inferior educational practices in black neighborhoods.[44] "We were demanding a fair share of the pie, that our children be educated the same way as everybody else's," Mallory recalled. She and the PC "decided that we would do something rather than just sit and complain among ourselves."[45]

Challenging City Hall

During the 1950s, Mallory surmised that many New Yorkers probably believed the maxim, "you can't fight city hall." But she and Baker proved how, in her words, "you can challenge city hall."[46] Mallory and Baker mobilized Harlem parents. Ella Baker worked on multiple fronts. In developing PAAED, Baker created an organization to implement a movement-building philosophy. With Parents in Action she showed parents how to become leaders themselves. Baker never developed dogmatic, doctrinaire approaches to activism. "New York City didn't act right after the '54 decision," she said. "It didn't have any reason to act so you had to help it realize it. I was asked to serve on the Mayor's Commission. They finally discovered the city wasn't integrated."[47]

That realization did not result in significant policy changes, however. In the three years after *Brown*, Baker and others became frustrated. They considered superintendent of schools William Jansen, and the entire BOE, to be untrustworthy on matters of racial segregation in the city's schools. The BOE refused to implement proposals like permissive zoning, which would have allowed students to attend schools of their choice outside their residential districts. In September of 1957, the BOE only adopted permissive zoning on a very limited basis. Permissive zoning would only apply to high schools, and the schools had to have seats available, though there would be relatively few since school was just about to begin.[48] Over the next few years, it became increasingly clear that the BOE was not interested in facilitating school integration, as the board was not implementing the policy recommendations of its own subcommissions. Few permissive transfers were granted and primarily at the high school level.[49]

Throughout 1957, PAAED pressured Mayor Wagner and Superintendent Jansen, and accused them of using the same strategies of obstruction that southern school boards employed to resist implementing *Brown*. Throughout the summer of 1957, Mallory's Parents Committee and Baker's PAAED, along with the Negro Teachers Association, worked together to recruit parents into the struggle, and request meetings with the mayor. Both groups planned to stage a protest that September.[50]

Ella Baker organized weekly meetings of parents throughout the city, "getting them to deal with the question of their schools, what was happening to their children."[51] Mae Mallory pointedly told Superintendent Jansen that her daughter's school was "just as 'Jim Crow' as . . . [those] . . . in Macon, Georgia."[52] Activist-intellectuals such as Baker and Mallory argued that racial school segregation was not unique to the South. By calling it Jim Crow, Mallory identified with accuracy and anger that the BOE consciously designed and maintained a racially segregated school system.

During the fall of 1957, as city officials' obstructions and delays continued, and activists' frustration mounted, parent activists marched. Their interpretation of the social and political situation signaled for them that nothing short of public action would move the needle of public opinion, or stimulate those with power to act, in ways that recognized the disadvantage that the city's Jim Crow education system put upon black students. On September 19, 1957, PAAED staged its rally to draw greater attention to the campaign. The *New York Times* gave poor coverage of the protest. Its reporter contended that only one hundred protesters participated, but Baker led a picket of over five hundred black and Puerto Rican parents in front of city hall to protest the beginning of another segregated school year.[53] PAAED called on the mayor for an equal share of experienced teachers compared to white schools, the end of part-time school days, smaller class sizes, a standard curriculum at each grade level, more remedial teachers, and the removal of the neighborhood school concept where it hindered immediate integration.[54]

Rather than recognize these conditions as products of a racist system, Superintendent Jansen instructed PEA researchers to use the word "separation" in their final report instead of the word "segregation." The word choice was tantamount to a denial that Jim Crow existed in New York City.[55] Official blindness to New York's Jim Crow system and their refusal to call racial segregation by its rightful name maintained New York as a Jim Crow city.

Baker also tried to get the NAACP to support direct-action tactics that underscored the urgency of improving black and Puerto Rican schools in New York City. The national office, concerned about potentially alienating its liberal white donor base, discouraged confrontational or "provocative" protest strategies against northern officials.[56] The NAACP desired direct access to the city's power brokers, and its national leaders undermined Baker, and members of more militant branches, who defined Jim Crow to encompass forms of northern discrimination. Baker wanted to cultivate leaders among the parents of Harlem. She educated them about their rights, helped them to develop tools to hold school and city officials accountable for their actions, and gave them the space to create their own protest movement for their children.[57]

The protesters threatened Mayor Wagner's reelection. Baker asked the mayor what would be done for the children in "subject schools," which were schools in "underprivileged" areas where the children were deemed to display "culturally deprived" behaviors.[58] "It seems mandatory that New York City, the world's leading city, should reflect the highest degree of democracy in its public school system," Baker said. "We know the ballot has speaking power and parents are concerned with what happens to their children."[59] For Baker, dissatisfied parents could channel their anger through their votes. She portrayed these blacks and Puerto Ricans as concerned parents, which challenged stereotypes about poor racial and ethnic minorities as inadequate parents, and their children as possessive of inveterate "cultural deprivation." Baker's arguments played to the city's image as a beacon of democracy to compel its leaders to provide quality, integrated education to all its students.

Baker honed her leadership philosophy of grassroots mobilization. "People have a right to participate in the decisions that affect their lives." She believed an activist had to "start with the people where they are." Baker traveled all over the city to educate and organize. The first step involved "organizing people around [breaking down school segregation] in terms of their level of understanding." Then, Baker said, "You try to reach from one level of understanding to another. Sometimes you may have to use different strategies to focus on the same question."[60] Political and social circumstances shaped how activists worked together. Poor people knew how to solve their problems, and Baker always saw herself as a pragmatist giving them the tools to change their own lives themselves.[61]

The multipronged and multilayered approach to leadership and movement building that Baker displayed during her time fighting for educational equality in New York was emblematic not only of her pragmatic and "radical democratic" method of operation but also of the way many other women activist-intellectuals, like Mae Mallory, participated in the black freedom struggle. These activists balanced an idealism that wished to eradicate racism in New York City, and the nation, with a pragmatism that focused on achieving tangible political victories against Jim Crow schools in Gotham. Their work as activist intellectuals enabled them to develop theories about how the Jim Crow North worked and about the most effective ways to create broad, democratic, flexible approaches for opposing it. These theories named northern racism as racism, not as something else, and they inspired direct-action protest.

Mallory and Baker participated in the planning and execution of the protests of 1957. Mallory also spoke out, and demanded action of city officials to improve Harlem's schools. She continued to demonstrate the agility of her theorizing, organizing, and activities in pressing a legal case to improve education in Harlem. This type of evolution of pragmatic activism, built from the ideals her family and community taught her and made real in her everyday life, grew from two fundamental truths that defined her political praxis and animated her actions: first, black people possessed esteem and value independent of what racist whites said and did; and second, New York City's systems and institutions promoted and perpetuated racism and segregation. From this intellectual foundation, this faith-filled reason, flowed her ability to fight racism in the Jim Crow North.

Unmasking the "Whole Segregation Myth" in the North

Mallory and Baker wanted the city's black and Puerto Rican children to live as first-class citizens, and to have the same opportunities for success white children had. In a more tangible sense, Baker and Mallory wanted schools rezoned, transfers between districts, more experienced teachers, an increased number of schools to end the practice of half-days for Harlem students, and rigorous curricula.[62] These plans would fix some of the structural inequities that perpetuated Jim Crow in New York City's schools. These proposals had come from multiple places, including the subcommission reports that Baker had helped write as part of the Commission on Integration, and Mallory's Harlem Parents Committee's own research. They were rooted in research, facts, and investigations. They represented these black women's intellectual work. They did not hide, obscure, or ignore racism in New York's public school system. They accepted the Jim Crow system as real and dealt directly with the social reality of a racially segregated education system.

In 1957, Mallory channeled this intellectual work into the first lawsuit against "de facto" segregation in the North. Her daughter, Pat, became civil rights attorney Paul Zuber's first client.[63] As Mallory put it, her lawsuit had "nothing to do with wanting to sit next to white folks, but it was obvious that a whole pattern of black retardation was the program of the board of education." Mallory's intellectual work proved that, in her words, "my children were going to the same school system [as white children and they] were coming out of school with less knowledge than I did. This isn't progress!"

Mallory, like Baker, challenged the racial structure of city life and the school system from multiple fronts. Mallory spoke to her children's principal, wrote letters to city officials, helped to establish a grassroots parents' organization, and protested in the streets in 1957. These actions did not grow from abstract theories about inequality, or political dogma regarding historical materialism and class struggle, but instead grew from the social realities of her everyday life. She did not need an abstract political theory to tell her that New York City was racist. One of her son's homework assignments snapped that reality into focus for her.

Her fifth-grade son came home with an assignment to count the pipes under the kitchen sink. Mallory's son's teacher took it for granted that her students had no career prospects beyond manual labor, and that their parents would not dare challenge the teacher's authority. Mae Mallory not only called out the teacher for assigning work with such low standards, but she also decided that the school's entire curriculum needed to change. Mallory's analysis of the problem started with her son and his teacher and their school, but she telescoped it out into an action that addressed the entire city's system. She recognized that low expectations led to the widespread miseducation of entire generations of black children. Such intellectual analysis of the Jim Crow North influenced the method, style, and explanations of her direct action.

Mallory's initial lawsuit, coupled with the 1957 protest, brought little change. A lengthy meeting with Mayor Wagner, Superintendent Jansen, BOE president Charles Silver, and other city officials offered more vague promises, but no tangible action. The Board of Education reported in October of 1957 that it was making progress toward integration, having rezoned fifty schools and transferred five thousand black and Puerto Rican students into formerly all-white schools.[64] Parents demanded that their children attend the school of their choice, not their zoned schools in Harlem. They also insisted that all one million students in the city's public schools, not just the black and Puerto Rican ones, share the burden for integration.

Parents' aggravation with inaction reached ever higher levels during the 1957–1958 school year. More protests occurred. Parents circumvented the established BOE process. They picked a fight with the BOE in the hope that their confrontations would force changes in the education system's practices, even incremental ones, to happen.[65]

In September of 1958, nine Harlem mothers, including Mae Mallory, removed their fifteen children from junior high schools. This act violated the state's compulsory education law. These mothers, initially nicknamed "the Little Rock Nine of Harlem," soon became known as the "Harlem Nine." As one mother described her growing exasperation, she echoed Ella Baker's sentiment from 1954. "Conference upon conference has procured nothing," the mother said. "We're going to see this through to the bitter end [even] if it goes to the Supreme Court."[66]

Mallory and the PC hoped litigation would pressure the BOE to speed up its timeline for desegregation. Most previous lawsuits about segregation in K–12 schools focused on southern places, and national discussions about desegregating schools only focused on the South. Mallory and the parents of the PC announced that segregation and educational inequalities plagued the North. Jim Crow education harmed northern children, and black and Puerto Rican parents should not be forced to send their children to inferior schools because of the zoned district.

In addition to filing suit against the BOE, the PC established an alternative school in Harlem. Civil rights lawyer Paul Zuber, Yale graduate Barbara Zuber, and other licensed teachers offered classes in English, French, math, science, social studies, world events, music, and art.[67] After operating this unlicensed school for more than a month, the PC and Zuber worried that the BOE would not take action against them because the alternative school functioned too well. The PC demonstrated that black parents, with community support, could develop a rigorous, culturally sensitive, and diverse liberal arts curriculum more effectively than the Board of Education. "Recognizing the irony of the situation, they decided to end the private tutoring" and filed a $1 million lawsuit against the city for "sinister and discriminatory purpose in the perpetuation of racial segregation in five school districts in Harlem."[68]

This action garnered the authorities' attention. Since the children had not been in their official schools for thirty-five consecutive days, the BOE charged the Harlem parents with violating the compulsory education law. The cases were heard in Domestic Relations Court, colloquially known as family court. Six of the cases were assigned to Judge Nathaniel Kaplan, who viewed the matter as simple truancy. He found four of the parents guilty. However, the cases of Charlene Skipwith and Sheldon Rector went before Judge Justine Wise Polier. She looked at the issues of gross inequality through a broader lens and considered the parents to be protecting, rather than endangering, the welfare of their children.

On December 3, 1958, less than two weeks after Kaplan had ruled against one set of parents, Polier ruled in favor of the parents, saying that children attending Harlem's junior high schools were getting "inferior education in those schools by reason of racial discrimination."[69] This signaled a significant victory for activist intellectuals like Baker and Mallory. The judge identified the problem they devoted their activism to defeating as "racial discrimination." The intellectual framework Baker, Mallory, and so many other activists in the Jim Crow North used to interpret the social problems of racism in New York became part of an official judge's ruling in a case on justice and equality in the city's public education system. Judge Polier charged the BOE with perpetuating the results of racial segregation and argued that the BOE could no longer shirk its responsibility to fix the problem. The Harlem Nine were vindicated.[70] The parents in Judge Kaplan's case appealed his decision. He delayed the case, and they escaped punishment.[71]

Mae Mallory noted years later that the school boycotts and legal cases underscored "the whole segregation myth" in the North. As historian Adina Back pointed out, "The boundaries between de jure and de facto segregation, between the North and the South, became blurred as the

Harlem Nine and their supporters called attention to inferior educational opportunities in the city's black schools. . . . [T]he North could no longer hide behind de facto segregation as an excuse for inferior educational facilities."[72]

Rather than enact reforms, accept the racism within the system, and adopt a framework for understanding racial inequities in public schools as systematic and endemic, the New York City BOE initially appealed Polier's ruling.[73] In February 1959, however, the new superintendent of schools, John Theobald, reevaluated the political damage the case had caused, overruled the board, and dropped the appeal.[74] Theobald allowed the children to attend JHS 43, the school of his choice, even though it fell outside their district. Theobald also agreed to an eight-point program designed to address the PC's demands to improve its district's schools. Reforms included an increase of licensed teachers, guidance counselors, reading specialists, and advanced classes. Theobald also created an advisory group of African Americans to counsel him on educational issues. For the first time, black leaders had direct access to the Board of Education. Their ideas about a Jim Crow racist city and education system mattered.[75]

The Harlem Nine compelled the BOE to reckon with the fact that black parents would not accept their children's consignment to inferior schools. With the help of women like Baker, these women organized themselves to develop their own movement philosophies and theories about racial inequity in New York City. Systematic racism embedded within politics created a Jim Crow public school system. Only direct action could address and reverse that political reality.

As time passed, the BOE did not implement the reforms it promised.[76] Its intransigence intensified school segregation. The BOE used several strategies to evade its responsibility to integrate public schools, including initially denying there was segregation in the schools; then renaming what was occurring; calling for studies of the school system in order to delay reforms; and, finally, not implementing the suggestions provided. The BOE broke promises to black New Yorkers, and then repeated these strategies as needed in order to perpetually maintain the city's Jim Crow education system, while also maintaining the city's liberal image.

And while the BOE continued to operate a Jim Crow system, the movement to integrate public schools also continued long after Mallory and Baker left New York City. Grassroots organizations such as Reverend Milton A. Galamison's Parents Workshop for Equality in New York City Schools, based in Brooklyn, carried the movement into the next decade. Galamison, who pastored one of the largest congregations in New York, had been at the forefront of the school integration battles since 1954, and became even more prominent after severing his ties to the Brooklyn NAACP in 1960. By the summer of 1963, he had helped establish the New York Citywide Committee for Integrated Schools, which included other grassroots groups, six branches of the NAACP, and several local chapters of the Congress of Racial Equality. This short-lived coalition was responsible for one of the most powerful protests for school integration, and the largest protest of the civil rights movement, when on February 3, 1964, more than 460,000 students boycotted the public schools. Many attended "Freedom Schools" for the day.[77] They sought freedom from Jim Crow in America's northern outpost of Jim Crow racism.

NOTES

1 Kristopher Burrell would like to thank Mr. Paul Torres, who served as a Research Assistant during the 2016–2017 academic year, as a result of a City University of New York Community College Research Grant for Mentored Undergraduate Research. Paul's assistance and diligence were valuable for improving the clarity of thought in this chapter. He would also like to thank the members of the North East Freedom North Writers Collective for all of the scholarly and emotional support.

2 On "hyper-segregation" see Douglas S. Massey and Nancy A. Denton, "Hyper-segregation in US Metropolitan Areas: Black and Hispanic Segregation along Five Dimensions," *Demography* 26:3 (1989), 373–91. For a vivid depiction of how hyper-segregation affected utilization of public schools in Brooklyn, New York, see "Some facts about segregated schools in Brooklyn, 1957 School Year," and "Utilization of Schools in the Borough of Brooklyn," maps for 1957, 1958, 1959, in Annie Stein Papers, Columbia University, Rare Book and Manuscript Division, MS#1481, Box 11.

3 *Brown v. Board of Education of Topeka*, 347 U.S. 483 (1954). *Brown v. Board of Education of Topeka*, 349 U.S. 294 (1955). In the United States, before 1954, seventeen states mandated segregation in schools: Alabama, Arkansas, Florida, Georgia, Louisiana, Mississippi, North Carolina, South Carolina, Tennessee, Texas, Virginia, Delaware, Kentucky, Maryland, Missouri, Oklahoma, and West Virginia. See Sean Farhang and Ira Katznelson, "The Southern Imposition: Congress and Labor in the New Deal and Fair Deal," *Studies in American Political Development*

19 (Spring 2005): 1, fn 1. On racial segregation and its effects on the City University of New York, see Tahir Butt, "'You Are Running a de Facto Segregated University': Racial Segregation and City University of New York, 1961–1968," chapter 7 in this volume.

4 Board of Education of the City of New York, *Toward Greater Opportunity: A Progress Report from the Superintendent of Schools to the Board of Education Dealing with Implementation of Recommendations of the Commission on Integration* (June 1960), 3, Box 5, Folder 41, Series 261, "Commission on Integration Papers," Board of Education Papers, Special Collections, Milbank Memorial Library, Teachers College, Columbia University, New York. This collection is now housed at the NYC Municipal Archives.

5 The Intergroup Committee on New York's Public Schools, "Children Apart: The Effects of Segregation on the Future of Young People in New York's Public Schools," 24 April 1954, 12, Box 56, Folder 2, Professional File, Subject File, Intergroup Committee on New York's Public Schools, Kenneth Bancroft Clark Papers, Manuscript Division, Library of Congress, Washington, D.C. Will be referred to hereafter as KBC Papers.

6 Four key studies that offer theories on the significance of histories of "local" activists in the civil rights movement are John Dittmer, *Local People: The Struggle for Civil Rights in Mississippi* (Urbana: University of Illinois Press, 1994); Charles M. Payne, *I've Got the Light of Freedom: The Organizing Tradition in the Mississippi Black Freedom Struggle* (Berkeley: University of California Press, 2007); Jeanne Theoharis and Komozi Woodard, *Groundwork: Local Black Freedom Movements in America* (New York: NYU Press, 2005); and Emilye Crosby, *Civil Rights History from the Ground Up: Local Struggles, a National Movement* (Athens: University of Georgia Press, 2011). On Milton Galamison, see Clarence Taylor, *Knocking at Our Own Door: Milton A. Galamison and the Struggle to Integrate New York City Schools* (New York: Columbia University Press, 1997). On Annie Stein, see Adina Back, "Up South in New York: The 1950's School Desegregation Struggles" (Ph.D. diss.: New York University, 1997). On Brooklyn CORE, see Brian Purnell, *Fighting Jim Crow in the County of Kings: The Congress of Racial Equality in Brooklyn* (Lexington: University Press of Kentucky, 2013). On community control see, Jerald Podair, *The Strike That Changed New York: Blacks, Whites, and the Ocean Hill–Brownsville Crisis* (New Haven, CT: Yale University Press, 2002); Heather Lewis, *New York City Public Schools from Brownsville to Bloomberg: Community Control and Its Legacy (New York: Teachers College Press, 2013)*, and Michael R. Glass, "'A Series of Blunders and Broken Promises': IS 201 as a Turning Point," *GOTHAM: A Blog for Scholars of New York City History,* August 1, 2016 www.gothamcenter.org.

7 Theoharis and Woodard, *Groundwork*, 2.

8 Darlene Clark Hine, ed., *Black Women in United States History* (Brooklyn, NY: Carlson, 1990); Belinda Robnett, *How Long? How Long? African-American Women in the Struggle for Civil Rights* (New York: Oxford University Press, 1997); Bettye Collier Thomas and V. P. Franklin, eds., *Sisters in the Struggle: African American*

Women in the Civil Rights–Black Power Movements (New York: NYU Press, 2001); Barbara Ransby, *Ella Baker and the Black Freedom Movement: A Radical Democratic Vision* (Chapel Hill: University of North Carolina Press, 2003).

9 Barbara Ransby, "Behind-the-Scenes View of a Behind-the-Scenes Organizer: The Roots of Ella Baker's Political Passions," in *Sisters in the Struggle: African American Women in the Civil Rights–Black Power Movements*, eds. Bettye Collier Thomas and V. P. Franklin (New York: NYU Press, 2001), 44, 47.

10 Ashley Farmer, *Remaking Black Power: How Women Transformed an Era* (Chapel Hill: University of North Carolina Press, 2017); Jennifer Scanlon, *Until There Is Justice: The Life of Anna Arnold Hedgeman* (New York: Oxford University Press, 2016); Ransby, *Ella Baker and the Black Freedom Movement*.

11 Paul Zuber, in Jeanne Theoharis, *A More Beautiful and Terrible History: The Uses and Misuses of the Civil Rights Movement* (New York: Beacon, 2018), 38; Matthew D. Lassiter, "De Jure/De Facto Segregation: The Long Shadow of a National Myth," in *The Myth of Southern Exceptionalism*, eds. Matthew D. Lassiter and Joseph Crespino (New York: Oxford University Press, 2010), 27.

12 Jennifer de Forest, "The 1958 Harlem School Boycott: Parental Activism and the Struggle for Educational Equity in New York City," *Urban Review* 40.1 (March 2008): 27.

13 Robert Wagner, Press Release, January 6, 1964, Roll 40054, Box 58, Folder 681, Discrimination (2), 1954, Office of the Mayor (Robert F. Wagner, Jr.), Subject Files, 1954–1965, New York Municipal Archives, New York, New York.

14 Adina Back, "Exposing the 'Whole Segregation Myth': The Harlem Nine and New York City's School Desegregation Battles," in *Freedom North: Black Freedom Struggles outside the South, 1940–1980*, eds. Jeanne F. Theoharis and Komozi Woodard (New York: Palgrave Macmillan, 2003), 68, 70.

15 Matthew F. Delmont, *Why Busing Failed: Race, Media, and the National Resistance to School Desegregation* (Oakland: University of California Press, 2016), 8–9.

16 Malaika Lumumba interview with Mae Mallory, February 27, 1970, 11–15, Ralph Bunche Oral History Collection, Moorland-Spingarn Research Collection, Manuscripts Division, Howard University, Washington, D.C. The collection will hereafter be referred to as the RBC. Barbara Ransby, "Cops, Schools, and Communism: Local Politics and Global Ideologies—New York City in the 1950s," in *Civil Rights in New York City: From World War II to the Giuliani Era*, ed. Clarence Taylor (Bronx, NY: Fordham University Press, 2010), 35.

17 Barbara Ransby, "Behind-the-Scenes View of a Behind-the-Scenes Organizer," 44, 47.

18 Lumumba interview with Mae Mallory, 10–1, RBC.

19 Sometimes a book stands as part of an intellectual, political movement, and representation of a historical moment. *But Some of Us Are Brave* is such a book in black women's history and literature. See Gloria T. Hull, Patricia Bell-Scott, and Barbara Smith, eds., *All the Women Are White, All the Blacks Are Men, but Some of Us Were Brave* (Old Westbury, NY: Feminist Press, 1982). See also, Darlene Clark Hines's

Black Women in America (New York: Oxford University Press, 2005), Belinda Robnett's *How Long? How Long?*, Bettye Collier Thomas and V. P. Franklin's *Sisters in the Struggle*; Jeanne Theoharis, "'We Saved the City': Black Struggles for Equality in Boston, 1960–1976," *Radical History Review*, 81 (Fall 2001): 61–93; Theoharis and Woodard, eds., *Freedom North*; Theoharis and Woodard, *Groundwork*; Dayo Gore, Jeanne Theoharis, and Komozi Woodard, eds., *Want to Start a Revolution? Radical Women in the Black Freedom Struggle* (New York: NYU Press, 2009); Jeanne Theoharis, *The Rebellious Life of Mrs. Rosa Parks* (Boston: Beacon, 2013).

20 Ransby, *Ella Baker and the Black Freedom Movement*, 79–81. Schuyler was then a leftist, but by the 1950s had become an arch-conservative.

21 J. Todd Moye, *Ella Baker: Community Organizer of the Civil Rights Movement* (Lanham, MD: Rowman & Littlefield, 2013), 70–71; Joanne Grant, *Ella Baker Freedom Bound* (New York: Wiley, 1998), 96; and Joanne Grant, *Fundi*, documentary, directed by Joanne Grant (1981), VHS.

22 Clarence Taylor, *Knocking*, 62.

23 Kenneth Clark, "Segregated Schools in New York City," 24 April 1954, 12, Box 56, Folder 5, Professional File, Subject File, Intergroup Committee on New York's Public Schools, KBC Papers.

24 Ibid., 7.

25 Intergroup Committee of New York's Public Schools, "Conference Report," 1.

26 Ransby, "Cops, Schools, and Communism," 37; Intergroup Committee on New York's Public Schools, "Children Apart," Program, KBC Papers.

27 Ransby, "Cops, Schools, and Communism," 37; Ransby, *Ella Baker*, 152–53.

28 Ransby, "Cops, Schools, and Communism," 37.

29 Ransby, *Ella Baker*, 153–54.

30 Ransby, "Cops, Schools, and Communism," 36.

31 Board of Education of the City of New York, *Toward Greater Opportunity*, 3; Lynn Farnol to Commission on Integration, n.d., Box 5, Folder 49, Series 261, "Commission on Integration Papers," Board of Education Papers, Special Collections, Milbank Memorial Library, Teachers College, Columbia University, New York.

32 Ransby, "Cops, Schools, and Communism," 37.

33 "Clark Cites Several Examples of School Segregation Here," *New York Herald-Tribune*, 21 October 1954; Kenneth Clark, "Steps toward Racial Integration: 'Segregation in New York City Schools,'" October 18, 1954, 3, Box 158, Folder 4, Professional File, Speeches and Writings, Speeches, KBC Papers; Taylor, *Knocking*, 81.

34 Taylor, *Knocking*, 116–17; Theoharis, *A More Beautiful and Terrible History*, 39–40.

35 David Rogers, *110 Livingston Street: Politics and Bureaucracy in the New York City Schools* (New York: Random House, 1968), 19–20.

36 Ransby, "Cops, Schools, and Communism," 36–37.

37 Lumumba interview with Mae Mallory, 3–4, RBC.

38 Ibid., 1–2.

39 Ibid., 5–6.

40 Ibid., 7–8.

41 Ibid., 10–11.

42 Ibid., 11–12.

43 Ibid., 12–13; Martha Biondi, *To Stand and Fight: The Struggle for Civil Rights in Postwar New York City* (Cambridge, MA: Harvard University Press, 2003), 137, 186, 209, 266; Brian Purnell, "Desegregating the Jim Crow North: Bronx African Americans and the Fight to Integrate the Castle Hill Beach Club," in *Afro-Americans in New York Life and History* 32.2 (2009): 47–78.

44 de Forest, "The 1958 Harlem Schools Boycott," 26.

45 Adina Back interview with Mae Mallory, New York City, 2000.

46 Lumumba interview with Mae Mallory, 14, RBC.

47 Ransby, "Cops, Schools, and Communism," 37.

48 Taylor, *Knocking*, 81.

49 Rogers, *110 Livingston Street*, 20; Taylor, *Knocking*, 81.

50 Night Letter to Mayor Robert Wagner from Ella Baker, Paul Zuber, and Richard Parrish, 16 June 1957; Telegram to Mayor Robert Wagner from Ella Baker, Paul Zuber, and Richard Parrish, 25 June 1957; Letter to Parents from Ella Baker, Paul Zuber, and Richard Parrish, 3 July 1957, Box 4, Folder 20, NAACP—NYC Branch Education Committee, 1956–1957, Ella J. Baker Papers, Schomburg Center for Research in Black Culture, New York Public Library, New York, New York. Will subsequently be referred to as the EJB Papers.

51 Back, "Exposing the 'Whole Segregation Myth,'" 70; Eugene Walker, interview with Ella Baker, September 4, 1974, Interview G-0007, Southern Oral History Program Collection, http://docsouth.unc.edu, accessed on November 10, 2015; Ransby, "Cops, Schools, and Communism," 38.

52 Mae Mallory, quoted in Adina Back, "Taking School Segregation to the Courts," unpublished manuscript, 1.

53 Sara Slack, "Don't Forget, N.Y. Has Its Own School Problem," *New York Amsterdam News*, September 28, 1957, 1.

54 "Parents Demand Integration Here," *New York Times*, September 20, 1957, Box 4, Folder 20, NAACP, NYC Branch Education Committee, 1956–57, EJB Papers.

55 Back, "Exposing the 'Whole Segregation Myth,'" 70.

56 Ransby, "Cops, Schools, and Communism," 38.

57 Ibid., 37–38.

58 Marie Lily Cerat and Whitney Hollins, "An Integration Plan That Never Was: Looking for *Brown v. Board of Education* in the New York City Board of Education's 1954 Commission on Integration," *Theory, Research, and Action in Urban Education* (n.d.), n. 4.

59 Slack, "Don't Forget," 1.

60 "Interview with Ella Baker," *Urban Review*, 20, EJB Papers.

61 Ransby, *Ella Baker*, 44–45.

62 Back, "Exposing the 'Whole Segregation Myth,'" 72; Melissa Weiner, *Power, Protest, and the Public Schools: Jewish and African American Struggles in New York City* (Newark, NJ: Rutgers University Press, 2011), 59.

63 Adina Back, "Taking School Segregation to the Courts," unpublished manuscript, 15.

64 Benjamin Fine, "Education in Review: Report on Integration in the City's Schools Shows Progress and Problems Ahead," *New York Times*, October 6, 1957.

65 Weiner, *Power, Protest, and the Public Schools*, 59.

66 Harlem parent Carrie Haynes, quoted in Back, "Exposing the 'Whole Segregation Myth,'" 73.

67 de Forest, 27–28; Back, "Exposing the 'Whole Segregation Myth,'" 73.

68 Back, "Exposing the 'Whole Segregation Myth,'" 74.

69 Justine Wise Polier, "Domestic Relations Court of the City of New York: Children's Court Division—County of New York," Docket No. 3913/58 and Docket No. 3945/58, December 1958, 27–8, Box 131, Folder 2382, "Race Discrimination, 1958–66," Pauli Murray Papers, Schlesinger Library, Radcliffe College, Cambridge, Massachusetts.

70 Polier, "Domestic Relations Court of the City of New York: Children's Court Division—County of New York," 26–27; Back, "Exposing the 'Whole Segregation Myth,'" 75–76; de Forest, 32.

71 Back, "Exposing the 'Whole Segregation Myth,'" 76.

72 Adina Back, "Still Unequal: A Fiftieth Anniversary Reflection on *Brown v. Board of Education*," *Radical History Review* 90 (2004): 67.

73 Back, "Exposing the 'Whole Segregation Myth,'" 77.

74 Ibid., 37–38.

75 Ibid., 38.

76 Weiner, *Power, Protest, and the Public Schools*, 63–64.

77 Taylor, *Knocking*, 141–42; Delmont, *Why Busing Failed*, 43.

4

Brown Girl, Red Lines, and Brownstones

Paule Marshall's Brown Girl, Brownstones *and the Jim Crow North*

BALTHAZAR I. BECKETT

In a 1969 *New York Magazine* cover story, Pete Hamill promoted Brooklyn as a "sane alternative" for the city's middle class. It was still possible, he held, "to buy a brownstone in reasonably good condition for $30,000, with a number of fairly good houses available for less, if you are willing to invest in reconditioning them." Hamill, one of the leading voices of the Brooklyn literary canon, employed nostalgia for Brooklyn's mythological past as a tool to render the borough palatable for investors. "There was something special, almost private, about being from Brooklyn when I was growing up," Hamill recalled about the 1930s and '40s, "a sense of community, a sense of being home." However, this idyll ended with the "white flight" in the context of "postwar decline in Brooklyn," which Hamill blamed on the fact that "black migration hit Brooklyn harder than any other part of the city." The author personified and vilified this immigration when Hamill wrote how "[t]he southern black man came to Brooklyn," and presented as "a badly educated rural black man." Hamill's framing of mid-twentieth-century Brooklyn left the real reasons for Brooklyn's social demise untouched. He culminated by describing how "[t]he streets became littered with broken bottles and discarded beer cans; the yards filled with garbage; drug arrests increased; hookers worked the avenues; there were knifings and shootings, and soon the merchants on Flatbush Avenue started folding up and moving away."[1]

Challenging such "nostalgic amnesia" that to this day permeates renderings of bygone Brooklyn, Brian Purnell argues that the way Jim Crow racism worked in the North was to make black people responsible for the social and economic effects of white racism. Purnell offers a corrective to this narrative when he reminds that "[t]he urban crisis that tore through American cities like a tornado after World War II was a product of decades of policies, bigotries, and fears directed against hundreds of thousands of black residents."[2] Yet despite such cautioning voices, many anthologies of twentieth-century literary Brooklyn still reinforce the borough's self-mythologization as "America's favorite borough" and an "inspiration to the world."[3] In so doing, scholarship remains silent about the distinctly northern patterns of racial segregation that have shaped Brooklyn—and that remain evident in its social dynamics today.

This is aggravated by the fact that texts that do highlight Brooklyn-style Jim Crow, such as Paule Marshall's *Brown Girl, Brownstones* (1959), are often framed in ways that distract from systemic racism at the heart of "the Brooklyn experience." Both the publishing history of Marshall's first novel and the scholarly response prioritize individual identity (the *Brown Girl*) over the context of policies around housing (the *Brownstones*) that shaped racial destinies in mid-twentieth-century Brooklyn. This omission calls for a reframing of Marshall's novel as an explicit commentary on the tenacious and ubiquitous mechanisms of a northern system of segregation, or a Jim Crow North, that emerged in the context of the New Deal.

Such a reframing is pivotal today because, as outlined by Hamill above, nostalgically distorted narratives of Brooklyn's past sanitize current processes of gentrification and conceal the origins of the equity gap that makes the current loss of black population in central Brooklyn possible. It disguises the numerous factors that conspired against aspiring black home owners in the 1940s persist into the present day.[4] "The New People, as they are called," Hamill wrote, bestowing a familiar northern liberal innocence onto early gentrifiers, many of whom had grown up in the suburbs, "saw Brooklyn fresh. They had not known it before, so they knew nothing about its decline."

Situating *Brown Girl* within the intricate system of redlining, financial divestment, and workplace discrimination that trapped black people, both migrants from the American South and immigrants from the West Indies, within Brooklyn's overcrowded, underfunded, and racially segregated Bedford-Stuyvesant neighborhood highlights the text's powers to dispel this amnesia. Freeing Brooklyn from its prison of nostalgia and returning it to its history of Jim Crow racism, *Brown Girl* shows how Brooklyn evolved into the magnet of gentrification and social inequity it has become during these first decades of the twenty-first century.

"That Life-Sore": Segregated Labor in Jim Crow Brooklyn

From a literary standpoint, few texts are more suited to challenge nostalgic narratives of midcentury Brooklyn than Paule Marshall's *Brown Girl, Brownstones* (1959), a thinly veiled roman à clef centered on the childhood experiences of Marshall's fictional stand-in, Selina Boyce, and her immigrant parents, Silla and Deighton. Arriving from Barbados after the First World War, Marshall's real-life parents settled in Brooklyn's Red Hook neighborhood before moving to Fulton Street in central Brooklyn, where the author was born in 1929. As she later explained, "For the West Indians of Brooklyn, the section of Fulton Street where I was born represented a step up from Red Hook. And no sooner had they arrived 'uptown' than they began eyeing the nearby white, middle-class neighborhoods of Bedford and Stuyvesant Heights, with their neat, tree-lined streets and row after row of handsome, high-stooped brownstone houses, some of them the finest in the city."[5] Brought up among Garveyites, Marshall joined the American Youth for Democracy (AYD) in 1946, a precursor of the Labor Youth League (LYL), which attracted other young black writers, such as Lorraine Hansberry and Audre Lorde. While she was also associated with John Oliver Killens's Harlem Writers Guild, in the 1950s Marshall became a principal figure in the Association of Artists for Freedom—a group that was "noted for its sharp attacks on the hypocrisy of white liberalism."[6] Scholars have failed to read Paule Marshall's work within the specific context of Jim Crow's northern incarnations. Instead, analysis situates Marshall's career within the context of southern forms of Jim Crow and a southern civil rights movement. "In 1960, one year after [. . .] [Marshall's] first novel (*Brown Girl, Brownstones*)," Darwin Turner writes, "sit-ins throughout the South attacked practices of segregation in public eating places and other public facilities."[7] Joyce Pettis observes that "[i]n 1959, when Paule Marshall's first novel, *Brown Girl, Brownstones*, was published, Rosa Parks had defied tradition and authority in Montgomery, Alabama, by refusing to relinquish her seat on a public bus and thus initiated the civil rights movement."[8] Aligning Marshall's life and career with a standardized civil rights narrative centered on a southern struggle bypasses her biographical and literary rootedness in the urban segregation of northern cities shaped by New Deal politics.

Brown Girl contains an indictment of northern liberalism. As Craig Wilder has noted, one central target of the "rise of Jim Crow in Brooklyn" that accompanied the in-migration of black residents to the borough in the 1920s and '30s was a "methodical struggle to subordinate black people as workers" as "[b]lack labor had to be degraded, if the triumph of exclusion was to be an advantage to white people."[9] Selina's parents are both caught up in a northern labor market based on racial disparities. Each morning, Silla and her friends take "the train to Flatbush and Sheepshead Bay to scrub floors. The lucky ones had their steady madams while the others wandered those neat blocks or waited on comers—each with her apron and working shoes in a bag under her arm until someone offered her a day's work. Sometimes the white children on their way to school laughed at their blackness and shouted 'nigger,' but the Barbadian women sucked their teeth, dismissing them."[10] Calling this process of precarious employment by its popular name, "slave markets," historian Harold Connolly details that "[w]hite housewives selected a likely prospect on the outward appearance of a strong body, sometimes even pinching a prospective victim to determine if muscle or fat was beneath her clothes."[11] Despite her low wages for domestic work, Silla serves as the breadwinner in the Boyce family.

Her husband, Deighton, has a tendency for lofty dreams and is prideful—yet his ambitions are routinely erased by employers' rejections of his applications. Because of numerous voices in the novel that are (to a certain extent justifiably) critical of Deighton's character, readers and scholars alike tend to subject his personality to harsh condemnation—and, in the process, neglect to scrutinize the larger context in which his failures happened. Thus, Connolly identifies the 1930s as a moment of "profound crisis in black male employment" caused by "[h]ostile employer attitudes, embodied in the acceptance of racial stereotypes and the outright refusal to hire blacks."[12] As a black man seeking labor, Deighton was barred from employment by most unions and denied entry to secure working-class jobs. It is prescient that Deighton only attains a job in a defense plant late in the war since, as historian Craig Wilder notes, "Black men remained a marginal force in the wartime economy" and "[w]hatever their gender, African-American laborers remained unskilled and they remained vulnerable."[13] Marshall dramatizes this vulnerability when Deighton gets injured and permanently disabled while working his defense job.

This is not to say that the novel is oblivious to the Jim Crow South. Rather, the text skillfully connects its treatment of racism from one geographical context to the other. Within a text that centers largely on Bajan-Americans, Miss Thompson, one of the tenants in Silla's brownstone, is representative of the tens of thousands of African Americans who migrated to Brooklyn during the Great Migration. Easily the most defining feature of Miss Thompson is, in Silla's words, "that life-sore 'pan she foot."[14] When the text first introduces her, readers witness how "[t]here was an ugly unhealed ulcer, yawning like a small crater on the instep of her foot, with a hard crust, pale center and slightly fetid odor. She sighed as she dressed it. This done, she leaned back and, for the first time in the twenty-four hours since she had been up, permitted herself to feel tired."[15] Miss Thompson's "life-sore" is connected to her economic precariousness and her exploitation as a laborer. Later in the novel, readers learn the origin of this wound. During a return visit down south, years ago, Thompson recalls, as punishment for perceived assertive behavior, a white, rural southerner "did take a piece clean outta my foot with that rusty shovel."[16] While this story of violence against African Americans visiting the American South from the North—published four years after the murder of Emmett Till—reiterates the narrative of the South as the primary site of American racism, the fact that Miss Thompson's wound does not close upon her return to Brooklyn and festers for decades challenges notions of northern liberalism as antidote to southern white supremacy.

In fact, during the pivotal scene in the novel, Selina experiences first-hand the virulent racism that lurks behind a distinctly northern liberal façade. Late in the novel, after excelling at a dance performance, she is taken to the Manhattan home of Margaret Benton, a white peer. Upon entry, Selina "hardly noticed the smiling woman [Margaret's mother] at the door, or how the smile stiffened as she entered"[17]— and later, how "the woman's mouth, eyes, the muscles under her pale powdered skin [shaped a] courteous, curious and appraising smile."[18] Still reveling in her successful dance performance, Selina merely senses that "[s]omething fretful, disturbed, lay behind [the woman's smile] and rove in a restless shadow over her face. She took Selina's hand between hers, patting it, and Selina could *feel* her whiteness—it was in the very texture of her skin."[19] The carefully arranged smile of the woman, whose position near the entrance door renders her as a figurative gatekeeper, represents the deceptive illusion of a white, northern liberalism—which is summarily unmasked in the subsequent scene.

Commencing with harmless small talk, Selina finds herself increasingly cornered by the woman, who enquires into Selina's residential and ethnic background, until, upon hearing that Selina's parents are from the West Indies, she declares, triumphantly, "Ah, I thought so. We once had a girl who did our cleaning who was from there."[20] Prior to this exchange, Selina had outperformed Mrs. Benton's daughter at dance— and thus temporarily upended the prevailing, white-supremacist racial hierarchy. Despite the woman's self-identification as a progressive ("I'm a real fighter when I get started!"),[21] this scene illustrates that racial liberalism cannot prosper in what is a racially segregated labor market. To Selina, the entire exchange feels "like an inquisition somehow, where she was the accused, imprisoned in the wing chair under the glaring lamp, the woman the inquisitor and Margaret the heavy, dull-faced guard at the door."[22]

Marshall brilliantly illustrates the rhetorical and affective violence that inscribes race onto Selina's body—which undermines the putatively liberal setting of this scene. "Those eyes," Selina agonizes, "were a well-lighted mirror in which, for the first time, [she] truly saw—with a sharp and shattering clarity—the full meaning of her black skin. And knowing was like dying—like being poised on the rim of time when the heart's simple rhythm is syncopated and then silenced and the blood chills and congeals, when a pall passes in a dark wind over the eyes." Unlike other race novels from the same era that feature liberals as white saviors (Harper Lee's Atticus Finch comes to mind), *Brown Girl* renders the interaction between white liberal and African American subject as a Hegelian life-and-death struggle. Selina senses that "this woman, the frightened girl at the door, those others dancing down the hall [...], all, everywhere, sought to rob her of her substance and her self."[23] Her racialization by New York's white liberal class is rendered in noticeably Hegelian terms. In his reflections on "lordship and bondage" (*Phenomenology of Spirit*), Hegel noted that the dominant entity, or "lord," achieves recognition of his being "an essential being" through "the sheer negation" of the other, which Hegel describes as a struggle to "[seek] the death of the other."[24] In other words, the lord renders the bondsperson as "the consciousness for which thinghood is the essential characteristic," as "an unessential, negatively characterized object."[25] Marshall's novel renders the underpinning of New York City's social landscape by a pernicious, structural white racism in terms of this master-slave dialectic. By rendering black New Yorkers as the servant-class foil to their own middle-class aspirations, liberal Manhattanites "sought to rob [Selina] of her substance and her self."

On her subway ride back to Brooklyn, Selina sees that "the shovel cutting [Miss Thompson's leg] like a scythe in the sunlight [. . .] was no different from the woman's voice falling brutally in the glare of the lamp."[26] Aligning Miss Thompson's physical wound inflicted by rural, southern white supremacists with her own psychological scarring by self-declared liberal Manhattanites, this passage challenges any illusion that white supremacy only blossoms south of the Mason-Dixon line. Expanding this analysis to include her neighborhood, Selina recognizes that she was "one with Miss Thompson, [. . .] [o]ne with the whores, the flashy men, and the blues rising sacredly above the plain of neon lights and ruined houses."[27] Here, Selina's analysis moves from individual to structural racism and a critical analysis of the "ghetto" that is growing around her—epitomized, here and elsewhere, by the centrality of Brooklyn's brownstones in the novel. Scholars are well-advised to follow the example of Selina's shift in critical outlook here.

Accentuate the *Brown Girl*, Blur the *Brownstones*

It is hard to ignore the emphasis that *Brown Girl, Brownstones'* social critique places on housing stock. Not only do Brooklyn's coveted brownstones feature prominently in the novel's title, where housing is inextricably linked to racialized identity, but the very cover of the novel's 1959 first edition by Random House features a nocturnal scene of a street corner, displaying several three-story row houses in typical Brooklyn fashion. Neighborhood residents are shown pursuing various errands (walking a dog, sweeping the sidewalk, or simply strolling), but their scale on the cover—vis-à-vis the brownstones—is too small for readers to come to any conclusions regarding these residents' individual identities. Clearly, the buildings are more central to the cover than the residents. Significantly, subsequent editions of the novel have diminished the importance of the title's *Brownstones* and foreground increasingly the role of the *Brown Girl*. A 1970 Avon paperback shows a young girl sitting on the stoop, while the 1981 and 2006 reissued paperbacks by the Feminist Press focus on a close-up painted portrait of a girl—with a blurred background. While both editions use the same cover image, the latter edition further obscures and smudges the image's backdrop. If these cover images are any indication of how publishers perceived Marshall's text, then the individual became more prominent, while the communal and political context faded, the further we move away from 1959. In creating this trajectory, publishers have been complicit in concealing the mechanisms of northern Jim Crow.

In keeping with this trend, scholarly essays have foregrounded questions of (black, female, immigrant) identity—and in turn pushed the underlying materialistic and political context to the back. Scholars thus focus on "the problems of black consciousness," "reconciling ethnicity and individualism," or "the construction of a black diaspora identity."[28] Frequently, critics have focused on the psychological, spiritual, or even metaphysical—noting, for instance, how Marshall "links problems such as identity, insecurity, and spiritual malaise to psychic fragmentation and moves toward acquiring wholeness through identification with African origins."[29] While each of these projects has merit, collectively, scholars of Marshall's work have downplayed *Brown Girl*'s concrete political context. Writing in the late 1980s, Darwin Turner even proposed that "Marshall tells the story of a Black family whose problems are not uniquely those of Black Americans."[30]

This is no coincidence. The Second World War marked a profound crisis for the legitimacy of white supremacy as the dominant ideology in the United States. (Importantly, *Brown Girl* presents racism as a global force by situating Marshall's portrayal of northern Jim Crow in the context of both Selina's parents' experiences in British-colonized Barbados and Selina's references to Anne Frank's diary.) As a result of this crisis, Jodi Melamed argues, white supremacy was replaced in postwar America by a series of official versions of antiracism—producing "a formally antiracist, liberal-capitalist modernity that revises, partners with, and exceeds the capacities of white supremacy without replacing or ending it." Within each of these antiracisms, literature and literary studies became "the most efficacious tool for Americans to describe, teach, learn about, and situate themselves with respect to racial difference and to know

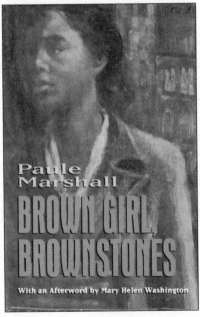
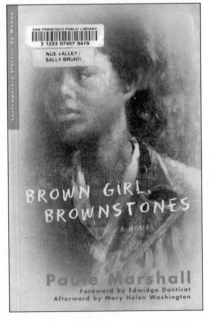

Figures 4.1a–4.1d. The covers of the 1959, 1970, 1981, and 2006 editions of *Brown Girl, Brownstones*.

the truth about the difference that racial difference makes (or does not make)." Racial liberalism, the first of these doctrines, dominated public discourse from the 1940s to the 1960s and conceived racism as personal, psychological prejudice—but left untouched the underlying material conditions that racialized capitalism both relied upon and intensified. In its emphasis on specific material realities, Marshall's novel goes decidedly against this ideology and the blueprint of many 1950s race novels. However, the fact that this is only rarely being acknowledged is due to a second, subsequent official racism, which Melamed labels "liberal multiculturalism." In the 1980s and 1990s, when scholarship about Paule Marshall flourished, this ideology promoted a "multicultural understanding of culture as aesthetics and identity—unmoored from materialism and the natural world." Multicultural literature becomes a vehicle for many privileged, middle-class, white students to learn about racial difference. Yet, while it "appeared progressive in contrast to neoconservative positions, it actually disabled effective antiracism, making it possible for people to satisfy their personal desire for racial equality while not knowing the institutional power and privilege they wielded in contemporary racial orders."[31] It is this officially sanctioned multicultural liberalism that informs many responses to *Brown Girl*.

To offset readings of *Brown Girl, Brownstones* that prioritize universalist themes and display moralist tendencies, the text—within both classrooms and scholarship—should be recontextualized within the concrete racial realities and segregationist policies of the 1930s and 1940s. The novel's opening pages alone hide, in plain sight, profound political commentary. "In the somnolent July afternoon," the novel begins, "the unbroken line of brownstone houses down the long Brooklyn street resembled an army massed at attention. They were all one uniform red-brown stone. All with high massive stone stoops and black iron-grille fences staving off the sun. All draped in ivy as though mourning."[32] Positioning Brooklyn's housing stock as more than just the backdrop to the plot that is about to unfold, this bleak and threatening image is at odds with many readers' own impressions of a street in Bedford-Stuyvesant in July—at least whenever I show my students a picture of such a street. Paradoxes and ambiguities like this permeate Marshall's text—and challenge readers to make sense of these perplexing and sometimes contradictory impressions. Without providing a ready-made explanation, the novel requires more exegetical effort than examples of 1950s protest novels that are less cryptic and more explicit than *Brown Girl*. Decoding puzzling moments—such as the mysteriously hostile atmosphere that is captured within the novel's opening—illustrates the potential this text carries to help readers understand the systemic complexity and long-term consequences of Jim Crown structures in the (mythologically liberal) urban Northeast.

Brownstones and Redlines

The novel's second page offers more concrete context for the eerie atmosphere that pervades the novel's opening. "First, there had been the Dutch-English and Scotch-Irish who had built the houses," the unnamed narrator describes, adding that "[t]here had been tea in the afternoon then and skirts rustling across the parquet floors and mild voices. For a long time it had been only the whites."[33] However, the story continues, "[N]ow in 1939 the last of them were discreetly dying behind those shades or selling the houses and moving away. And as they left, the West Indians slowly edged their way in. Like a dark sea nudging its way onto a white beach and staining the sand, they came."[34] These statements—which students and scholars alike frequently summarize with the seemingly straightforward designation "white flight"—need some unpacking. Remarkably for an autobiographical novel written by a Barbadian-American novelist, West Indian immigration is described as an act of racial contamination: "[l]ike a dark sea nudging its way onto a white beach." Seemingly paradoxically, Marshall's novel here cleverly echoes popular xenophobic (and eugenicist) texts of the early twentieth century. White-supremacist writer Maddison Grant employed similar rhetorical images in *The Conquest of a Continent; or, The Expansion of Races in America* (1933), when he noted that "[i]n America the events of the last hundred years, especially the *vast tide* of immigration, have greatly impaired our purity of race and our unity of religion and even threatened our inheritance of English speech."[35] With the coming of the West Indians, Marshall's narrator comments, similarly focusing on linguistic change, "[T]here was no longer tea in the afternoon, and their odd speech clashed in the hushed rooms."[36] The text here illustrates—albeit in a very playful and subtle manner—the author's familiarity with anti-immigrant rhetoric and white-supremacist logic.

It takes this context to explain fully the above described hostility and defensiveness of the line of brownstones on Selina's street. In his revealingly titled *Rising Tide of Color: The Threat against White World-Supremacy* (1920), Grant's disciple Lothrop Stoddard outlined that the "inner dikes (the areas of white settlement) [. . .] should be defended to the last extremity no matter if the costs involved are greater than their mere economic value would warrant. They are the true bulwarks of the race, the patrimony of future generations who have a right to demand of us that they shall be born white in a white man's land."[37] Reflections of this early-twentieth-century nativism inform the novel's cryptic opening image of an "unbroken line of brownstone houses [. . .] resembl[ing] an army massed at attention." This seemingly impenetrable line of row houses, *Brown Girl* suggests, constitutes the (now breached) dikes against a rising tide of non-Anglo-Saxon immigration. It is this nativist segregationist machinery that Marshall captures, when her narrator later notes that "[u]nder the enveloping night the brownstones reared like a fortress wall guarding a city, and the lighted windows were like flares set into its side."[38] The virulent white-supremacist rhetoric of Grant and Stoddard was mirrored by actual efforts in Brooklyn. In the case of Bedford-Stuyvesant, aside from a brief flourishing of the Ku Klux Klan, neighborhood associations, such as the infamous Gates Avenue Association, attempted to create a bulwark against nonwhite newcomers, fearing, as their archives indicate, "the colored invasion."[39]

But personal bias was not the only driving force behind this opposition. In addition to cultural fears, Harold Connolly notes, "Only total exclusion of Negroes offered a satisfactory solution and stable realty values."[40] In this sense, the narrator's facile statement that in 1939 white Brooklynites were "selling the houses and moving away" demands contextualization. This brief reference conceals what the term "white flight" often hides, namely, the complex, government-sanctioned mechanisms that caused this radical demographical change. The backstory to this larger context (which is absent from all but a few scholarly essays on Marshall) is the defining role of the Home Owners' Loan Corporation (HOLC), established in 1933 as part of the New Deal, which divided Brooklyn into sixty-six communities and assigned each a grade—purportedly to assess their safety for real estate investment. Because the underlying rationale determining each block's security was racial composition, Craig Wilder explains, the resulting discriminatory lending practice (which is best known as "redlining") "drew middle-class white people to South Brooklyn and the suburbs and forced African Americans and Caribbeans into North Brooklyn, drawing a line of racial separation across the heart of the borough."[41]

Marshall places the Boyce family's brownstone on Chauncey Street near Fulton Park—a short distance from where she herself grew up at 501 Hancock Street. An "Area Description" from October 1937 cautioned that the neighborhood was exposed to detrimental influences, such as "[o]bsolescence and poor upkeep. Infiltration of Negroes." Likewise, a "Residential Security Map" that was being produced in cooporation with HOLC's Appraisal Department, situates both addresses within an area colored a deep red and labeled "Hazardous." Published on April 1, 1938, the map precedes the opening of the novel by little more than a year—and it effectively singles out the neighborhood that adolescent Selina finds herself in for divestment and decline.[42]

Whiteness and Black Antineighbors

Redlining and home ownership were crucial to the workings of Jim Crow in the purportedly liberal urban north, and *Brown Girl* recognizes the central role they played in the (re)articulation of "whiteness" and the creation of a perpetual urban underclass. The novel's second paragraph poses a significant riddle for its readers: "[Y]ou thought of those joined brownstones as one house reflected through a train of mirrors, with no walls between the houses but only vast rooms yawning endlessly one into the other," the narrator muses about Selina's block. "Yet, looking close," the narrative adds, "you saw that under the thick ivy each house had something distinctively its own. Some touch that was Gothic, Romanesque, baroque or Greek triumphed amid the Victorian clutter. [. . .] Yet they all shared the same brown monotony. All seemed doomed by the confusion in their design."[43]

Rendered simultaneously uniform and unique, this portrayal is informed by a profound ambiguity, a sense of incompatibility of contradictory ideas: The buildings, so crucial to the novel, are both distinctive and monotonous. What Marshall captures here (once again cryptically) is a pivotal moment in the history of race within the United States—in which housing played a crucial role. In the early twentieth century, European mass immigration had led to a fracturing of whiteness into a plurality of subgroups, which were the focus of scientific racism. Yet in the wake of the first wave of the Great Migration, Matthew Frye Jacobson argues, "[W]hiteness was reconsolidated: the late nineteenth century's probationary white groups were now remade and granted the scientific stamp of authenticity as the unitary Caucasian race—an earlier era's Celts, Slavs, Hebrews, Iberies, and Saracens, among others, had become the Caucasians so familiar to our own visual economy and racial lexicon."[44] Now, "[T]he regime of Anglo-Saxon or Nordic supremacy," Jacobson asserts, gave way to "a pattern of Caucasian unity" and "the ascent of monolithic whiteness."[45] Paule Marshall captures this very process, albeit by expressing it in architectural terms, connecting racial identity to urban policies—and, more explicitly, to Brooklyn's brownstones. Real estate was central to the dynamic of, as Ta-Nehisi Coates phrases it, "washing the disparate tribes white."[46] *Brown Girl* recognizes that the creation of a new, monolithic whiteness out of disparate subgroups was intricately connected to the transformation of urban space she observed during her childhood in Brooklyn. Further, having witnessed, by 1959, the rise of ethnically homogeneous suburbs and volatile urban ghettos, Marshall also acknowledges, at the end of the above quoted paragraph, that this American apartheid is "doomed in [its] design."

Decades ahead of such scholarly assessments, *Brown Girl* is clearly cognizant of and dedicated to engaging these racial dynamics, as is made clear in the introduction of its main protagonist. Introducing Selina, the narrator notes that "[h]er house was alive to [her]" as she "listen[ed] to its shallow breathing"—thus creating an intricate bond between "brown girl" and "brownstone." Adding to this that Selina's eyes "were not the eyes of a child" and that they "were weighted, it seemed, with scenes of a long life,"[47] the narrator employs a sense of the supernatural to offer a broader, longer, and more systemic social critique—thus cleverly extending the otherwise limited perspective of the young focalizer. This central theme of the text refutes attempts—as presented in the analysis of the novel's covers above—to remove the individual from the larger context. In fact, pushing the boundaries between the self and broader historical forces, the novel then stages a ghostly encounter between Selina and the brownstone's former inhabitants. We thus see Selina rise, "her arms lifted in welcome, and quickly the white family who had lived here before [. . .] glided with pale footfalls up the stairs. Their white hands trailed the banister; their mild voices implored her to give them a little life. And as they crowded around, fusing with her, she was no longer a dark girl alone and dreaming at the top of an old house, but one of them, invested with their beauty and gentility."[48] Selina's imaginative identification clearly reflects associations between home ownership, whiteness, and gaining acceptance through citizenship, respectability, and middle-class status.

Yet this illusion is temporary. Structurally, the building, despite now being inhabited by mostly black residents, still reflects the politics of whiteness. "It was," as the narrator points out in oxymoronic terms, "the museum of all the lives that had ever lived here. The floor-to-ceiling mirror retained their faces as the silence did their voices."[49] It is in this very mirror that Selina comes face to face with the structural permanence of whiteness—and with her own role in this racial rehearsal. "The mood was broken," she comments as she sees her reflection. "The illusory figures fled and she was only herself again. A truculent face and eyes too large and old, a flat body perched on legs that were too long. A torn middy blouse, dirty shorts, and socks that always worked down into the heel of her sneakers. That was all she was."[50] Deepening this commentary on the incommensurability of white power structure and aspirational black body, the narrative voice adds, "She did not belong here. She was something vulgar in a holy place. The room was theirs, she knew, glancing up at the frieze of cherubs and angels on the ceiling; it belonged to the ghost shapes hovering in the shadows. But not to her."[51]

Marshall's depiction of Selina's self-perception as "a vulgar item in a holy place" echoes the preface of *The Souls of Black Folk* (1903), which opens with W. E. B. Du Bois's declaration that "[b]etween me and the other world there is ever an unasked question: [. . .] How does it feel to be a problem?"[52] In terms that reverberate in Marshall's prose, Du Bois held that "[i]t is a peculiar sensation, this double consciousness, this sense of always looking at one's self through the eyes of others, of measuring one's soul by the tape of a world that looks on in amused contempt."[53] Rather than merely containing a clear reference to Du Bois's seminal text, however, Marshall clearly connects Selina's alienation—her existence as "brown girl" in a white world—to the actual building she inhabits. Even though white flight is in full force and black Brooklynites move into brownstone buildings, *Brown Girl* reveals the sway that white power structures still have over the new inhabitants. "Why did God," Du Bois asked, "make me an outcast and a stranger in mine own house?"[54] Selina's experience here poses a similar question, but Marshall frames the encounter not as an interlocution of a deity, but of the relationship between her main protagonist and the actual housing stock she finds herself in. Central to the New Deal's white-washing of new European immigrants was the permanent exclusion of nonwhite citizens and immigrants alike from what David Roediger has called "the wages of whiteness." Central to this was the private home, which, as he notes, "increasingly defined as a 'white' house, became a key site for the making of race," casting African Americans as "antineighbors."[55]

Selina therefore is "a stranger in [her] own house," or, as Marshall phrases it, "a vulgar item in a holy place," because her presence (as an "antineighbor") has been rendered dangerous by the language of HOLC maps. Having determined neighborhood value in terms of racial occupancy, the Federal Housing Administration (FHA) also encouraged collective racial vigilance and policing of neighborhood boundaries among whites. Selina's rejection of her own reflection in the context of her imaginative, ghostly encounter with the brownstone's former owners here clearly demonstrates that she has internalized an understanding of the way her own nonwhite body ("the vulgar object") threatens the whitening powers of racially exclusive urban space ("the holy place"). She recognizes that her racialized body (the "brown girl") has the ability to alter the racial designation of the space (the hitherto white houses) she inhabits. Various scholars have noted that neighborhood borders were routinely defined racially, not geographically. Bedford-Stuyvesant, one study deduced, is "wherever Negroes happen to live."[56] The neighborhood's contours were fluid and expanded with black in-migration. While Selina playfully and temporarily escapes the realities of race in her daydream, her racialized body ("the vulgar item") holds—not because of pathology, as Pete Hamill suggested, but, to use Ta-Nehisi Coates's terms, as "the correct and intended result of policy"[57]—the power to turn the brownstone (the erstwhile "holy place") into what Connolly identifies as a growing "black ghetto."

A Ghetto Grows in Paule Marshall's Brooklyn

"[G]iven hindsight," Connolly noted in *A Ghetto Grows in Brooklyn* (1977), "one can see in skeletal form by 1930 the outline of the future Brooklyn ghetto."[58] Various references throughout *Brown Girl* chronicle this downward spiral—beginning with subtle references to redlining. "Every decent white person's moving away, getting out," argues the daughter of the bedridden, sole remaining white tenant, in 1939. Citing a newspaper advertisement, she notes that "they're building inexpensive houses on Long Island" and that "[i]t says anybody can afford one. I could get a loan."[59] As this quotation makes clear, "everybody" here means "white." The novel's black protagonists' comprehension of the housing market is noticeably different. "[Y]ou got to start buying," Deighton's friend Seifert Yearwood implores. "Go to the loan shark if you ain got the money."[60] Similarly, when Silla and her friends discuss strategies for "buying house," Florrie Trotman lists the predatory, disadvantageous, or outright desperate venues that are open to black Brooklynites: "They doing it some of every kind of way. Some working morning, noon and night for this big war money. Some going to the loan shark out there on Fulton Street. Some hitting the number for good money. Some working strong-strong obeah. Some even picking fares."[61]

Later in the novel, Deighton responds to Silla's insistence on buying a brownstone by suggesting that "[t]here's plenty of loan sharks out there on Fulton Street waiting for you house-hungry Bajans" who are "only too glad to make you a loan at 6 percent and keep yuh in debt the rest of your life."[62] Yet, despite this abundant fiscal context, scholars rarely interpret Silla's fateful decision to sell Deighton's land in Barbados (a decision that sets in motion a series of events that ultimately lead to his deportation and death) in light of this financial quarantine. On the contrary, by reading this act as an expression of Silla's "ruthless determination," of the "materialistic ambitions which the fast-moving, competitive, at best amoral 'New World' proliferates and spurs," of an ill-fated "belief in this mythic American Dream," of a "portrait of the negativity of materialism," or of her "integration into white bourgeois capitalism,"[63] scholars routinely ignore the lack of viable alternatives to escape poverty or downplay the socioeconomic stakes of the 1930s housing market.[64]

None of these scholars crunch the numbers. Without access to subsidized government mortgages, the nine hundred dollars from the sale of Deighton's land would have offered a major economic life-line for the family. According to the classifieds in the *Brooklyn Daily Eagle*, the going rate for three-story brownstone buildings on Hancock Street (where Marshall grew up) was $6,500 in 1939—for buildings that, according to the ads, had been assessed at twice that price, indicating the downward spiral the neighborhood was slated to take. That price plummeted to around $5,000 in 1940, $4,500 in 1941, and as low as $3,250 (asking for $750 dollars down payment) in 1942. To properly assess these figures, one has to take into account the family's income: At the opening of the novel, Silla and her friends reflect on how, while cleaning houses in South Brooklyn, "Their only thought was of the 'few raw-mout' pennies' at the end of the day which would eventually 'buy house.'"[65] Specifying what these "few raw-mout' pennies" amount to, Harold Connolly details that "[w]ages for scrubbing, washing, ironing, dusting, ranged from twenty to thirty-five cents per hour, although most offers rarely exceeded a quarter. A full day's work would thus net a worker two dollars on the average." That said, many employers "preferred to limit such employment to fewer than eight hours, and it was not unusual for a 'slave' to work two hours for a total wage of forty cents."[66]

While Silla does temporarily gain more lucrative employment in a defense plant, this opportunity is fleeting. The narrative only hints at the fact that by the first postwar winter, Silla "studied a course in practical nursing, since she worked in a hospital now that the war plant had closed."[67] As usual, Marshall's factual line hides a larger development: As Wilder notes, while "[b]lack women [initially] seized the opportunity in defense industries to sustain their families and communities, [. . .] they had virtually no opportunity to jump from defense work to organized labor" since "as white veterans returned to their jobs, nonwhite industrial workers were laid off."[68] Classified ads in the postwar volumes of the *Eagle* advertised jobs as "hospital workers," which includes "tray girls," "nurses' aides," and "laundry helpers"—indicating that Silla has rejoined a precarious and underpaid workforce. To increase her income, she wonders how to "make upstairs into smaller rooms and charge little more"[69] and eventually evicts her erstwhile tenants to raise the rent. Frequently read as excessive materialism, Silla's approach is to be reconsidered given the financial quarantine to which central Brooklyn was subjected. Having bought up housing stock under advantageous conditions provided by white flight, according to Connolly, predatory realtors "resold the brownstone [. . .] homes to black newcomers for large profits. To afford the high interest rates and exorbitant mortgages, black homeowners cannibalized properties to accommodate multiple rental units."[70] Any criticism of Silla's alleged "integration into white bourgeois capitalism" needs to be situated within this specific low-wage economy, government-sanctioned ghettoization, and actual material and fiscal conditions. Prices for brownstones stabilized towards the end of the war, and by 1947 the going rate for a building on Chauncey Street, where Silla leases her brownstone, had risen to $10,000 even though by then the neighborhood was in steep decline in terms of its infrastructure. The opportunity that nine hundred dollars presents to Silla in 1945 is as precious as it is fleeting.

Remarkably, even those studies that directly engage the novel's "brownstones" show significant blind spots. Kimberley Benston's frequently cited essay "Architectural Imagery and Unity in Paule Marshall's *Brown Girl, Brownstones*" rightly identifies the "binding power of architectural imagery,"[71] but falls short because it treats architecture as mere metaphor—devoid of actual context of federal housing policy. Benston condemns "Silla's continued monomania of 'getting house'" and notes that "[w]hile the brownstones themselves are 'indifferent,' their occupants turn them into forces of life and death, symbols of aspiration and success."[72] Benston misses an important point, since it is not the occupants, but American racial politics that have turned home ownership into "forces of life and death, symbols of aspiration and success." Marshall's own criticism of materialism must not overshadow her larger critique of systemic racism in urban policy. Benston, after all, wrote in 1975, when decades of systemic divestment had turned Bedford-Stuyvesant into "Bed-Stuy, Do or Die," trapping its inhabitants in a world of exorbitant rent, decaying infrastructure, underfunded schools, and resulting crime. Commenting on Silla's ultimate ambition to purchase property on Long Island, Benston remarked that "the quality of life will be the same, the vision of 'buying house' having lost its grandeur while retaining its underlying misdirection."[73]

This statement is, of course, blatantly untrue. While central Brooklyn had been targeted for ghettoization, parts of Long Island—planned communities that pioneered modern (white) suburbia—were destined for prosperity, middle-class comfort, and growing equity. The trajectories of Bedford-Stuyvesant, on the one hand, and Levittown, on the other, illustrate the fallacious nature of this statement. Certainly by 1975, when Benston wrote, Bedford-Stuyvesant and the suburbs of Long Island did not provide the same quality of life. Further, Benston fails to acknowledge the policies that triggered this urban decline when he equates the "'ravaged, ruined' brownstones" at the end of *Brown Girl* with "the bankruptcy of the values which [Selina's] parents suffered because of their empty value structure."[74] Benston's interpretation, connecting urban decline with the community's moral bankruptcy, is complicit with one of the persistent myths of ghettoization in the United States, namely, according to historian Craig Wilder, "this idea that black people, Puerto Ricans, and non-white folk generally moved into neighborhoods and destroyed them." Neighborhoods like Bedford-Stuyvesant, Wilder offers as a corrective, "had actually been targeted for destruction before the victims of that destruction ever arrived."[75] Benston's reading of black residents as self-destructive disregards these structural forces. In his misappraisal of neighborhood decline, Benston is not alone. The neighborhood's dramatic decline, in terms of its housing stock *and* living conditions for its residents, is frequently neglected. Clearly, when the novel opens, in 1939, the brownstones "owned or leased by the West Indians look[ed] almost new with their neat yards, new shades and fresh painted black iron fences."[76] Yet, towards the end of the war, Selina is depicted walking "past the despoiled brownstones that had been converted into rooming houses, glancing at the roomers who stared like prisoners from the windows of their cubicles while their children chalked their names on the stoops."[77] Selina's final glance at her community reflects the collective social tragedy of this redlined neighborhood: "Faces hung like portraits in her mind as she walked down Fulton Street," the narration describes. "Suggie and her violated body, Miss Mary living posthumously amid her soiled sheets, Miss Thompson bearing the life-sore and enduring, Clive and his benign despair, her father beguiled by dreams even as he drowned in them, the mother hacking a way through life like a man lost in the bush."[78]

Marshall's mapping of decline on buildings, bodies, and social relations alike continues until the final scene of the novel, presumably taking place in fall of 1947, when Selina reminisces that the once respectable Fulton Park has become "a ruined park which belonged to the winos who sat red-eyed and bickering all day, to the dope addicts huddled in their safe worlds and to the young bops clashing under the trees and warming the cold ground with their blood." Studying "the ravaged brownstones," Selina notes that unlike a decade before, when the streets were quiet at night, "Now, the roomers' tangled lives spilled out the open windows,"[79] indicating the increasingly crowded conditions in this part of Brooklyn. Testifying to the decline of Bedford-Stuyvesant and to its new function as a warehouse of poor people of color, Marshall wrote in *Reina* (1962) that the places that were central to her childhood "no longer matter that much since most of them have vanished. [. . .] Our house even, a brownstone relic whose halls smelled comfortingly of dust and lemon oil, the somnolent street upon which it stood, the tall, muscular trees which shaded it were leveled years ago to make way for a city housing project—a stark, graceless warren for the poor."[80]

Yet the novel's ending is as invested in central Brooklyn's imminent future as it is in its recent past. Offering a glance at the politics of urban renewal, the book closes with the image of "a vast waste—an area where blocks of brownstones had been blasted to make way for a city project [where] [a] solitary wall stood perversely amid the rubble, a stoop still imposed its massive grandeur, a carved oak staircase led only to the night sky."[81] These ruins contrast tellingly with the book's opening description of an "unbroken line of brown stone houses [. . .] with high massive stone stoops and black iron-grille fences staving off the sun," giving off "the impression of formidable height."[82] Looking beyond the ruins of a city block at newly erected public housing projects, Selina gets a cursory look at a dystopian urbanity. "[T]hose monolithic shapes," she observes, "seemed to draw near, the lighted windows spangling the sky like a new constellation. She imagined she heard footsteps ringing hollow in the concrete halls, the garbled symphony of radios and televisions, children crying in close rooms: life moving in an oppressive round within those uniformly painted walls."[83] Almost a half-century later, writing in the aftermath of Hurricane Katrina, Henry Giroux observed the emergence of a new form of biopolitics "in which entire populations are now considered disposable, an unnecessary burden on state coffers, and consigned to fend for themselves."[84] *Brown Girl* illustrates that this form of American biopower has deeper roots.

Reading the ruined city block as a symbol of a social tragedy, Selina "turn[s] away, unable to look any longer. For it was like seeing the bodies of all the people she had ever known broken, all the familiar voices that had ever sounded in those high-ceilinged rooms shattered—and the pieces piled into this giant cairn of stone and silence."[85] As a final act in the novel's last paragraph, Selina tosses one of her two silver bangles across her shoulder, producing "[a] frail sound in that utter silence."[86] Read—as Selina's character so often is—as divorced from the specific urban realities of a Jim Crow North, this act has been interpreted as "emblematic of her final ambivalence and self-division" or as reflecting "a kind of hybrid ethnicity."[87] However, when read within the context of northern urban segregation and decline, the book's final words—"[a] frail sound in that utter silence"—is also to be read as a reflection of the novelist's intention to produce a sound in the silence surrounding this planned destruction of a neighborhood. "In an historical sense, blacks in Brooklyn have long suffered from a triple disability [. . .] which taken in conjunction rendered its victims almost invisible," Harold Connolly holds. "What," he asks, "can the history of Brooklyn teach us about the process of ghettoization? What, if anything, could have prevented the creation of some of these demographic and socioeconomic tragedies that litter America's urban landscape?"[88] Paule Marshall's novel offers some compelling answers to this question. Rather than being solely preoccupied with questions of self and identity, as her work is often understood to be, Marshall's continued chronicling of the rise and fall of Bedford-Stuyvesant (from the opening page of *Brown Girl* to today) serves as an important contrapuntal voice to the nostalgic canon of literary Brooklyn.[89]

NOTES
1 Pete Hamill, "Brooklyn: The Sane Alternative," *New York Magazine*, July 14, 1969.
2 Brian Purnell, *Fighting Jim Crow in the County of Kings: The Congress of Racial Equality in Brooklyn* (Lexington: University Press of Kentucky, 2013), 26.
3 The past thirty years have seen a proliferation of anthologies endeavoring to represent twentieth-century Brooklyn. All too frequently, within these volumes, black Brooklynites are either invisible—or even vilified. Popular works such as *When Brooklyn Was the World, 1920–1957* (1986), *The Brooklyn Reader: Thirty Writers Celebrate America's Favorite Borough* (1994), *Brooklyn: A State of Mind* (2001), *Song of Brooklyn: An Oral History of America's Favorite Borough* (2008),

Brooklyn Was Mine (2008), *In the Country of Brooklyn: Inspiration to the World* (2008), and *Literary Brooklyn: The Writers of Brooklyn and the Story of American City Life* (2011) reveal a noticeable imbalance towards Irish, Italian, and Jewish experiences and a resulting nostalgic yearning for a (white) working-class past of the borough in the first half of the twentieth century.

4 "Blacks Still Face a Red Line on Housing." Editorial, *New York Times*, April 14, 2018.

5 Paule Marshall, "Rising Islanders of Bed-Stuy," *New York Times*, November 3, 1985.

6 A. M. Wald, *American Night: The Literary Left in the Era of the Cold War* (Chapel Hill: University of North Carolina Press, 2012), 198.

7 Darwin Turner, "Introduction," in Paule Marshall, *Soul Clap Hands and Sing* (Washington, DC: Howard University Press, 1988 [1961]), xvi.

8 Joyce Pettis, *Toward Wholeness in Paule Marshall's Fiction* (Charlottesville: University of Virginia Press, 1995), 9.

9 Craig Wilder, *A Covenant with Color: Race and Social Power in Brooklyn* (New York: Columbia University Press, 2000), 137.

10 Paule Marshall, *Brown Girl, Brownstones* (New York: Feminist Press of the City University of New York, 1981 [1959]), 11.

11 Harold X. Connolly, *A Ghetto Grows in Brooklyn* (New York: NYU Press, 1977), 116.

12 *Ibid.*, 115.

13 Wilder, 169 and 171.

14 Paule Marshall, *Brown Girl, Brownstones* (New York: Feminist Press at the City University of New York, 1981), 27.

15 *Ibid.*, 28.

16 *Ibid.*, 216.

17 *Ibid.*, 283.

18 *Ibid.*, 285.

19 *Ibid.*

20 *Ibid.*, 287.

21 *Ibid.*, 288.

22 *Ibid.*, 287.

23 *Ibid.*, 289.

24 Georg Wilhelm Friedrich Hegel, *Phenomenology of Spirit*, trans. A. V. Miller (Oxford: Oxford University Press, 1927 [1807]), 111, 116, and 113.

25 *Ibid.*, 115 and 113.

26 Marshall, *Brown Girl, Brownstones*, 292.

27 *Ibid.*, 292.

28 Gavin Jones, "'The Sea Ain' Got No Back Door': The Problems of Black Consciousness in Paule Marshall's *Brown Girl, Brownstones*," *African American Review* 32.4 (1998): 597–606. Martin Japtok, "Paule Marshall's *Brown Girl, Brownstones*: Reconciling Ethnicity and Individualism," *African American Review* 32.2 (1998): 305–15.

29 Joyce Pettis, *Toward Wholeness in Paule Marshall's Fiction* (Charlottesville: University of Virginia Press, 1995), 11.

30 Turner, xii.
31 Jodi Melamed, *Represent and Destroy: Rationalizing Violence in the New Racial Capitalism* (Minneapolis: University of Minnesota Press, 2011), 6–7, 2, xxii, 92.
32 Marshall, *Brown Girl, Brownstones*, 3.
33 *Ibid.,* 4.
34 *Ibid.*
35 Madison Grant, *The Conquest of a Continent; or, The Expansion of Races in America* (New York: Scribner, 1933), 5. Emphasis mine.
36 Marshall, *Brown Girl, Brownstones*, 4.
37 Lothrop Stoddard, *The Rising Tide of Color against White World-Supremacy* (New York: Scribner's, 1921 [1920]), 226.
38 Marshall, *Brown Girl, Brownstones*, 34.
39 Qtd. in Connolly, 8.
40 Connolly, 60.
41 Wilder, 193–94.
42 For the HOLC "Security Map" and "Area Description" see *Mapping Inequality*, https://dsl.richmond.edu.
43 Marshall, *Brown Girl, Brownstones*, 3.
44 Matthew Frye Jacobson, *Whiteness of a Different Color: European Immigrants and the Alchemy of Race* (Cambridge, MA: Harvard University Press, 1998), 8.
45 *Ibid.,* 91–93.
46 Ta-Nehisi Coates, *Between the World and Me* (New York: Spiegel & Grau, 2015), 8.
47 Marshall, *Brown Girl, Brownstones*, 4.
48 *Ibid.,* 5.
49 *Ibid.*
50 *Ibid.,* 5–6.
51 *Ibid.,* 6.
52 W. E. B. Du Bois, *The Souls of Black Folk* (Chicago: A.C. McClurg, 1903), 1.
53 *Ibid.,* 3.
54 *Ibid.*
55 David Roediger, *Working towards Whiteness: How America's Immigrants Became White* (New York: Basic, 2005), 8–9.
56 Qtd. in Michael Woodsworth, *Battle for Bed-Stuy: The Long War on Poverty in New York City* (Cambridge, MA: Harvard University Press, 2016), 47.
57 Coates, 17.
58 Connolly, 55.
59 Marshall, *Brown Girl, Brownstones*, 36.
60 *Ibid.,* 39.
61 *Ibid.,* 74.
62 *Ibid.,* 131.
63 Japtok, 310; Kimberley Benston, "Architectural Imagery and Unity in Paule Marshall's *Brown Girl, Brownstones*," *Negro American Literature Forum* 9.3 (Autumn 1975): 68; Kathlene McDonald, "Paule Marshall's Critique of Capitalism and Cold

War Ideology: *Brown Girl, Brownstones* as a Resistant Working-Class Text," *Black Scholar* 30.2 (Summer 2000): 26–33, 26; Joyce Pettis, "Qualities of Endurance: Paule Marshall's *Brown Girl, Brownstones*," *Black Scholar* 30.2 (Summer 2000): 15–20, 18; Susan Willis, *Specifying: Black Women Writing the American Experience* (Madison: University of Wisconsin Press, 1987), 75.

64 Some scholars have recognized, in general terms, the centrality of home owner-ship: Vanessa Dickerson observes that the text provides an exploration "of the relations of a Black woman to real estate." See, Vanessa Dickerson, "The Property of Being in Paule Marshall's *Brown Girl, Brownstones*," *Obsidian II* 6.3 (Winter 1991): 1–13, quotation on 2. Gavin Jones argues that the houses "offer the only means of escape from financial exploitation for the Barbadian immigrants" (600); Barbara Christian has noted that owning a brownstone constitutes "a bulwark against poverty, racism, failure." See, Barbara Christian, *Black Feminist Criticism: Perspectives on Black Women Writers* (New York: Teacher's College Press, 1985), 82. Martin Japtok reads efforts to buy homes "as a wish to protect and shelter the younger generation against an essentially hostile white world" (311); Francis Donette notes that the novel "identifies homeownership as one strategy Barba-dian immigrants deploy to mediate the racial hostility of America." See, Donette Francis, "Paule Marshall: New Accents on Immigrant America," *Black Scholar* 30.2 (Summer 2000): 21–25, quotation on 21; and George Lipsitz reads *Brown Girl* as representative of "the decapitalization of Black communities that simultaneously subsidized asset accumulation for whites." See, George Lipsitz, *How Racism Takes Place* (Philadelphia: Temple University Press, 2011), 189. Yet apart from Lipsitz, commentators have been vague about the specific historical context within which these developments took place.

65 Marshall, *Brown Girl, Brownstones*, 11.

66 Connolly, 116.

67 Marshall, *Brown Girl, Brownstones*, 200.

68 *Ibid.*, 174.

69 *Ibid.*, 201.

70 Connolly, 11.

71 Benston, 68.

72 *Ibid.*, 68 and 69.

73 *Ibid.*, 70.

74 *Ibid.*

75 Qtd. in Kelly Anderson (dir.), *My Brooklyn*, 2012.

76 Marshall, *Brown Girl, Brownstones*, 53.

77 *Ibid.*, 178.

78 *Ibid.*, 307.

79 *Ibid.*, 309.

80 Paule Marshall, *Reena and Other Stories* (New York: Feminist Press, 1983), 72.

81 Marshall, *Brown Girl, Brownstones*, 309.

82 *Ibid.*, 3.

83 *Ibid.*, 310.
84 *Ibid.*, 186 and 174.
85 Marshall, *Brown Girl, Brownstones*, 310.
86 *Ibid.*
87 Jones, 604; Japtok, 312.
88 Connolly, xi and xiii.
89 Thank you to Brian Purnell, Salimah Hankins, and Shaina Hammerman for the many careful edits and thoughtful responses to earlier drafts of this essay.

5

"Let Those Negroes Have Their Whiskey"

White Backtalk and Jim Crow Discourse in the Era of Black Rebellion

LAURA WARREN HILL

On the whole . . . these migrants are not lazy, shiftless and desperate as some predicted that they would be. They generally attend church, save their money and send a part of their savings regularly to their families. They do not belong to the class going North in quest of whiskey.
—Carter G. Woodson, 1918

Let those negroes have their whiskey.
—J. S. Johnston of Tallahassee, Florida, 1964

On July 27, 1964, Olive LeBoo, a long-time resident of Rochester, New York's third ward, wrote to the city's mayor, Frank Lamb, "as a citizen and a Rochesterian, in the hope that [Lamb] as an official will stand firm and not jelly out on the Negro problem."[1] Her letter, and many others like it from white citizens across the nation, came just days after Rochester's uprising—an outpouring of social unrest that resulted from longstanding social tensions in the city's two predominantly Black wards. Overpatrolled and underemployed, Black Rochester exploded when police with dogs arrested a Black man at a community dance. The uprising became an expression of discontent directed at three related social issues: police brutality, employment discrimination, and educational inequality. Yet, from LeBoo's perspective "the Negro problem" resulted from the migration of "transient undesirable Negros,"[2] and the appropriate solution was law and order. Many Americans, in and out of Rochester, would come to share LeBoo's views.

In 1964, LeBoo was fifty-four years old. She had owned her home on Fitzhugh Street in the third ward—an area hit particularly hard by the uprising—for at least ten years, an accomplishment in which she took great pride. Having noted that her family "was poor by financial standards" but learned "to make the best of a home that was available, cleaning a little paint hear [sic] and there,"[3] LeBoo understood home ownership as a contribution to society and a political responsibility. Some forty years prior, when LeBoo was in her late teens, her father—a millwright, also born in Rochester and named after the politician and newspaperman Horace Greeley, died, leaving her mother and older brother to fend for themselves. When her brother married and moved out, LeBoo and her mother continued moving between apartments. By the time she purchased her home, she had settled as an office clerk for a local company. From her perch on Fitzhugh Street, she read the newspaper daily and kept abreast of city policy and practice. Much about Rochester's black population troubled her.

In the year preceding the revolt, LeBoo began to communicate her demographic concerns to her councilwoman, Constance Mitchell—the first elected Black official in Rochester. She also wrote regularly to the local and national NAACP, where she struck a conciliatory tone, noting that there existed in her neighborhood some "good respectable negro families" whom she "found it necessary in many instances" to defend.[4] She acknowledged that rent in her neighborhood was too high, but legitimated the practice as it affected the races equally, and simply insured property owners against the damage done by the "plague of locusts" moving in.[5] In her own telling, then, LeBoo was not anti-Black, but rather hoped to stop the flood of "transient riff raff . . . that are unspeakably filthy, use the streets for toilets, loud, have some sort of music or radio in the window and playing to be heard 4 blocks away," were "unmarried," lived in "pig styes [sic]," and did not know "what a broom or soap was for."[6] She was a veritable expression of Jim Crow whiteness in the North, convinced that she was entitled to consideration and respect as a constituent.

LeBoo's correspondents included Rochester's police chief, and several city officials. She demanded accountability on urban renewal projects and took aim at the creation of the Police Review Board, formed in 1963 after several highly publicized instances of police brutality, including one investigated by the Justice Department. And, as expected, she received responses regularly. Ms. Mitchell met with her in her home to discuss her concerns; and, city officials responded to her inquiry satisfactorily regarding urban development plans. When she complained to Chief Lombard about the review board, "an insult to our Police Department," he directed her to contact the Fraternal Order of Police, headquartered in Philadelphia, rather than defend the organization. When writing the Fraternal Order of Police, LeBoo evinced none of the conciliation she reserved for the NAACP, noting that "all the very undesirable elements" are "95% negros [sic] and believe [her] some are pretty bad."[7] Regardless of how forthcoming she was about her view of African Americans, LeBoo expected that as a white citizen and home owner, her communications to her city officials mattered. By all accounts, they did. As the 1964 uprising suggests, this was an entitlement reserved for white constituents, however. Black residents were afforded no such consideration for their growing concerns.

Whether she was aware or not, LeBoo had entered a national conversation—a Jim Crow discourse—taking place around migration, labor, race, and rights throughout the twentieth century. Rochester would become prominent in this national conversation when in the postwar era southern Black migrants first moved to the city in significant numbers. As indicated by LeBoo's correspondence, their arrival in that northern outpost, the 1964 uprising, and the subsequent white response make visible a form of white backtalk, which expressed fears about the changing world and the explosive dangers of race and racial construction, locally and globally. While the historian Carol Anderson notes the structural and political policy making inherent in white rage, white backtalk happens in homes, among friends, in local newspaper editorials, signaling to officials and courts that white rage will be supported.[8]

LeBoo was not alone. Accompanying her letter to Mayor Lamb was another that began with the familiar, "Dear Frank," and then explained, "We will make a deal with you Rochester people but on our terms. We will take back into Dixie all 35,000 of your negroes for $150,000 each and in cash—no checks,"[9] wrote J. S. Johnston of Tallahassee, Florida. With its crass tone, Johnston's letter contrasts with the often polite segregationism evident in the North. Yet, in the face of such commentary, a reporter for a Rochester newspaper summarized, "[W]e are beginning to realize that discrimination, Northern style, can be even meaner in some ways than anything designed by the most unreconstructed Southerner," meaner, it seems, because it was so insidious.[10]

Some forty-five years prior to these Rochester events, scholar Carter G. Woodson had defended southern migrants against this Jim Crow discourse, as both moved north. LeBoo and Johnston illustrate this attack on the migrants' work ethic and morals, attributing their struggles to Black pathology, rather than structural racism. Woodson rejected this position, lauding the migrants' collective desire to save money, attend church, and support their families. The vast majority of these sojourners, he rejoined, had not traveled north "in quest of whiskey."[11] Nevertheless, these letters to Lamb some four decades after Woodson wrote reveal how rooted this trope had become. Johnston rebuked the mayor for banning the sale of liquor during the 1964 Rochester rising. Given that Blacks would not act properly if sober, as the Jim Crow discourse went, Johnston implored the mayor, "Let those negroes have their whiskey."[12]

LeBoo and Johnston were just two of many who targeted officials with such Jim Crow discourse following the rebellion. One hundred and four such letters have survived in a municipal archive—letters penned by ordinary white people, from progressive liberals to fiscal conservatives who describe themselves variously as moms, NAACP supporters, taxpayers, and citizens, and who fervently believed in American democracy and justice. Collectively, they circulated ideas and tropes about Black life, evincing their authoritative right as white people to the body politic, and ultimately mainstreaming this discursive backlash. Like LeBoo, they believed in their ability to influence events, and indeed official speeches and policies enacted subsequently seem to suggest their impact. While a more outlandish letter such as Johnston's could be dismissed as histrionics, the majority reflect the earnest engagement of citizens insisting on their entitlement to the political system as well as their anxiety at the disruption of their racial realities. Having stayed abreast of current events, they felt not just empowered but entitled to inform and advise their elected leaders. Thus, the white backtalk generated in these letters both mirrored and informed reporting, local and national. And while Rochester officials claimed fear of "a 'white backlash' of resentment against Negroes," as one told *U.S. News and World Report*, "'We have to find a way to avert the backlash; we have received phone calls at

City Hall that would make your hair stand on end,'"[13] such sentiments were widespread locally in newspaper editorials, in official documents from business associations, in speeches by city officials, and even in the analysis of psychologists.

Here, the Rochester archive suggests that far from inventing it, the law-and-order theme that became the centerpiece of Richard Nixon's 1968 presidential campaign simply capitalized on a grassroots movement that took root earlier in the decade. In 1963, Alabama governor George Wallace received, much as Mayor Lamb had, letters and telegrams from all over the country applauding his stand blocking Black children from white schools. As the legal scholar Ian Haney Lopez observed, "Hostility against Black advancement wasn't confined to the South." Wallace realized, "'They all hate black people, all of them. They're all afraid, all of them. Great god! That's it! They're all Southern. The whole United States is Southern.'"[14] And while Nixon's tactics have popularly been called the "Southern Strategy," the Rochester archive suggests it was anything but a regional campaign, as is further evidenced by Nixon's subsequent victory.[15]

Of the 104 surviving letters to Lamb, and to his city manager, Porter Homer, women authors comprised one third, occasionally cosigning en masse. Men authored forty-three letters, while twenty-three were unsigned or were indecipherable, either because of a gender-neutral name or the use of initials. Organizations submitted the final thirteen letters. As one might expect, more than half of the letters (54 percent) arrived from Rochester. Another 36 percent of the letters originated in twenty different states, half from below the Mason Dixon line. Non-Rochester northerners provided another 10 percent while midwestern and western residents supplied another 8 percent. It is impossible to decipher where the final 10 percent originated. Only three authors self-identify as African American, an indication that they were not assured that their perspectives mattered.

This compilation of correspondence, evidence of a national conversation regarding race and migration, is likely one of many such collections housed in local archives. Yet, there is surprisingly little scholarship on the voices of average whites in response to the urban revolts that swept the nation in the 1960s and early 1970s. One explanation for this lacuna is that municipal archives are generally not well advertised, as national, state, and university archives tend to be, and are often difficult to access. A second potential explanation for the dearth of scholarship on the white response to Black rebellion is that scholars of civil rights and Black Power rightly privilege Black organizing, expectations, and efforts. The way white folks felt about or discussed Black strategies for transformation bears little on their work. Another possibility is that scholars have not recognized northern anti-Black discourse in the same ways that scholars such as Matthew Lassiter, Joseph Crespino, and Jason Sokol have studied in the South.[16] Northern anti-Black discourse remains largely invisible because northerners were not expected to have a racially defined consciousness. Yet, revealing the Jim Crow discourse as it took place on the ground helps to uncover just that. The conditions in which African Americans in the North lived and worked and the attitudes and beliefs they confronted rivaled those in the South. Despite its benevolent image, it is clear from these letters that the North was not the Promised Land.

Recent work by scholars, including Matthew Lassiter and Joseph Crespino, is useful for analyzing such letters.[17] "The most insightful observers of southern history," they posit, "have always insisted that the region is inseparable from the nation, that the South is not the antithesis of a progressive America but, rather, has operated as a mirror that reveals its fundamental values and practices."[18] In this sense, letters such as LeBoo's and Johnston's, which made demands, shared advice and strategies, and called for a halt to black migration, offer scholars a glimpse at how white citizens across regions understood themselves. They also reveal both white fears and the contextualization of these fears in contemporary events. Grace Hale, a historian, notes that "[a]fter World War II, broad historical changes long underway—migration to cities and suburbs, the rise of white-collar corporate employment, the growth of government and corporate bureaucracies, and the changing nature of family life—continued to erode middle-class whites' sense of control over their lives and their feelings of rootedness in place and community." According to Hale, "African Americans' growing demand for greater rights only increased middle-class white fears."[19] The urban historian Khalil G. Muhammad argues that this began with Black emancipation in 1865: "African American freedom fueled far-reaching anxieties among many white Americans."[20] Such letters, then, demonstrate that in moments of rapid global change, when "the categories of power" are "destabilized,"[21] white people of various political persuasions mitigated their anxieties by marking and defining Blackness, subsequently stabilizing and bolstering their own whiteness. The uprisings of the 1960s prompted white citizens to talk back racially. Whites constructed Blackness as the "Negro problem" rather than the Jim Crow conditions they perpetuated all while reasserting their racial priorities.

And Rochester was experiencing rapid change. The city's Black population had grown exponentially, increasing 780 percent from 1940 to 1970.[22] Racially exclusionary practices such as redlining, that pernicious practice that confined Black newcomers to the two city wards traditionally home to immigrants, created tensions.[23] In fact, "A study of race relations in five major New York State cities revealed in 1958 that Rochester had the most rigid barriers against the sale of houses in the suburbs to Negroes."[24] Like LeBoo, the Rochester newspaper encouraged a change in housing policy and practices, not for the sake of equality or to guarantee civil rights but to prevent "the slums [from] sink[ing] into jungle conditions, real 'ghettos' where even the police fear to tread."[25] This jungle trope recurs throughout the paper's reporting and can be found in correspondence to the mayor. The city's failure to reallocate resources, other than police, severely strained municipal services, housing stock, parks, and schools in the increasingly Black and segregated wards. Inevitably, conditions deteriorated. Meanwhile, the dwindling number of white residents in these increasingly Black wards developed a siege mentality.[26] The local paper reported, "Suddenly the Negroes seemed all around us—and not just in the big cities, but right here in Rochester. They took over the slums and the slums began to spread."[27]

Despite this documentation of conditions, many claimed the Rochester rebellion came as a surprise to white folks, causing one "civil leader" to publicly bemoan, "Why here—of all places?"[28] This refrain was not unique to Rochester, but rather served as a generic reaction to racial unrest in cities outside the South. Historian and biographer Jeanne Theoharis argues that such rejoinders were part of a willful shock and a "strategic response by northern white officials and residents to deny [longstanding] black grievances."[29] Likewise, Lassiter and Crespino cogently argue that "[s]cholars, journalists, and politicians compartmentalized outbreaks of racial backlash in the 'non-South' by drawing on a reliable reservoir of southern metaphors," and thus contributed to the sense that social conditions were not to blame for Black dissatisfaction. Such a framework, Lassiter and Crespino continue, "attributes episodes of racism and racial violence inside the South to the social and political structures of the region, while portraying similar events elsewhere as anomalous incidents that really should have happened down in Mississippi or Alabama."[30] Asking "why here, why us" further hitched the regional issues purportedly endemic to the South to Rochester, much as Johnston's letter, and others to the mayor, suggested. "The city seems to have become a victim of its own generosity," the same unnamed official opined, in language reminiscent of LeBoo's, "Rochester is known as a soft touch for welfare and relief chiselers. As a result, there has been a large influx of shiftless Negroes with no real desire to work for a living. They are the people who live in squalor, who won't try to better themselves, whose main interest seems to be where the next bottle of booze is coming from."[31]

The local papers continued to publish articles and editorials that while focusing on demographic changes, simultaneously shared a language for the racial problems in the city.[32] Later entitled "The Road to Integration," this editorial compilation charted the growing animosity of many whites in Rochester to African Americans. Highlighting Black migration to the North, the compilation of articles posited that "Mr. Average Rochester Citizen (white)," wondered "why the Kennedy administration hasn't done something about the city of Washington, which should be the nation's showplace and which seems to be on the way to becoming a jungle." Another article in the collection drew connections between citizenship and welfare: "The white should open all the doors and say, 'Now that you have all the rights, accept the responsibilities and do the job.' The white man should not want to carry the welfare loads of Negroes."[33]

As the decade progressed, some would come to see Black grievances in the North as legitimate civil rights issues. The federal government lent credence to this view when, in 1968, it sanctioned the Kerner Report, which highlighted conditions found in Rochester and elsewhere, though it would subsequently bury the findings and decry the report's more systemic conclusions.[34] In 1964, however, the Rochester *Times-Union* rejected the notion that racist structural policies and practices contributed to the rising. "This is rot, and every responsible Rochesterian knows it," the paper editorialized. "The riots were the result of unreasoning hoodlumism. They occurred in spite of the fact that Rochester has as progressive a record in advancing civil rights, urban renewal and minority opportunity programs as almost any community in the country."[35] In 1964, Black pathology remained the more palatable official explanation for uprisings.

As news of the Rochester rising spread across the country, such editorials and articles fueled a national frenzy. *Newsweek* would report, "The preceding week of tumultuous rioting had already set in motion a groundswell of anti-Negro 'white backlash' sentiment."[36] The archived letters provide evidence for how this Jim Crow discourse unfolded. When Dr. Benjamin Pollack, the assistant director of the Rochester State Hospital, for example, was quoted in a *U.S. News and World Report* article calling for "armed force . . . as the only way to deal with a rioting mob" and counseling that "[y]ou can't appeal to reason . . . it's deeds, not words, that count when you're dealing with primitive emotions let loose. You've got to show strength," because "they know that here in Rochester they can live on relief handouts and city charity without doing a day's work," people responded.[37] Lamb and Homer received an influx of letters from people eager to apply this discourse to Rochester, the nation, and the world. Drawing on that *U.S. News and World Report* article, a Florida woman wrote to Lamb, "I think the free handouts and welfare checks have made parasites of many. . . . If this is not promoting illegitimacy I don't know what is. It may be all right to help out with the first child but if they were fined for any thereafter that would put a stop to so many babies."[38] Letters such as this not only reinforce whiteness and mark Blackness; they also highlight the authors' fears regarding national and global changes taking place at midcentury and beyond. Scholar Kathleen Gray offers that this type of conversation is indicative of a larger process. "What people say about race and how they say it reflects more than just individual racial attitudes: the way people talk about race constructs and deconstructs the racial status quo . . . what is expected, acceptable, meaningful, and good when it comes to the definitions and treatment of different racial groups," she argues.[39] A letter written from one part of the country to another offers more than just the perspective of a single author. Certainly those writing letters from around the country felt their voices should matter more than the African Americans about whom they wrote. As sociologist

Dean Harper summarized a year after the Rochester events, "What the riots did for many whites, then, was to permit the public expression of hostile attitudes. . . . [T]his was a time for people with hostile attitudes to express their hostility without feeling guilty."[40]

For discursive purposes, these voices are here organized into two categories. It should be noted, however, that these categories are not clearly delineated in the letters, and that the correspondents seamlessly moved among white backlash tropes in this Jim Crow discourse. Their diversity and complexity speak to the deep-seated anti-Blackness of the era, a mindset that was never confined to the white South. The letters further reveal the anxiety that many whites felt in the wake of the urban rebellions, and in challenges to white supremacy nationally and globally.

The first method for marking Blackness doubled as a commentary on welfare policies that had evolved since implementation in the earlier part of the century. Several writers suggested that national welfare policies, a catch-all phrase that actually referred to Aid to Families with Dependent Children (AFDC), were the root cause of Black misbehavior. If only the state and national governments would revoke welfare benefits for African Americans who asserted citizenship rights, they declared, then Black uprisings would come to an end, and order would be restored. The second method for marking Blackness posited that the inherent nature of Black folk was "African." Writers pointed alternatively to a childlike nature as well as to an essential animalism or jungle-like behavior. Many made unflattering connections to anticolonial rebellions and activities, especially the struggle for independence in the Congo, and expressed a broad unwillingness to coexist with America's Black population.

Once Blackness had been marked in these ways, the correspondents sought to bolster white supremacy, by theorizing events in Rochester and the nation, and by outlining methods to perpetuate racial segregation.[41] The letters demanded law and order, and reasserted the imperative of white control. The correspondence reveals further the surprise of white northerners at the uprisings, and the glee of white southerners, eager to highlight northern white hypocrisy on the race question. "You Yankees will listen to us one day but it will be too late," warned one white southerner.[42] In the end, whites in the North and South looked longingly, if uncomfortably, for a new national consensus, a Jim Crow America, based on a shared understanding of whiteness.

In Rochester, citizen response to the rebellion was a complicated outgrowth of long-held paternalist beliefs and a thinly veiled distaste for "transient undesirable Negroes" or, more pointedly, "this low down hoodlum negro element," as Olive LeBoo put it.[43] But the 1964 uprising gave citizens from around the country the opportunity to espouse their views on the causes and cures of Black insurgency more forcefully to Rochester officials. Most white correspondents agreed that an overly generous welfare system contributed to Black "misbehavior," reflecting a surprising awareness of national policy debates underway regarding the AFDC program. AFDC began in Roosevelt's New Deal era as Aid to Dependent Children (ADC) a program to support children in families that lacked a primary male caregiver due to death, absence, or inability to work. As conceived and enacted, the program allowed states to curtail dependent children not living in "suitable homes," a euphemism for "children of never-married or African American mothers."[44] It also allowed states, rather than the federal government, to set funding levels— all of which restricted Black access to the social safety net.

State-controlled ADC yielded surprising payment differentials for families who migrated, so that when thousands of southern Black migrants settled in Rochester, white people believed high welfare payments had attracted them. A family coming from Sanford, Florida, would have received $7.30 per child in benefits before migrating, but a whopping $24.15 per child after arriving in Rochester. Still, these Florida children were in a much better position than families who remained in Kentucky, Mississippi, and Texas, states that refused to participate in the federally funded program at all.[45] As a result of migration, white fears of "welfare sucking Negroes" gained currency. And when race rebellions erupted across the country, white citizens increasingly employed welfare to mark Blackness in the North. One need only recall the unnamed civil official who told a national news outlet, "Rochester is known as a soft touch for welfare and relief chiselers. As a result, there has been a large influx of shiftless Negroes with no real desire to work for a living."[46]

Another Rochester author, who identified him/herself only as "an irate tax payer," demanded that welfare payment to "all Nergros [sic]" be withheld until the merchants were repaid for damage done during the uprising. This same writer anticipated the 1965 Moynihan Report, which insisted that white families were stable while Black families were not. "We, the people . . . have provided good housing projects, paid relief for the unemployed, even paid extra for all the illegetement [sic] children they have produced over the years,"[47] ignoring or erasing the existence of the Black taxpayer, of course. Connecting welfare payments and illegitimate children was a related tactic. "Promiscuity in having children then pawning them off on welfare should not be tolerated," harped another Rochester citizen in 1964. "[P]roof of marriage and dependents (legal) should be required to draw welfare."[48] Daniel Patrick Moynihan echoed such beliefs a year later, in his 1965 report entitled *The Negro Family: The Case for National Action*. "The steady expansion of this welfare program, as of public assistance programs in general," he argued, "can be taken as a measure of the steady disintegration of the Negro family structure over the past generation in the United States."[49] In an attempt to convince President Lyndon Johnson to give racial inequality more attention, Moynihan reified this trope of Black pathology, a key tenet of white backtalk.

Importantly, these perceived connections between welfare and Blackness translated into a call for limiting Black citizenship. Bobby Baker, from Chicago, who signed his letter "Against Johnson the nigger lover for Votes," suggested to Lamb that individuals who received government aid should be prohibited from exercising their constitutional rights. "[A]dults and families on relief that demonstrate" should be advised that "these relief checks will be stopped at once." Baker indicated that Lamb could then "[w]atch good results."[50] While Baker felt that withdrawing welfare could be used to punish activists, another Rochester resident felt that welfare payments contributed to the rising "I can't see when you politicians are going to wake up that they are savages," he wrote. "You pay them $300 per month relief money besides medical care, extra surplus goods and clothes. They use the money to buy liquor and say they are ill fed. I'm just interested to see what steps you are going to take against them but as usual I'm sure appeasement."[51] When a *Times-Union* editorial assessed conditions two years after the uprising, it demonstrated the hold that such views had over Rochester: "The feeling that Negroes shouldn't be given something whites have had to work hard for is widespread. . . . It's been said of the bitter white reaction touched off in the past two years that people are simply expressing prejudices they've always held."[52] Such letters exhibit the long debate over migration, welfare, and race that heated up in the 1950s and rolled to a full boil in the 1960s.

While many interlocutors determined that Black folk were too dependent upon welfare, others suggested that they were simply too "African" for integration into American culture. In seeking integration, the United States set itself up to face events similar to the racially charged disturbances then occurring in Africa. Despite their many obvious differences, these theorists shared with Black Power practitioners the view that uprisings in the United States paralleled anticolonial struggles in Asia and Africa, including the violent undertakings in Congo and Kenya. Giving a speech in Rochester in 1965, Malcolm X provided the history of such logic: "Until 1959 the image of the African continent was created by the enemies of Africa. Africa was a land dominated by outside powers. A land dominated by Europeans . . . it was they who created the image of Africa that was projected abroad." To his largely Black audience, Malcolm emphasized, "They made us think that Africa was a land of jungles, a land of animals, a land of cannibals and savages. It was a hateful image."[53]

Now, as African decolonization unfolded, this trope was picked up in the letters sent to Rochester. A set of pamphlets sent to the mayor by a group calling itself "185 Million Americans" articulated this "Africa argument":

> The origin of the Negro is, I believe, quite well-known, but in case it is not, let us recall it. Africa was made the home of all Anthropoids and Apes, such as gorillas, monkeys, baboons, negroes, orang-a-tang, maus, and many other jungle tribes . . . There [sic] numbers were regulated by jungle environment. It is not unkind to remind him of his true place in creation. . . . He has a different body from us. It is black, it is strong in many ways solely to equip him for life in the jungle where we could not survive. . . . Jungle brains can only understand jungle laws. Has the world ever before seen such a disgraceful spectacle in any civilized country as has occurred in America? . . . They have taken over until we all bow to their will. We can expect much worse results soon.[54]

If perhaps this group had not connected "Negroes" with animals clearly enough in its first pamphlet, it echoed the sentiment in a second. Blacks, the second pamphlet commanded, "will drop no more of their offspring here on this land and claim they are American. Being born in a stable doesn't make you a horse. Wherever they are born they remain offspring of a black African jungle tribe. . . . Let us take a look at the Congo!" Both pamphlets equate Africa, or being African descended, with inhumanity.

Likewise, a postcard sent to Rochester pithily drew such connections to Africa. The card simply proclaimed, "Happy Congo!"[55] People of African descent everywhere, these writers suggested, inevitably would revert to the laws of the jungle without firm white governance and control, a point underscored in the pre-uprising articles warning Rochester about its ghettoes. Other correspondence highlighted what was seen as the fixed nature of Blackness. One interlocutor mailed the article from *U.S. News and World Report* on the uprising with handwritten comments that included, "Finest schools in the whole wide world cannot take the jungle out of the apes."[56] At once, this reasoning, long associated with places such as Mississippi, asserted the fundamental incapacity of Blacks to integrate into American life while simultaneously rejecting Black strivings for equality. The collection of letters reveals that in the North, too, invoking the "African jungle" to question African American aspirations was but one of many responses to the Black uprisings.

Yet not all correspondents subscribed fully to the "African jungle" depiction. Some conceded the humanity of Black folk, but denied their capacity for full development. African Americans, according to this argument, were a childlike people. William Leuco, of nearby Pennsylvania, believed that "negroes are not capable of any kind of organized violence. An individual negro with gun or knife can be dangerous, but a group of negros [sic] are like a group of children. All they can do is a little window breaking and make a lot of noise."[57] Consequently, Black citizens should neither be feared nor taken seriously; instead, they should be subject to law and order until they accept the leadership and guidance from white betters. Along these lines, another letter declared, "They are like children. They want attention. So, they are getting their glory by people printing their riots."[58] The belief that Black people were the moral and intellectual equivalent of children produced the following prescription, articulated by Mrs. Joseph H. DeNoon: "The rioters cannot be reached with reason or money, but like a child, only with discipline."[59] In this way, perhaps, Blacks were elevated above animals, where some of Lamb's correspondents placed them, and accorded humanity, albeit of a childlike variety.

These attitudes were not confined to letters. We see these tropes permeate public discussions surrounding civil rights issues in Rochester throughout this era. Two related debates playing out in the local papers in 1963 and 1964 surrounded Black speech patterns and Black reproductive rights. The local schools were heavily criticized for leaving the correction of "[substandard] Negro colloquial speech . . . up to classroom teachers to correct." Apparently many in Rochester felt that African Americans were denied jobs not because of racist hiring policies but because "[f]orty-five percent of the Negro youths entering Rochester high schools do not know how to speak proper English." They concluded that Rochester City Schools needed to implement a program.[60] Likewise, one of the local papers, the *Democrat and Chronicle*, weighed in on debates over the placement of Planned Parenthood centers, calling for "intolerance of any further obstruction to setting up Planned Parenthood centers in underprivileged areas . . . for the tragic clock-like spawning of unwanted children locks families into permanent poverty."[61] Thus the notion that Black Rochesterians were too African, too childlike, and incapable of solving their own issues had appeared in public debates around schooling and health care years earlier, a discourse evident in the post-uprising letters to officials.

Mayor Lamb's correspondents strove toward several ends. First, they offered well-worn tropes from the Jim Crow discourse—liquor, the jungle, welfare, Africa, and Blacks' "childlike" nature—to mark Blackness. In so doing, they promoted Black inferiority and its corollary, white superiority. Having affirmed white supremacy, they made a case for Black restriction and exclusion by demanding "law and order."

This cry for law and order simultaneously calls into question Rochester's, and perhaps the North's, racially benevolent image. At one end of the spectrum, some merely desired "stricter enforcement of liquor laws and control of taverns" in the areas where the rebellion took hold.[62] At the other end of the spectrum was the increasingly frustrated Olive LeBoo. Immediately after the uprising she chastised Lamb, "Our police force should have shot to kill instead of accepting the going over they did. Appeasment [sic] will just call for more of the same."[63] LeBoo was not alone in her call for a heavy-handed response. Frederick Drury, writing from the University of Rochester, echoed her call, but with the caveat that he did "not mean this to sound like a 'white backlash.' I feel very

---

sorry for the too few negroes who have worked hard to better themselves and get out of the ghettos. They are the ones who suffer. As for the rest, I say they should have been shot, as any other looter would have been. Enough is enough!"[64] Such responses were in no way confined to Rochester. Writing from Maryland, John Floyd sent Lamb a Washington, D.C., editorial making similar arguments. The editorialist declared, "[T]he American people are beginning to see that the looting of stores, with damages running into the millions, has very little to do with the merits of any 'civil rights' question but has everything to do with the age-old problem of crushing crime by any measure of law enforcement deemed necessary to protect life and property."[65]

Others agreed with LeBoo that the civilian police review board, created in the months preceding the uprising, tied the hands of the Rochester police during the revolt. Rochester was one of the few cities that had a civilian review board at that time, though it would quickly fade into obscurity in the aftermath given its lack of popularity with many whites. Indeed, most cities refused to create similar panels, though activists often demanded them. Rochester resident William Myers was among those who believed that the police review board contributed to the revolt. "In my opinion there is no mystery for the riot," he wrote. "It looked to me as if the hands of your policemen were tied and with a hundred more handcuffed police you would have still had the riot. Why not admit it. . . . Without full law forcefully enforced, you have the law of the jungle, that is what we had in the riot."[66] For Myers, the police were responsible for containing the subhuman, "African" nature of Black Rochester, and they should be fully empowered to do so. Otherwise, civilization itself would be imperiled. This was the view of psychologists and businessmen alike. The aforementioned Dr. Benjamin Pollack counseled, "You can't appeal to reason. It's deeds, not words, that count when you're dealing with primitive emotions let loose. You've got to show strength."[67] J. Wallace Ely, president of Rochester's Security Trust Company, in a rather personal letter to "Frank and Porter," that is, Mayor Lamb and City Manager Homer, counseled,

> Any criticism directed toward the police effort is sadly misplaced. They may have been outnumbered or overwhelmed and they may have been under some foolish restrictive orders with respect to the amount of force,

or under the impossible handicap of living under an impractical "Review Board." The fault lies not with the Police department but with those who have failed to comprehend. When a police force is under restrictive orders, there are evil forces that take advantage of their position. I feel strongly that we are either going to have law and order (regardless of what force is required to maintain law and order) or we are going to have civilization replaced by civil war and anarchy. We have gone too far in building up a "sacred cow" status around certain groups, which, obviously, take advantage of their privileged status.[68]

Not everyone demanding law and order required shoot-to-kill orders. Others demonstrated both restraint in language and the possibility for law and order in moderation. Joseph Hockenos of Rochester, for example, simply asked that it be impressed upon "all citizens that they respect the badge of law and order worn by policemen. . . . [I]t is good to impress upon those who think they are oppressed to start their climb back first by respecting the law and order that all other citizens respect."[69] A group of eleven Rochester residents protested the suspended sentences that participants in the uprising received. They collectively declared, "If instead of suspended sentences, given to these rioters, they were made to spend a few weekends in jail, it would give them something to think about and might help to prevent any more of this disgrace which they have caused in our city."[70] Interestingly, most of those suspended sentences resulted from illegitimate arrests involving violations of the "riot curfew," which city officials later determined they had no legal right to impose.

In response to such demands from the white citizenry, Mayor Lamb insisted publicly "that law and order shall prevail in Rochester. Any violations will be dealt with, and dealt with swiftly, harshly and conclusively."[71] Homer echoed this sentiment. "I want to make it crystal clear," he announced, "that we will not be sandbagged by any pressures from any person or persons, whether from Rochester or outside our city." He did attempt to soften this message with the following: "I wish to tell you that despite the apparent sternness of the administration with respect to the preservation of law and order, we will recognize the legitimate rights of our citizens, whether members of a minority group or not."[72] He failed to say which "legitimate rights" would be respected.

Behind the scenes, Lamb and Homer were working with chief of police William Lombard on a new Emergency Mobilization Plan. Lombard later notified his subordinates that "[i]n addition to what has already been issued to the officer, additional weapons such as tear gas, riot guns and ammunition for same will be issued to each squad, post or unit." The new plan also allowed for "a supply of night sticks to be issued to field personnel."[73] While many attribute the weaponization of police forces to the Watts uprising in 1965, the Rochester archive demonstrates an earlier response. Such changes in official policy responded directly to calls such as the one published in *U.S. News and World Report* wherein one "Rochester industrialist" complained that the "police—inhibited by fears of 'brutality' charges—didn't start using their nightsticks soon enough."[74] Likewise, such changes reflected research that Lamb had done on "riot control," including an article published in *Ordnance* a year before Watts by Lieutenant Rex Applegate, who suggested that "[t]he long baton is much superior to an empty gun or sheathed bayonet and also more effective since the man confronting the mob can use it with any degree of force indicated to achieve the desired result and, at the same time, personally perform in the kind of aggressive manner that maintains his morale and offensive spirit."[75] Mayor Lamb undoubtedly felt that Applegate was speaking directly to him, given criticism he faced nationally from news outlets such as Florida's *Sun Sentinel*, which reported, "The 180 guardsmen, part of the 1,000 called to duty, carried unloaded bayonet-tipped rifles but did not have ammunition."[76]

While white northerners attempted to explain urban rebellions, white southerners delighted in what they saw as northern white hypocrisy. Like J. S. Johnston, who with Olive LeBoo began this story, Mrs. Christine Drone (Louisiana) was among those who seemed to savor the ironic moment created by the Rochester rising. She sent a clipping about the revolt from her local paper suggesting that Rochester officials unwittingly reproduced the language of their southern counterparts: "Rochester's City Manager sounds strangely southern in his protestations that 'outsiders' have stirred up that New York town and that—left alone—whites and Negroes could work out decent race relations. That, of course, is what the South has been saying all along, but we don't recall any protestations . . . in the North when the first 'freedom riders' caused such strife in various Alabama towns."[77] Drone rhetorically poked along the bottom of the clipping: "Ha, Ha, Ha! What was that you said about Mississippi?"[78] Other letters highlighted a key message implied in such a communication: Black rebellion in northern cities created the potential for white solidarity across the Mason-Dixon line. Evelyn Powell, writing to both Mayors Lamb and Wagner of New York City, was among those offering such advice. "If it were not so tragic, we in the South would derive some compensation from the race troubles you are having in New York," Mrs. Powell began. Such trouble could be avoided if northern whites were willing to learn from the experience of their southern counterparts. "We have been indignant that people in the North, who do not KNOW the Negro have had the audacity to presume to tell us what to do about the Negro problems, when we have been dealing with the Negro and trying to help him for over 200 years!" Such urban rebellions offered the possibility of a white racial accord, nationally. "There is something Southerners know about the Negro which may be of help to those trying to control delinquency among the Negroes" in the North, the sage Mrs. Powell concluded. "That is that he respects only strength and force. The more one treats the Negro as an equal, the more he takes advantage of that person."[79] While southerners' remarks are often and easily dismissed as disingenuous, the Rochester archives make clear that they pointed to something real, even if their motives were questionable.

Not all those engaged in the Rochester correspondence and beyond believed white supremacy was ever in serious danger. J. S. Johnston pointed to two of the era's most poignant symbols—whiskey and the police dog—summarizing what he viewed as the nationally shared plight and preserver of white America. His advice to simply "[l]et those negroes have their whiskey" was reminiscent of an old southern strategy recorded by Frederick Douglass: "[B]y far the larger part [of the enslaved population] engaged in such sports and merriments as playing ball, wrestling, running foot races, fiddling, dancing and drinking whiskey and this latter mode of spending the time was by far the most agreeable to the feelings of our masters." Johnston simply pointed to Douglass's observation made a century earlier: whiskey intoxication was "among the most effective means in the hand of the slaveholder in keeping down the spirit of insurrection."[80] Johnston believed this strategy would work equally well in the North if only white northerners would embrace it. For a community startled by a "new breed of Negroes," Johnston proffered, "It's no new breed. You have just what we have had in Dixie for 343 long years, but you Yankees have 10,000+ long hot summers ahead of you."[81]

The 1960s was a turbulent era around the globe, particularly for colonialism and white supremacy. For Black folk worldwide, it was a moment of possibility. Any and every tactic was used to secure freedom and justice. In the United States, not since the Civil War had whiteness been given such a run. African Americans had integrated schools and universities, increased access to public space, and secured legislation to protect their political and economic rights. Increasingly, too, they rejected and challenged police efforts to limit and control their movements. Black equality was conceivable in such a moment.

Thus, many whites, north and south, rallied to uphold white supremacy. Using the familiarly perilous tropes—liquor, welfare, Africa, and animalism—they agitated around Black inferiority and the insecurity it created for the state. Having done so, they sought to protect the privileges of whiteness under the cloak of other threats. The most visible manifestation culminated in a local and national entreaty for law and order, calls that would be realized ultimately in the election of Richard Nixon in 1968. Along the way, white northerners and southerners negotiated a common cause, seizing an opportunity to bridge regional differences by joining once again on the race question. The 1964 Rochester uprising and the subsequent correspondence provide a window through which to observe this national Jim Crow discourse as it unfolded.

NOTES

1 LeBoo to Lamb, 12/27/64. Rochester City Archives (herein RCA), Frank Lamb Collection (herein FLC), BIN 1274, Riots of 1964. (All subsequent letters from LeBoo are from this collection; all RCA documents found in BIN 1274 unless otherwise noted.)

2 LeBoo to Lamb, 7/27/64.

3 LeBoo to Wilkins, 12/13/63.

4 LeBoo to Wilkins, 11/5/63.

5 LeBoo to Morrison, 10/1/63.

6 LeBoo to Wilkins, 12/13/63.

7 LeBoo to Fraternal Order of Police, 10/21/63.

8 Carol Anderson, *White Rage: The Unspoken Truth of Our Racial Divide* (New York: Bloomsbury, 2016).

9 J. S. Johnston to Lamb, 7/28/64, RCA, FLC.

10 Vincent S. Jones, "The Background: The Road to Integration," *Rochester Democrat and Chronicle*, April 15, 1965.

11 Carter G. Woodson, "The Exodus during the World War" (1918) in Malaika Adero, ed., *Up South: Stories and Letters of This Century's African-American Migrations* (New York: New Press, 1993), 11.

12 Johnston to Lamb.

13 "Crisis in Race Relations: Rochester; Where a Race Riot Hit a 'Model' City," *U.S. News and World Report*, August 10, 1964, 38.

14 Ian Haney Lopez, *Dog Whistle Politics: How Coded Racial Appeals Have Reinvented Racism and Wrecked the Middle Class* (New York: Oxford University Press, 2014), 16.

15 Suburban Rochester overwhelmingly supported Nixon's campaign. In fact, 58 percent of suburban Monroe County voters (where Rochester is located) pulled the lever for Nixon while another 3.6 percent voted for George Wallace. On Nixon's campaign, see, Reg Murphy and Hal Gulliver, *The Southern Strategy* (New York: Scribners, 1971); Glenn Feldman, ed., *Painting Dixie Red: When, Where, Why, and How the South Became Republican* (Gainesville: University Press of Florida, 2011); and, Thomas A. Johnson, "Negro Leaders See Bias in Call of Nixon for 'Law and Order,'" *New York Times*, August 13, 1968, 27.

16 Matthew Lassiter and Joseph Crespino, *The Myth of Southern Exceptionalism* (New York: Oxford University Press, 2010); and, Jason Sokol, *There Goes My Everything: White Southerners in the Age of Civil Rights, 1945–1975* (New York: Knopf, 2007).

17 Lassiter and Crespino.

18 Lassiter and Crespino, 7.

19 Grace Elizabeth Hale, *A Nation of Outsiders: How the White Middle Class Fell in Love with Rebellion in Postwar America* (New York: Oxford University Press, 2011), 5.

20 Khalil G. Muhammad, *The Condemnation of Blackness: Race, Crime, and the Making of Modern Urban American* (Boston: Harvard University Press, 2010), Kindle edition.

21 Grace Elizabeth Hale, *Making Whiteness: The Culture of Segregation in the South, 1890–1940* (New York: Pantheon, 1998), 6.

22 See, Laura Warren Hill, "'We Are Black Folk First': The Black Freedom Struggle in Rochester, NY, and the Making of Malcolm X," *The Sixties: A Journal of History, Politics, and Culture* 3, no. 2 (December 2010), 165.

23 For more on redlining, see, Antero Pietila, *Not in My Neighborhood: How Bigotry Shaped a Great American City* (Chicago: Ivan R. Dee Press, 2010); Gregory D. Squires, *Privileged Spaces: Race, Residence, and the Structure of Opportunity* (Boulder, CO: Rienner, 2006); Beryl Satter, *Race, Real Estate, and the Exploitation of Black Urban America* (New York: Metropolitan, 2009); and, Dianne Suzette Harris, *Little White Houses: How the Postwar Home Constructed Race in America* (Minneapolis: University of Minnesota Press, 2013).

24 Blake McKelvey, "Housing and Urban Renewal: The Rochester Experience," *Rochester History* 27, no. 4 (October 1965), 22.

25 Editorial, *Rochester Democrat and Chronicle*, August 25, 1963.

26 See, Laura Warren Hill, *"Strike the Hammer While the Iron Is Hot": The Black Freedom Struggle in Rochester, NY, 1940–1970* (Ithaca, NY: Cornell University Press, forthcoming).

27 Vincent S. Jones, "The Background: The Road to Integration," *Democrat and Chronicle*, April 15, 1965.

28 "Crisis in Race Relations: Rochester; Where a Race Riot Hit a 'Model' City," 38.

29 Jeanne Theoharis, "Hidden in Plain Sight: The Civil Rights Movement outside the South," in Lassiter and Crespino, 54.

30 Lassiter and Crespino, 9.

31 "Crisis in Race Relations: Rochester; Where a Race Riot Hit a 'Model' City."

32 See, "The Road to Integration: Selected Art and Articles from a Continuing Program Which Has Won a Pulitzer Citation for Public Service for the Gannett Newspapers," RCA, FLC.

33 Ibid.

34 *The Kerner Report: The 1968 Report of the National Advisory Commission on Civil Disorders*. 1st ed. (New York: Pantheon Books, 1988).

35 "How to Rescue a Good Image," *Times-Union*, August 3, 1964, RCA, FLC.

36 "Civil Rights: Calculated Risk," *Newsweek*, August 10, 1964, 27.

37 "Crisis in Race Relations: Rochester; Where a Race Riot Hit a 'Model' City."

38 Mrs. John Parker Montgomery to Mayor Lamb, 8/10/64, RCA, FLC.

39 Kathleen Bulger Gray, "Negotiating Race Talk: How Whites Hide Racial Privilege and Structural Inequality" (PhD diss., University of Pittsburgh, 2012), 1.

40 Dean Harper, "Rochester: The Effects of a Riot." Subsequently published as "Aftermath of a Long, Hot Summer," *Trans-Action* 2, no. 5 (July 1965), 7–11. RCA, Riot Emergency 1964 Report to Council, BIN 301, Box 4&5.

41 This term was coined by David Roediger, *The Wages of Whiteness: Race and the Making of the American Working Class* (New York: Verso, 2007).

42 Johnston to Lamb.

43 LeBoo to Lamb, 7/27/64, RCA, FLC. See also, citizen residing at 230 Trafalgar St., Rochester to Lamb, 7/29/64, RCA, FLC. This letter was signed, but the signature was removed during photocopying.

44 Susan W. Blank and Barbara B. Blum, "A Brief History of Work Expectations for Welfare Mothers," *Welfare to Work* 7, no. 1 (Spring 1997), 28–38.

45 Richard Sterner, *The Negro's Share: A Study of Income, Consumption, Housing, and Public Assistance*, ACLS Humanities E-Book (New York: Harper, 1943), 285.

46 "Crisis in Race Relations: Rochester; Where a Race Riot Hit a 'Model' City."

47 Office of Policy Planning and Research, United States Department of Labor, *The Negro Family: The Case for National Action* (March 1965), 5; and "an irate taxpayer" to "Whom It May Concern. Dept. Public Welfare" 7/26/64, RCA, FLC.

48 Rochester citizen to Lamb, undated, RCA, FLC.

49 Office of Policy Planning and Research, 14.

50 Bobby Baker to Lamb, 7/27/64, RCA, FLC.

51 Citizen residing at 230 Trafalgar St., Rochester, to Lamb.

52 "Race Relations '67: Where Do We Stand?" *Times-Union* (1967) reprint, RCA, City Manager Subject Files "C" Box 4&5 Combined, BIN 0301.

53 Malcolm X, "Not Just an American Problem, but a World Problem," Corn Hill Methodist Church, Rochester, New York, February 16, 1965, in Bruce Perry (editor), *Malcolm X: The Last Speeches* (New York: Pathfinder Press, 1989), 145–73.

54 Pamphlets from "185 Million Americans," n.d. JRCA, FLC.

55 A. R. Boling to Lamb, n.d., RCA, FLC.

56 *U.S. News and World Report* article, RCA, FLC.

57 William Leuco to Lamb, 7/26/64, RCA, FLC.

58 Unsigned to Lamb, undated, RCA, FLC.

59 Mrs. Joseph H. DeNoon to Lamb, 7/28/64, RCA, FLC.

60 Bob Spellman, "The Speech Barrier: The Road to Integration," *Gannett Newspapers*, April 15, 1965.

61 Clifford E. Carpenter, "Wanted: A New Kind of Intolerance," editorial, *Democrat and Chronicle*, July 28, 1964; *Democrat and Chronicle*, November 6, 1968, 1A.

62 Sidney Lindenberg, Baden Street Settlement, Addenda to Board and Committee Members, 7/28/64, RCA, FLC.

63 LeBoo to Lamb, 7/27/64, RCA, FLC.

64 Frederick H. Drury to Lamb, 7/30/64, RCA, FLC.

65 John P. Floyd to Lamb, 7/28/64, RCA, FLC.

66 William A. Myers to Lamb, 8/10/1964, RCA, FLC.

67 "Crisis in Race Relations: Rochester; Where a Race Riot Hit a 'Model' City."

68 J. Wallace Ely to Lamb and Porter, 7/31/64, RCA, FLC.

69 Joseph L. Hockenos to Lamb, 7/31/64, RCA, FLC.

70 "Undersigned and taxpayers" to Lamb, undated, RCA, FLC.

71 Transcript of Joint Address given by Mayor Lamb, Commissioner Corbett, and City Manager Porter, RCA, FLC.

72 Ibid.

73 William Lombard, Chief of Police, to All Police Personnel. Emergency Mobilization Plan, 8/3/64, RCA, FLC.

74 "Crisis in Race Relations: Rochester: Where a Race Riot Hit a 'Model' City."

75 Lt. Col. Rex Applegate, "New Riot Control Weapons," *Ordnance*, July–August 1964, 68.

76 "Rochester Plagued 3rd Night: Molotov Cocktails Hurled in Brooklyn," *Sun Sentinel*, August 27, 1964, RCA, FLC.

77 Mrs. Christine Drone to Lamb, 8/6/64, RCA, FLC.

78 Ibid.

79 Mrs. Evelyn Powell to Robert Wagner, 7/31/64, RCA, FLC.

80 Frederick Douglass, *Narrative of the Life of Frederick Douglass, An American Slave, Written by Himself*, 2nd ed., edited by David W. Blight (Boston: Bedford/St. Martins, 2003), 90.

81 Johnston to Lamb.

6

Segregation without Segregationists

How a White Community Avoided Integration

MARY BARR

The school bell rang as Anita Darrow, a suburban housewife, and her young daughter, Anne, drove by it. Seconds later, the doors were flung open. Students poured out. When Anne screamed, "Mommy, I didn't know there were black *children*," Darrow was overcome with guilt for raising her kids in the lily-white suburb of Winnetka, Illinois. Recalling the incident years later, she said it inspired her to join a small group of concerned mothers determined to desegregate Chicago's suburbs. Together the women would become the force behind a 1965 open housing campaign known as the North Shore Summer Project (NSSP).

Collectively, the communities of Evanston, Wilmette, Kenilworth, Winnetka, Glencoe, Highland Park, Lake Bluff, and Lake Forest are known as the North Shore. By 1910, railroad lines leading from Chicago made possible the growth of these chic residential suburbs. As wealthy whites left the city, the number of black southerners moving north grew. Whites acted quickly to contain these new migrants on Chicago's South and West sides. Black people who managed to move into the city's designated white neighborhoods were met with intimidation.[1] Rather than turn to violence, North Shore residents enacted measures of exclusion that kept their public image intact while ensuring that their neighborhoods remained off limits to African Americans not employed by white families. Service workers would have been the only black people Anne encountered before the drive into the city changed her worldview.

Most North Shore residents opposed fair housing. To keep their communities white, they turned to race-neutral policies such as strict zoning rules and land-use laws that prohibited construction of apartment complexes. This tactic froze out blacks and other working-class people, and enforced segregation. By framing housing discrimination in the language of liberalism, they disguised racial motivations with market interests.[2]

Blaming developers who added racial clauses to deeds, real estate agents who refused to work with black home buyers, and white neighbors whom they claimed not to want to upset, North Shore residents pretended they believed in integration while simultaneously they maintained Jim Crow suburbs. Only rarely did they say outright that they did not want black neighbors.[3] Yet, when fair housing activists tried to bring change to the North Shore, homeowners made sure they did not succeed. Their high social class enabled them to subdue pressures to integrate without appearing racist. Residential segregation in the North did not happen through individual prejudices, or because black people preferred black neighbors. It was a racial system embedded in social institutions and cultural practices.[4]

While the subtleties of northern discrimination could be difficult to prove, William Moyer, director of the American Friends Service Committee's (AFSC) Chicago fair housing program, saw similarities between northern real estate discrimination and southern lunch counter discrimination.[5] Moyer developed the idea for a suburban housing movement after participating in a voting rights campaign in Mississippi in 1964. "Chicago's system of separation of the races differs from Mississippi's only in degree," Moyer explained. "In Mississippi, the Ku Klux Klan burns churches. [In 1964,] in Chicago, three houses were burned to the ground because they were purchased by black citizens."[6] In both Mississippi and Chicago, specific culprits could be identified, making a direct-action campaign viable. Believing that the problem stemmed from misunderstanding, the North Shore movement set out to end discriminatory housing practices through education and peaceful persuasion.

Darrow's neighbor Henrietta Boal Moore, president of the Winnetka Human Relations Committee, was one of the North Shore liaisons for the AFSC's Home Opportunities Made Equal, Inc. (HOME), a listing service for minority buyers that included suburban properties. In 1964, a year before the North Shore campaign, she joined other wealthy socialites in the southern civil rights project, Wednesdays in Mississippi, a program that allowed affluent northern women to travel to Mississippi.

Like Moyer, Moore returned home ready to increase pressure on suburban homeowners unwilling to rent or sell to African Americans.

If not for a small bronze marker set in a stone base on the corner of the Winnetka Village green, residents living on the North Shore today would not know about the local movement that attempted to end residential segregation. The community commemorates Project organizers, but refuses to acknowledge that most local people opposed integration. The media is partly at fault for sugarcoating northern racism. During the summer of 1965, local presses covered fair housing campaign activities, but ignored resistance against it. The national media either turned a blind eye, or portrayed liberal whites as sympathetic to racial-justice initiatives. A *New York Times* article covered Martin Luther King Jr.'s visit to Winnetka and celebrated the large white audience eager to hear his message.[7] This chapter tells the underreported story of the 1965 North Shore Summer Project, the first direct-action civil rights movement in a suburban area, and the white "frontlash" resistance it inspired.[8]

North Shore residents hoodwinked integration activists, hid their true feelings, and signed petitions for open housing, but then opposed the effort. These deceptive acts undermined the Summer Project's educational strategy. Organizers set out to inform what they believed was a naive public about the suburban realities of segregation. The educational approach disregarded two fundamental realities: most white people did not want blacks as neighbors, and many black families did not want to subject themselves to humiliation and ostracism just to live in hostile communities. Finally, education tactics as a means of advancing racial integration ignored a structural reality, namely, that no matter their credit history, African Americans had trouble securing mortgages to purchase homes.[9] It was not individual naivety, but calculated perniciousness that advanced racial separation in the suburbs.

In the twenty-first century, less than 1 percent of the North Shore's population, excluding Evanston, is African American. These segregated communities ignore the histories that created them: most North Shore residents did not want to live with blacks and defended housing segregation tooth and nail, even while purporting to be against it. Chicago's North Shore continues to reflect this history of northern Jim Crow.

Thursday Afternoon Meetings (1961)

Henrietta Boal was born in Winnetka in 1915. She grew up in a rambling, big house built in 1879 for her grandfather, Lorenzo Johnson, a railroad tycoon, and attended Vassar College.[10] A member of the class of 1937, she belonged to a generation of women that was empowered in ways that others were not.[11] Still, she was not expected to put her degree to practical use and, in 1938, married a Harvard man, Philip Wyatt Moore Jr.[12] Taking care of her five children occupied most of Moore's time until her husband died unexpectedly of a heart attack in 1954. At this transformative moment, Moore, now thirty-eight years old and a single mother, took over his business, unusual for the time. She found companionship with other North Shore women who were also confident, well-educated, and independent.

In 1961, Moore joined a small group that included Anita Darrow, Dora Williams (also Vassar alumnae), and Jean Cleland, whose husband was a HOME board member. All had been involved in the AFSC's Chicago fair housing program and were frustrated by the slow pace of their work, so they decided to act privately and reach out to neighbors who were selling homes. The *Wilmette Life*, a weekly newspaper, listed local sales in its real estate section. The paper was published every Thursday. So the women met later in the day to gather the names and numbers of residents who had listed homes for sale. They would then call and ask homeowners to sell their property on a nondiscriminatory basis. More times than not, the calls were cut short when the person hung up, indicative of what people really thought about integration. The origins of the 1965 North Shore Summer Project can be traced back to these weekly meetings.[13]

A mission to create more diversity for their children's cultural enrichment as well as a tradition of noblesse oblige drove these women's pursuit of justice in open housing. Darrow's grandfather, the founder of Weiboldt's department store, established a philanthropic foundation in 1921.[14] Moore's family had railroad money, and Williams was heir to the DuPont chemical company fortune. With resources and a shared purpose, the group was well positioned to bring about social change. In February 1963, they sponsored a full-page advertisement in the *Winnetka Talk*, another local paper, calling for fair housing on the North

Shore and pointing out that though a century had passed since the signing of the Emancipation Proclamation, black people had not reaped the full benefits of citizenship. Sixty-seven Winnetka residents signed the letter—many of whom did not see their own discriminatory actions as denying rights to others.[15]

For most black activists, integrating the suburbs was not a high priority. In Chicago, twenty miles south of Winnetka, anger over public school policy was the principle source of black unrest.[16] The Coordinating Council of Community Organizations (CCCO), a broad interracial coalition of Chicago civil rights, religious, and community groups, founded in 1962 by Al Raby, targeted school superintendent Benjamin Willis, who had become the symbol of Chicago segregation by placing mobile classrooms near overcrowded black schools to avoid integrating less crowded white schools.

Other civil rights organizations such as the Temporary Woodlawn Organization (TWO) focused on repairing the ghetto. TWO formed in 1962 and sought to eliminate slums in Chicago's Woodlawn neighborhood using rent strikes as its tool for change. To be sure, some black civil rights organizations supported fair housing initiatives. Traditional race advancement organizations such as the National Association for the Advancement of Colored People (NAACP) and the Urban League sought change through legislation and joined forces to support passage of an Illinois State fair housing law. Using direct-action tactics, Chicago chapters of the Congress of Racial Equality (CORE) also pushed for open occupancy. CORE staged sit-ins in Hyde Park beginning in 1962 and sponsored demonstrations favoring open occupancy in the North Shore suburb of Deerfield in 1963. These civil rights activities did not garner change from North Shore residents, who were experts at concealing their own prejudices and liked to use the media to support the fiction that southerners were the culprits of racial injustice.

The biggest news stories of 1963 included protests of downtown businesses in Birmingham, Alabama.[17] Searing images of police officers attacking protestors with water hoses overshadowed efforts both in Chicago and in Mississippi where the Council of Federated Organizations (COFO), a coalition of major civil rights groups, including the Student Non-Violent Coordinating Committee (SNCC), was trying to empower voters. To gain media attention, and thus a national audience, members of SNCC made the controversial decision to recruit white students from northern colleges to be part of an elaborate voter registration campaign named the 1964 Mississippi Freedom Summer Project (MFSP). Moore's oldest son, Phil, a senior at Harvard, and his classmate, Geoff Cowan, volunteered. The boys' mothers mobilized to support them with a plan that would join Jim Crow North and South.

Wednesdays in Mississippi (1964)

Polly Spiegel Cowan was a prominent New Yorker and social activist. She was also the volunteer executive director of Wednesdays in Mississippi (WIMS), a civil rights initiative sponsored by the National Council of Negro Women (NCNW). In the spring of 1964, Cowan and Dorothy Height, president of NCNW, came up with the idea of sending teams of middle-aged northern women south to support COFO initiatives. They thought WIMS participants could mediate racial tensions by befriending southern women.

Cowan grew up in Kenilworth, Illinois. As with other North Shore suburbs, Kenilworth's founders acted early to keep minority groups out. In 1889, developer Joseph Sears purchased land that would become the Village of Kenilworth. To ensure an elite class of residents he wrote building restrictions into the founding documents, including large lot sizes, high standards of construction, and sales to "Caucasians only."[18] A Jewish couple, Lena and Modie Spiegel (of Spiegel catalogue fame), took advantage of Sears's vague language when they bought a house in Kenilworth to raise Polly and her three siblings sometime around 1910. Over the years, and although the family achieved a degree of stature among their peers, "they remained outsiders."[19] According to sociologist James Loewen, "It is generally thought that one outcome [of the Spiegels] was to buttress the practice of enforcing restrictive covenants," clauses that specified "white protestants only."[20] Kenilworth residents had closed ranks and loopholes. Growing up in the segregated North shaped Cowan's racial consciousness and future activism.

As the WIMS project coordinator, her job was to assemble interracial, interfaith teams of prominent northern and midwestern women, members of what she called the "Cadillac crowd."[21] To do that, she drew from her own social circle. Henrietta Moore was an ideal candidate; like other WIMS members, she was a middle-aged college graduate and a member of various community boards and social-welfare organizations, including AFSC's HOME and the Winnetka Human Relations Committee. Going to Mississippi to support her son pushed the geographical and ideological boundaries of her activism.

Seven teams visited Mississippi in the summer of 1964. Cowan asked Moore to be the coordinator for Chicago Team 6, which was scheduled to visit Mississippi August 11–13. The interracial team consisted of six white women from the North Shore (including Moore; sisters-in-law Jean and Miriam Davis, who were also open housing advocates; Lucy Montgomery, a SNCC fundraiser; Narcissa King, and Sylvia Weinberg), and two African American civic leaders, Chicagoans Etta Moten Barnett and Arnetta Wallace. Two years earlier, Barnett and Wallace had sat together at the head table of a Human Rights Dinner sponsored by the interracial American Friendship Club. Barnett, whose husband was the founder of the Associated Negro Press, was a well-known entertainer and philanthropist. Wallace was a member of the National Council of Negro Women's executive committee. Although their stories are not as well known, northern blacks, like their southern counterparts, were also active in trying to overcome racism in their hometowns.

The flight carrying the Chicago team arrived in Jackson on the evening of Tuesday, August 11. Local WIMS staff greeted the ladies, who were whisked away to drop off luggage and eat dinner. Once they landed, local Jim Crow laws required the women to separate. The next morning, they drove to Canton, Mississippi, where they visited a freedom school, voter registration project, and community center. On Thursday, they returned home, where Chicago's segregated housing policies required them to separate again.

Back on the North Shore, the white women did not abandon Mississippi. They continued to support COFO projects by giving lectures, fundraising, and holding book drives. With a heightened awareness of racial struggle, they had gained new ways of seeing their own community problems. Chicago had its own variant of Jim Crow segregation, undergirded by separate and unequal housing, and at its core was not different from the communities they had witnessed in their travels. "Many of us who live here have expressed our deep concern and indignation about events in Alabama and Mississippi, but are unwilling to address the closed communities we call home," the women wrote.[22] The prospect of a summer project was beginning to take form. What they did not expect was that, in parallel ways, North Shore residents would resist change as strongly as white Mississippians.

The great majority of people living on the North Shore did not want to be considered bigots. Individually, they agreed that African Americans should have equal opportunities in Winnetka and elsewhere. Suburbanites expressed sympathy for integrated schools or voting rights—targets of the southern civil rights movement—but deep down did not see open housing as an equivalent. On the surface, there seemed to be widespread support for integration. This was not a coincidence, according to Thomas Sugrue, a leading historian on the northern civil rights movement. "[M]any of the towns [in the North] with the most vocal open housing organizations . . . had little affordable housing stock."[23] The irony was that while black people could not buy property in Winnetka, they could work there. Most large homes in the area had servants' quarters. This explains why the 1960 census recorded 252 black residents in Winnetka out of a total population of 13,368.[24] North Shore Summer Project organizers saw no reason to doubt their neighbors' integrity and were convinced they could counter misperceptions with facts. They believed that the segregated society of the North Shore reflected the wishes of only a small percentage of the community, demonstrating how successfully northern racism was able to mask itself. They underestimated their neighbors' bigotry.

The North Shore Summer Project (1965)

The American Friends Service Committee (AFSC), an international civil rights organization founded by Quakers in 1917, organized its Chicago Housing Opportunity Program (HOP) in 1951 after a white mob of four thousand attacked an apartment building housing a single black family in Cicero, Illinois. In 1960, under the leadership of William Moyer, HOP created HOME, Inc., a listing service for minority buyers that served as a channel for suburban sellers and minority buyers to make contact and whose philosophy resembled WIMS's bridge-building philosophy. HOP also established fair housing committees in about twenty-five suburbs to keep a record of houses that were for sale or rent on a nondiscriminatory basis. On Chicago's North Shore, the committees were scattered through what was to become the Summer Project area.[25]

Working with property owners to make individual suburban homes available for sale to black families met with modest success. HOP records indicated that there were twenty thousand qualified black families in Chicago who wanted to buy homes, and North Shore agents had serviced only .025% of that total in recent years.[26] Moyer thought more could be accomplished if the independent housing committees redirected their energies to develop a joint program. At the invitation of Reverend Buckner Coe, fair housing advocates met at the First Congregational Church in the North Shore suburb of Wilmette on January 21, 1965. It was at this meeting that the idea of the North Shore Summer Project took shape.[27] A steering committee consisting of AFSC staff and local community members was assembled. During the meeting, the group evaluated the slow pace of their work. The open-housers trusted their neighbors and thought they could rally them to demand a change in real estate practices. The real estate industry was cast as an enemy that had to be conquered.[28]

Virtually all brokers operating on the North Shore belonged to one trade organization, the Evanston–North Shore Board of Realtors (ENSBR). If the extent of its overall authority was in doubt, its role in effectively backing housing discrimination was clear. The board controlled its members' policies through a written constitution, a central office, and a monthly newsletter. With its far-reaching power, ENSBR effectively kept homes out of the reach of minority buyers: through a multiple listing service (homes listed for sale by member agencies); by refusing to list homes for sale on a nondiscriminatory basis; and by declining to service black home seekers. Statistical data illustrate the results of these discriminatory practices. The board listed over two thousand homes for sale in 1964, yet only five black families moved to the North Shore that year. Realtors relied on a conservative rhetoric of individual rights to defend their policies. Arguing that "nobody wants to sell to Negros," "the community isn't ready for it," and "the owner has the right to sell to persons of his choice," they claimed to be acting simply as agents for their clients and therefore powerless to do anything about it.[29] Because brokers projected blame for their actions on residents, open housing advocates concluded that agents might adopt nondiscriminatory policies with reassurance from residents.

Local residents were not ready to give such a mandate because they did not care if there was a problem or not. An almost insurmountable obstacle confronting the housing committees was the apathy of most suburbanites regarding racial discrimination. Residents were white and prosperous, and free to buy any home they could afford. They did not see the racial composition of their suburbs as being related to urban ghettos where inadequate housing, high unemployment, poor schools, and poverty were the flip side of affluence. Social isolation ensured that North Shore residents lacked cross-racial understanding and therefore made decisions based on stereotypes and prejudice. While it was the exclusion of nonwhite families from North Shore suburbs that had created these ghettos, the media's distorted portrayals of black people let whites believe otherwise. In a rare transparent moment, a North Shore resident wrote a letter to a local paper explaining why he opposed integration: "We cannot afford to have Negroes moving in on us in the suburbs. I understand they are lazy, shiftless, and uninterested in community affairs."[30] Still, Summer Project leaders believed that housing discrimination stemmed largely from misunderstanding and only in part from prejudice and bigotry, both of which could be remedied by gently educating North Shore communities.

Project members set out to challenge the collective conscience of the North Shore, a goal that was based on the liberal premise that compassionate white Americans would see racism as a travesty of justice once they truly understood its impact on black families.[31] At the same time, organizers were careful not to accuse residents of wrongdoing for fear they might alienate them. The group set its mild-mannered agenda:

> (1) Publicly dramatize the fact that Negro citizens are being denied the right to choose where they want to live in Chicago's North Shore. (2) "Register" white home sellers to sell their houses on a nondiscriminatory basis. (3) Encourage North Shore citizens and organizations to publicly demand that the real estate system serve all citizens without regard to race, color, creed or national origin. (4) Work with Negro families as they try to live in the North Shore neighborhoods of their choice.[32]

Organizers decidedly linked Mississippi to Chicago's North Shore. The Summer Project was designed to dramatize the issue of the closed community in the North much in the same way that Mississippi's closed society in the South had been illuminated. Black people were asking to be served by realtors and treated like first-class citizens, but they were being turned away, just as courthouses in the South turned them away. Northerners had expressed outrage at southern racists believing they were superior. Organizers drew parallels to southern Jim Crow, hoping whites would take a look at themselves in the mirror. At every turn, North Shore organizers sought to identify with the Mississippi Freedom Summer Project.

The tactical and ideological imprint of the Mississippi Freedom Summer Project was everywhere evident in NSSP's agenda. The name "Summer Project" itself was inspired by the Mississippi campaign and consciously copied in an attempt to transfer its glamour to quiet, tree-shaded suburban streets.[33] As with MFSP, student volunteers provided manpower for the North Shore Project, but instead of registering voters, they registered homeowners willing to sell on a nondiscriminatory basis. The organization's prospectus drew connections to the South even when the comparison was not warranted. For example, it exaggerated the risk students would take when stating that volunteers would need to dig deep to summon "the same courage, stamina and guts that enabled COFO workers not to give up last summer when the going got rough."[34]

The most obvious connection between the two movements was the returning volunteers. Most of the suburban participants had attended either a march or a rally and had witnessed nonviolent direct action, alongside such civil rights giants as Martin Luther King Jr., John Lewis, and Fannie Lou Hamer. In 1962, Dora Williams had worked with King in Albany, Georgia. Henrietta Moore drew from a broad repertoire of educational and persuasive techniques and activities that she had learned in Mississippi with WIMS. North Shore women had marched in Selma for voting rights, in March 1965, alongside Viola Luizzo, a housewife from Detroit, murdered by the Ku Klux Klan following a King rally in Montgomery. Back safely at home, the women did not fear for their lives. Instead they were ostracized and faced bitter resentment from neighbors who smiled and pretended to be on their side. As a reminder that she had accomplished the impossible twice before, Williams carried a typewritten note in her purse that read, "Age 18: Suspended from Vassar for breaking the college rules (they don't have them anymore). Age 50:

Jailed in Georgia for breaking the Jim Crow rules (they don't have them anymore either)."[35]

What these organizers had seen down South convinced them of the need to bring the struggle for racial justice home to their local communities. But it was easier to go to far-off places in the South to confront racism than it was to confront neighbors at home. The hypocrisy was not lost on them. Mississippi had been described as a "closed society." "The same could be said about white neighborhoods in the North that excluded Negro families."[36] At some point they must have also faced their own complicity and to their credit they decided to do something about it. As the Summer Project's founding documents laid out, "Now it is time to do something about our own hometown."[37]

The North Shore Project was well thought out and tightly organized. As in the South, women led civil rights organizing in the Midwest, often doing much of the day-to-day work. In the suburban context, unlike in the South, most women were white. Even as the Summer Project empowered women, it still held rigid views of the roles they could play. With the exception of Henrietta Moore, who served on both the steering and executive committees, men were assigned to key positions at the top. Reverend Emory G. Davis of Bethel AME Church in Evanston was appointed chairman of the steering committee, and William Moyer, who headed HOP, was named executive director.[38] Because women had been on the ground locally as members of AFSC housing committees, they were named town chairs for each of the participating suburbs. Women also oversaw most essential tasks divided among ten subcommittees. Representatives from the subcommittees formed an executive board that assumed overall responsibility for the project.

Recruiting and caring for the student volunteers was regarded as women's work. Informational flyers were sent to colleges and universities. Organizers targeted the Chicago area: "The primary sources of potential candidates will be through colleges on the North Shore, students whose homes are on the north shore, but who go away to school, and Negro students who live in Chicago."[39] Students had to be intelligent and articulate in their interactions with homeowners. They would also bear a heavy responsibility for the program's success and would have to cope with a variety of difficult and important situations. After careful review, a short list of applicants received in-person interviews. Nearly one hundred students were chosen. Jean Cleland, who, with Moore and Williams, had made phone calls to homeowners in 1961, oversaw the maintenance committee charged with housing, feeding, and transporting student volunteers.[40]

Moore's daughter, Lesley, was among the few high school graduates recruited. She planned to start Pitzer College in the fall of 1965. A few students from outside the area received room and board from North Shore residents. The Moore family hosted Grace Meigs Dammann, also a recent high school graduate. The clear majority of young people were college students. Of this number, nearly everyone attended colleges in the Chicago area. A few students from northern colleges had enrolled in exchange programs with southern institutions. Almost all the students were from the North Shore, either residents or in college there—carrying out the position that "this is a local problem with local people working to solve it."[41] Organizers hoped to recruit an equal number of white and black college students, believing it was "important to have persons in its project representing a wide variety of religions, nationalities, and races."[42]

Recruiting black students proved difficult. One reason why most volunteers were white was that students had to be able to forego summer jobs. Black students did not live in the area and would have to pay the extra expense, above their ten-dollar weekly stipend, of commuting from Chicago or lodge with a North Shore family. As a result, most of the volunteers were white, upper-middle-class college students for whom the issue of money was not a concern.

On June 25, 1965, student volunteers arrived for orientation. For a week, they were schooled on race and housing on the North Shore. They learned local real estate practices and terminology. Henrietta Moore and AFSC staff gave workshops on the history and methods of nonviolence. Steering committee member and chair of the Winnetka committee, Dora Williams, who had also been part of the 1961 group, hosted a reception for students at her Winnetka home. Williams, like the other women, had the support of their politically involved husbands. In 1964, Dora's husband, Lynn Williams, unsuccessfully challenged incumbent Donald Rumsfeld for a seat in Congress. The Williamses invited Lerone Bennett Jr., senior editor at Chicago-based *Ebony Magazine*, to give a welcome speech. His words inspired the crowd: "All Americans are indebted to you for taking up this fight in this place and at this time. For white liberals cannot convert anyone in America until they convert themselves and their constituencies. It is something to send money to Selma, but it is more to give Negroes jobs in Chicago and to fight for open occupancy on the North Shore. It is something to march on Montgomery, but it is more to march through the heart of the church and in the streets of Winnetka."[43] Real estate discrimination had restricted black housing choices. Brokers would not make their listings available on a nondiscriminatory basis without consensus from a misinformed community. The time to educate homeowners had come.

For the next eight weeks, students interviewed white homeowners about their willingness to participate in an open market. Beginning on July 5, they followed a daily routine that was highly structured. Each of the participating suburbs had rented a storefront and placed a large banner outside that read, "North Shore Summer Project Freedom Center (town name) Headquarters."[44] Students arrived by 9:00 a.m. to receive lists of families selling homes through ENSBR. Student canvassers then visited home sellers in pairs. They were instructed to be polite, use friendly persuasion to get answers, and leave gracefully if faced with resistance. When student volunteers arrived on doorsteps they introduced themselves by name, explaining that they were NSSP fieldworkers, and then conducted their interviews.

Students were instructed not to veer from the well-designed questionnaire. Data collected by students would be compiled into a report and released to the public in August through the media. Homeowners had received letters about the project before it started. Students began each interview by asking residents if they had any questions about the letter. Then they asked, "Will you show your home to any buyer your realtor brings regardless of the buyer's race, color, creed or national origin?" If homeowners answered "yes," they were asked to sign pledge cards (eventually shown to brokers and African American buyers) and petitions. Homeowners who answered "no" were asked to explain their decision. Students gave a scripted response: "If we overcome this (these) objection(s) will you show your home to any buyer regardless of the buyer's race, color, creed, or national origin?"

Drawing from information received during orientation, students had plenty of evidence to counter resistance to fair housing. For example, if a resident expressed concern about plummeting property values, students cited findings from *Property Values and Race* by Dr. Luigi Laurenti, who had concluded that when nonwhites enter a previously all-white neighborhood consisting primarily of single-family homes, prices of residential property in the area will probably not decline and may very well rise.[45] If a homeowner produced a property deed stating that the home must be sold to Christian Caucasians, students reminded owners that the 1948 Supreme Court decision in *Shelley v. Kraemer* held that courts could not enforce racial covenants. If homeowners feared that a sale to one black family would open the floodgates to other minorities, students explained that North Shore property was too expensive for blockbusting to be a real possibility. Rapid block-by-block change and neighborhood transition happened in relatively low-income areas usually adjacent to large black ghettos bursting at their seams.

A number of students commented on the hostility they faced. During an interview conducted in southeast Evanston, a student volunteer reported that a woman became "very emotional." She stood behind her screen door and scolded him: "Negroes want to live next door so they can 'marry our daughters.'" According to another student, there were no "violent reactions" per se; instead persons opposed to selling to minorities had been "polite in their refusal."[46] Overall, northerners practiced a greater subtlety of justification for their bigotry than southerners. Property owners knew how to be discreet. They said they were opposed to an open market by projecting blame on racist neighbors. By blaming neighbors, realtors, or extolling "rights," they avoided responsibility for their own choices. They persuaded themselves and others that segregation came to them from without.

African American home buyers were another important component of the Summer Project. They were sent into the field to test realtors and record anecdotal evidence of residential discrimination. Their stories were used to expose and publicize injustices. As was the case with black students, the Project struggled to recruit "pioneers," or black middle-class couples that would be the first to buy houses in white neighborhoods. African American families did not necessarily want to live where they were not welcome and feared for their children's safety if they happened to be successful. Reflecting on the summer, Moore wrote, "The problem was that there were very few Negro homeseekers with the time and the special courage necessary to face the rebuffs, the equivocations they met in real estate offices."[47]

Harriett Robinet and her husband, a physics professor at the University of Illinois, who had been living in a small, cramped Chicago apartment for five years, wanted to live in Winnetka and were one of the few black couples willing to give it a try. Schools were a priority, and the North Shore had the best. The couple was refused by three realtors before giving up. Eventually, they bought a house in Oak Park, a suburb west of Chicago. Robinet described the precautions that her family had to take when moving into their new home:

> The Illinois Commission of Human Relations suggests that neighbors not see the Negro family near the house before the actual moving day. I hadn't even been inside our new home yet. The moving must be fast and professional, done in the middle of the day, in the middle of the week—no weekend idlers nearby. And the white neighbors must be completely informed before the move-in takes place. Two hours before we arrived, everyone on the block received a mimeographed notice from the village manager, explaining that a Negro family was buying a house on the street from a Presbyterian minister and his wife. Then to dispel rumors about us, the notice described our family and our background briefly but thoroughly.[48]

The Robinet family would always be a spectacle to their neighbors, and they would constantly have to prove their worth. The question was, were good schools and safe neighborhoods worth it?

Collecting the data was one thing. Disseminating information to make a difference was another. While northerners still reveled in the notion that they were not as bad as the southerners on the issue of civil rights, the proponents of NSSP still yearned for a similar national spotlight on their movements. Therefore, organizers made every effort to associate the Summer Project with the national black freedom struggle. But the Summer Project could not count on racist police to manufacture drama and sympathy. Housing segregation did not make for compelling television. Viewers had come to expect violent bodily injuries, and when violence was enacted against property, it did not have the same effect.

They also could not count on the media. Weekly suburban newspapers provided coverage, but the national media failed to report it. In the summer of 1965, outbreaks in Los Angeles and on Chicago's Westside, after a black woman was killed by a firetruck, made headline news.

The daily metropolitan news did not pay much attention to the North Shore fair housing struggle. A fulltime NSSP publicity director could get attention from the local community presses but was unable to gain the interest of the national media. Usually the voice of the status quo, these smaller community presses did help the women publicize Project events and activities. Since the national media were also the northern media, editors may have lost some of their enthusiasm for pointing out the region's flaws. Instead, Summer Project workers doubled down to give the project visibility. Notable scholar-activists headlined public meetings. Such luminaries included Reverend C. T. Vivian, renowned historian John Hope Franklin, and the most popular civil rights leader of the time, Martin Luther King Jr. These educational events were well attended by project participants, but they never reached the whole community, except the King rally.

The rally that featured Martin Luther King Jr. was the Project's logistical tour de force. Ten thousand people attended the rally without incident. The Winnetka police chief directed a brigade of police who controlled traffic and crowds efficiently and effectively. The relatively high social class of Winnetka's residents meant that they subscribed to a certain standard of public decorum, and they had the resources to ensure it. King, who was then president of the Southern Christian Leadership Conference (SCLC), was in Chicago as part of his ten-day people-to-people tour of northern cities. Demonstrating a strong emphasis on labor and economic challenges, this tour signaled the civil rights icon's increasing focus on the urban ghettos of the North and his insistence on including more prominently northern challenges in the ongoing southern-based civil rights struggle. Indeed, his visit was timely for NSSP, a movement whose existence underscored that trend. With the local attention it received, it was described as the Project's greatest tangible accomplishment. The rally enabled the Summer Project to associate itself with the national civil rights movement in a way that it had never done before and to take advantage of Dr. King's charismatic appeal.

"You Would Do Us All a Big Favor If You'd Just Move out of Winnetka to the West Side of Chicago. We Wouldn't Miss You at All."

A civil rights march through the North Shore villages on August 29, 1965, marked the end of the North Shore Summer Project. It was a beautiful Sunday afternoon and Selma-styled, confrontational nonviolent tactics were on full display. The pace was brisk. Moyer, John Lewis, who was then president of SNCC, and Reverend Davis led a line of marchers that stretched a couple of blocks. Demonstrators walked four abreast. There was no sign of Moore or the other North Shore women who had spear-headed the campaign at the front of the line. When marchers reached Evanston, they paused for silent prayer in front of the Evanston–North Shore Board of Realtors' offices. The crowd then descended on Bent Park to celebrate two months of fair housing advocacy work. Reverend Davis addressed the crowd: "The North Shore Summer Project ends. But the civil rights movement is on the North Shore to stay. We've proved we can march at home as well as in Selma." John Lewis was also a featured speaker at the rally. There is nothing wrong with being an agitator, he said, "if you're agitating for the right thing." He continued, "It's like a washing machine shaking dirt out of the clothes."[49] The crowd sang several civil rights songs, including "We Shall Overcome," the anthem of the southern civil rights movement.

The event was not merely about exhibiting solidarity. Organizers used the event as a forum to present a ten-page report reflecting the outcomes of eight weeks of intensive research that revealed the realities in a racially segregated society. At a press conference after the march, organizers and volunteers continued to distribute the report. This detailed report laid bare the salient facts backed by solid statistical details. Four hundred and sixty-two homeowners with property for sale were interviewed, 73 percent of whom said they were willing to show their homes on a nondiscriminatory basis. Fifty-seven percent said they had never discussed the issue with their agent, because they did not place restrictions themselves and they assumed that their home was being shown to all potential buyers. Of the respondents, 322 said they were not influenced by the racial or religious composition of a prospective neighborhood. There were 209 homeowners who had refused to be interviewed; however, even if they had responded negatively, that would still mean that 50 percent of homeowners were in favor of nondiscriminatory selling. Additionally, of the 1,560 property owners who were interviewed and did not have homes for sale, 1,277 said that "if a Negro moved next door to them they would not move, not agitate for removal, nor 'do anything.'" Of owners who were not moving, 82 percent said they would accept Negroes as neighbors. These numbers represent "only a willingness *not* to move out and *not* to protest if a black family moved next door," according to Phyllis Palmer's study of a white neighborhood in Washington, DC. "Passive acceptance did not indicate a willingness to take positive action."[50]

In a nutshell, the report concluded that the realtors were the primary culprits of racist housing discrimination: "The realtor has obviously conducted his business according to his own fears and prejudices, not according to the unknown wishes of the seller."[51] Reverend Davis personally presented the report to Louis A. Pfaff, president of ENSBR. The dissemination of the report and its submission to the main culprits of the problem marked the end of the North Shore Summer Project.

With help from local college student volunteers home for school break, and black home buyers wanting to move to the suburbs, organizers had worked to diversify the North Shore through door-to-door interviews and weekly lectures given by prominent civil rights activists. White suburbanites had refused to budge. While organizers borrowed from and were influenced by the southern movement, they also had their own distinct and unique strategies. Their approach was mild-mannered and polite. A rally that featured King seemed to appease residents more than challenge them. Nonviolent tactics employed by the group had the additional benefit of placating local leaders who were more concerned with public image than diversification. Student volunteers used a "softsell" approach aimed at convincing people to do the right thing but never confronted them with their inaction. The community at large had been encouraged to attend educational events, but most people never bothered. Twelve thousand and fifty-nine North Shore residents had signed a pledge stating their support of open housing but no homes were sold or rented to African Americans that summer. Whites were skilled at explaining to themselves and others that segregation was not their fault. By focusing their civil rights news on the southern states, the national media affirmed the false perceptions northerners had of themselves.

A commitment to fair housing exacted a high price on movement actors. Throughout the summer, organizers received hate mail and threatening phone calls. Henrietta Moore was more able than the others to shrug off intimidation and liked to joke that she was going to sell her home to Dr. King just to annoy her detractors. After the civil rights leader visited Winnetka, Dora Williams received this anonymous note: "Mrs. Williams—You would do us all a big favor if you'd just move out of Winnetka to the west side of Chicago. We wouldn't miss you at all. . . . May God have mercy on your soul. If you have so much leisure time, put it to good use instead of causing your neighbors trouble. The white boys are dying for their country while the negroes are demonstrating. WAKE UP SISTER"![52] Jean Davis lived next door to the Rumsfelds (politician Donald Rumsfeld's parents). They shunned her family and scrutinized every move Davis made. Although they never said it, Davis knew they were worried that she might sell her house to a black family. These reprisals were mild in comparison to those faced by African American home buyers and religious leaders.

Very few African American home buyers were involved, and those who were faced indignation and dehumanization. Emory Davis was forced to resign from Evanston's historically black Bethel AME Church. The congregation disagreed with the minister over the role of the church in civil rights activities. According to a church spokesperson, "[W]e don't believe that demonstrations accomplish very much. Civil rights will be advanced when people's hearts are changed, and demonstrations won't do that."[53] Yet changing the hearts and minds of residents is exactly what the Summer Project had tried to do. Two months earlier, Reverend Buckner Coe had been forced out of Wilmette's all-white First Congregational Church. Members had made it clear that they thought he had "gone too far" in speaking out for integrated housing.[54] Northerners had fashioned themselves as different from southerners, but their actions spoke louder than their words.

Nevertheless, the Summer Project had a lasting effect on its participants, who intensified their commitment to civil rights and remained active throughout their lives. It drew attention to closed housing issues and inspired Martin Luther King Jr.'s Chicago Freedom Movement the following year. The North Shore Project was also important because it was a *northern* project. By transferring the summer project idea to the North and by focusing attention on the white community, the North Shore Project underlined the truth that the race problem in America is a white one and a national one.

NOTES

1 Andrew Wiese, *Places of Their Own: African American Suburbanization in the Twentieth Century* (Chicago: University of Chicago Press, 2004), p. 25; see Allan H. Spear, *Black Chicago: The Making of a Negro Ghetto, 1890–1920* (Chicago: University of Chicago Press, 1967), especially chapters 1 and 11; William M. Tuttle Jr., *Race Riot: Chicago in the Red Summer of 1919* (Chicago: University of Illinois Press, 1996); Stephen Grant Meyer, *As Long as They Don't Move Next Door: Segregation and Racial Conflict in American Neighborhoods* (Lanham, MD: Rowman & Littlefield, 2000), especially chapters 2 and 7.

2 David Freund, *Colored Property: State Policy and White Racial Politics in Suburban America* (Chicago: University of Chicago Press, 2007).

3 See Eduardo Bonilla-Silva, *Racism without Racists: Color-Blind Racism and the Persistence of Racial Inequality in America* (Lanham, MD: Rowman & Littlefield, 2018), for more on how whites justify racial inequalities.

4 For an in-depth look at a northern city that boasts an image of racial harmony even as it continues to produce racial disparities, see Mary Barr, *Friends Disappear: The Battle for Racial Equality in Evanston* (Chicago: University of Chicago Press, 2014).

5 On the North Shore they advocated for an interracial housing development in Deerfield in 1959. They established Home Opportunities Made Equal, Inc. (HOME), a fair housing listing service for minority buyers that included suburban properties. The organization understood that both local leadership and grassroots participation were necessary for long-term change in all-white communities.

6 James R. Ralph Jr., *Northern Protest: Martin Luther King Jr., Chicago, and the Civil Rights Movement* (Cambridge, MA: Harvard University Press, 1993), pp. 99–100.

7 Austin C. Wehrwein, "Dr. King Attends Winnetka Rally: Wealthy Suburb of Chicago Fails to Halt Address," *New York Times*, July 26, 1965, p. 12.

8 Michael Barkun and James Levine, "Protest in Suburbia: Case Study of a Direct-Action Movement," *Syracuse Law Review*, 21 (1968–1969).

9 Beryl Satter, *Family Properties: How the Struggle over Race and Real Estate Transformed Chicago and Urban America* (New York: Picador, 2009).

10 "Upper-class WASP families educated their children at colleges such as Harvard, Princeton, Yale, and Vassar," according to E. Digby Baltzell in *Judgement and Sensibility: Religion and Stratification* (Piscataway, NJ: Transaction, 1994), p. 8.

11 Nevitt Sanford, *Self and Society: Social Change and Individual Development* (Palo Alto, CA: Atherton Press, 1966), p. 257.

12 "Henrietta Boal Becomes Bride of Philip Moore: Repeat Vows on Staircase of Winnetka Home," *Chicago Tribune*, November 27, 1938.

13 Gail Schecter, "The North Shore Summer Project: 'We're Going to Open Up the Whole North Shore,'" in *The Chicago Freedom Movement: Martin Luther King Jr. and Civil Rights Activism in the North*, eds. Mary Lou Finley et al. (Lexington: University Press of Kentucky, 2016).

14 "Wieboldt Left a Legacy That Returns Favor: Foundation Set Up by Retailer Gives Back to the Community," *Chicago Tribune*, May 19, 1996.

15 *Winnetka Talk*, February 23, 1963. Also see WTTW broadcast "Civil Rights on the North Shore: Bringing the Movement Home," by Rich Samuels, January 2002.

16 James R. Ralph Jr., *Northern Protest: Martin Luther King Jr., Chicago, and the Civil Rights Movement* (Cambridge, MA: Harvard University Press, 1993), p. 14.

17 Gene Roberts and Hank Klibanoff, *The Race Beat: The Press, the Civil Rights Movement, and the Awakening of a Nation* (New York: Vintage, 2007), chapter 19.

18 Colleen Browne Kilner, *Joseph Sears and His Kenilworth: The Dreamer and the Dream* (Kenilworth, IL: Kenilworth Historical Society, 1969).

19 Michael H. Ebner, *Creating Chicago's North Shore: A Suburban History* (Chicago: University of Chicago Press, 1989), p. 230.

20 James W. Loewen, *Sundown Towns: A Hidden Dimension of American Racism* (New York: New Press, 2005).

21 Debbie Z. Harwell, *Wednesdays in Mississippi: Proper Ladies Working for Radical Change, Freedom Summer 1964* (Jackson: University Press of Mississippi, 2014), p. 46.

22 "A Statement of Purpose," n.d., University of Illinois–Chicago Archives, North Shore Summer Project Collection, Box 1, Folder 13.

23 Thomas Sugrue, *Sweet Land of Liberty: The Forgotten Struggle for Civil Rights in the North* (New York: Random House, 2009), p. 424.

24 1960 US census.

25 "Housing Opportunities Program," n.d., University of Illinois–Chicago Archives, American Friends Service Committee Records, Box 46, Folder 17.

26 "Prospectus of the North Shore Summer Project," n.d., University of Illinois–Chicago Archives, North Shore Summer Project Collection, Box 1, Folder 12.

27 Letter inviting members of HOME, Inc., to Wilmette meeting, written by William Moyer, executive director, American Friends Service Committee Archives Philadelphia, n.d.

28 Letter to Mr. Lewis Pfaff, President, Evanston–North Shore Board of Realtors, written by Emory G. Davis, Chairman, NSSP Steering Committee, Martin Bickham Papers, University of Illinois–Chicago Archives, June 29, 1965.

29 "Evanston Real Estate Brokers' Council Adopts Policy against 'Forced Housing,'" *Evanston Review*, May 27, 1965, p. 19.

30 *Winnetka Talk*, Public Forum, March 1964.

31 Gunnar Myrdal alleged that northern whites were generally ignorant of the situation facing African Americans. He noted, "[T]o get publicity is of the highest strategic importance to the Negro people," given the pivotal role of the press in the civil rights movement. Roberts and Klibanoff, *The Race Beat*, p. 6.

32 "Student Recruitment Brochure," n.d., University of Illinois–Chicago Archives, North Shore Summer Project Collection, Box 1, Folder 13.

33 Michael Barkun and James Levine, "Protest in Suburbia: Case Study of a Direct-Action Movement," *Syracuse Law Review*, 21 (1968–1969), p. 23.

34 "Prospectus of the North Shore Summer Project," p. 3.

35 James Janega, "Dora DuPont Williams, 90: North Shore Woman Aided Liberal Causes," *Chicago Tribune*, March 29, 2002.

36 "What about Chicago's North Shore?" informational brochure, n.d., University of Illinois–Chicago Archives, North Shore Summer Project Collection, Box 1, Folder 13.

37 "A Statement of Purpose."

38 Moyer spent time in Mississippi and must have known some of the northern volunteers because he was listed as a reference on at least one application. Doug McAdam, *Freedom Summer* (New York: Oxford University Press, 1988), p. 159.

39 "Prospectus of the North Shore Summer Project," p. 4.

40 Kathy Routliffe, "Jean Cleland Helped Open Housing on North Shore," *Wilmette Life*, November 4, 2013.

41 "Report to the Field Foundation on Chicago Metropolitan Area Housing Opportunities Program," October 1, 1964–September 30, 1965, American Friends Service Committee Archives, Box: CRD 1965 Housing Program Con't, Folder: Regional Offices, Chicago—Housing Opportunities Prog.

42 "Student Participant Application Form," n.d., University of Illinois–Chicago Archives, North Shore Summer Project Collection, Box 1, Folder 15.

43 Full text of speech reprinted in *North Shore Summer Project* newsletter, July, 23, 1963, University of Illinois–Chicago Archives, North Shore Summer Project Collection, Box 1, Folder 3.

44 "A Statement of Purpose."

45 Luigi Laurenti, *Property Values and Race* (Berkeley: University of California Press, 1960).

46 "'Neighbors Would Object,' Respond Whites Opposed to Selling to Negro," *Evanston Review*, July 29, 1965, p. 14.

47 "Report to the Winnetka Human Relations Committee—The NSSP in Winnetka," written by Henrietta Moore, October 1965, University of Illinois–Chicago Archives, North Shore Summer Project Collection, Box 1, Folder 5.

48 Harriet Robinet, "I'm a Mother—Not a Pioneer," *Redbook Magazine*, February 1968.

49 "Rally, Report End Summer Project," *Evanston Review*, September 2, 1965, p. 83.

50 Phyllis Palmer, *Living as Equals: How Three White Communities Struggled to Make Interracial Connections during the Civil Rights Era* (Nashville, TN: Vanderbilt University Press, 2008), p. 98.

51 "North Shore Summer Project Summary Report," August 29, 1965, University of Illinois-Chicago Archives, North Shore Summer Project Collection, Box 1, Folder 5.

52 Interview with Dora Williams's children posted on www.open-communities.org.

53 "Negro Cleric Quits Church," *Fon du Lac (WI) Commonwealth Reporter*, August 10, 1966.

54 "Views on Race, Poverty Too Strong; Pastor Quits," *Jet Magazine*, June 2, 1966.

7

"You Are Running a de Facto Segregated University"

Racial Segregation and the City University of New York, 1961–1968

TAHIR H. BUTT

Introduction

On June 12, 1963, Martin Luther King Jr. addressed an estimated fifteen thousand New Yorkers at the 117th commencement of the City College of New York. For those gathered that day, the focus was understandably on the southern movement against the racial injustices of Jim Crow. Early that same morning, Medgar Evers had been murdered in Jackson, Mississippi. The tragic event was, King reminded, just the most recent example of the "ruthless denial" characteristic of Mississippi: the state where Emmett Till had been killed as well as the home of the segregationists who violently protested James Meredith's enrollment at the state university.[1]

Only days before commencement, President John F. Kennedy had deployed the National Guard to the University of Alabama to protect Vivian Malone and James A. Hood as they integrated another southern state university. The all-white campus was an important setting for the struggle for civil rights; it situated the noble aims of desegregating higher learning against the backwardness of "separate but equal" public education. In fact, the legal challenge against the segregation of public higher education in the South, begun in the 1930s, had laid the foundation for the assault at the elementary and secondary levels. The story of segregation in higher education came to be told as a southern tale: the efforts to enroll Black students, in the ones and twos, who were qualified for admission but were excluded to preserve segregation.

For City College graduates in 1963, the denial of justice at southern colleges could have been a distant though distressing legacy of American slavery. But, as King implored them to see, racial injustice was "not merely a sectional problem" but a national one. He called upon them to "see that the de facto segregation of the north is as injurious to the Negro student as the legal segregation of the south."[2] Segregation in New York City had worsened in the years following *Brown v. Board*. The municipal colleges, as an extension of the K–12 system, were part and parcel of a segregated system of education.

There were probably fewer than three dozen Black graduates seated among the twenty-eight hundred graduates when King spoke at the 1963 commencement—less than 2 percent of the graduates.[3] The audience that day in Harlem, the capital of Black America, was blindingly white. In 1964, an editorial in the Black newspaper *New York Amsterdam News* attacked the policies of City College for producing a campus as "lily-white as the University of Mississippi campus was before Miss ever heard of a young man named James Meredith."[4] Later that year, a Republican assemblyman from Long Island, no friend of the public colleges of the city, nor of the Black poor, told a gathering of alumni that the university's policies were a "deprivation of opportunity." To the chairman of the university's board, he had been more bold: "You are running a de facto segregated university."[5]

In a city where people come to "make it," the City University has long been associated with opportunity, particularly for its urban poor. Today, City College is one of twenty-four colleges and professional schools in the City University system, which as a whole enrolls over 270,000 students, making it the third-largest public university system in the country. Nearly a quarter of its students are Black, and a little less than a third are Hispanic. Their success has been interpreted as a realization of the democratic mission to which the municipal colleges have been committed for over a century.

The Free Academy, the predecessor to City College, began in 1847 with a bold vision of democratic education: "Open the doors to all—Let the children of the rich and the poor take their seats together and know of no distinction save that of industry, good conduct, and intellect." Central to its democratic mission was a free tuition policy, which was maintained until 1976. Unlike private colleges that catered to an "aristocracy of wealth," the founders of the Free Academy, and early boosters of City College, sought to create an "aristocracy of talent." Though tuition-free college education lowered economic barriers, meritocratic hurdles were erected early on to keep academic standards comparable to what was available at private institutions. Later, in the context of the racial conflict of the 1960s, a color-blind meritocracy became a powerful racial myth that enabled city officials and administrators to deflect responsibility for racial injustice.

In the 1960s a color-blind meritocracy at City College transformed a tuition-free college education into a public subsidy hoarded by white New Yorkers but paid for by all New Yorkers. Over the course of the decade, university administrators, city officials, and white residents deflected charges of racism at the City University and shifted responsibility onto prior educational inequalities or onto the individual students. When a few reforms did develop to increase minority enrollments, they happened on the margins of the institution. CUNY's defenders, who refused to recognize the racial biases embedded within the institution, were typical of northern liberals who justified Jim Crow conditions at home even as they decried them below the Mason-Dixon line. Northern liberals, like those at City College, marshalled democratic and meritocratic ideals to excuse themselves and their institutions of any wrongdoing in maintaining the racial status quo.[6]

Their failure to act was ultimately challenged by a historic series of events at the end of the decade. On April 21, 1969, two hundred Black and Puerto Rican students at City College began a two-week occupation of its south campus. They demanded that the university reflect the demographics of the urban populations for which it had been founded. Black and Puerto Rican students accounted for less than 10 percent of the total enrollments across CUNY, though they together comprised nearly half of the public school students. Under pressure from multiple fronts, the Board of Higher Education finally agreed to lower admission requirements and initiated the Open Admissions policy by which all graduates of the city's public high schools would be assured entry to the municipal colleges with remediation if necessary.

Open Admissions transformed the university by opening its doors to many who had previously been excluded. But the events of 1969 were not the fulfillment of the historic mission of City College. Instead, as historian Martha Biondi has noted, "[T]he campus tumult of the late 1960s reveals the snail's pace of court-mandated integration and the stunning lack of preparation for it on American campuses."[7] City College was no exception to this pattern. Inseparable from a segregated system of public education, the policies of the City University actively undermined equal opportunity. High admission requirements effectively excluded most of the city's growing Black population trapped in inferior schools.

"The Problem Has Nothing to Do with Race"

In 1959, the Board of Higher Education, the local governing body of the municipal colleges, convened a special committee. The city's public colleges had struggled throughout the decade with budgetary crises. At a time when other states, most notably California, were building up their public systems, New York's public colleges languished without adequate state aid. The funding of the municipal colleges was still a responsibility of the city government. In the wake of a recession in 1957, the city pinched its purse strings, causing the municipal college administrators to seek a new way forward.

At the center of the committee's concern was the persistent space problem that had saddled the colleges. In asking for more state aid, the special committee recommended a major reorganization of the colleges to increase efficiency and cut costs. With an eye to its budgetary problems, the committee recommended consolidating the loosely coordinated municipal colleges in the hopes that any efficiencies gained could lower overall costs, as well as increase the maximum number of students given the existing facilities. The four-year colleges, of which there were four, and the two-year community colleges, a total of three, were reorganized into the City University of New York (CUNY) in 1961.[8]

Whereas the committee was most concerned with the problem of space, it also addressed the seeds of another problem it found in the changing demographics of the city. Between 1950 and 1958, 835,000 southern Blacks and Puerto Ricans moved to the city just as 1,285,000 city residents, mostly white, moved out.[9] City College had historically admitted freshmen based on their high school grade averages and, more recently, standardized test scores. Furthermore, the application for admission contained no place to fill in one's race, ethnicity, or religious affiliation. The admissions process was celebrated both for its high standards and for the absence of social biases in its definition. This latter point was no small feat at the time. Even though New York was the first state to pass a fair educational practice law, a federal commission found that 76 percent of its colleges in 1960 still required a personal interview where implicit biases could disadvantage minority groups.[10]

For the Black southerners and Puerto Ricans swelling in numbers at the city's public schools, the color-blind admissions process of City College presented a formidable barrier to access. Many of the new migrants to the city arrived from rural backgrounds. Because of decades of residential segregation, these two minority groups also arrived into the inferior schools of New York ghettos. But the cause for concern that the committee expressed was not the fate of these minority groups. Instead, they raised a warning for the municipal colleges. Migration patterns were causing the average high school grades to drop and thus threatened the possibility that fewer students would be qualified applicants for admissions to the municipal colleges. Instead of easing selectivity, the committee warned that lower grade requirements "will substantially increase the number of students who will have to vie for seats in already crowded classrooms."[11]

The recommendations of the special committee report in light of the city's demographic changes follow a template used by city officials to dismiss charges of segregation. One of the sharpest critics of the Board of Education was City College professor Kenneth B. Clark. "While school officials may not deliberately tolerate segregation," he wrote, "there is no evidence that they have zoned to encourage bringing about integrated schools."[12] Whereas the Board of Education absolved itself of responsibility by pointing to residential segregation, the Board of Higher Education could escape fault by asserting the prior inequality of schooling at the primary and secondary levels. And, the municipal college administrators absolved themselves on the basis of the color-blindness of their admissions policies.

In August 1963, Mayor Robert F. Wagner Jr. appointed Benjamin F. McLaurin to the Board of Higher Education. McLaurin, a Black trade unionist and long-time leader in the Brotherhood of Sleeping Car Porters, was only the second Black member of the board. Early the following year, McLaurin spoke at a meeting of the City College faculty union. He took the occasion to propose a reform to admissions policies that could increase the number of Black students. McLaurin proposed that

5 to 10 percent of the freshman class every year not be admitted based on their high school averages but instead on their "potential." Those students exempted from the usual admissions policies would be nominated by their high school principals for admission. Though the policy was color-blind by definition, McLaurin hoped that the city's racial and ethnic minorities would disproportionately benefit from it.[13]

McLaurin's proposal generated a telling response from the defenders of "color-blind" admissions. The day after McLaurin's proposal was reported in the New York Times, the chairman of the Board of Higher Education, Gustave Rosenberg, categorically denied that a racial problem even existed. Rosenberg retorted that the municipal colleges, in fact, had the largest percentage of Black and Puerto Rican undergraduates of any university in the country. But Rosenberg admitted that any demographic figures, even his own, were only estimates since the university was not permitted to record such information. Still, he dismissed the basis of McLaurin's plea since "anyone . . . who spends an hour on the campuses of the colleges" would find some of the estimated 6,300 to 8,600 Black and Puerto Rican students enrolled across the university, a figure he had produced by personally consulting faculty. Not simply content with absolving the institution of wrongdoing, Rosenberg suggested that it had done more than most for the cause of racial equality.

Whereas Rosenberg simply denied the existence of a problem, others admitted that racial disparities at the municipal colleges were troubling but dismissed the idea that they amounted to segregation. In 1963, the Brooklyn College president defended the university in the Amsterdam News against charges of discrimination: "We are not restricting the opportunity to go to college. . . . The problem has nothing to do with race or breed—or with the middle class structure of some of our students. . . . It is a question of space."[14] The problems of space and overcrowded classrooms were certainly real challenges for the municipal colleges for many years. But, that this scarcity justified the persistence of racial inequality reinforced the myth of color-blind meritocracy.

In 1964, the newly appointed chancellor, Albert Bowker, reasserted the correctness of the university's color-blind policies. In the preface to CUNY's first master plan, he wrote how the master plan addressed the reality that "the major weakness of the City University today is the physical plant" but claimed that "another bold aspect" of the plan was that it was "color-blind." The problem, at least as the chancellor of CUNY saw it, was not with race-neutral admissions policies but with prior educational inequalities. The "major erosion" of public schools required a "massive upgrading" of the public school system.[15]

Bowker oversaw the university during a massive expansion over the following decade. Between 1960 and 1970, total enrollments nearly tripled, from 85,000 to 250,000. According to one account of this period, "Bowker brought the disadvantaged minorities into public higher education with a bold stroke that captured the sense of the times."[16] At the end of the decade, Bowker was instrumental in the initiation of Open Admissions after students of color occupied City College. As the name suggested, the new policy guaranteed graduates of the public high schools admission to CUNY. The admission requirements across the four-year and two-year colleges were lowered, and those students who still fell below the lower bar were provided remedial courses and counseling services. However, the policy had recast the student demands for increased Black and Puerto Rican enrollments by forging a policy that would also benefit other social groups, particularly the city's white ethnics. Since the turn of the century, the students of City College and the other senior colleges had been predominantly Jewish. Though Open Admissions increased Black and Puerto Rican enrollments, other major beneficiaries of the policy were white Catholics, Italian Americans and Irish Americans, who had also struggled to compete for admission. Ultimately these white ethnic groups were better positioned for enrolling in college out of racially segregated public schools.

The color-blindness of Open Admissions, as well as the policies it transformed, did more than just disproportionately benefit white residents. Under the cover of universalism, the unequal outcomes resulting from a color-blind admissions policy gave the lie to the liberal racism of the institution. Municipal college administrators were willing to acknowledge racial inequality but located the problem away from the locus of its manifestation. In higher education, the onus of responsibility was shifted to the educational inequalities inherited from residential segregation or, even, to the individual students. Though Bowker had noted inferior public schools in impoverished neighborhoods, he also concluded that these schools, as well as the colleges, "must say to these

youngsters that they are expected to succeed and that there will be opportunities for them beyond the high school." As a consequence, color-
blind policies directed attention away from the institution where those
policies were set and enforced.

Though administrators explained the unequal outcomes from color-
blind policies as a product of scarcity, the 1960s was also the decade of
the greatest expansion of the municipal colleges in U.S. history. Overall, the postwar period is considered a "golden age" in American higher
education since enrollments climbed from 1.5 million before the Second
World War to 7.9 million by 1970.[17] The expansion of public colleges accounted for most of that growth. But New York State, and the municipal
colleges, were exceptionally late to the national trend. New York ranked
at the bottom in terms of state support for higher education. The state
finally began to develop the state university system in earnest after the
1958 election of Nelson A. Rockefeller as governor. During Rockefeller's
fifteen years in office, the share of total enrollments at public colleges in
the state doubled from 30 to 60 percent. With the state borrowing $2 bil-
lion for construction, the State University grew from forty-six colleges in
1960, enrolling 41,000 students, to sixty-four colleges, enrolling 357,614.
The City University benefited much less from the state's largess but still
grew enormously in the 1960s, from seven colleges enrolling 85,269 students in 1960 to twenty colleges enrolling over 250,000 by 1970.

Still, overcrowding was a reality for the institution since demand for
college education was far outpacing the rate at which new seats were
being added. The rhetoric of overcrowding and lack of funds to push
back demands for increasing Black minority enrollments served as a
racial myth since it absolved the institution of having a hand in systemic
racism. Based on yearbook photographs, from 1950 to 1970 the number
of City College graduates identifiable as Black grew from only thirty to
just sixty. An estimated 375 Black students graduated over the course of
the 1960s.[18] The structure of racial inequality at City College remained
rigid even as the CUNY system went through a massive expansion.

When confronted with these racial disparities in enrollments, liberal
defenders of the status quo argued for gradualism. The education editor
of the New York Times at the time, Fred Hechinger, personified an optimism in the gradual erosion of racial inequality. Hechinger is particularly relevant here since he regularly took to the pages of the Times to

advocate on behalf of his alma mater, City College. In 1960, Hechinger explained how low college enrollment of Puerto Rican newcomers to the city was due to the fact that they were "not yet wealthy enough to be able to afford even tuition-free daytime study." According to such logic, the municipal colleges could do little for the first postwar generations of newcomers, be they Puerto Ricans or southern Blacks. Hechinger assumed that the prospects of class mobility for the new immigrants would not diverge from the experience of prior immigrant groups. Enrollments would gradually increase as "the latest wave of newcomers has been sufficiently educated."[19] Six years later, Hechinger still remained optimistic about racial progress in CUNY enrollments. "If present admission standards are maintained, then it will probably be a matter of several years before the Negroes and Puerto Rican minorities will start rushing in, in numbers comparable to the immigrant minorities before them."[20]

Hechinger's optimism belied his opposition to the local grassroots desegregation efforts. In 1963, when local activists threatened to boycott the public schools over the failure of the Board of Education to desegregate, Hechinger dismissed them as having misunderstood local conditions. "Although efforts are made—paradoxically both by Southern segregationists and Northern integration spokesmen—to make it appear as if the Northern issue could be equated with segregation in the South, this is a distortion of facts," he concluded.[21] The following year, as civil rights activists pushed forward with the boycott, Hechinger continued to write about the "confusion" that "blurred" the distinction between the South and New York City, particularly in the context of "open enrollment" policies adopted by the board in 1960. "Thus, in contrast to the South, no Negro child would be kept out of any school, if his parents moved into the school's area."[22] Since the problem, according to Hechinger, was underlying residential segregation, any plan to achieve "racial balance" through "rapid integration" would be doomed to fail.

However, liberal moderation and gradualism in expanding higher education opportunities for the city's minority populations were contradicted by the fact that racial inequality persisted in a period of massive expansion of the municipal college system. When demographic data on the students was finally collected in 1967, it revealed just how close the "northern issue" was to southern segregation.[23] Though enrollments grew three-fold over the decade, the rising tide did not lift all boats. At the four-year senior colleges—City College, Hunter College, Brooklyn College, and Queens College—Black students accounted for only 3.6 percent of the matriculated enrollment. Moreover, the majority of Black matriculants were in the less selective community colleges, where they accounted for 13 percent of the total. Yet, the most revealing finding of the survey was that most of the Black students attending the municipal colleges were never in fact admitted to the degree programs at the four-year or two-year colleges. Instead, close to 60 percent of the Black students, more than half, were enrolled in courses as nonmatriculants. Therefore, for the few Black students who did enter the doors of the municipal colleges, most entered its lower tier, either into the less selective programs or as part-time nonmatriculants.[24]

Contrary to popular perceptions that City College, the "Harvard of the Poor," had been free to all, the lower tier of the City University where most of its Black students enrolled was not in fact free. Throughout its history, tuition from an increasing number of students enabled the municipal colleges to expand opportunity and add much-needed revenue. The Free Academy Act of 1847 authorized the city "to establish a free academy in the city of New York . . . for the purpose of extending the benefits of education gratuitously." In the twentieth century, however, the municipal colleges extended the "benefits of education gratuitously" to a fraction of its enrolled students by adding tuition-paying students. Initially this was done through the addition of evening courses and extension programs for adults, both of which charged "instructional fees" to students. Later, community colleges added tuition-paying students since, by state law, a third of the revenue for new community colleges was to come from tuition fees. Matriculated students in the community college of CUNY were charged tuition until 1965, when the city finally agreed to cover the fraction collected from students.[25]

Indeed, a majority of the enrolled students in the 1960s at CUNY were charged tuition. In 1950, though twenty-six thousand students attended tuition-free at the municipal colleges, nearly forty-five thousand paid for their education. By 1967, tuition-free students accounted for just 42 percent as the total enrollment skyrocketed to 150,000 across CUNY. And, at its peak in 1965, the revenue from students accounted for 20.3 percent of the total budget.[26]

Meritocratic admission policies and a free tuition policy for a privileged few meant that for most of the Black students who entered through the doors of the City University before Open Admission, there was a price for entry.[27] Of the nearly eighty thousand tuition-free matriculated students in 1967, white students were the overwhelming majority, at 87 percent of the total, while Black students accounted for less than 6 percent. Black students were more likely paying tuition as nonmatriculants, where they accounted for 18.9 percent. Black students enrolled in the City University were thus three times more likely to be paying as nonmatriculants than they were to be attending tuition free as matriculated students in the day session.[28]

The addition of new community colleges broadened opportunity to more Black high school graduates, but again at a cost.[29] In 1967, a fifth of those enrolled at the city's community colleges were Black students, close to four times their numbers at the senior colleges. The growth of two-year colleges far outpaced the expansion of four-year colleges—so much so that by the end of the decade they accounted for 30 percent of the total enrollment whereas they had only accounted for 11 percent in 1961. Yet, that expansion added tuition-paying students since nonmatriculants at the community colleges continued to pay tuition.

The structure of inequality at the City University penalized the city's Black students twice. High admission requirements for tuition-free college meant that the poor, who were disproportionately Black, were excluded from the benefits of universal public subsidy. For those who still enrolled, they did so as tuition-paying students. But in so doing they disproportionately bore the burden of adding much-needed revenue for sustaining the world-class tuition-free education from which they had been excluded.

"Democracy Is Interested in All of Its Treasures"

The high admissions requirements at the City University effectively transformed free tuition into a scholarship for the select few. Upon the release of the Master Plan of 1964, the Senate Committee on the Affairs of the City of New York called on a prominent civil rights leader, Lester Granger, to review whether its free tuition policies were in the best interests of the city's minority youth. Granger had been the national executive secretary of the National Urban League from 1941 to 1961. Published in November 1964, the report assessed the plan within the context of the contemporary social and economic dislocations that had given rise to an era of racial conflicts, most notably the Harlem riots of that summer.

Granger explained the explosive social conditions by the "inadequate education" and "outmoded work skills" available to low-income Black and Puerto Rican residents. On these counts, Granger concluded that the proposed plan was a "disturbing document" since "not only is it true that the Colleges of the City University have been unable to handle this job in the past; there is no indication in the Master Plan of any program to accomplish it in the predictable future." Moreover, the free-tuition policy of the municipal colleges of City University, which the plan proposed to maintain, was found to "discriminate unfairly against those very groups who are supposed to be aided." Instead, the preservation of a free tuition policy meant "no public degree–education for thousands of young members of minority groups."[30]

In challenging CUNY's policies, Granger took aim at one of the dominant myths of northern racism: southern exceptionalism. The evidence on the municipal system revealed a "bitterly ironic" comparison of local conditions to those in the Jim Crow South. The Black population of New York City was approximately the same as it was in all of Louisiana, Granger observed. But the senior colleges of the municipal system enrolled only a thousand Black students while Louisiana's state colleges enrolled more than ten thousand. Though Granger admitted that the city's education was "superior" to Louisiana's, it was no good for "a racial group or one of its members against whom college entrance doors are barred."[31]

Given the structural inequality of segregated public education in New York City, Granger proposed a dramatic change to meritocratic criteria used in admissions. Rather than one metric for all students, Granger recommended that students be measured according to the high schools where they were educated. Black students were unable to compete with their white counterparts educated in better-resourced schools and given the necessary college preparation. Of the two types of public high schools—academic and vocational—only students at academic high schools had the opportunity to take courses in preparation for college. Students at the city's vocational high schools had no chance of gaining college admission. In 1967, Black students accounted for only 3.7 percent of high school graduates eligible for admission to CUNY, even though they comprised over 20 percent of students at the academic high schools.[32] Thus, Granger proposed that students be admitted on the basis of their rankings within a school, rather than in competition with all of the city's graduates. Like McLaurin before him, Granger did not stipulate any racial or ethnic criteria for admission. Yet, while the board's color-blind policies sought to increase competition, Granger's policies sought to level the playing field without an explicit racial criterion.

Granger's findings offered upstate Republican legislators new fodder for their attack on the city's budget. One of the Republican leaders of this campaign was Joseph F. Carlino, the assembly speaker from Nassau County. Along with Rockefeller, Carlino had helped expand the student aid programs across the state in place of tuition-free public colleges. In 1963, when the State University imposed a uniform tuition to reap the benefits of the new student aid programs, Democratic legislators from New York City attacked SUNY's Board of Trustees for creating a barrier for minority students. But Carlino countered them by calling free tuition a "myth." Rather than providing opportunity to students from "culturally deprived low income groups," the City's tuition-free colleges catered to an "academically elite group whose families are far better able to meet tuition payments than those who attend the City's night schools or are enrolled at its community colleges where tuition is charged."[33] Later that year, he called free tuition a "deprivation of opportunity," claiming that only 1.9 percent of the student body at the City University was Black.[34]

As upstate Republicans used the mantle of civil rights in their continued attack on free tuition, a coalition of local forces came to its defense. Central to the successful defense of free tuition was the Alumni Association of City College. Upon the release of Granger's report, the Alumni Association wrote a five-page rebuttal attacking the proposal as lowering the quality of higher education. The *Amsterdam News* quoted its executive secretary, who effectively called Granger's proposal racist: "Mr. Granger, . . . implying that able Negro and Puerto Rican youngsters are incapable of competing on an equal level with the rest of the population for college admission if adequately prepared or given remedial work to compensate for earlier educational deprivation, is contributing to the myth of Negro and Puerto Rican inferiority."[35] City College was not the problem; leveling the playing field by changing the standards was the greater racial injustice.

Moreover, the Alumni Association's framing of free tuition had been for some time more meritocratic than egalitarian. When Rockefeller signed into law an expanded student aid program and ended the legally mandated free tuition in 1961, the Alumni Association began a political campaign to restore the mandate. In the next issue of its magazine, the Alumni Association president reminded readers that the high academic standards of the college were the result of 113 years of development and must not be undone by Rockefeller. The author warned that tuition charges at the municipal colleges would "open the door to further attempts to impose an artificial and damaging uniformity at the 'lowest common denominator.'"[36] Thus, any effort to broaden access, even those to increase minority enrollments, was equated with lowering educational standards. While the alumni dismissed Granger for contributing to the myth of Black inferiority, they cautioned against lowering admission requirements on the grounds that doing so would damage academic standards.

In the postwar period, free tuition had come to be understood more as a scholarship for the most deserving than as an education for those who could not afford to pay. According to the Alumni Association president, the free tuition policy was "the equivalent of four-year tuition free scholarships to those who are best able to profit from them."[37] The positive portrayal of free tuition as a scholarship was counterpoised to the negative connotations associated with welfare. The four-year scholarship at the municipal colleges was not "a matter of charity" for the alumni who came to its defense. Rockefeller's scholarship program required a student to prove his or her inability to pay tuition. Means-test scholarships were "a dressed up version" of the "pauper's oath," particularly "degrading and demoralizing" to those able students from low-income groups. For the children of Black and Puerto Rican families, changing tuition policy would have the opposite effect that its opponents were suggesting. The Black and Puerto Rican children "ask only for a chance to make their own contribution to the fabric of American society" but come from "underprivileged homes where, in many instances, a college education is still a strange concept."[38] Contrary to what upstate Republicans were pushing, the alumni argued that student aid would reinforce a "culture of poverty," while free tuition alone held the promise of escaping poverty. By defending the meritocratic ideals underlying free tuition, City College alumni concluded that the promise of an American dream was enough for the Black and Puerto Rican families otherwise trapped in poverty.

Though alumni of the municipal colleges stood to benefit from high academic standards more than most, the reality of a tuition-free scholarship created a problem for the democratic ethos of the institution. The Republican Joseph Carlino had criticized admissions policies to the tuition-free colleges as requiring students to "have high school grades which approach the genius level."[39] Even the *Times* decried how City College favored academic elites in an editorial published after Benjamin McLaurin's proposal in 1964. The *Times* accepted the basis of McLaurin's challenge: "[F]ree college education for the excellent student" was unjustly depriving the students "who have grades that would have admitted them a decade ago and who cannot afford to go elsewhere."[40] The Alumni Association president countered, as administrators had done in years prior, that high admission requirements were "determined by a shortage of facilities in the face of expanded enrollment pressures." As additional funds and facilities would be secured, the college could "roll back admission grades" and fulfill "the college's historic role of providing free higher education for all qualified students."[41] On this, the *Times* agreed: "Until New York City can build a large enough City University with a special emphasis on two-year community colleges to hold all who can benefit by a free college education, there seems no alternative to discrimination, of one kind or another." In place of immediate action, liberals simply acquiesced to discrimination.

For its ardent defenders, restricting admission to tuition-free CUNY to the most qualified was not only a necessity but also virtue. On the one hand, lack of public funds had made the public subsidy a scarce commodity, one that could not be realistically available to all qualified. On the other hand, that scarcity had become a virtue of the system, as "tuition-free" was recast as a "free scholarship." A concern for tuition-paying students was tellingly absent from the discourse employed by defenders of free tuition and high academic standards. Instead, their promotion of the virtues of a "free scholarship" cast off any supposed universalism of free tuition and the egalitarianism of its democratic mission.

What emerged at the municipal colleges was a liberalism more committed to excellence than equality. That meritocratic mutation of the original mission had disastrous consequences for the city's Black and Puerto Rican youth in postwar New York. Their absence was not an indictment of the institution, as Granger, and McLaurin before him, had concluded. A letter to the *Times* written by a Hunter College student in response to McLaurin best captured how the democratic mission of the institution had been reshaped by its meritocratic ideals. The City University should treat Black and white alike as long as they are qualified: "Democracy is interested in all of its treasures and not the color of its jewels." "That City College is situated in a Negro area," the student emphasized, "does not entitle Negroes to admission."[42] By dismissing McLaurin's proposal as an effort to "entitle" Black residents of the city's ghettos, the student affirmed the legitimacy that only the city's "treasures" deserved to be educated by its free public colleges.

CUNY's policies marked most of the city's Black youth as undeserving of a tax-supported, tuition-free college education. Test scores were accepted as valid criteria for admissions, even though many in higher education had concluded that those test scores were failing Black students. In the fall of 1959, the College Entrance Examination Board (CEEB), the producers of the Standardized Achievement Test (SAT), gathered leading educators in Harriman, New York, to discuss college admissions. The colloquium produced a report, "The Search for Talent," that was published the following summer. The report roundly criticized the social biases implicit in the use of test scores for admissions to higher education, favoring "students from the right side and from the right schools." The foreword to the report decried how "so rich and fat a country as ours" could "be starving the educational and personal development of tens of thousands of able children whose only fault is that they are poor, or a wrong color."[43]

Among the participants in Harriman was Kenneth B. Clark, who had joined the psychology faculty at City College in the early 1940s as the first tenured Black professor. Clark had grown up in Harlem, but before the neighborhood's public schools were segregated with the exodus of its white residents. While at City College, Clark gained national recognition for his testimony to the Supreme Court in *Brown v. Board of Education*. Locally, he was a leading public advocate for desegregation and a vocal critic of an intransigent Board of Education. Clark's efforts also extended to higher education, where his contributions can be seen as a rejection of the meritocratic myth at his own City College.[44]

To appease desegregation activists like Clark, the Board of Education began to experiment with programs to improve the quality of education at segregated schools. The Demonstration Guidance program, as well as its successor, the Higher Horizons Program, were premised on providing "disadvantaged" students with academic training, remedial work, and counseling services. One of the two schools where the pilot program was conducted was Junior High School 43 (JHS 43), located at 129th Street and Amsterdam Avenue, which was only a few blocks from City College. The junior high school reflected the demographics of Harlem: 40 percent of students were Puerto Rican and 45 percent were Black. The pilot program at JHS 43 was conducted by the Northside Center for Child Development, the center cofounded by Clark with his wife, Mamie Phipps. Its success would be evident when six times as many of the school's students went to college because of the support they received.[45]

In his contribution to the CEEB colloquium report, Clark considered the hurdles to democratizing access in higher education moving into a new decade. Long before white opposition would be cast as a racial backlash, Clark addressed the opposition by whites to opening the doors to higher education for racial minorities. He observed how social groups that had benefited from public education in the past were now doubting that other social groups, particularly the new Black residents, could benefit from the same opportunities. These older groups wielded "the power of decision and control of fiscal and educational policies and procedures" they had obtained. Particularly relevant to the story at City College, Clark concluded that these groups stood against democratizing access to higher education since it would "lower and dilute academic standards."[46] In other words, a myth of meritocracy—those who benefit from college education are deserving of their gains—was deployed in attacking broadening access.

Clark offered City College as a counterexample to such white opposition. "Certainly," Clark noted, "the experience of unquestioned academic success of the municipal colleges of the city of New York—colleges which were founded to provide a tuition-free education to the disadvantaged groups of the past—refutes this argument that a more democratic higher education would necessarily be less effective academic education."[47]

The following decade at the City University affirmed Clark's prescient critique of the meritocratic myth. The municipal college system was already among the most selective public colleges in the country.[48] By 1961, when CUNY was created, the municipal colleges required a high school average above 85 for admission. The cut-scores for admission put tuition-free CUNY out of reach of the majority of graduates from the city's public schools. According to estimates from 1970, when the grade average requirements were finally lowered as part of the Open Admission policy, only 12.7 percent of Black graduates at the academic high schools had averages above 80 percent, compared to 45 percent of their white classmates.[49] Since 1957, the municipal colleges had supplemented high school grades with SAT scores to give some students a second chance based on their intellectual ability.[50] However, as Clark's own research would conclude, Black high school students were far less likely than their white counterparts to have taken the SAT and, if they had, were on average scoring well below white students.[51]

Clark's contribution to higher education exposed the meritocratic myth at the core of northern liberal racism. He worked to extend the Demonstration Guidance Project into the university, with the creation of College Discovery Program at the community colleges and the Search for Education, Evaluation, and Knowledge (SEEK) Program at the senior colleges. These subsequent experimental programs added further evidence that "disadvantaged" students were capable of academic success, contrary to the liberal fears of irrevocable damage to academic standards.

Unmasking Segregation

The memory of City College is not marked by segregation. The failure to reckon with the past was evident at the 2013 commencement of City College, fifty years after King had addressed its graduates. Matthew Goldstein, the chancellor of the City University of New York, was among the graduates in 1963 who had heard King speak. In his memorializing of the 1963 speech, Goldstein recounted his "awakening" upon witnessing King's call to "moral clarity" and "action." The chancellor's speech was excerpted and printed in the university magazine alongside a feature article that detailed the events of that fateful year in the civil rights movement. But King's challenge to northern racism, so central to his address, was left untouched in both contributions to the magazine. Indeed, though the feature article mentioned that Goldstein was seated next to one of the "relatively few Black students" at the 1963 commencement, the fact failed to warrant further comment.[52]

In part, segregation at City College can be papered over because that story does not fit into the dominant framing of segregation in higher education by way of exclusionary practices associated only with the South. An exclusively southern framing has obscured the exclusion of New York City's Black youth from tuition-free college education. No George Wallace stood at the gates of lily-white City College; no federal troops would be deployed to the college on the hill on behalf of the Black poor living in its shadow. City College lacked the drama of segregated higher education in the South.

But the story of a segregated City College remains difficult to unmask since it requires a radical questioning of the social order, the sort called for by King in 1963. To admit the charge of segregation, defenders of color-blind meritocracy, then as now, would have to question the basic legitimacy of educating only those already deemed qualified and admit the hoarding of resources by a generation of whites. The liberal opposition to the desegregation of New York's public colleges in the 1960s requires a revision not only to its history but also to the limits of liberal democracy itself.

NOTES

1   Martin Luther King Jr., "City College Commencement Address," June 12, 1963. Digital Archives. City College of New York. http://digital-archives.ccny.cuny.edu.

2   Ibid.

3   "Black Alumni," Department of Special Programs/SEEK Program Records, 1968– (ongoing), City College of New York, New York, New York.

4   James L. Hicks, "Education Gets Higher!" *New York Amsterdam News*, May 9, 1964.

5   Judith S Glazer, "A Case Study of the Decision in 1976 to Initiate Tuition for Matriculated Undergraduate Students of the City University of New York" (unpublished doctoral dissertation, New York University, 1981), 279.

6 For relevant case studies of the problems of liberal racism in New York, see Clarence Taylor, *Knocking at Our Own Door: Milton A. Galamison and the Struggle to Integrate New York City Schools* (New York: Columbia University Press, 1997); Adina Back, "Blacks, Jews, and the Struggle to Integrate Brooklyn's Junior High School 258: A Cold War Story," *Journal of American Ethnic History*, 2001, 38–69; Jeanne F. Theoharis and Komozi Woodard, eds., *Freedom North: Black Freedom Struggles outside the South, 1940–1980* (New York: Palgrave Macmillan, 2003); Adina Back, "Exposing the 'Whole Segregation Myth': The Harlem Nine and New York City's School Desegregation Battles," in Theoharis and Woodard, eds., *Freedom North*, 65–92; Matthew F. Delmont, *Why Busing Failed: Race, Media, and the National Resistance to School Desegregation* (Oakland: University of California Press, 2016).

7 Martha Biondi, *The Black Revolution on Campus* (Berkeley: University of California Press, 2012), 117.

8 Thomas C. Holy, *A Long-Range Plan for the City University of New York, 1961–1975* (New York: Board of Higher Education, 1962).

9 Fred M. Hechinger, "City Schools Cite Integration Gain against Big Odds: Population Shifts and Fiscal Curbs Reported Limiting Combined Program City Schools Cite Integration Gain," *New York Times*, June 28, 1960.

10 United States Commission on Civil Rights, "Equal Protection of the Laws in Public Higher Education" (Washington, DC: United States Commission on Civil Rights, 1960), 155–56.

11 Holy, *A Long-Range Plan*, 82–88, 114.

12 "Dr. Clark Blasts Zoning of Negro as Schools' 'Out,'" *New York Age*, November 12, 1955; for detailed account of Clark's role in local desegregation campaigns, see Adina Back, "Up South in New York: The 1950s School Desegregation Struggles" (unpublished doctoral dissertation, New York University, 1997).

13 Charles G. Bennet, "Mayor Naming Negro Unionist to Board of Higher Education," *New York Times*, August 8, 1963; "New Policy Urged in City University," *New York Times*, January 3, 1964.

14 "N.Y. Colleges Color Blind, Says President," *New York Amsterdam News*, November 23, 1963.

15 Board of Higher Education of the City of New York, *Master Plan of the Board of Higher Education for the City University of New York, 1964* (New York: Board of Higher Education, 1964).

16 Sheila C. Gordon, "The Transformation of the City University of New York, 1945–1970" (unpublished doctoral dissertation, Columbia University Teachers College, 1975), 266.

17 John R Thelin, *A History of American Higher Education* (Baltimore, MD: Johns Hopkins University Press, 2011).

18 Conrad M. Dyer, "Protest and the Politics of Open Admissions" (unpublished doctoral dissertation, City University of New York, 1990).

19 Fred M. Hechinger, "City University," *New York Times*, December 18, 1960.

20 Fred M. Hechinger, "Crisis in Our Municipal Colleges," *City College Alumnus,* January 1966.

21 Fred M. Hechinger, "Issue of Balance: Segregation Protest in the North Obscures Educational Problems," *New York Times,* September 8, 1963, editorial section.

22 Fred M. Hechinger, "Education Cities in Crisis: The Northern Integration Issue; Crash Programs or Boycotts?" *New York Times,* January 12, 1964, sec. news background editorials, http://search.proquest.com.

23 Office for Civil Rights, "Undergraduate Enrollment by Ethnic Group in Federally Funded Institutions of Higher Education, Continental U.S.A., Fall, 1968" (Washington, DC: U.S. Dept. of Health, Education, and Welfare, Office of Civil Rights, Research and Data Analysis Branch, 1969).

24 Office of Institutional Research and Assessment, "1967–1968 Data Book" (New York: City University of New York, 1968).

25 Donald P Cottrell, "Public Higher Education in the City of New York: Report of the Master Plan Study" (New York: Board of Higher Education of the City of New York, 1950), 170, Baruch College, Stack IX Side B. Baruch College Archives and Special Collections; Florence Margaret Neumann, "Access to Free Public Higher Education in New York City: 1847–1961" (unpublished doctoral dissertation, City University of New York, 1984), 164.

26 Glazer, "A Case Study of the Decision in 1976," 275, 465, 264.

27 The demographic survey report did not break down students as tuition-free and tuition-paying. Instead, a breakdown was reported by the matriculated status of students. Though matriculated status did not translate directly to tuition status, disparities within the matriculant and nonmatriculant groups point to the structured racial inequality across the system. Only matriculated students in the day session attended the City University tuition-free. Those students who matriculated in the evening session were on the other hand charged tuition. Furthermore, at the more selective senior colleges, Black students were only 3.6 percent of the matriculants.

28 Office of Institutional Research and Assessment, "1967–1968 Data Book," appendixes III–IV.

29 Unlike California, where an extensive junior college system had developed before 1960, New York City had few community colleges when the City University was established in 1961. The first community college in the city had been started by the state government in 1946. The first community college sponsored by the municipal government, Staten Island Community College, was not established until 1955; the addition of Bronx Community College came in 1959 and Queensborough Community College in 1960. The extension of free tuition to the community colleges added eleven thousand tuition-free students to the municipal system, but the maintenance of the free tuition policy came at a cost to the system. In 1963, the board of the State University replaced free tuition at its public colleges with a uniform tuition charge of three hundred dollars in part to benefit from state student aid money. Since the City University did not charge tuition to its full-time

undergraduates, many of its students were excluded from receiving state and federal student aid.

30 Lester Blackwell Granger, *A Report on the City University and Its Proposed 1964 Master Plan* (New York: New York Senate Committee on the Affairs of the City of New York, 1964).

31 By comparison, Alabama, Mississippi, and Louisiana together accounted for just 4.1 percent of the national total. Of all the Black students enrolled in college nationwide, 6.1 percent were enrolled in Louisiana, 4.9 percent in Mississippi, and 4 percent in Alabama. Most of New York's Black college students attended colleges in New York City, which by 1960 already had 1,417,511 Black residents, accounting for 8.4 percent of the total city population. Of the 11,367 Black college students in New York, 4,145 (over a third) attended CUNY. SUNY, which had received far more public funding, enrolled only 1,167 Black students, nearly a third of whom were at a single campus in Buffalo. More than half of all Black college students in New York were enrolled in private institutions. Public colleges in New York were failing to provide opportunity found in southern state colleges. By comparison, Louisiana's public colleges enrolled almost 13,000 Black students, and in Mississippi the total was over 9,500. By 1968, New York had accounted for 7.6 percent of all students attending college across the country, but enrolled just 4 percent of the country's Black college students. The City University accounted for a third of the total Black enrollment in the state. See Office for Civil Rights, "Undergraduate Enrollment by Ethnic Group."

32 Robert Birnbaum and Joseph Goldman, *The Graduates: A Follow-Up Study of New York City High School Graduates of 1970* (New York: Center for Social Research, City University of New York, 1971).

33 Joseph F. Carlino, "Press Release" (Letter, March 11, 1963), Manfred Ohrenstein, Box 4. New York State Library.

34 "Carlino Says Free Tuition Ideal Is 'a Deprivation of Opportunity,'" *Observation Post*, December 3, 1963, City College of New York.

35 "CCNY Alumni Support Free Tuition Policy," *New York Amsterdam News*, December 12, 1964.

36 Clifford O. Anderson, "A Reply to the Heald Report," *City College Alumnus*, January 1961.

37 Ibid.

38 Clifford O. Anderson, "The Case against Tuition Fees," *City College Alumnus*, October 1959.

39 Carlino, "Press Release."

40 "City University for All?" *New York Times*, January 15, 1964.

41 Max Greenberg, "Shortage of Facilities," *New York Times*, January 23, 1964.

42 Xenia Penry, "Negroes at City Colleges: Dissent Expressed with Proposal to Admit More to University," *New York Times*, January 16, 1964.

43 College Entrance Examination Board, *The Search for Talent* (New York: College Entrance Examination Board, 1960); Gene Currivan, "Colleges' Social Bias Bars

Able Entrants, Panel Says: Colleges Scored on Entry System," *New York Times*, June 26, 1960.

44 Gerald E. Markowitz and David Rosner, *Children, Race, and Power: Kenneth and Mamie Clark's Northside Center* (Charlottesville: University Press of Virginia, 1996); Back, "Up South in New York."

45 Kenneth B. Clark, *Dark Ghetto: Dilemmas of Social Power* (New York: Harper & Row, 1965).

46 Kenneth B. Clark, "Discrimination and the Disadvantaged," in *The Search for Talent* (New York: College Entrance Examination Board, 1960), 12–19.

47 Ibid.

48 During the Depression, the Board of Higher Education had increased admission requirements, due to shortages of space, increased demand, and lack of adequate municipal and state funds. In addition to nonmatriculants, some matriculants were also charged tuition. In a practice first introduced in 1932 as a temporary measure during the Depression, the municipal colleges had begun matriculating students with lower scores on admissions tests into associate degree programs in the evening session, for which they were charged per credit hour as nonmatriculated students had been.

49 Neumann, "Access to Free Public Higher Education," 278; Birnbaum and Goldman, *The Graduates*, 56.

50 Beginning in 1941, the municipal colleges began to use a composite score by weighting and combining high school averages and standardized test scores. One of the goals was to provide intellectually able students on the lower end of the grade averages another measurement to be judged upon. In fact, the registrar of the college remarked at the end of the 1950s that fewer students with grade averages above 90 were gaining admission, suggesting increased competition for those clustered in the high 80s. Robert L. Taylor, "The Changing Academic Pattern," *City College Alumnus*, March 1958.

51 Kenneth Bancroft Clark and Lawrence Plotkin, "The Negro Student at Integrated Colleges" (New York: National Scholarship Service and Fund for Negro Students, 1963); College Entrance Examination Board, "On Further Examination: Report of the Advisory Panel on the Scholastic Aptitude Test Score Decline and Appendices" (New York: College Entrance Examination Board, 1977).

52 "Martin Luther King Jr. at City College 50 Years Ago: A Historic Commencement," *CUNY Matters*, 2013, www1.cuny.edu.

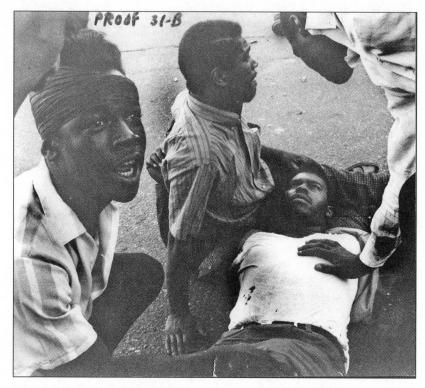

Wounded Hunters Point Residents, 1966. San Francisco History Center, San Francisco Public Library.

8

A Forgotten Community, a Forgotten History

San Francisco's 1966 Urban Uprising

ALIYAH DUNN-SALAHUDDIN

Awakenings

Near 3:00 p.m. on September 27, 1966, in San Francisco's Bayview-Hunters Point (BVHP) community, Alvin Johnson, a fifty-one-year-old veteran police officer, shot sixteen-year-old Matthew "Peanut" Johnson in the boy's back. Johnson died.[1] The shooting unleashed three days of conflict between BVHP residents, local police, and nearly two thousand National Guard troops. "I remember the day. It was warm. . . . and people was having balloon fights on Third Street. . . . [C]ommon typical day in an urban setting in America," remembered Menelek Walker, a life-long resident of Hunters Point, "but underneath all that outward expression was the feeling of being mistreated. . . . [I]t was a direct result of built-up frustration, fear, anger, and no ways to express it."[2]

While less known than the 1965 Watts Uprising, the BVHP Uprising informed the Black Power movement of the West. Two months after the 1966 Hunters Point Uprising, the Black Panther Party formed in Oakland, California. In 1968, a year-long student strike at San Francisco State University created the nation's first School of Ethnic Studies. The 1966 Uprising, like these events, served as culminations of longstanding Jim Crow practices in the San Francisco Bay Area. The Hunters Point Uprising of 1966 is a little-known part of an interconnected web of activism that defined San Francisco's civil rights history.

Historians have skimmed over Black political struggles in the Bay Area that predated the Black Panther Party. The 1966 Hunters Point Uprising was a turning point in this history. Victories in this struggle brought state and federal attention to address specific needs of Black San Franciscans, such as housing conditions and unemployment, but they failed to bring structural changes to iniquitous social conditions that affected Black San Franciscans. The 1966 Hunters Point Uprising confirmed that the lives of Black Americans in the North were as vulnerable to terrorism as they were in the South.

Perhaps the Hunters Point Uprising was forgettable because it took place in the heart of one of the country's most liberal cities. San Francisco's ethnic diversity has long concealed the fact that it practiced segregation in housing, employment, and policing. California's liberalism also masked the history of Jim Crow in San Francisco. World War II's end decreased the state's need for laborers. Decommissioning of industries hit African American workers hard, and the city's policies and institutions in housing and policing hurt African Americans. Prior to the 1940s, San Francisco did not have "a large industrial black working class like Chicago, Cleveland, Detroit, Pittsburgh, or Milwaukee, although the number of Blacks in industrial jobs did increase steadily after 1910."[3] During the mid-twentieth century, racist attitudes previously employed towards Japanese, Chinese, and Mexicans targeted the emerging Black communities of San Francisco. Although it is a place that defies the simple black-white binary that often frames civil rights history, San Francisco's rich diversity did not produce social equality. On the contrary, racism limited opportunities for social mobility. The 1966 Uprising brought attention to the fact that liberalism could coexist with, and perpetuate, racism.

The 1966 San Francisco Uprising was not an isolated event. Newspapers and political officials often treated it and other uprisings that way, but the history of this event shows how it was a protest against longstanding practices of economic disenfranchisement, police brutality, and deplorable housing conditions. To get to this larger history of grievance and struggle that predated the uprising, this essay draws on the voices of community members, newspapers, TV news coverage, police reports, and a 1963 film report by the American novelist James Baldwin, called *Take This Hammer*. In that film report, Baldwin journeys to San Francisco to "pay his dues," arguing that "what is really crucial is whether or not the . . . people in the country . . . are able to recognize that there is no moral distance . . . between the facts of life in San Francisco and the facts of life in Birmingham."[4] Baldwin understood fundamentally that Jim Crow was not limited to the South. The same social forces that disenfranchised African Americans in the South also existed in the North and the West. The uprising against Matthew Johnson's murder was a reckoning with this history of the Jim Crow North.

Origins of Black Bayview–Hunters Point

The World War II era facilitated the growth of a strong Black, working-class community in San Francisco's BVHP. African Americans from mainly Texas, Louisiana, Arkansas, and Oklahoma embarked on the longest route of the Great Migration, and planted their roots in the unfamiliar soil of the West. Historian Isabel Wilkerson wrote that "the people who ultimately made lives for themselves in the North and West were among the most determined of those in the south, among the most resilient of those who left, and the most resourceful of Blacks in the North."[5] Florence Richardson, an African American migrant to San Francisco, viewed the city as "the path to gold."[6] But, it was not only San Francisco's beauty that brought African Americans to the Bay Area; they came for jobs. The construction of San Francisco's Hunter's Point Naval Shipyards, purchased by the Navy in December 1939, operated primarily as a ship-building and -repair facility from 1945 to 1974, transforming BVHP from a thriving diversified economy of butcheries, breweries, truck farms, and fisheries to a war-based economy dependent upon thousands of migrant workers. The San Francisco Bay Area became the biggest single shipbuilding center in the nation, employing nearly 240,000 people at its peak in 1943.[7]

Various ethnic populations were allowed to be laborers in the West, but not full citizens. Despite the immediate financial gains presented by the war industry, San Francisco lacked adequate housing and services needed to meet the demands of a growing population of workers, many of whom were Black. African Americans came to San Francisco in the thousands, and both formal and informal Jim Crow practices in the private and public housing sectors confined them to primarily the Bayview–Hunters Point and Fillmore/Western Addition districts of San Francisco. In 1942 the San Francisco Housing Authority (SFHA) erected a large, fourteen-thousand-unit housing development for the families and employees of the Hunters Point Navy Shipyard. Fearing integration, the SFHA placed African Americans in separate units.[8] This area, known as Hunters Point, would become permanent and primarily Black. The Hunters Point Housing development, and the private residential area around it, would become Bayview–Hunters Point. That same year, Executive Order 9066, which called for the removal and internment of Japanese, created housing opportunities for African Americans in the Western Addition/Fillmore neighborhood of San Francisco. By the 1950s the Black population of San Francisco would increase dramatically, making African Americans the second largest ethnic population, growing from 4,846 in 1940 to 43,502 by 1950, reaching its peak in 1970 at 96,078.[9] Opportunities for young people coming of age in the West in the 1960s would become increasingly scarce. As an unidentified Hunters Point youth in 1963 explained, "[T]he white man [is] not taking advantage of you out in public like they doing down in Birmingham, but he's killing you with that pencil and paper, brotha."[10] That "pencil and paper" symbolized an overall lack of local and federal will to ensure the economic and social equality of Black San Franciscans as the war industries declined.

The uprising of 1966, and others that took place in that decade, clashed with and fueled the rising tide of a burgeoning conservative movement in northern and central California. The 1964 Republican National Convention, held in San Francisco's Cow Palace, brought out fully hooded members of the Ku Klux Klan in support of Republican nominee Barry Goldwater, and local NAACP counterprotesters to the steps of San Francisco's City Hall. One year prior, the California Fair Housing Act, or Rumford Act, was passed, intended to address longstanding practices of racial discrimination in the rental or sale of property. In 1964, the act was nullified by the overwhelming passage of Republican-backed Proposition 14 on grounds that it violated the rights of private owners. The passage of Proposition 14 amid the election of Barry Goldwater reflected the rise of racial conservatism in California, weakening the prospects for a new generation of young people. The shooting of Matthew "Peanut" Johnson and the subsequent uprising of '66 were consequences of the city's and state's failure to adequately address Jim Crow in the North.

Black San Francisco's 1960s Struggles in Housing

African Americans could be laborers, but not neighbors. They would experience residential restrictions and racial discrimination in both the public and private housing sectors. Racial segregation was practiced and defended by city officials in San Francisco. Following the model of the Navy, the San Francisco Housing Authority unanimously adopted a resolution stating that it "shall act with established uses, customs, and traditions of the community" in mind, and would not "enforce the commingling of races, but shall insofar as possible maintain and preserve the same racial compositions which exist in the neighborhood where a project is located."[11] On May 28, 1942, the housing authority also adopted what came to be referred to as a "neighborhood pattern," which used race to determine the occupancy of the federally funded housing communities. In 1946, the San Francisco Housing Authority expanded these plans with the development of five additional permanent low-income housing communities throughout the city, utilizing this "neighborhood pattern." Out of the six housing projects available to applicants—Westside Court, Holly Courts, Potrero Terrace, Sunnydale, Ping Yuen, and Valencia Gardens—Black tenants were only admitted to Westside Court and Chinese applicants were similarly segregated to the Ping Yuen Housing Projects.[12]

Laws meant to protect African Americans were weakly enforced. In 1949 the San Francisco Board of Supervisors cast a vote to oppose racial discrimination or segregation in any programs undertaken by the city's Redevelopment Agency; but due to opposition, an ordinance that would make discrimination a misdemeanor was struck down under the State Community Redevelopment Act.[13] Toni Carpenter recalls that "the whites stayed on the upper part of Hunters Point and we stayed down on the lower part near the slaughter yards, the junk yards."[14] There was no need for signs that read "colored" or "white," when racist policies and practices at the local and state levels predetermined what spaces people inhabited. Ms. Florence Richardson experienced blatant racial discrimination in her search for housing in San Francisco. When responding to an ad for a rental unit, she recalled the property manager's reaction, saying, "[H]e just outright told me he wouldn't rent to colored or Chinese."[15]

Opposition grew against such practices. In October 1947, the newly formed California Federation for Civic Unity (CFCU), comprised of forty-six interracial civic and community groups from all over the state, adopted a platform that called for a statewide committee to fight "restrictive covenants by which property owners refuse to sell houses to Negroes and other 'minority' group members" and to implement educational programs and local discussions of police brutality, discrimination, and unemployment of "Negroes in major industrial areas [who] suffered three times as much unemployment as white persons."[16] By 1952, this growing political opposition laid the foundation for a groundbreaking civil rights case. NAACP attorney Terry Francois took the lead on the case of Mrs. Mattie Banks and James Charley Jr., an African American couple, who sued the San Francisco Housing Authority after unsuccessfully attempting to gain access to the North Beach Housing Project, another permanent public housing community.[17]

In October of 1952, Superior Court Judge Melvin L. Cronin ruled in favor of Banks and James Charles Jr. The judge found that the Housing Authority was acting unconstitutionally by "excluding Negroes from five of the six housing projects and segregating them to West Side Court."[18] Legal proceedings continued into the next year.

In testimony taken under oath, the executive director of the San Francisco Housing Authority, John Beard, openly admitted to segregating tenants by race. When asked "if a Negro with the best types of qualifications, say it is a Negro veteran who has been disabled, veteran who has been displaced, and who applied for housing in Holly Court [one of the four housing developments designated for whites], under your instruction would you admit him to Holly Court?" Beard replied,

A: We have no displaced Negro applicants.
Q: If such applicant would apply, would you admit him to Holly Courts?
A: No.
Q: Because he is a Negro, is that correct, or because he is non-white is that correct?
A: Yes, I would prefer to put it that way because he is non-white.[19]

Community organizations such as the San Francisco Branch of the NAACP, the Council for Civic Unity, the Japanese American Citizenship

League, and the Urban League formed coalitions to challenge the San Francisco Housing Authority's practice of following what they referred to as a "neighborhood pattern." The San Francisco Housing Authority filed a countersuit to appeal Cronin's ruling but lost the appeal, marking a major civil rights victory for the NAACP, Mattie Banks, and all Black San Franciscans.

* * *

Neighborhood covenants and discrimination were also used to maintain Jim Crow segregation in San Francisco's private housing sector. The local NAACP president, John Adams Jr., and field secretary, Lester P. Bailey, observed that "segregated islands of residency were springing up all over the city."[20] In 1957, the city gained national attention when world-famous centerfielder for the San Francisco Giants, Willie Mays, was denied the right to buy property near the city's affluent St. Francis Wood neighborhood. This came to be known as the "Willie Mays Incident."[21] The property owner argued that he "was under tremendous pressure from the neighborhood not to sell to Negroes." Mays was only able to finalize the purchase of his home after much public pressure. In an effort to maintain the liberal image of San Francisco, mayor George Christopher, offered Mays haven in his own home. Mays respectfully declined, and following the purchase, the mayor seemed relieved "that this city of St. Francis has retained its reputation as an understanding and progressive city."[22] Yet, for the majority of Black San Franciscans, these practices continued outside of the eye of the press, concentrating Black San Franciscans primarily in the Hunters Point and Fillmore districts.

In addition to segregation in public housing and discrimination in private housing, the quality of public housing for Black San Franciscans remained an ongoing issue, especially in Hunters Point, where the conditions of the public housing were often unbearable. This barracks-style housing, originally meant to temporarily house employees of the Navy Shipyard, was isolated from stores, other non–public housing residences, transportation, and public services (emergency and nonemergency). These permanent public-housing communities were spread throughout the entire city, and sometimes literally next door to privately owned or more affluent residences. A handful of these permanent public housing communities, such as the Alice Griffith, Sunnydale, and West

Point communities, were severely isolated and hidden within pockets of the city. In October of 1965 the local news periodical the *Spokesman* quoted a resident tenant who observed that "rats as big as coke bottles can be found running about the Alice Griffith project just before the sun goes down."[23] Another tenant, Ethelene Wilson, recalled that "she could hear rats in the walls, and that her young children have found the filthy rats dead in the streets and sidewalks."[24] The newspaper predicted that the residents of the Alice Griffith Project located in BVHP "will do something to force the Housing Authority to do something about this deplorable living condition."[25]

The residents of BVHP, unwilling to accept these conditions, made many attempts to engage local officials in order to improve conditions. On October 14, 1965, concerned citizens from the Sunnydale and Yerba Buena Plaza housing projects joined the tenants of the Alice Griffith Project to inundate the regular Thursday meeting of the San Francisco Public Housing Commission. A lifetime resident and community organizer of BVHP, Ms. Osceola Washington, "entered the complaints of residents of the Alice Griffith [development] with regards to rats and the lack of any sort of 'community' facilities including a child care center." The crowd, which "represented unions, block clubs, church groups, and many other organizations," accused "the Housing Authority . . . of failures in dealing with problems of pest control, repairs and services, unjust or degrading rules and regulations, and insufficient concern for the tenants as people instead of names on a card."[26]

These forms of civic-minded activism and protest were well documented in San Francisco and took place both before and after the 1966 Uprising. On March 8, 1966, fifteen BVHP residents staged a sit-in, preventing the forceful eviction of Alice Griffith Project tenant Ollie Wallace, father of two, who was awakened by the sheriff and movers. Wallace was not being evicted because of failure to pay rent on time but because he failed to pay erroneous fines, including "court fees for the eviction, as well as the cost of the movers for the furniture, both of which he was not made aware of."[27] In addition, he had already paid his rent to the Housing Authority, so it was a great surprise to him that he was being evicted. These types of evictions were common, and the community continued its organization against such practices. The following day, March 9, 1966, sixty BVHP residents took over a special meeting of the San Francisco Housing Authority and demanded that their grievances be heard. The small boardroom was packed wall to wall, as Housing Authority official Steven Walters quickly attempted to adjourn the meeting, exclaiming, "[W]e are not going to discuss the Hunters Point problem today."[28] Community members then blocked the exits as George Earl, chairman of the Inter-Block Council (a grassroots BVHP community organization), spoke on a microphone provided by the press, stating, "We have long complained and long been ignored. We again rehearse our complaint. Number one: evictions can no longer be done in the highhanded manner, which has become routine. We protest any evictions which is done without exhausting all methods of resolving the principle problems involved." After the statement was read, "the group sang 'we shall overcome' [allowing] the commission to leave, and [then they] proceeded to demonstrate outside."[29] Following this action, the Housing Authority agreed to halt further evictions and all disposed actions, pending a reexamination of their policy.

Activism and civic engagement were strategies used by BVHP residents both before and after the uprising of 1966. In October of 1966, less than a month after the 1966 Hunters Point Uprising, residents from various housing projects in BVHP formed the Hunters Point Tenant Union and threatened a rent strike, demanding "covers on all drains, extermination of roaches and rats, installation of at least one detachable window screen for each room in each apartment, establishment of coin operated washer and dryer in various locations throughout the Hunters Point area, establishment of a more responsive, courteous and effectual relationship between Housing Authority and Tenants."[30] This collective response in the form of a strike reflects the deep determination of Hunters Point residents to fight against Jim Crow practices in the West. But their grievances went largely unmet. The 1966 Uprising happened because the activism of the BVHP community, in the years before the uprising, was ignored by city officials and policy makers, who also ignored the impact of Jim Crow.

Black San Francisco's Employment Struggles

The rapid industrialization as a result of World War II proved to be fruitful for Black migrants coming west, but a sharp economic decline followed the end of the Korean War. As a young man in BVHP, Toni Carpenter "realized you can't just live in a neighborhood without being a part of the economical base."[31] Donna Jean Murch concurs with this view, positing that "in Oakland, and for much of the Black population in Richmond, Hunters Point, and South Berkeley, five short years of boom developed into several long decades of bust."[32] In 1966 alone, four of California's Special Youth Employment Offices estimated at least twelve thousand unemployed youths, the majority of whom were African American.[33] Additionally, in 1960, the largest concentrations of low-income residents with low levels of educational attainment, and the highest levels of unemployment in all of San Francisco, resided in Hunters Point.[34] While this new generation of youth had more access to education than their parents and grandparents, they still would live under the yoke of Jim Crow. There has been much more scholarship on the Black experience in Oakland; because the population was smaller, San Francisco has not been as associated with the Black freedom struggle.

San Francisco's system of Jim Crow yielded opportunity to Blacks when doing so benefited the city economically, but the city lacked the willingness to ensure that Black San Franciscans would have any sustained economic and employment opportunity. The San Francisco Navy Shipyard employed close to eighty-five hundred civilians by the mid-1950s, and in the Bay Area, as a whole, "over 70 percent of Black newcomers found work in the shipyards, and Black female employment tripled."[35] However, as the war drew to a close, employment opportunities dwindled for Black migrants and their children, who were coming of age in the city. As a local Hunters Point resident explained in 1963, "[Y]oung people go to school together, they graduate off the same stage and then when it comes to jobs, the black face is not qualified, but they graduate and then my daughter has to clean up the same girl's house that she graduates [with] on stage."[36]

In 1960, the San Francisco Commission on Equal Employment Opportunity reported that "discrimination in San Francisco may be less overt . . . but it exists."[37] One complaint of discrimination, filed with the commission, involved a transportation company that transferred part of its business to a subsidiary, thereby eliminating a number of positions. The subsidiary then rehired the white terminated employees and denied all ten formerly employed African Americans any consideration for employment.[38] Denial of positions in skilled labor, denial of access into higher-paying industries, and discriminatory hiring practices were not openly sanctioned by the law, but were in fact the lived experiences of African Americans in San Francisco.

Black San Francisco's Struggles with Police Brutality

The killing of Matthew Johnson was not an isolated incident, nor was it the singular cause of the 1966 Hunters Point Uprising. It was but a spark that ignited longstanding frustrations with housing, unemployment, and police brutality. Instances of police brutality were well known and common in San Francisco, reinforcing visceral feelings of anger and oppression. Understanding the fragility of police-community relations in Black San Francisco, Police Chief Thomas J. Cahill created a Police-Community Relations Unit in April 1962 to "project a different image of the department to the community."[39] By 1962, the San Francisco Police Department (SFPD) had committees set up in four police districts. The SFPD understood that the weakened police-community relations were not "confined to police problems, but they run the gamut from community to personal."[40] Despite these efforts, modes of policing BVHP led to highly publicized instances of brutality, diminishing any gains made by Cahill's efforts, which were too little, too late, and failed to address the deeper institutional problems that would create the reality of the 1966 BVHP Uprising.

On December 14, 1964, San Francisco mail clerk Issac Hinton called the police to the residence of an unidentified female friend, after an ex-boyfriend arrived and threatened them both. Hoping that the police would prevent the situation from escalating, Hinton was surprised when police arrived and he was "told to shut up and dragged to police car . . . driven to the vicinity of Pine and Lyon Street [in San Francisco] while trying to explain he was the person that placed the call. The four officers then beat him with black-jacks, night sticks, and kicked him about the face and body."[41] Hinton was beaten so badly that the four police officers took him to San Francisco General Hospital, where, Hinton reported, "he was beaten" again by officers.[42] Hinton was later found not guilty of resisting arrest in municipal court. Hinton could not return to work for six weeks after the incident and sued SFPD for seventy-five thousand dollars. This incident, two years before the uprising, is but one in a long pattern of injustice.[43]

The next year another highly publicized incident of police brutality brought attention to the terrorism experienced by Black San Franciscans. In July of 1965, one year before the uprising, thirty-one-year-old Ralph Newman voluntarily went to the San Francisco Hall of Justice for traffic warrants amounting to sixty-nine dollars. He was subsequently taken to the city prison; when Newman refused to empty his pockets, an officer struck him. "A second policeman, according to Newman, asked to be given a turn at punching him, to which his colleague readily consented." After having suffered a beating from both officers while being detained, Mr. Newman "began to vomit blood" and was taken "to Mission Emergency Hospital."[44] Newman's wife demanded his release, so he could be transferred to a private hospital for treatment. The police denied his release because of the sixty-nine-dollar warrant, and only after several hours was he transferred to Mt. Zion Hospital, where he required surgery.

Consistent acts of police brutality leading up to the San Francisco Uprising would make the 1966 murder of Matthew Johnson a tinderbox situation. In the fall of 1965, the better-known Watts Uprising acted as a warning to Jim Crow cities all over the country and illustrated a definitive shift towards self-defense and self-determination. Uprisings are never a chosen political destination but the byproduct of the consistent denial of basic human rights. Americans, both Black and white, understood that Watts did not happen in a vacuum; similar acts could happen anywhere, even in San Francisco.

In mid-July of 1966, two months prior to the Hunters Point Uprising, there was a "near riot" in San Francisco's Fillmore District after off-duty African American police officer Herman George shot robbery suspect Frank Jackson in the stomach. A crowd of 200–250 young people gathered at the scene of the shooting and threw bottles at Officer George. African American youth Larry Scott warned, "[O]ur brothers in Hunters Point, Daly City, the Bayview and the Fillmore know that was just a warm-up too. You know what happened in Watts and Chicago, man? Well that's gonna happen here too."[45] People in Hunters Point and all over the country knew that social conditions had reached a tipping point.

The summer of 1966 in San Francisco was one of the hottest.[46] In July of 1966, at a press conference in San Francisco, Dr. Martin Luther King Jr. had made clear that "our nation's summers of riots are caused by our nation's winters of delay and as long as justice is postponed, as long as these problems are there, we are on the verge of social disruption and it hurts not only the Black man, it hurts our nation as a whole."[47]

On September 27, 1966, sixteen-year-old Matthew "Peanut" Johnson was shot in the back and killed by fifty-one-year-old veteran police officer Alvin Johnson. The shooting of Matthew Johnson took place in broad daylight on "the Hill," an area encircled by low-income housing units. Shot from behind, Matthew fell down the hillside and died lying face down in the dirt. A registered nurse of the Economic Opportunity Center, Mrs. Louise Williams, attempted to administer first aid, but there was no chance of saving his life. Word spread throughout Hunters Point, and a crowd of nearly 150 children, adults, and youth looked down into the ravine at his lifeless body. This was the breaking point. People began to gather along Third Street, and as the evening approached, "throughout the area small groups could be seen congregating on every corner discussing the tragedy that had happened only hours before."[48]

Understanding the potential for violence, young community organizers and activists from the Bay View Community Center and the Local Youth for Service organization attempted to get people off the streets and to organize a meeting among youth, the mayor, and the police chief. They wanted to meet specifically with Mayor Shelly to discuss the immediate release of the officer who shot Johnson. The Youth for Service would later become the Peace Patrol, whose goal was to get young people out of harm's way during the uprising.[49] They established peaceful community patrols in Hunters Point and in other neighborhoods throughout the city, in Chinatown, North Beach, the Mission, and the Fillmore, understanding that "many of the youth [would] get hurt if the riot continues, because we can't win trying to fight the National Guard or the Police."[50] The mayor did not comply with these early requests, losing an important opportunity for peaceful intervention with these concerned young people. Like many activists engaged in the Black freedom struggle throughout the country during this time, they found themselves acting as buffers between the anguish of the Black community and a police force fully committed to restoring "law and order" through often indiscriminate and violent means.

Thomas C. Fleming of the *Sun-Reporter,* the city's oldest and largest Black-owned newspaper, recalls getting word of the shooting in BVHP and immediately heading to the area with the NAACP president Thomas Nathaniel Burbridge, to try to help mediate the situation. They called the mayor's office to come and address the group of youth, but the mayor refused. They then headed to the Potrero Hill Police Station, where they found Mayor Shelly and Chief of Police Thomas Cahill assessing the situation. Meanwhile, local police and groups of youth continued to gather on Third Street as tension increased.[51] These were the crucial hours in which the uprising could have been prevented, but instead city officials prepared for armed conflict.

Calls for police and government officials to come to the area, by youth activists and community members, continued to be unheard as the evening turned to night. In the absence of the mayor, the Potrero Hill police chief, following the direction of Mr. Greenville Jackson and Mr. Walter Scott of the Human Rights Commission, were escorted to the Economic Opportunity Center, where a group of forty to sixty youth organizers were already meeting. The youth demanded to know if the shooting officer, Alvin Johnson, had been charged or arrested for the killing. Chief Jackson made it clear that he could not comment on the investigation of the shooter, Officer Johnson.[52] This only fueled the frustrations of many youth, who personally knew Matthew Johnson and considered him a close friend. Chief Jackson's inability to communicate any significant information did little to lessen the tension within the community. The situation continued to escalate.

Eventually, Mayor Shelly decided to address the people of Hunters Point and was escorted by a small group of heavily armed police officers to the Bay View Opera House.[53] The crowd at the opera house consisted of both youth and a wider range of concerned community members. According to the local paper, *The Spokesman,* Mayor Shelly was unable to address the crowd because "by this time things were not quiet. Even the news of his coming was like so many of the remote promises that reflected in the open despair now turned to anger on the faces of every youth that Tuesday night."[54] Fleming recalled the crowd throwing eggs and vegetables at the mayor, who was booed by the crowd. The community had had enough; they demanded justice for Matthew. A frustrated

Shelly left the opera house to meet with Governor Pat Brown at the San Francisco Hall of Justice, where Officer Johnson was being sequestered. Prior to entering the Hall of Justice, Governor Brown held a press conference with the local media, stating, "We cannot have revolution in this country and I can assure the people of my state that I will do everything within my power to see that law and order is observed and the rights of person and property are carefully protected. And I'll tell you this—we're going to meet force with force."[55] The determination of the government to use the power of the state to inflict violence on the Hunters Point community, as opposed to using the power of the state to address the conditions of the Hunters Point community, reflected the inherent bias within the city's systems of governance towards communities of color.

The 1966 Uprising was a direct response to the longstanding social inequity and violence experienced in the daily lives of Black citizens in America. These types of violent social responses are the product of long-term exposure to Jim Crow. Local civil rights activist Carlton B. Goodlett urged citizens to

> never forget the fact that San Francisco has followed a national pattern in which racial violence has been triggered by police-Negro community confrontation . . . and in this instance, the slaying of sixteen-year-old [Matthew "Peanut" Johnson], nobody has gone before the citizenry and said "this police officer will be brought to justice."[56]

No matter the size of the community, if it was poor and Black, the response by the state would be the same, as then Governor Pat Brown was quoted earlier [saying] they "would meet force with force." Dr. Goodlett criticized the SFPD; even those who tried "to solve this on a citizen-by-citizen basis have been roughed up by the police" and "are the victims of [an] incensed feeling on the part of the police department."[57] He himself was threatened with a shotgun twice while attempting to get people off the street.

As time passed, small altercations took place between police and groups of youth, who continued to congregate in the streets. Rocks and bricks were thrown at police and firemen and a car set afire. A storefront window was smashed at the Rexall Drug Store near Third and Palou, along with several others of "white owned businesses," according to the local *Spokesman*. After a whole evening of unrest, there was still little to no acknowledgment of wrongdoing, further fueling feelings of injustice. Local and state officials had already committed themselves to violence as a means of resolution. Four days after the shooting of Matthews, the chief deputy attorney general, Charles O'Brien, even suggested the attorney general look into "studies in the development of specialized weapons for use by police officers," such as tranquilizer guns that would be "safe for human use" during riots.[58] O'Brien even used the circumstance of Matthew's death, insinuating that if "an officer came upon a boy stealing a car, the tranquilizer gun would be used—if needed." A younger generation was coming of age as civil rights commitments to nonviolent strategies waned, and violence was seen as a justifiable means to "contain" the Black population. A youth worker in BVHP complained that he had "been begging and pleading for seven years and all it's got me is a $1.35 an hour job, but you gotta' do better than this because I won't beg anymore."[59] Jim Crow in San Francisco successfully disenfranchised and marginalized Black San Franciscans to the point of desperation; Matthew's slaying brought the community to a breaking point.

Wednesday, September 28 was characterized by an increased police presence. Every corner had armed police and rifled officers occupying rooftops. Governor Brown declared a state of emergency. Curfews were implemented in both the Fillmore and BVHP districts. Following the governor's proclamation, nearly two thousand members of the National Guard, California Highway Patrol, and local police were deployed to the BVHP district over the course of three days.[60] Youth leaders, who earlier formed the Peace Patrol, hoping to mediate tension and get people out of harm's way, continued to push for meetings with the mayor. Although there were radio broadcasts that reported violence in the Fillmore, the staff of *The Movement* (the publication of the Student Nonviolent Coordinating Committee [SNCC]), found nothing but a few broken windows.[61]

In a check-in with the San Francisco Police in the BVHP area one day after the initial incident, according to local station KNTV, "[T]hey described the 18-block area of Third Street as jungle warfare."[62] This description of the community as a "jungle" ignored the root causes of the uprising, further dehumanized BVHP residents, and justified the use of force. As the *Los Angeles Sentinel* reported, "This cosmopolitan, sophisticated city by the Bay reverberated with racial tremors today, the aftermath of the worst ethnic-based violence in local history."[63] Even in Los Angeles, the idea that such racial unrest and oppression existed in San Francisco seemed surprising. Newspapers from all over the country chronicled the turmoil, but the community of BVHP and its history were still rendered invisible. The San Francisco Uprising of 1966 was a confirmation that the complex forces known as Jim Crow existed in the West, but this was not the story that made headlines.

The situation escalated more when rumors of a sniper among protesters circulated. A police officer in a passing squad car who was hit by a rock yelled, "I'm hit, I'm hit." The driver reporting to police headquarters did not clarify what he meant by "hit," and it was assumed that he was shot by a sniper. A battle line was drawn near the Bayview Community Center, where a large crowd of unarmed youth gathered. The police then shot into a group of roughly thirty youth outside the community center, where it was reported that children were inside. The director of the center, Harold Brooks, recalled, "[W]hen the firing broke out, bedlam followed, until I got them to lie down. I went out the front door to get them to stop firing and let the kids out." Seven people were wounded outside the building, including those clearly marked as Peace Patrol members. Adam Rodgers was one of those organizers desperately telling people on a bullhorn to get off the streets before he was shot in the back, asking, "Why did they shoot me?" No guns were found in the building, and no sniper was found.[64]

By Thursday, the last day of unrest, 161 people were reported injured, the majority of those injuries sustained by civilians, ten from gunshots. Many police and firemen were injured from bottles and rocks that were thrown, but the police report fails to indicate specifically what those injuries were. No police, firemen, Guardsmen, or Highway Patrol officers were reported shot, stabbed, or assaulted in the 128-hour period. Four hundred and fifty-seven persons were arrested throughout the entire city in connection to the incident, and property damage totaled $135,782.[65] The city of San Francisco and the community were stunned. Local and state officials felt they had successfully prevented "another Watts," but as the dust settled the community members of BVHP were left traumatized. The tragedy of Matthew's death began to sink in and the community mourned not only the loss of his life but also the sheer lack of empathy for their plight after years of organizing peacefully for social change in BVHP.

Over a thousand people attended the funeral of Matthew "Peanut" Johnson, whose procession passed on the same streets where battle lines had been drawn a few days earlier.[66] The procession of cars, which stretched as far as the eye could see, slowly made its way up Third Street, reflecting the long fight for Black freedom in Hunters Point, and in America. The news cameras waited anxiously in the neighborhood, suspecting that more violence would result from the funeral, but all they were able to capture were the sullen, tear-soaked faces of residents of a deeply wounded community.

The coroner cleared Officer Alvin Johnson, and he was reinstated to the police force with full pay. Although curfews were lifted by Friday, September 29, and the police and National Guard began to withdraw from the area, the people of BVHP knew the battle for justice was far from over. The ideals of self-defense and self-determination that would characterize the coming Black Power movement had taken root in Black San Francisco.

The 1966 uprising did not, however, completely diminish the will of the people to make change in their communities. It further politicized them and helped to foster important collaborations between local communities and political organizations. One year after the BVHP Uprising, in May of 1967, U.S. senators Robert Kennedy, George Murphy, and Joseph S. Clark visited San Francisco as part of their Poverty Tour to assess the effectiveness of the programs implemented under the War on Poverty. In a public hearing held in the Bay View Community Center one year after the uprising, Senator Kennedy asked, "Have the conditions that brought that about, have they changed over the period of the last 12 months?" The crowd unanimously stated, "No." Mrs. Osceola Washington, a long-time resident and community organizer, exclaimed "No . . . these men have grew up in this situation, police brutality, poor schools, poor education. . . . [I]f you are from Hunters Point you get no chance at all."[67] The morale was low, but Matthew Johnson's spirit lived on in the continued efforts of the community to create change in their lives.

In July of 1967 the Bayview Community Center lost its lease due to its inability to secure funding for its one-thousand-dollar rent. Similar grassroots organizations in BVHP that played a huge role in servicing youth had no real financial support from the city of San Francisco. Ruth Williams, an activist and member of the board for the Bayview Community Center, expressed her frustrations at a press conference in June of 1967, where she tearfully stated, "[F]or so long we have been appealing to other funding agencies for money, and it always seems as though it's something wrong with this particular organization, and I think it's just because we're poor people trying."[68] This is one of many key resources that dwindled in the wake of the uprising. The conversation with Bobby Kennedy a few months prior would come to represent the continued lack of commitment of the local, state, and federal government to poor Black communities such as BVHP in America. Ronald Reagan, who would ride this wave of conservatism to the governorship of California, serving two terms from 1967 to 1975, criticized "those that would trade our freedom for the soup kitchen of the welfare state."[69] Calls for "law and order" replaced antipoverty rhetoric, and excessive militarized violence against urban Black communities became the immediate solution to deeply rooted systemic issues of unemployment, police brutality, and inadequate housing.

Despite the deep wound caused by the 1966 uprising, the BVHP community and Black people all over the Bay Area recommitted to work together in common cause. In 1968, at San Francisco State University, students of all socioeconomic backgrounds, BVHP community members, and political organizations, like the Black Panther Party (formed roughly two months after the 1966 Uprising) would successfully strike for the first School of Ethnic Studies in the nation. BVHP mother, resident, and activist Eloise Westbrook spoke passionately at a rally in support of the strike on campus, in December of 1968, proclaiming, "I want you to know that I am a Black woman, I'm a mother, and I have 15 grandchildren, and I want a college that I can be proud of . . . . [W]hen I die I'm dead and you better believe it, but I'm dying for the rights of people."[70] She knew that the struggles of Bayview–Hunters Point were the struggles of all oppressed people. Her words are echoed by her comrade, Ruth Williams, who unapologetically declared, "I'm here to say I'm from the ghetto community. . . . [W]hen I rise up just about the masses of Hunters Point rise up too."[71]

NOTES

1 Ford E. Long and Richard Trueb, *128 Hours: A Report of Civil Disturbance in the City and County of San Francisco* (San Francisco: San Francisco Police Department, 1966), 2–4. Available at https://archive.org (accessed January 2017).

2 Alonzo Menelek Abdul Raheem Walker oral history interview (film), conducted by Aliyah Dunn-Salahuddin, San Francisco, California, January 20, 2017 (in author's possession).

3 Albert S. Broussard, *Black San-Francisco: The Struggle for Racial Equality in the West, 1900–1954* (Lawrence: University Press of Kansas, 1993), 221–28.

4 Richard O. Moore, *Take This Hammer*, 16mm b&w optical sound film. San Francisco: WNET/KQED, 1964. San Francisco Bay Area Television Archive, San Francisco State University DIVA Collection. Video, https://diva.sfsu.edu (accessed March 2018).

5 Isabel Wilkerson, *The Warmth of Other Suns: The Epic Story of America's Great Migration* (New York: Random House, 2010), 264.

6 "Florence Richardson, oral history interview conducted by Albert S. Broussard, 1976-7-12." San Francisco Public Library, San Francisco History Oral History Project Collection. Transcript. San Francisco History Center, Neighborhood Files.

7 Boyden, Richard, "Where Outsized Paychecks Grow on Trees: War Workers in San Francisco Shipyards," *Prologue: The Journal of the National Archives* 23 (Fall 1991): 253.

8 Richard Rothstein, *The Color of Law: A Forgotten History of How Our Government Segregated America* (New York: Liveright, 2017), 27–30.

9 Bay Area Census, African-American Population 1940–1970, (accessed February 19, 2010), www.bayareacensus.ca.gov.

10 Moore, *Take This Hammer*.

11 Broussard, *Black San-Francisco*, 222–23.

12 Bernard Taper, "Housing Authority Urged to Give Up Segregation," *San Francisco Chronicle*, June 7, 1953. From News Bank, http://infoweb.newsbank.com.

13 "Supervisors Vote to Ban Race Bias in Housing Plan," *San Francisco Chronicle*, May 7, 1949. From News Bank, http://infoweb.newsbank.com.

14 Claude (Toni) Carpenter oral history interview, conducted by Aliyah Dunn-Salahuddin, San Francisco, California, January 20, 2017 (in author's possession).

15 "Florence Richardson, oral history interview."

16 "Racial Discrimination in State Hit by Civic Unity Federation," *Berkeley Daily Gazette*, October 20, 1947.

17 Broussard, *Black San-Francisco*, 223.

18 "Supervisors Vote to Ban Race Bias in Housing Plan," *San Francisco Chronicle*, May 7, 1949.

19 Bernard Taper, "Housing Authority Urged to Give Up Segregation," *San Francisco Chronicle*, June 7, 1953. From News Bank, http://infoweb.newsbank.com.

20 Ibid.
21 "Willie Mays Buys Home after Race Dispute," *San Francisco Chronicle*, November 15, 1957.
22 Ibid.
23 "Rats Run Rampant in Project," *Spokesman* (San Francisco, CA), October, 15, 1965.
24 Ibid.
25 Ibid.
26 John Pittman, "Beard Blasted: Public Housing under Fire," *Spokesman* (San Francisco, CA), October 15, 1965. From San Francisco Public Library, San Francisco History Center.
27 John Pittman, "Residents Stop Eviction," *Spokesman* (San Francisco, CA), March 19, 1966. From San Francisco Public Library, San Francisco History Center.
28 *Bayview Community Speak Out at Housing Authority Meeting.* B&w negative/magnetic sound film. San Francisco: Young Broadcasting of San Francisco, Inc. March 9, 1966. From San Francisco Bay Area Television Archive, San Francisco State University DIVA Collection. Video, https://diva.sfsu.edu (accessed September 16, 2018).
29 Ibid. and "Housing Commission Forced to Listen," *Spokesman* (San Francisco, CA), March 19, 1966. From San Francisco Public Library, San Francisco History Center.
30 "Rent Strike," *Spokesman* (San Francisco, CA), October 15, 1966. From San Francisco Public Library, San Francisco History Center.
31 Claude (Toni) Carpenter oral history interview.
32 Donna Jean Murch, *Living for the City: Migration, Education, and the Rise of the Black Panther Party in Oakland, California* (Chapel Hill: University of North Carolina Press, 2010), 31–40.
33 "A Suspicion—and Chaos Followed," *San Francisco Chronicle*, September 29, 1966. District edition, sec. B, p. 20.
34 United States Department of Labor, "Income, Education, and Unemployment in Neighborhoods," Maps I & II Correspondents between Tracts with Low Family Income and those with High Unemployment, April 1960. Print. San Francisco Public Library, Government Center.
35 Murch, *Living for the City*, 36.
36 Moore, *Take This Hammer*.
37 San Francisco Commission on Equal Employment Opportunity, *Final Report of the Commission on Equal Employment Opportunity of the City and County of San Francisco* (San Francisco, 1960), 1–2. From San Francisco Public Library, Government Center. Print (accessed March 2016).
38 Ibid.
39 John Pittman, "Police Community Relations in Poverty Office," *Spokesman* (San Francisco, CA), February 3, 1966. From the San Francisco Public Library, Magazine and Newspaper Center (accessed July 2017).
40 Ibid.

41 Thomas C. Fleming, "Four SF Policeman Sued For 75,000-Assault," *Sun Reporter* (San Francisco, CA), July 10, 1965. From the San Francisco Public Library, Magazine and Newspaper Center (accessed July 2017).

42 Ibid.

43 Ibid.

44 Fleming, "Four SF Policeman Sued."

45 Paul T. Miller, *The Postwar Struggle for Civil Rights: African-Americans in San Francisco, 1945–1975* (New York: Routledge, 2010), 88–89.

46 Long and Trueb, *128 Hours*, 1.

47 "Rev. Dr. Martin Luther King Jr. on Civil Unrest." 16mm, b&w. San Francisco: CBS5 KPIX-TV, 1966. From the San Francisco Bay Area Television Archive, San Francisco State University DIVA Collection. Sound film. https://diva.sfsu.edu (accessed March 2017).

48 McKinze Morris and Phil Kay, "The Outbreak: Moment to Moment," *Spokesman* (San Francisco, CA), October 8, 1966, editorial, p. 4.

49 Ibid.

50 "Youth for Service Press Conference (Hunters Point)." B&w negative/magnetic sound film. San Francisco: Young Broadcasting of San Francisco, Inc., September 30, 1966. From San Francisco Bay Area Television Archive, San Francisco State University DIVA Collection. Video, https://diva.sfsu.edu (accessed July 2014).

51 Chris Carlsson, "Thomas C. Fleming on the 1966 Hunters Point Riot," San Francisco: Shaping San Francisco, 1999, http://www.foundsf.org (accessed September 16, 2018).

52 Long and Trueb, *128 Hours*.

53 The Bay View Opera House is a historic building in BVHP that continues to serve as a meeting place and venue for local community members and organizations located near the Bayview Community Center, a geographically central location of the 1966 Uprising.

54 Morris and Kay, "The Outbreak."

55 "Governor Pat Brown speaking on Bay View Hunters Point Social Uprising." 16mm b&w optical sound film. San Francisco: CBS5 KPIX-TV, 1966. San Francisco Bay Area Television Archive, San Francisco State University DIVA Collection. Video, https://diva.sfsu.edu (accessed June 26, 2016).

56 Ibid.

57 "Carlton B. Goodlett on Police Behavior." B&w sound film. San Francisco: Young Broadcasting of San Francisco, Inc., September 29, 1966. The DIVA Project: San Francisco Bay Area Television Archive, San Francisco State DIVA Collection, https://diva.sfsu.edu (accessed June 26, 2016).

58 "Advanced Units of the California National Guard Are Moving into Candlestick Park to Camp Out for Possible Riot Duty in the City," September 28, 1966. San Francisco: KNTV, 1966. Digital copy KNTV News (Shot Logs). From the San Francisco Bay Area Television Archive, San Francisco State University DIVA Collection, San Francisco Bay Area Television Archive (accessed June 26, 2016).

59 John Pitman, "Young Leadership in Crisis," *Spokesman* (San Francisco, CA), October 8, 1966.

60 Long and Trueb, *128 Hours*, 36.

61 "Hunters Point—Cops Shoot into Community Center Sheltering 200 Children," *Movement* 2, no. 9 (October 1966), cover.

62 "Bayview Hunters Point Uprising, 9/28/66." KNTV Shot Logs. From the San Francisco Bay Area Television Archive, San Francisco State University DIVA Collection. https://diva.sfsu.edu (accessed June 2015).

63 "Riot Creates Tensions in Troubled Bay Area," *Los Angeles Sentinel*, September 28, 1966.

64 "Hunters Point—Cops Shoot into Community Center."

65 Long and Trueb, *128 Hours*, 114.

66 "Hunters Point—Cops Shoot into Community Center."

67 "Robert Kennedy Visiting with Black Community," archival news film. San Francisco: Young Broadcasting of San Francisco, Inc., May 10, 1967. From the San Francisco Bay Area Television Archive, San Francisco State University DIVA Collection. Video, https://diva.sfsu.edu (accessed September 29, 2015).

68 "Bayview Community Center Eviction." 16mm b&w negative. San Francisco: Young Broadcasting of San Francisco, Inc., June 19, 1967. From the San Francisco Bay Area Television Archive, San Francisco State University DIVA Collection. Silent/sound film, https://diva.sfsu.edu (accessed May 2016).

69 Ronald Reagan, US Archives and Records Administration: Ronald Reagan and Presidential Library and Museum. Accessed June 15, 2017. From the San Francisco Bay Area Television Archive, San Francisco State University DIVA Collection. www.reaganlibrary.gov (accessed June 2017).

70 "Bayview Hunters Point Community Support SF State Strike."16mm b&w film. San Francisco: CBS5 KPIX-TV, July 28, 1967. From the San Francisco Bay Area Television Archive, San Francisco State University DIVA Collection. Archival news film. https://diva.sfsu.edu (accessed May 2016).

71 Ibid.

Recorder's Court Judge George W. Crockett Jr., February 1968.
Walter P. Reuther Library, Archives of Labor and Urban
Affairs, Wayne State University.

9

"The Shame of Our Whole Judicial System"

George Crockett Jr., the New Bethel Shoot-In, and the Nation's Jim Crow Judiciary

SAY BURGIN

[African Americans] had no rights which the white man was bound to respect.
—Supreme Court Chief Justice Roger Taney, 1857

[T]here is no equal justice for black people in our criminal courts today . . . because our judges, by their rulings, make it so.
—Recorder's Court Judge George Crockett Jr., 1971

In the early morning hours of Sunday, March 30, 1969, in an unused office in Detroit's First Precinct police station, Recorder's Court judge George Crockett Jr. announced that court was in session. A few hours earlier, he had received reports that one white officer had been killed and another wounded in a "shoot-out" outside the New Bethel Baptist Church. Police had sprayed the church with gunfire and arrested all 142 African American men, women, and children inside. Crockett learned that these individuals were being held incommunicado, unable to contact attorneys. Worried that police were denying black Detroiters their constitutional rights, he hurried to the precinct and, right there in the station, assembled habeas corpus proceedings. In the intense weeks that followed, amid much misreporting, Detroit police and news outlets mounted a campaign against Crockett, whom they accused of being an activist judge and impeding police work. An opposing camp of Crockett supporters quickly assembled, including a forty-group coalition called the Black United Front. At stake for both Crockett and his supporters was nothing short of a righteous blow to a criminal court system that claimed color-blindness but enacted highly racialized forms of "justice."

At the time of the New Bethel shoot-in,[1] Crockett had practiced law for thirty-five years, including over twenty years in Detroit, and had served on the Recorder's Court bench (Detroit's criminal court) for over two years. During that time, he watched unequal justice operate as the judicial norm. Such was the necessary effect of a Jim Crow judiciary—a court system that was as old as the nation itself but that had become increasingly visible as African Americans shouldered a disproportionate bulk of the prison time associated with the doubling of crime rates throughout the 1960s.[2] A Jim Crow judiciary aimed less at the social separation codified through *Plessy v. Ferguson*—that 1896 Supreme Court decision mandating "separate but equal"—and more at creating a two-track system in which the courts maintained the constitutional rights of whites and the economically comfortable while abridging those of poor and black defendants. Indeed, it was the Supreme Court's 1857 *Dred Scott* decision that became the more enduring guide for the nation's judiciary: African Americans "had no rights which the white man was bound to respect."

To see the Jim Crow judiciary is to see that the ideal of judicial autonomy has operated as a mirage. At a distance—in our high school social studies classes—the bench is viewed as distinct, separate from the other major players in the courtroom, including the defense, prosecution, and police. It is seen as a check on police abuse and prosecutorial overreach. With closer examination, however, that sense of separateness evaporates. Theoretically, judicial independence and impartiality are supposed to ensure black defendants' due process rights and check the excesses of police and prosecutors. Yet, this ideal is not the reality, and these three arms of the state more often work as allies than as adversaries, more codependently than independently. That judicial neutrality is crucial to the way fairness and equality under the law are ostensibly guaranteed indicates the state's own investment in the mirage of judicial autonomy.

Ideologically, judges across the country have leaned heavily upon—and reproduced—racist ideas that twinned criminality and blackness.[3] In practice, they leaned on police and prosecutors. Judges enacted unequal justice every time they acted on the assumption that they should take their cues from and act in the interests of the police, what Crockett

referred to as "the old habit of *accommodating* the police and the prosecutor's office."[4] Thus, Jim Crow justice was enacted precisely *through*
relinquishing judicial autonomy and becoming the enforcement arm of
the police. Such "accommodation" inevitably entailed abandoning the
ideal of an adversarial courtroom—one in which the very existence of
oppositional powers was meant to ensure fairness and due process. It
also meant disposing of presumptions of innocence because "accommodating" prosecutors and police in their desires—for instance, for
high bail or deference in submitting evidence—necessarily involved
accommodating their efforts to demonstrate a defendant's guilt. With
the railroading of defendants' due process rights at a time—the 1960s—
when African Americans were becoming an even larger proportion of
criminal defendants, a Jim Crow judiciary ensured highly racialized outcomes in terms of key facets of the justice system, including habeas corpus, bail, sentencing, probation, and parole. A Jim Crow judiciary, thus,
laid the groundwork for the mass incarceration of African Americans
in the 1980s and beyond. When judges like Crockett actually exercised
independence and detached themselves from the wishes of police and
prosecutors—as happened in the wake of the New Bethel shoot-in—
they were accused of being unfair. By the time Crockett made his stand
in the spring of 1969, "[T]he erosion of constitutional rights and liberties" had gone on "for so long," he said, "that to most of us, the violation
of the law is the law."[5]

A double standard of justice could be seen in courtrooms across the
North throughout the 1960s. One New York judge, in 1969, gave a suspended sentence to a white man who pled guilty to illegally trading $20
million, but a few days later sentenced a black man to one year in jail
after he stole a television worth $100.[6] In 1967, a Cook County judge
sentenced the three white men who killed seventeen-year-old Jerome
Huey in the Chicago suburb of Cicero to a mere nine to twenty years
in prison. A *Chicago Defender* reader vented her frustrations with a reminder that in 1965 another Chicago judge had sentenced one black defendant, Charles Evans, to "67 to 130 years" for burglary and aggravated
assault.[7] Untold individual cases appeared through statistics. One study
of misdemeanor cases in Detroit's Recorder's Court in 1969 found that,
even with legal representation, judges sentenced African Americans to
jail at twice the rates of whites; that whites were twice as likely to receive

a fine as a penalty (rather than the harsher outcomes of jail time or probation); and that "black defendants were more likely than whites to have received no proper indication of the charge, the right to testify, or the right to call and cross-examine witnesses."[8]

The Black Power era was responsive to these injustices and produced powerful critiques of the nation's courts. The Black Panthers, for one, declared that "the many Black and poor oppressed people now held in U.S. prisons and jails have not received fair and impartial trials under a racist and fascist judicial system."[9] People also responded to the abuses carried out by police and courts during urban uprisings. Black Detroiters fought for justice after police killed three young black men during the July 1967 uprising, while Crockett spoke out from the bench about the railroading of black Detroiters' rights by his peers. His actions during the uprising made clear that police brutality required the consent of judges—that his colleagues chose to overlook illegal arrests and testimony of police violence. He made clear that judges allowed for the overprosecution of black folks, failing to check prosecutors. Such disruptions from court insiders took place throughout the 1960s and '70s as the numbers of black judges grew. By 1971, African Americans comprised a paltry 1 percent of judges on local or state benches—255 out of 21,294—roughly 90 percent of whom resided outside of the South.[10] Yet among this small band were vociferous critics of the bench whose rulings resisted Jim Crow dictates.

As Crockett's actions demonstrate, such resistance often met with swift reprisals from the police, prosecutors, lawmakers, and the larger public. Conservatives, including the Detroit News and the Detroit Police Officers Association (DPOA), led the way. Having served as unofficial Crockett watchdogs since he assumed the bench, they accused him of antipolice bias and racism. They sought his removal from office. Moderates and liberals, too, disregarded the critique of unequal justice that Crockett made in his actions. White officials like Governor William Milliken and Mayor Jerome Cavanaugh, along with the city's other white daily, the Detroit Free Press, focused criticism on the Republic of New Africa and framed Crockett's actions as "unorthodox." Black Detroiters had denounced the city's criminal justice system for years, reproaches that had heightened in the wake of the July 1967 uprising. Liberals repeatedly ignored these criticisms. That they did so again in the spring of 1969 meant they not only diverted time and attention away from the focus of Crockett and his supporters—a two-track system of justice. They also contributed to the justifications of Jim Crow in the North.

Northern-based judges like Crockett fit uneasily into a narrative of the black freedom movement that stresses southern segregation because of that narrative's emphasis on the Supreme Court. It stands in as a northern hero and savior-promoter of civil rights—as in *Smith v. Allwright*, *Shelley v. Kraemer*, and, especially, *Brown v. Board of Education*. When segregation is firmly located in the South, northern courts win easy praise and escape scrutiny; their judges do not require the kinds of checks that must be placed on southern counterparts. Consequently, while a boom in mass incarceration studies has inspired research into the intersection of civil rights/Black Power and criminal justice, the role of judges needs much more attention. Crockett's stance showed that segregated court outcomes were as much a reality in the North as in the South, for judges got the ultimate say in the denial of African Americans' civil liberties. Judges sealed the deal—police brutality and prosecutorial overreach could not stand without them. Crockett and his supporters understood this all too well. In the years that proved foundational to mass incarceration in America, black freedom activists understood that they could not wage war against northern inequalities without taking on the criminal justice system—and not just the police and prosecutors but the judges too.

Crockett would ultimately spend more than a decade criticizing the actions of his judicial peers. But of his many unpopular legal decisions, his actions in the New Bethel hearings most starkly demonstrated the high costs of opposing northern racial injustice. There were immediate calls for his impeachment, as well as threats to his life. But Crockett refused to back down. He repeatedly pointed out that the nation's unequal justice centered on the unfair practices of judges: "[T]here is no equal justice for black people in our criminal courts today, and what's more, there never has been. And this is the shame of our whole judicial system. . . . And this is so, not because the written law says it shall be so, rather it is so because our judges, by their rulings, make it so."[11] Governmental and legal bodies eventually declared that Crockett's actions in the New Bethel cases were legal and proper. Yet the campaign mounted against Crockett demonstrated that equal justice under the law would be as elusive to African Americans in the North as it was in the South.

* * *

Roughly 150 people remained at the New Bethel Church on the night of Saturday, March 29, 1969. They had gathered to celebrate the Republic of New Africa's (RNA) first anniversary. Founded by Detroit-based brothers Gaidi and Imari Obadele, the separatist group sought the secession of five southern U.S. states into a new black nation. By its one-year anniversary, it had established consulates in a handful of northern cities—and caught the attention of several surveillance divisions of the Detroit Police Department (DPD), Michigan State Police, and the Federal Bureau of Investigation. At around 11:30 that night, two white rookie policemen, Michael Czapski and Richard Worobec, pulled up to the church. Despite Michigan's open-carry laws, Worobec later claimed they were suspicious of armed men outside the church. Like many crucial details of this story, what happened next depended upon the storyteller. The DPD insisted that RNA members opened fire on the officers.[12] The RNA, however, testified that it was Czapski and Worobec who, without any provocation, initiated gunfire on RNA members outside the church, who then shot back in self-defense.[13]

Police back-up arrived quickly and in huge numbers after Worobec radioed that he and Czapski had been shot. On arrival, police fired off scores of rounds into the church, wounding four RNA members, including seventeen-year-old Abdul Bobo of Chicago.[14] Even the young man who would become the prosecution's star witness, nineteen-year-old David Brown Jr., attested that he had been "repeatedly kicked in the head by officers in the church."[15] Without knowing who shot Worobec and Czapski, but insisting the shooters had fled inside the church, police decided to arrest all 142 people in the building, including many children. Meanwhile, Czapski was pronounced dead on arrival at Henry Ford Hospital.

Gaidi Obadele, who had been driving away from the church at the time the first shots were fired, contacted Michigan House representative James del Rio, who, alongside Reverend C. L. Franklin—New Bethel pastor and Aretha Franklin's father—arrived at the station and saw a situation that reminded them of the abysmal detention conditions during Detroit's July 1967 uprising. Three and a half hours after being taken into custody, police still held all RNA arrestees incommunicado in the parking garage of the precinct. It appeared that the police had not even begun to process the arrestees, let alone allow them to make phone calls or contact lawyers. So, after ensuring that the women and children were brought out of the makeshift garage-prison, Franklin and del Rio went to the house of Judge George Crockett.[16]

In Crockett, the men knew RNA arrestees would find a judge whose first concern was equal justice under law. Crockett had been elected to Detroit's thirteen-judge Recorder's Court in 1966—one of that court's three black judges. Yet, years before, he had made a name for himself as a champion of the constitutional rights of groups who were rarely assured equal justice. He served as a defense attorney for the Communist Party in 1948–49 when its leaders were indicted under the Smith Act. Cited for contempt during this case, he served four months in a federal prison in Kentucky in 1952, saying he "regarded it as a badge of honor to be adjudicated in contempt for vigorously prosecuting what I believe to be the proper conception of the American Constitution."[17] When the House Committee on Un-American Activities came to Detroit in the 1950s, Crockett defended black trade union organizers. As one of its longstanding members, he pushed the National Lawyers Guild to create the Committee for Legal Assistance in the South (CLAS), which provided free legal assistance to civil rights workers in the 1960s.[18]

Crockett directed CLAS during the 1964 Mississippi Freedom Summer, and as Ernie Goodman, Crockett's white law partner, recalled, this work led Crockett "to the conclusion that he could become more directly and effectively involved in the struggle for justice and equality" by running for office.[19] In 1965, he made a bid for Detroit's Common Council, his platform centering on black Detroit's housing, employment, and civil liberties. In his campaign materials, he vowed to "separate and divorce the Police Department from the Prosecutor's Office."[20] Unsuccessful in this election, Crockett later learned that the FBI's Counter-Intelligence Program had aided conservatives in red-baiting him. The Bureau's Detroit office mailed anonymous letters to conservatives in the area in which it alluded to Crockett and his "communist background" and called him a "charlatan." Despite losing the election, Crockett did not think the FBI's foul play had cost him the election, though he did suspect further harassment the following year when he ran for Recorder's Court.[21] That time, Crockett later reflected, the FBI's dirty tricks "nearly cost him the court race."[22] Still, in 1966 voters sent Crockett to the Recorder's Court, which they continued to do until he retired in 1980.

Crockett's experiences as a lawyer had taught him that, when it came to civil rights and civil liberties, rather than "checking" their excesses and oversights, the judiciary often aided the executive and legislative branches. In the 1940s and '50s, judges chose not to uphold Communists' First Amendment rights; in the '50s and '60s, their decisions enabled unsafe conditions for civil rights workers. In Detroit, the cozy relationship between Recorder's Court and the police was an open secret. Crockett recalled to one interviewer that, when he was a lawyer, there were countless occasions when he had requested a habeas corpus or bail hearing, "And I would be told, 'Counsel the police tell me that they can complete their investigation within 48 hours, so I think I'm going to put this whole thing over for 48 hours.' . . . I was determined when I got on the bench that I would not be accused of following that practice."[23]

To Crockett, a different kind of judiciary was necessary if the rights of unpopular defendants—including political dissidents and African Americans—were to be upheld.

Detroit's July 1967 uprising gave him ample opportunity to be a different kind of judge. That event laid bare the bench's collusion with police and prosecutors. Judicial conduct during the uprising illustrated that police brutality could not stand without the support of judges. At the outset, Wayne County prosecutor William Cahalan signaled to the Recorder's Court his plan to arrest as many people as possible by authorizing 98 percent of warrants requested, including thousands who were charged with looting despite a lack of evidence. His office also failed to reject what were in fact hundreds of illegal arrests for curfew violations. The city's original curfew proclamation did not stipulate that breaking the curfew would result in a misdemeanor charge. Yet police made curfew arrests illegally anyway, Cahalan processed the warrants, and most judges chose to detain those individuals.[24]

Cahalan explicitly requested that judges impose high bails—up to ten thousand dollars—to keep "off the streets" the seventy-two hundred individuals arrested during the week-long revolt. Executive Judge Vincent Brennan did him one better by urging his peers to set bails up to twenty-five thousand dollars. Most willingly complied. They systematically violated Eighth Amendment protections, failing to inquire into individual circumstances such as community and employment ties, as well as prior offenses. The *Michigan Law Review* estimated that at least half of arrestees were held on bonds exceeding ten thousand dollars, and its legal observers reported seeing a judge line up "fifteen or twenty unrepresented prisoners" to tell them they were all charged with looting and would each be held on ten thousand dollars' bond. The judge then called the next group and said, "You heard what I said to them, the same applies to you."[25] Brennan even ordered the sheriff not to honor *any* bonds so that bail could be reviewed and, potentially, raised further.[26] If by midweek some of Detroit still thought the bench acted independently, Judge Robert Colombo set them straight: "What we're trying to do here is keep them off the streets. . . . In a way we're doing what the police didn't do."[27]

To Crockett, the bench's actions constituted a "wholesale denial of the constitutional rights of virtually everyone who was arrested during that disturbance."[28] It was perhaps the clearest example of the way judges enacted a Jim Crow judiciary—the way they perpetuated it through their protection of police brutality and police and prosecutorial corruption. In their violations of Fifth, Sixth, Seventh, and Eighth Amendment rights, Crockett's peers refused to draw on the full arsenal of due process protections for black and poor defendants. As just one indication of the corruption in the criminal justice system during the uprising, by spring of 1968, with half of the thirty-two hundred "looting" cases cleared, 60 percent had resulted in dismissal and only two of the original charges had resulted in convictions.[29]

Crockett refused to be drafted into their efforts. In response to Brennan's request that judges impose bails of twenty-five thousand dollars, Crockett reminded his colleagues that they had a duty to uphold protections for reasonable bail: "I intend to exercise that responsibility." While ten Recorder's Court judges disallowed legal representatives in their courtrooms, Crockett took up an offer of legal advice from the Office of Economic Opportunity–funded Neighborhood Legal Services. Its members interviewed defendants and used phones that Crockett had brought in to verify information that could not be ascertained from missing case files. Crockett thus individualized bail levels. He released roughly one in ten prisoners who came before him on their own recognizance; an estimated six out of ten saw bail levels of two thousand dollars or less. Crockett's bail levels that week never exceeded five thousand dollars, which he applied in a handful of cases. He also threatened to hold the sheriff in contempt of court if he did not honor bail bonds.[30]

Though he later admitted that, even as the "lowest in the Court," his bails "still were much higher than they should have been," he spoke out against the "high bail policy."[31] Hundreds of innocent people, he said, had been "separated from their unknowing families and jobs and incarcerated in our maximum security detention facilities . . . without benefit of counsel, without an examination, and without even the semblance of a trial."[32] "Racist?" he posed: "Try to imagine what our system of justice—and those who administer it—would have required if these defendants had been white or rich. Hundreds of cases can be cited to show that for such defendants personal recognizance would be the only requirement for their immediate release."[33]

Crockett's own actions met with praise from many black Detroiters, the *Michigan Law Review*, and the *Detroit Free Press*. In May 1968, the *Michigan Law Review* published a scathing report of judicial conduct during the uprising but consistently singled out Crockett as a justice who prioritized due process rights.[34] This report prompted the *Free Press* to admit that "Judge Crockett proved that even under trying circumstances it was possible for the courts to be what they ought to be."[35]

Crockett's judicial integrity was the reason del Rio and Franklin turned to him a year and a half following the uprising—Sunday, March 30, the morning following the New Bethel shoot-in. Arriving at the precinct, he discovered that police still had not brought charges and that, though those being detained had not yet been able to make phone calls, police had begun fingerprinting and administering nitrate tests. Police had not granted detainees recourse to legal counsel nor made them aware of their right to counsel. Meeting with Police Commissioner Johannes Spreen, Crockett discovered that police did not even have a list of those detained. This he demanded, as well as an improvised courtroom and a prosecutor. He would begin habeas corpus hearings in the station itself.[36]

Throughout that morning and into the afternoon, police and prosecution released 130 individuals against whom they had no evidence. Prosecutor Cahalan wanted nine of the remaining individuals to be detained as "key suspects," including some individuals whose nitrate tests produced positive results. In a move that become hotly contested and

woefully misunderstood—the decision around which much controversy would swirl—Crockett ordered their release because, he argued,
the nitrate tests had been unconstitutional. Indeed, denying counsel to
all those arrested, let alone conducting nitrate tests on individuals who
had been held incommunicado, constituted violations of the Supreme
Court's recent *Miranda* ruling, he asserted. To Crockett, that decision
had been "drastic" but vital to "stop[ping] police from running rough-
shod over the rights of the accused."[37] Almost as if to prove his point,
Cahalan ordered the rearrest of one person, James Wheeler. Crockett
fired back, ordering Cahalan to appear later in court to show why he
should not be held in contempt.[38]

Beginning immediately and lasting throughout the month, conservative forces mounted a campaign against Crockett. They perpetuated the
erroneous claim that Crockett had released nearly all the prisoners. The
DPOA and the white daily *Detroit News* charged that Crockett had acted
out of step with the law and aided Worobec and Czapaski's shooters. The
Detroit News had long been criticizing Crockett's judicial conduct, particularly what it saw as Crockett's habit of providing light sentences to
black defendants.[39] It framed the New Bethel events as another example
of Crockett's misjudgments and gave little space to the question of police misconduct. "Police Fear Crockett Ruined Hunt for Killer," ran one
front-page headline. It seemed likely that Crockett "stretched his own
authority beyond its legal boundary" in "his haste to release the prisoners," the paper opined. It called for "an investigation into Judge Crockett's
conduct by the state judicial tenure commission."[40] In the week following the events, the *News* criticized black leaders for not condemning the
RNA or Crockett's actions, compared the RNA to the Ku Klux Klan, and
insisted that Crockett saw himself as an "advocate" for black defendants.
A cartoon it ran called "Next Case" pictured the release of several militarized militants—suited and booted in fatigues and berets—right under a
judge's (Crockett's) apathetic nose; a prosecutor (Cahalan) looks aghast.
Racism had nothing to do with the actions taken by police at the church
or police station, the *News* maintained; it was Crockett who turned the
whole affair into a race war.[41]

Meanwhile, police groups sought Crockett's removal from the bench,
portraying him as in cahoots with black "militants." A few days after
the habeas corpus hearings, off-duty officers and their families picketed

outside the Recorder's Court building, their placards reading, "Crocket Justice? Release killers. Prosecute prosecutors. Give license to kill policemen." Their petitions called for investigations into Crockett's conduct, alleging that he "conspired with known revolutionaries who planned the overthrow of the government."[42] The DPOA twice ran a full-page advertisement in the *Detroit News* that claimed to provide "the complete story of the assassination of patrolman Czapski." They accused Crockett of barring press from the habeas corpus proceedings at the police station, producing a writ on legally faulty grounds, and demonstrating a history of bias in support of black defendants. "Justice that is either all Black or all White," the ad concluded, "is not justice at all."[43] By the middle of April, the DPOA had mounted a campaign to see Crockett removed from office on grounds of "gross misconduct . . . persistent failure to perform his duties . . . and conduct clearly prejudicial to the administration of justice."[44]

Anti-Crockett forces were aided by the tamer criticisms of white moderates and public officials who, rather than charge bias, minimized the racialized dimensions of the events. Mayor Cavanagh backed the police and claimed that their actions ensured that another riot did not occur— apparently forgetting that the 1967 uprising began with the mass arrest of black Detroiters. He joined Governor Milliken and several Michigan State lawmakers in calling for the newly formed Judicial Tenure Commission to investigate Crockett, which it did starting in mid-April. One congressman from Detroit, Representative E. D. O'Brien, called for Crockett's outright removal from the bench.[45] The Motor City's other white daily, the *Detroit Free Press*, similarly supported police actions. More measured in tone than the *News*, it called the RNA "an irrational extremist group," asserted that Crockett did not act in accordance with "standard" procedures, and claimed that Crockett had impeded the police's investigation (though not irrevocably).[46] Disregarding the DPD's history of wrongfully arresting black Detroiters, the *Free Press* concluded that "the question of capricious or unnecessary arrest has been bothering civilized men for a long time," but that was no excuse for Crockett's actions.[47]

Thus, while conservative forces tended to blame all of black Detroit— for allowing for the creation of an "extremist" group like the RNA, for not condemning Crockett's actions, or for *being* Crockett—moderates lamented the RNA's existence but focused blame on Crockett's "hasty" and unorthodox judicial conduct. Common to both camps, though, were practices necessary to the maintenance of a Jim Crow judiciary: taking the police at their word, presuming that the role of the judge is to support the police, and assuming bias, if not blatant deceit, on the part of African Americans. Hence, as Crockett later pointed out, it took several days before any media outlet actually "requested a copy of my certified report of the habeas corpus proceedings."[48] Likewise, as angry citizens penned letters to New Detroit—the organization that was founded after the 1967 uprising and that sought to bridge the growing divide over Crockett—they persistently backed the DPD and assumed no legal grounding for Crockett's actions. One sarcastic note scoffed, "I'm sure the policeman must have been wrong. They always are though time and time again they give their lives in the line of duty."[49] Another called Crockett "a menace to the general public" who "carried out a personal vendetta against the police."[50]

That the police might have acted illegally, that they fired so many rounds at innocent people (and into a place of worship), and that black Detroiters had constitutional rights that could have been violated— these notions garnered little research, let alone press or sympathy from much of white Detroit. Crockett's actions were so out of step with the longstanding custom of judges enacting the will of police and prosecutors that many white Detroiters assumed he was waging an antipolice crusade.

And yet, as immediately as Crockett's detractors swung into action, his supporters organized to defend him. Foremost in their minds were the failures of the police and courts during the uprising that led them to fight their own battles for justice. "A sizeable delegation representing Detroit's Black community," Crockett wrote, "protest[ed] against the flagrant denials of their civil rights and liberties," adding pressure that ultimately caused the Recorder's Court to release most of the uprising's detainees on personal bonds.[51] Black Detroiters had taken justice into their own hands when police killed three young black men—Carl Cooper, Aubrey Pollard, and Fred Temple—at the Algiers Motel during the uprising. Because the state initially refused to indict the officers involved, local activists like SNCC staffer and city employee Dan Aldridge set up a People's Tribunal, in which a jury and the public were invited to hear evidence and judge the guilt or innocence of the DPD. Held a month after the uprising with an audience in the thousands, the people's jury found the officers guilty. Black Detroiters had a history of fighting for equal justice, and they valued Crockett. As the RNA's defense attorney, Kenneth Cockrel, contended, "We don't have independent judiciary in [Recorder's Court]. Probably the only one we got is Judge Crockett."[52]

The RNA and Reverend Franklin wasted no time in speaking out about the events. Both made statements to the press on March 31, the day after the habeas corpus hearings. Franklin censured the "slanted" journalism, stating that it "results in giving the white community a distorted and misleading view of the black community which . . . add[s] to the many brutal experiences that the black community has suffered."[53] He reconfirmed his belief in the RNA's legitimacy, saying he would lend his church to the group again.[54] Meanwhile, at the RNA press conference, Gaidi Obadele criticized Mayor Cavanagh for accepting the police officers' version of events. He took issue with the notion that it was police who had been endangered and asked, "What about those black women and children who were assaulted in a Christian church?" Not only did he reveal that the RNA believed that police had provoked a gun battle outside of New Bethel but he also insinuated government surveillance of the group when he announced that they "suspect[ed] some planning" on the part of police beforehand.[55] While many Detroiters scoffed at the idea, a later Senate investigation revealed that the group had indeed been infiltrated and that there was undercover law enforcement in the church at the time of the mass arrest.[56]

For a few days, Judge Crockett stayed quiet—in no small part because threats against his life mounted and he had to be put under police protection (which would be necessary for months).[57] Four days after the habeas corpus proceedings, Crockett broke his silence in a powerful press statement. Correcting the many errors in journalists' accounts, he went over the facts of the case and stressed that prosecutors had moved to release nearly all the arrestees. When it came to the question of the prosecution's desire to hold several men on the grounds of positive nitrate tests, he reiterated that constitutional rights took priority: "I am most anxious that criminals be apprehended, tried and brought to justice. But I will not lend my office to practices which subvert legal processes and deny justice to some because they are poor or black."[58] He defended his actions as "legal, proper and moral" and made clear that the unconstitutional practices against black defendants had gone on for so long that his very upholding of rights provoked a backlash:

> Indeed, it is precisely because I followed the law, equally and without partiality, that questions and accusations are being raised. . . . An angry prosecutor [Cahalan], lacking police evidence or testimony which might produce a probable suspect, and resentful that ordinary and undemocratic police practices were challenged, chose to divert public attention to Judge Crockett. And some of the media, particularly the *Detroit News*, picked up that lead and began their campaign to help the police and the Prosecutor's office continue their efforts to dominate and control the courts.[59]

Crockett concluded by reminding his audience of the double standard by which constitutional rights were applied: "Can you imagine the Detroit Police invading an all-white church and rounding up everyone in sight to be bussed to a wholesale lockup in a police garage? . . . Can anyone explain in other than racist terms the shooting by police into a closed and surrounded church? If the killing had occurred in a white neighborhood, I believe the sequence of events would have been far different."[60] Crockett's press statement, thus, highlighted multiple practices that constituted a Jim Crow judiciary: the normatively "undemocratic" behavior of police that was ignored by judges who were expected to work *with* prosecutors and police in ways that limited black defendants' due process rights. As Ernie Goodman recollected, Crockett's statement was so powerful because "he pulled away the façade of impartiality which shielded the legal system."[61]

What Crockett was less explicit about in his press statement but later made clear was that his own blackness worked to condemn him. "[T]hey also got upset," Crockett told an *Ebony* reporter, "because a black judge had protected the rights of black people."[62] Indeed, attacks on constitutionally minded black jurists persisted in the 1960s and '70s. In 1965, as a new appointee on Chicago's criminal courts, Judge George Leighton, stood accused of being prejudiced against police after he ruled that two Mexican men could not be found guilty of resisting arrest by plainclothes police because the police had used excessive force. Leighton weathered pressures that presaged Crockett's: aided by the white press, police called for Leighton's removal from the bench while state legislators sought to impeach him.[63] Amid great pressure, he maintained his position: "Why if I give in now, especially since I am right, no other Negro judge in Chicago would be safe from having his every decision regarding white people reversed by the *Chicago Tribune* and that crowd."[64]

In the early 1970s, New York police began calling Judge Bruce Wright "Turn 'Em Loose Bruce" after he defied the Manhattan district attorney's suggestion of one hundred thousand dollars' bail in the case of Joseph Grutolla, who stood accused of shooting a policeman. The DA, Wright said, "presented no evidence that the defendant would fail to appear on any adjourned date."[65] Wright set bail at five hundred dollars; police called for his removal from the bench. When, on appeal, a white judge set a bail that Grutolla could also meet, "not a whisper of protest was heard from the police," wrote Wright.[66]

Racist double standards and easy charges of racial bias account for some of the backlash experienced by judges like Crockett, Leighton, and Wright. Yet, these judges were also targeted because notions of guilt and innocence had been rewritten in the context of a criminal court system that put "efficiency" above due process rights. Across the country, criminal courts had generally not expanded in line with the spike in crime throughout the 1960s. Judges felt this squeeze in terms of career progression: they might be able to move up the judicial hierarchy if they ran "efficient" courtrooms.[67] To do so, however, meant forsaking due process rights in this, the era of the "due process revolution." Throughout the 1960s, the Supreme Court shored up criminal defendants' rights in myriad ways, including guarantees that police read arrested persons their rights and assurances against unlawful search and seizure. Simultaneously, however, judges enacted what ethnographer Nicole Gonzalez Van Cleve refers to as "due process for the undeserving"—practices that flattened due process rights like the right to a jury trial and instead emphasized plea bargaining as a way to "efficiently" dispose of cases.[68] Indeed, it was in the 1960s that the guilty plea came into wide use; legal scholar Donald Newman's landmark 1966 book *Conviction* showed that 90 percent of those convicted of a crime plea bargained.[69] Judges directly contributed to pressures to plea and waive rights to jury trials. Recorder's Court judges gave little time to cases, hearing 40 percent of them in less than three minutes and 80 percent in less than ten minutes.

Boston judges were found to "threaten a higher sentence if [a] defendant appeal[ed]" their decision.[70] These and other forms of judicial misconduct led citizens to tell Kerner Commission interviewers that courts "dispense[d] 'assembly line' justice."[71] When judges like Crockett slowed down the court system by, for instance, observing *Miranda* rights, they demonstrated that it was possible to run courts differently and yield equal justice.

Crockett's supporters understood this well and did not waste a minute defending him. New Detroit's newly appointed president, William Patrick, wrote privately to Crockett, "Your insistence on the full utilization of the law as a servant of this community in a time of great stress was remarkable. I think you may well have spared our community of most disastrous consequences as a result of your forthright stand." Meanwhile, from his position in the Michigan State Senate, Coleman Young condemned the resolutions being introduced to investigate Crockett's actions, referring to the effort as "a Senate lynching session."[72] Claudia Morcom, Neighborhood Legal Services director, headed a Committee to Honor Judge Crockett. It gathered signatures for a support statement and printed "Support Judge Crockett" bumper stickers.[73] For his part, Representative del Rio provided an "eyewitness" account and reprinted the entire transcript from the court proceedings.[74]

A mass mobilization joined these distinguished supporters, the Black United Front (BUF). Formed on April 1—two days after the habeas corpus hearings—BUF consisted of over forty local groups aiming to mount "a concerted drive against police oppression."[75] Coming together were organizations as diverse as churches, the League of Revolutionary Black Workers, the Detroit Black Panthers, and the Guardians—Black Police Officers for Equal Justice. They appointed as acting chairman Dan Aldridge, who said the group would take aim at a criminal justice system run by police and prosecutors: "This solidarity of Black citizens stems from the indignation at the continued demonstration of racism not only on the part of members of the police department but on the part of the Prosecutor in his attempt to usurp the authority of Judge Crockett."[76] BUF ensured that Crockett's detractors did not dominate street protest. When off-duty officers picketed with their anti-Crockett signs, student groups countered with placards that read "Justice Is Judge Crockett" and "Black People Need Crockett."[77] On April 3—the day prior to the one-year anniversary of MLK's assassination—BUF brought supporters out in the hundreds, including many high school students who had staged walkouts, to demonstrate outside the Recorder's Court building. To better highlight the significance of police support for Crockett, the Guardians held a separate rally at Kennedy Square a few blocks away.[78]

Significantly, a critical mass of white supporters leapt to Crockett's defense. People Against Racism (PAR) was a party to BUF's April 3 demonstration, as was the Ad Hoc Action Group. Founded by future Detroit City councilwoman Sheila Murphy, Ad Hoc's white suburbanite membership originally came together as a police watchdog group in 1968.[79] As the controversy whipped up, Ad Hoc partnered with PAR to maintain white pressure on the police. The two groups distributed flyers pointing out that, during the uprising, it was Prosecutor Cahalan who suspended constitutional rights by asking judges to exact high bails, while the DPD's history of criminality was clear: "The people of Detroit remember the Algiers execution."

As with Franklin's statement, the BUF demonstration, and other black-led efforts, prejudiced and erroneous media reporting proved a key rallying point for Crockett's white supporters. PAR quickly drew up a report on the first week's coverage of the "New Bethel Incident" within the pages of the *News* and *Free Press*. Entitled *Mass Media, a Racist Institution*, it charged the dailies with "unquestioning support of the police" and demonizing the RNA. The *News'* longstanding "vendetta" against Crockett meant that, over the years, it purposely "created the impression that he has 'flooded' the streets of Detroit with known criminals." The report concluded that white Detroit had shown itself incapable of addressing the city's history of unequal justice for black Detroit: "In short, when it comes to crimes against black people, whites have traditionally been totally paralyzed in administering punishment against themselves."[80]

Crockett's supporters did their own reporting, too. *The South End*, the Wayne State University newspaper that had been taken over by radicals like Dodge Revolutionary Union Movement member John Watson, gave over its entire April 3 issue to the events and "reprinted statements from all sides, including those of Crockett, del Rio, Franklin, the DPOA, and anti-Crockett reporters."[81] Both it and the *Michigan Chronicle*, the Detroit-based black weekly, remained diligent in their coverage. Meanwhile, two largely white faith-based groups decided a television program could serve as an additional, crucial medium. They worked with the local public television station to put together an hour-long special on Crockett and the New Bethel case—and they did it in a hurry. The special aired the evening of Monday, April 7, a mere nine days on from the mass arrest.[82]

* * *

In the end, Crockett's actions were widely, if not always enthusiastically, proclaimed appropriate and legal. A number of legal associations, including the National Lawyer's Guild and the Wolverine Bar Association (an organization of black attorneys), declared Crockett's actions constitutional.[83] By mid-April, the *Free Press* expressed "regret" that both it and the *News* had erred in their reporting.[84] Soon after, the mayoral office's Commission on Community Relations released its report on the events, which, without clearly backing Crockett, slammed the actions of the police: "The DPOA premises of 'support law and order and remove George Crockett' have emerged to symbolize the spect[er] of the police state and paramilitary government of a colonial people."[85] Then, on April 25, New Detroit's Law Committee issued a report that found that Crockett's actions could not be read with "even the slightest implication of incompetence or impropriety."[86] Later on in the year, in a close 5–4 decision, the Michigan Judicial Tenure Commission put the matter to rest: Crockett was in the right. Much of the initial turmoil died down on the back of so much prominent support for Crockett—and as attention shifted to the two trials stemming from Czapski's and Worobec's shootings. Upstart defense attorney Kenneth Cockrel, who "repeatedly tried to push the city's legal system to its progressive limits," often by going on the "offensive," eventually saw to the acquittals of all four defendants: Alfred 2X, Kirkwood Hall, Raphael Viera, and Chaka Fuller.[87]

Those few, tempestuous weeks did not temper Crockett's denunciations of unequal justice; nor did they alter his judicial conduct. When former vice president Spiro Agnew got off lightly for tax evasion in October 1973, Crockett declined to sentence a defendant with jail time, stating, "I really don't feel like giving any time to anybody this morning when I see what the judge down in Maryland did with respect to [Agnew]. . . . Those who are rich enough to get high-priced counsel and influence the court, they get away with just a tap on the hand. Someone like [the defendant in front of him], if you don't throw the book at him then you're accused of being soft."[88]

It would be his decisions with the New Bethel arrestees, though, that most clearly demonstrated the contours of the nation's Jim Crow judiciary: a court system that surrendered its independence in the service of prosecutors and police, producing unequal adherence to constitutional rights and highly racialized outcomes. Crockett and his supporters used the attack on him to shine a light on this segregated system, for to do so was necessary for the northern black freedom movement. When it was expected that judges would dispense Jim Crow justice by treating the court as the enforcement arm of the state, black defendants were denied their constitutional rights, prisons were crammed with black bodies, and Black Power groups were gunned down in houses of worship.

Crockett was attacked because he maintained his independence from police and prosecutors, because he assumed the Constitution's universal application, and because he did both while being black. Crockett felt that, as a black judge, he had been entrusted with a difficult but important duty. "I think a black judge, by nature," he said, "in this historical period has got to be a reformist—he cannot be a member of the club. The whole purpose for selecting him is that the people are dissatisfied with the status quo and they may want him to shake it up, and his role is to shake it up."[89] Crockett did not see the courts as a site in which America's mistakes and inequalities were filtered out; he did not count on his peers on the bench to purify the North or the South of racism. He understood that the decisions taken by himself and some other northern black judges would be unpopular, even put them in danger. But he worked in the knowledge that "the shame of the whole judicial system"—the nation's history of unequal justice for African Americans—required a different kind of judiciary. He demonstrated what kind of independent judiciary was possible.

NOTES

1 I use the term "shoot-in" in this essay for two reasons: (1) it reflects the language that many of Detroit's black communities use when they refer to this episode; and (2) it more accurately describes the events that took place. While the police claimed there was a "shoot-out" that took place outside the church prior to their storming of the church, the RNA denied that a "shoot-out" necessarily took place. What was clear to the RNA and black people in Detroit was that police shot into

the church many times. So, the language of "shoot-in" is more accurate in this regard.

2 Michelle Alexander, *The New Jim Crow: Mass Incarceration in the Age of Color-blindness* (New York: New Press, 2010), 41. The doubling of crime rates seen in Detroit in the late 1960s might have had more to do with police manipulation of crime statistics than an actual rise in crime. See Heather Ann Thompson, "Rethinking the Politics of White Flight in the Postwar City: Detroit, 1945–1980," *Journal of Urban History* 25(2) (January 1999): 163–98 (178–79).

3 On the historical relationship between notions of blackness and criminality see, Alexander, *New Jim Crow*; and Khalil Gibran Muhammad, *The Condemnation of Blackness: Race, Crime, and the Making of Modern Urban America* (Cambridge, MA: Harvard University Press, 2010).

4 Charles Sanders, "Detroit's Rebel Judge Crockett," *Ebony*, August 1969, 114–24 (116), emphasis in original.

5 George Crockett, "The Role of the Black Judge," *Journal of Public Law* 20 (1971): 391–400 (397).

6 Glynn Mapes, "Unequal Justice," *Wall Street Journal*, 9 September 1970, 1, 17.

7 Sun Bae Lee, "Unequal Justice Is Seen in the Huey Case," *Chicago Defender*, 27 May 1967, 10. See also, "Burglar Who Beat Nun Gets 3 Long Terms," *Chicago Tribune*, 27 July 1965, 5.

8 Mapes, "Unequal Justice"; and Derrick Bell Jr., "Racism in American Courts: Cause for Black Disruption or Despair," *California Law Review* 61(1) (January 1973): 165–203 (176).

9 Robyn Spencer, *The Revolution Has Come: Black Power, Gender, and the Black Panther Party in Oakland* (Durham, NC: Duke University Press, 2016). For another critique, see, Carlyle Douglas, "How Justice Shortchanges Blacks," *Ebony*, October 1974, 76–84.

10 "The Black Judge in America: A Statistical Profile," *Judicature* 57(1) (June–July 1973): 18–21.

11 Crockett, "Role of the Black Judge," 394.

12 Lee Winfrey, "Two Charged after Slaying of Policeman outside Church," *Detroit Free Press* [hereafter, *DFP*], 31 March 1969, 1, 4A; and Gary Blonston, "RNA's Goal: Black Nation," *DFP*, 31 March 1969, 1, 10A.

13 Dan Georgakas and Marvin Surkin, *Detroit I Do Mind Dying: A Study in Urban Revolution* (Chicago: Haymarket Books, 1975), 66–67.

14 Winfrey, "Two Charged after Slaying," 1.

15 Heather Ann Thompson, *Whose Detroit? Politics, Labor, and Race in a Modern American City* (Ithaca, NY: Cornell University Press, 2001), 134.

16 James del Rio, "Representative James del Rio Gives on-the-Scene Account," *24th District Reporter: Del Rio Reports*, 2 April 1969, 1–3.

17 Quoted in Ruth Martin, "'They feel the beams resting upon their necks': George W. Crockett and the Development of Equal Justice under Law, 1948–1969," *Michigan Historical Review* 39(2) (Fall 2013): 51–75 (59).

18 Martin, "'They feel,'" 60–65; and Steve Babson, Dave Riddle, and David Elsila, *The Color of Law: Ernie Goodman, Detroit, and the Struggle for Labor and Civil Rights* (Detroit, MI: Wayne State University Press, 2010), 383–84.

19 Ernie Goodman, "An Unofficial, Incomplete Biographical Sketch and a Few Personal Recollections of Congressman George W. Crockett Jr.," 4–5, in Ernest Goodman Papers, Part 2, Box 88, Folder 12, Walter Reuther Library, Wayne State University [hereafter RL].

20 Crockett campaign materials in George Crockett Jr. Papers, Series 2, Box 1, Folder 27, RL.

21 Chris Parks, "Crockett, 2 Others on FBI Smear List," *DFP*, 14 February 1977, 3, 10.

22 *Ibid.*, 10.

23 Quoted in Goodman, "An Unofficial, Incomplete Biographical Sketch," 34–35.

24 George Crockett, "Recorder's Court and the 1967 Civil Disturbance," *Journal of Urban Law* 45 (Spring/Summer 1968): 841–47 (842); and "The Administration of Justice in the Wake of the Detroit Civil Disorder of July 1967," *Michigan Law Review* 66(7) (May 1968): 1542–1630 (1554).

25 "The Administration of Justice in the Wake of the Detroit Civil Disorder," 1547–49.

26 *Ibid.*, 1550–51, footnote 30.

27 *Ibid.*, 1550.

28 Crockett, "Recorder's Court and the 1967 Civil Disturbance," 841.

29 *Ibid.*, 847.

30 *Ibid.*, 1550–55; and Martin, "'They feel,'" 68.

31 Crockett, "Recorder's Court and the 1967 Civil Disturbance," 841.

32 *Ibid.*, 846.

33 George Crockett, "A Black Judge Speaks," *Judicature* 53(9) (April–May 1970): 360–65 (362).

34 "The Administration of Justice in the Wake of the Detroit Civil Disorder of July 1967."

35 "U-M's Court Study Shows Value of Keeping Cool," *DFP*, 7 October 1968, 8.

36 Crocket, "Black Judge Speaks," 363; and del Rio, "Del Rio Gives on-the-Scene Account," 2.

37 Quoted in William Serrin, "Judge Crockett: The Man behind the Controversy," *DFP*, 6 April 1969, 3–4 (4).

38 Tom Delisle and John Griffith, "Crockett Angered: Cahalan Cited for Contempt," *DFP*, 31 March 1969, 4; and Winfrey, "Two Charged after Slaying," 4 (Crockett quotation).

39 See for instance, Richard Ryan, "Slayer's Victim 'Old'—Crockett Cuts Term," *Detroit News* [hereafter *DN*], 23 February 1969, 22A.

40 *DN*, 1 April 1969. Quotations from "Judge's Conduct Questioned: An Abuse of Power?" 18A.

41 *DN*, 2 April 1969, 18A; "Crockett's Role: Advocate or Judge?" *DN*, 6 April 1969, 18A.

42 Lee Winfrey, "Cavanagh Calls Shootings 'Unprovoked, Senseless,'" *DFP*, 1 April 1969, 1, 2A; and "Probe of Crockett's Actions Is Asked by State Senate," *DFP*, 2 April 1969, 1, 8.

43 *DN*, 18 April 1969, 2B.

44 William Serrin, "DPOA Opens Drive to Oust Crockett," *DFP*, 15 April 1969, 3–4 (3).

45 John Griffith, "Cavanagh Defends Police Acts," *DFP*, 2 April 1969, 1; and "Milliken Asks for Probe of Crockett," *DFP*, 3 April 1969, 1–2.

46 "Keep Isolated Incidents within Narrow Limits," *DFP*, 1 April 1969, 6A.

47 "Questions to Be Answered," *DFP*, 3 April 1969, 6.

48 Crockett, "Black Judge Speaks," 364.

49 M.C. to Max Fisher, 8 April 1969, Folder 6, Box 185, New Detroit, Inc. Papers, RL [hereafter, NDP].

50 Jim Roy Brown to New Detroit Committee, 26 April 1969, Folder 6, Box 185, NDP. Emphasis in original.

51 Crockett, "Recorder's Court," 846.

52 "Statements of Milton Henry and Kenneth Cockrel," *South End*, 12 May 1969, 8.

53 C. L. Franklin Statement to the Press, Folder 6, Box 185, NDP.

54 Christian Davenport, *How Social Movements Die: Repression and Demobilization of the Republic of New Africa* (New York: Cambridge University Press, 2014), 227.

55 "Cavanagh Calls Shootings 'Senseless,' 'Unprovoked,'" 2.

56 Davenport, 234.

57 Sanders, "Detroit's Rebel Judge Crockett," 114.

58 Transcript of statement by Judge Crockett, 3 April 1969, Folder 10, Box 10, Detroit Industrial Mission Records, RL [hereafter, DIM Records].

59 *Ibid.*

60 *Ibid.*

61 Goodman, "An Unofficial, Incomplete Biographical Sketch," 7.

62 Sanders, "Detroit's Rebel Judge Crockett," 116.

63 "Chicago Judge Slaps Back," *Jet*, 15 April 1965, 8–9; and "Judge Produces Furor by Freeing of Two in Attack," *Chicago Tribune*, 7 March 1965, 1–2.

64 "Chicago Judge Slaps Back," 9.

65 Bruce Wright, *Black Robes, White Justice* (Secaucus, NJ: Lyle Stuart, 1987), 69.

66 *Ibid.*, 122.

67 Isaac Balbus, *The Dialectics of Legal Repression: Black Rebels before the American Criminal Courts* (New York: Russell Sage Foundation, 1973), 15–25.

68 Nicole Gonzalez Van Cleve, *Crook County: Racism and Injustice in America's Largest Criminal Court* (Stanford, CA: Stanford University Press, 2016), 73.

69 Donald Newman, *Convicted: The Determination of Guilt or Innocence without Trial* (Toronto: Little, Brown, 1966).

70 Bell, "Racism in American Courts," 176–77.

71 Quoted in *ibid.*, 174.

72 "Probe of Crockett's Actions," 8.

73 Letter to New Detroit from A Committee to Honor Judge Crockett, 3 April 1969, Folder 6, Box 185, NDP. On Claudia Morcom, see, Babson, Riddle, and Elsila, *Color of Law*, chapters 10–11.

74 *24th District Reporter*, especially, "Rep. James del Rio Gives on-the-Scene Account," 2 April 1969, 1.

75 "Black United Front to Fight Injustice," *South End*, 3 April 1969, 1.

76 *Ibid.*

77 "Probe of Crockett's Actions," 8.

78 Gene Goltz and John Griffith, "Hundreds Demonstrate in Support of Crockett," *DFP*, 4 April 1969, 1, 12.

79 "Ann, Sheila Honored as Leaders," *DFP*, 30 December 1968, 21, 23.

80 PAR, *Mass Media, a Racist Institution: Coverage of the New Bethel Incident by the Detroit News and the Detroit Free Press, March 30–April 3 1969*, Folder 10, Box 10, DIM Records.

81 Georgakas and Surkin, *Detroit I Do Mind Dying*, 69.

82 James Campbell to William Patrick Jr, 17 April 1969, Folder 10, Box 10, DIM Records.

83 "Bar Groups Counsel Restraint," *DFP*, 5 April 1969, 1–2.

84 "Detroit Cannot Afford to Follow DPOA Lead," *DFP*, 16 April 1969, 8.

85 Detroit Commission on Community Relations, Memo on the New Bethel Incident, 5–6, 16 April, Folder 6, Box 185, NDP.

86 Quoted in "DPOA Raps Report Backing Crockett," *DFP*, 26 April 1969, 5.

87 Thompson, *Whose Detroit?* 129–35 (129).

88 "Erratic Justice," *Wall Street Journal*, 26 October 1973, 1, 23.

89 Crockett, "Role of the Black Judge," 398.

10

"We've Been behind the Scenes"

Project Equality and Fair Employment in 1970s Milwaukee

CRYSTAL MARIE MOTEN

On May 25, 1971, Gloria Watkins submitted a formal complaint to the Wisconsin Department of Industry, Labor, and Human Relations (DILHR) accusing her employer, the Milwaukee County Department of Welfare, and her union, the American Federation of State, County, and Municipal Employees Local 594, of racial discrimination. Watkins, an African American woman, had been hired in 1968 as a general caseworker with the Department of Welfare. After more than a year on the job, Watkins heard of a job opening for a more specialized caseworker position, one that had a reduced caseload, but that allowed workers to give more attention to individual cases. Because there would be no pay increase, and Watkins had the necessary experience and qualifications for the job, she figured the transfer process would be fairly simple and straightforward. She was wrong. Watkins submitted her transfer request in April 1969, and by November her supervisor still had not approved the transfer, although the requests of three white caseworkers, who had submitted their requests after Watkins and who had less seniority, had been approved by May 1969. Through February of 1970, Watkins's supervisor continued to transfer white workers and ignore Watkins's request.

Frustrated by this, Watkins filed a grievance with her union, but the union refused to fully process the complaint. Undeterred, Watkins submitted an official complaint to the DILHR that accused both her union and the Milwaukee County Department of Welfare of racial discrimination. Six months after Watkins filed her complaint, but before the DILHR heard the case, the Milwaukee County Department of Welfare transferred Watkins to her requested position. Despite this, Watkins did not rescind her complaint, and her case was heard by the DILHR. At the hearing, examiners dismissed Watkins's case, stating that her recent transfer nullified any claims of alleged discrimination. After the case was dismissed, Watkins appealed and the case went to the circuit court of Dane County and eventually the Wisconsin Supreme Court, which did not rule in her favor.[1] The Wisconsin Supreme Court sided with the DILHR, arguing that the body did not need to hear the case since Watkins eventually received the job transfer she requested.

Watkins's case was representative of the employment experiences of black workers in Milwaukee and the urban North. By the late 1960s, as a result of the legal breakthroughs of the civil rights movement, some black workers were able to obtain jobs in sectors that had previously been closed to them. However, once on the job, they endured racist and discriminatory treatment from supervisors and coworkers who saw them as inferior and unqualified, and, as a result, devalued their labor. Black workers relied on the state of Wisconsin's fair employment apparatus, which was an outgrowth of President Roosevelt's 1941 Executive Order 8802 and the resulting federal Equal Employment Opportunity Commission (FEPC), to submit formal complaints regarding their treatment. This process rarely resulted in economic justice for black workers because with no federal, or many times local, funding allocated, the FEPC had little enforcement power. While some workers across the country benefited from the national FEPC and its local equivalents, widespread employment discrimination continued.[2]

The case of Gloria Watkins disrupts historical and historiographical narratives about economic-justice activism in the urban North. When we usually think of employment discrimination in the urban North, particularly in the cities of America's industrial heartland, the typical stories that are told revolve around organized factory workers agitating for worker rights. The workers in these stories are, by default, men, and their actions become the typical way of understanding worker activism in the urban industrial North.[3] However, this narrative erases the experiences of black women workers as well as the work they were doing to combat racism in the workplace. In many cases, their activism was neither flashy nor immediately successful. It resembled Gloria Watkins's experience—a mixture of triumph and challenge.

The employment struggles and activism of women like Gloria Watkins often go unnoticed, but much can be learned from examining the responses of women like her. Gloria Watkins's experiences at the Milwaukee County Department of Welfare reflect the nature of Jim Crow employment discrimination in the city. Because of her race, the Department of Welfare refused to transfer her to a position with more responsibility, flexibility, and impact; instead, it reserved those prized positions for white caseworkers. The department knew it had been engaging in discriminatory practices, and when faced with a complaint and possible repercussions, it transferred Watkins to her desired position in order to invalidate her claims and silence her. This was exactly how Jim Crow employment discrimination operated in the North. Some employers could say they hired black employees, but they restricted these employees to the least desirable jobs; outright harassed them; and refused to promote them. When black workers dared raise their voices or submit complaints, they were subjected to an arduous investigation process that ultimately found no fault with the business or company being investigated—thus simultaneously hiding and perpetuating structural employment discrimination. This was precisely why activists devised new strategies to both expose and eradicate structural employment discrimination.

In the Milwaukee context, activists established a local chapter of Project Equality (PE), a private, nonprofit organization that aimed to address systematic racial inequality in urban employment. Organized nationwide in 1965, PE was brought by activists to Milwaukee in 1970 after civil rights activists saw its success in persuading employers to adopt affirmative action practices, which would address racial discrimination and in turn increase the number of workers of color. From its inception in Milwaukee until the early 2000s, black women ran the office. Bringing PE into the story of worker rights and economic justice disrupts the narrative that defines economic justice as an exclusively male domain, especially in the urban, northern, Milwaukee context.

In the beginning, Project Equality started out as a Catholic social action program but grew into an interreligious program that provided an opening for black women to take the lead in matters of economic justice, especially in the Milwaukee office. The program's main focus was to urge Catholics to use their immense buying power for economic justice. The primary tool PE used was its popular *Buyer's Guide*. The *Buyer's Guide* could be described as a compendium, a Yellow Pages of sorts, of companies across the nation committed to affirmative action. PE encouraged its Catholic constituents to only use the *Buyer's Guide* when purchasing goods or services. Companies as large as national airlines, hotels, and department stores could be included in the *Guide*, if they had an active affirmative action policy. On the local level, smaller businesses and firms could be included if they affirmed fair employment practices and certified this with a local office. In short, the national popularity and reach of the *Buyer's Guide*, coupled with the buying power of Catholics across the nation, second only to that of the federal government, made it so that no company wanted to be left out of the annual publication. Thirty million members had access to the *Guide*, and by 1970, Project Equality had twenty local offices in urban areas across the nation and had expanded its religious reach to include Protestant churches, as well as synagogues across the country. The Wisconsin office, with its headquarters in Milwaukee, would go on to be one of the longest-running offices in the nation, a testament to the tenacity of the primarily black female activists who ran the office and the intractable nature of employment injustice in the city.

This chapter illuminates the nature of Jim Crow employment, how businesses and the state were implicated in the perpetuation of employment discrimination, and what some black activists did to combat it. Focusing on the work of Project Equality Wisconsin (PE-W), which ultimately was a quintessential affirmative action program, shows how entrenched Jim Crow was (and continues to be). Instead of focusing on the individual experiences of racism workers experienced, PE-W's goal was to eliminate the deeply entrenched structural and systematic employment discrimination that lay at the core of the corporate world. PE's goals were to generate compliance, create accountability, and promote equality—goals that the state employment agency had but could not fulfill. Project Equality became a fruitful mouthpiece for economic justice, especially because it was also armed with the national *Buyer's Guide* and a local Wisconsin supplement, which proved to be an effective tool in pressuring companies to comply with affirmative action standards. On the local level, through the work of the executive director, who provided the day-to-day leadership of the office, PE-W aimed to expose how employment discrimination was embedded in the structure of most Milwaukee-area businesses. PE did this through its administrative compliance process and through the education it provided in its monthly newsletters. PE worked well on the local level because of its intentional self-definition as a nonantagonistic, cooperative, affirmative-action management-consulting firm. PE assisted businesses in complying with the law before being threatened with a complaint or with noncompliance by the federal government.

Although PE described itself as "friendly" and "cooperative," the black women who ran the PE-W office did the work of exposing the nature of Jim Crow in the North, especially as it related to employment discrimination. Part of this work was bringing to light the false ideas that bolstered racial inequality in the jobs economy. Supposedly, a "culture of poverty" developed among black city dwellers as a result of their maladjustment to urban, northern city life.[4] The behaviors of black people and not structural discrimination were the reason black people could not rise above urban poverty and join the ranks of the American middle class. Employers' belief in these ideas meant that they assigned black workers the hardest and dirtiest jobs, while providing few training opportunities and little to no chance of advancement. For so long, businesses placed the blame on black workers for their employment difficulties, but the black women who ran the PE-W office sought to change the narrative surrounding black workers in the city. In essence, PE-W put the onus on businesses and employers as they insisted that it was the responsibility of businesses to change their beliefs and policies surrounding black workers.

The story of PE has not been fully told, mostly because employment justice still remains elusive, but examining the liberal activism of PE matters. Whereas the state's equal employment office reacted by responding to employment complaints only if they were filed, PE was proactive and aimed to help employers address and eliminate employment discrimination before the state needed to step in. Additionally, examining PE and the black women who led the office in Milwaukee highlights the nature of black women's economic activism in the urban North. Their organizing did not always result in tremendous media attention. Yet, day by day, they engaged in the slow, tedious work that they believed would help chip away the walls of injustice. For example, Betty Thompson, one of the executive directors of PE-W, knew that the work she did was often "behind the scenes," and slow, but she knew that it was important, not because it was always successful but because it endeavored to shift the narrative surrounding employment injustice in the city.

Despite the work of the black women of Project Equality–Wisconsin, African Americans continued to face employment difficulties in the city and the state. By the 1980s, as the toll of deindustrialization and a recession set in, this toppled an already-precarious black working class. Tens of thousands of jobs disappeared from the city, replaced by lower-paid service jobs. PE's leaders recognized this and continued with its message of employment justice—a message that remained relevant as the employment outlook worsened for people of color in the city in the 1980s and 1990s.

The Struggle for Fair Employment in a Jim Crow Northern City

The struggle for fair employment has long roots in Wisconsin. By the mid-1940s, the state passed state laws and created state-level bodies to address employment discrimination in the state. In 1945, the Wisconsin state legislature passed the state's first fair employment law, which banned discrimination in employment on the basis of race, color, national origin, or ancestry. In addition to the fair employment legislation, the governor of Wisconsin, Walter S. Goodland, created the Governor's Commission on Human Rights, which functioned as a special body, but had no funding or paid staff. Still, the mission of the commission was to dedicate "all our energies to the elimination of all discriminatory practices," as well as "to sustain with vigor the free exercise of human rights by all people everywhere."[5] In 1965, Wisconsin expanded its Fair Employment Practices Division (FEDP) to the Equal Opportunities Division in order to administer Wisconsin's newly passed fair housing law. By 1967, the state consolidated the work of the Governor's Commission on Human Rights and the Equal Opportunities Division into the Equal Rights Division, which became responsible for administering state law as it related to discrimination wherever it occurred and in whatever form.

Despite Wisconsin's lengthy history in attempting to address employment discrimination, African Americans rightly believed that the state law "had no teeth," especially since little changed for black workers in the state. In fact, in 1957 Virginia Huebner, the director of the Employment Practices Division, told the *Milwaukee Defender*, "[W]hile resistance to the principles of fair employment practices in Wisconsin may be decreasing, nevertheless, the actual practice of discrimination in employment because of race, creed, color, national origin or ancestry has not, in the same degree, lessened."[6] Over a decade after its existence, the Fair Employment Practices Act had no power. Democratic congressman Henry S. Reuss, a member of the Governor's Commission on Human Rights, said as much on a public radio broadcast. "The present law," Reuss asserted, "actually permits discrimination in employment against Negroes. The court can do no more than interpret the law. It is the Republican dominated legislature which is to blame for having an unenforceable [fair employment] act on the books."[7]

Despite a Fair Employment Practices law on the books, employers blatantly discriminated against, intimidated, or harassed African Americans because they knew they would not face any repercussions. Edris Washington's story is a prime example.[8] In 1958, Washington filed a complaint with the Milwaukee Urban League regarding her experiences at the law offices of Bass and Goldstein. Eighteen-year-old Edris Washington heard of a clerical job at the firm and sought employment. After an initial positive interview, Washington was hired and told to report to work. When she arrived to work, she reported to Goldstein, her supervisor. In her official complaint, Washington noted that Goldstein was "in another office apparently dressing." She went into another room until he finished, and afterwards he called her into his office where he, once again, explained to her what the duties of the job would be, information she had received in her initial interview. In addition to recounting information she had already been told, Washington wrote, he spoke to her "in some detail of his rape and illegitimacy cases." These remarks made Washington uncomfortable so she left his office to practice her skills on the office's stenographic equipment. While she was working in the other room, Goldstein asked her to retrieve a paper towel from the ladies' room, and when she entered his office, she realized he did not have on any clothes. In her complaint Washington noted that she ignored his state of undress and left his office. When he was dressed, Goldstein called Washington back into his office to discuss the job duties again. During the meeting, Goldstein noticed that Washington was quiet. The meeting soon ended with Goldstein telling Washington to think more about the job and that he would call her to follow up. After this, Washington left the office and never returned.

This horrific experience of sexual intimidation and harassment speaks to the intersectional experiences of African American working women in the labor force. Edris Washington went to the Milwaukee Urban League to register her complaint, and it was filed as a racial complaint. While there was no way to indicate sexual harassment, Washington was correct to read Goldstein's tactics as employment intimidation. Washington's decision not only to tell her story but also to have it certified by a notary public highlights that not all black women were bound by a culture of dissemblance that would have them remain silent in the face of sexual mistreatment.[9] Unfortunately, the record is not clear regarding the Urban League's response to this case. This case is significant, nonetheless, because it provides another layer to the employment-related injustice black women endured in Milwaukee's labor force. Black women's employment complaints abound in the record, and taken together they tell a story of exclusion and marginalization, but also resistance.[10]

Because many black workers like Edris Washington routinely went to the Urban League to lodge their complaints, in 1963, the FEPD partnered with the Milwaukee Urban League in an effort to bolster its efforts against employment discrimination in the city.[11] Local Congress of Racial Equality (CORE) activists did not believe much would come from the partnership because of the state's record up to that time.[12] Despite the FEPD's existence, neither local businesses nor local companies had been held accountable for discriminating against or harassing black workers and this, according to CORE activists, led African Americans to distrust the state's work on behalf of fair employment.

While the state, at the very least, recognized the existence of employment discrimination, the city of Milwaukee crafted a narrative of African American economic progress. Authorized by Milwaukee mayor Henry W. Maier in 1963, the Milwaukee Commission on Community Relations published a short report, "The Negro in Milwaukee: Progress and Portent, 1863–1963."[13] The report, a succinctly packaged narrative of progress, claimed that the status of African Americans had improved nationwide during the hundred years since the passage of the Emancipation Proclamation. The report, divided into two sections, "The Nation" and "Milwaukee," used "statistics [to] tell the heartwarming story" of African American advancement. Data related to life expectancy, employment, political representation, and education proved the central claim of the report: "America has made great strides toward true racial equality." While the report contended that life for African Americans across the nation had substantially improved, could the same be said for African Americans in Milwaukee?

According to the report, African Americans in Milwaukee enjoyed access where it mattered most: employment. African Americans worked in "practically every type of occupation, practically every industry, and in practically all categories of general employment." Comparing 1950 to 1960, the commission used census data to illustrate the increased number of African American engineers, teachers, nurses, technicians, craftsmen, and those employed in industry. For example, in 1950, there were 177 African American professional and technical workers compared to 704 in 1960. There were 264 clerical workers in 1950 and 997 in 1960. Similarly, there were 626 craft workers in 1950 and nearly three times as many in 1960. The number of manufacturing operators doubled, from a little over 3,000 to around 6,700. In addition to increased employment opportunities, the report also described progress in politics—there were African American members of the state assembly, a member of the Common Council, and a member of the school board, all from Milwaukee. Additionally, seven African Americans served on city boards, commissions, and committees. Patting itself on the back, the report also noted the eighty-five African Americans employed by the city. "We can be proud of our record," the report concluded.

A closer look at these raw numbers indicates a major flaw—the numbers did not take into account the dramatic 187% increase in the African American population that occurred between 1950 and 1960. Taking this into account, for example, the paltry jump from one African American engineer in 1950 to seventeen in 1960 was not progressive at all. African Americans remained underrepresented in all employment categories. Milwaukee's employment record was nothing to be proud of, but the report told a different story. Building upon the fiction of African American progress in employment, the report then failed to make connections between lack of quality housing opportunities and a failing public education system. The report hid structural inequality, racism, and discrimination in language that minimized the responsibility of the state while highlighting the responsibility of individuals to "maintain good citizenship." The report concluded that the city "must realize that Negroes of low income, still unaccustomed to life in a Northern city, do not have a long heritage of culture and an ethical tradition on which to build their lives."[14] The report effectively blamed African Americans for the racial and economic inequality they experienced—inequality that was built into the very fabric of the urban industrial landscape.

African Americans workers understood this and utilized the black press to tell their stories of employment discrimination. In January 1970, one of Milwaukee's African American weekly newspapers, the *Greater Milwaukee Star*, headlined the story of L. C. Tyars, who believed he was unfairly fired from Allen-Bradley, one of the city's largest manufacturing companies. Allen-Bradley Company, which specialized in industrial controls and electronic components, was well known for its hostile relations with African Americans in the city. Over the preceding decade, black community leaders tried to pressure the company to increase the number of blacks it hired. By the mid-1960s, the company only employed one hundred African Americans out of six thousand workers. In 1968, the NAACP Youth Council Commandos, along with a coalition of Hispanic activists, protested racial discrimination at the company. While Allen-Bradley and the Youth Council came to an agreement that Allen-Bradley would hire more people of color, some felt the agreement had not gone far enough. Well-known civil rights activist Father James Groppi believed that while Allen-Bradley said it would hire more blacks and Hispanics, the community should not trust this without some form of accountability.[15] Two years later, the case of L. C. Tyars illustrated that the problem of employment in Milwaukee was not only that African Americans were not being hired but also that they were being unfairly fired, as well as badly mistreated on the job.

After being fired from the company, Tyars went to the black press to tell his story. The *Star* ran the story on its front page, describing Tyars as "reacting like a man to extreme provocation."[16] According to Tyars, on January 6, he came back from his lunch break and was reprimanded by a white coworker, Robert Walszak. Although Walszak had no more seniority than Tyars, Walszak argued with Tyars about arriving back late from his lunch break. Tyars told Walszak to leave him alone and take his complaints to their supervisor, but Walszak refused, escalating the confrontation with abusive language. At this point, Tyars pushed Walszak, and he finally retreated. Soon after, the foreman called Tyars to his office and fired him. After going to the *Star's* office, Tyars filled out a complaint with his union steward and contacted the NAACP.

According to the *Star* article, Robert Walszak only received a written warning for his behavior while Tyars, "a black man, who was wounded three times in Viet Nam, is without a job for being a man." Tyars commented, "It looks like the company gets rid of Black employees by having a man harassed to a boiling point. I feel after all I went through in Vietnam, I'm entitled to more than this." After a three-week grievance process, and as a result of pressure from the press and the NAACP, and with the union's support, Allen-Bradley rehired L. C. Tyars. The union was not able to compel the company to give Tyars back pay for the unfair firing. Unhappy about this outcome, Tyars did not press the issue because he understood the nature of Jim Crow employment in the city: "[T]he company knew I needed money," he said, "and figured I'd have to be satisfied with things as they are."[17] Tyars's comment regarding the incident further exposed the insidious nature of Jim Crow employment in the city. Not only were black workers expected to accept intimidation from white workers; they were also expected to stay in their place, which was beneath white workers. Any attempt to disrupt this hierarchy led to termination. Like many veterans, Tyars thought his military service would earn him rights and status upon his return. He was sadly mistaken and stated, "It's hard for me to understand the wounds I suffered in Vietnam, when I come back and face this. Allen-Bradley cuts off my pay, while permitting the white employee to go right on earning the God almighty dollar."

Vietnam veteran L. C. Tyars's experience at Allen-Bradley illustrates what was common knowledge to black workers in the city: Jim Crow permeated the labor market and affected employment on a structural level. Workers hired by one of the city's many manufacturing companies went so far as to describe work in the industrial labor force as a "caste system" or as a "master-slave" relationship.[18] African American workers had the lowest status with no way to progress. Even white workers who had the same job titles as black workers believed they were superior to black workers, as illustrated by the case of L. C. Tyars. Jim Crow's insistence on keeping black workers at the bottom of the workforce meant that although manufacturing work paid more than jobs in the city's service industry, black workers could not climb the ranks into higher positions, which would increase their earning power. Two reports, published in the late 1960s, illuminate the employment landscape for African Americans in the city. The 1968 Equal Employment Opportunity Report, published by the state's Department of Industry, Labor, and Human Relations, found that the majority of African Americans in the workforce labored as semiskilled operatives, unskilled general laborers, or service workers.[19] In a survey of over five hundred companies in Milwaukee County, the report also revealed that 98 percent of the managerial and professional force at these firms was white. African Americans accounted for less than 1 percent of the managerial and professional rank. A 1969 report published by researchers from the University of Wisconsin–Madison and sponsored by the Office of Education at the Bureau of Research in Washington, DC, found that "the reality of employment for blacks in Milwaukee remains bleak. . . . Job opportunities seem to be limited to low-paying, low-status, dead-end jobs."[20]

Project Equality in Wisconsin

In the 1970s, as illustrated by the examples above, racial discrimination and intimidation in employment remained entrenched after decades of struggle. African American workers knew they did not have allies in either big companies or the state. Therefore, when the private, religious organization Project Equality emerged on the scene and gained early success in large urban areas such as Detroit and Saint Louis, activists in Milwaukee decided to try the program in their locale. Although PE-Wisconsin's initial Board of Directors consisted of white men, they understood the importance of African American leadership for the state office and hired African American civil rights activist Helen I. Barnhill as the office's first executive director. Prior to working with PE-W, Barnhill served as executive secretary for the Milwaukee Citizens for Equal Opportunity (MCEO), which was a civil rights organization that focused on fair housing. Her work with MCEO led to a job with the Wisconsin Equal Rights Division, where she investigated instances of housing discrimination. Barnhill had also worked with the Milwaukee Urban League as a counselor. In this position, she assisted working-class families with their housing needs. By the time she began work in 1970 as PE-W's executive director, she was well known in the community.

The heart of Project Equality was a concern about discrimination in employment, and its organizers thought that the best way to tackle employment discrimination was to target employers. Additionally, because federal and state equal employment commissions were backlogged with complaints, PE served as a voluntary nonprofit compliance organization. PE developed a compliance review that determined whether a business or organization had a proactive antidiscrimination, affirmative action employment process. It was not enough to simply have an equal employment clause on an application or job description; because employment discrimination was structural, companies had to identify concrete steps to rectify economic injustice. Any business that signed on with Project Equality agreed to an annual compliance review and also received support from local PE offices to help implement their affirmative action plans. This commitment allowed PE-W to publish information about the company in the national *Buyer's Guide* and its local supplement. A company did not have to be in perfect standing to be listed in the *Buyer's Guide*; it simply had to make a commitment to the annual compliance review process and make continual progress toward equal employment.

Helen Barnhill laid the foundation for PE-W as its first executive director. The executive director was responsible for guiding the daily activities of the office, representing PE-W on the local, regional, and national levels, as well as developing and offering affirmative action training workshops. Most importantly, however the executive director played a large role in undertaking compliance reviews, which determined whether companies were making sufficient progress toward their affirmative action goals. The results of these compliance reviews determined whether companies would be included in the national annual buyer's guide. Compliance reviews took two forms: the desk audit and the site visit. With the desk audit, companies sent Project Equality the necessary documents that would allow the organization to determine whether the company was equal-employment-opportunity compliant. Documents included the company's "affirmative action plan, including goals and timetables; work force report, which breaks down the total number of employees by race sex, and job level; log of applicants; equal employment opportunity policy statement; list of resources used for hiring; copies of tests used; job application forms; purchasing policy; advertising materials; employee handbooks; union contracts; benefit statements; and any other items the company feels have relevance to their total EEO stance."²¹ If the results of the desk audit uncovered major areas of noncompliance, then a site visit would be scheduled to develop a plan of action. The PE compliance review officer would meet with the owner of the company if it was a small business, or executive management if it was a larger firm. After the site visit, PE would make explicit recommendations and provide the company with a timeline for achieving the recommendations. Upon making successful progress, the company could then be listed in the *Buyer's Guide*.

The *Buyer's Guide* was PE's ultimate tool in encouraging Christians to push for affirmative action through their consumer choices. Samuel Wong, associate executive secretary of the United Methodist Church's Commission on Religion and Race, wrote, "[I]f buyers are intentional about equality, they will examine the employment practices of their suppliers and do business with firms that share their commitment to equal employment practices." "Equality," Wong felt, was "everybody's business." Christian consumers could make their "mission follow [their] money" by writing to their suppliers to request that they participate in Project Equality. After participating in the compliance process, they could join the thousands of businesses nationwide in the *Buyer's Guide*, which would then be sent to over two dozen religious denominations representing thirty million members.²²

Although the executive director ultimately answered to a Board of Directors, she set the agenda for the local office. By 1973, Helen Barnhill resigned as executive director, and after hiring a temporary executive director for one year, the Board of Directors hired Betty Jean Thompson, an African American woman who grew up in Milwaukee. Thompson's belief in equal employment for all people of color and her Christian faith prompted her to join PE-W in 1973. In the PE-W newsletter announcing her new position, she wrote, "Employment opportunity for all minorities is one of the principle starting points in the struggle for liberation from oppression."²³ Growing up in segregated Milwaukee, on the predominantly African American north side, Thompson knew her family was "poor materially, but not spiritually."²⁴ It was this belief that prompted her to get involved with demonstrations for open housing led

Project Equality Buyer's Guide 1972

WORDS MUST BE MADE INTO DEEDS

PROJECT EQUALITY

Figure 10.1. Cover of 1972 *Project Equality Buyer's Guide* (image courtesy of Department of Special Collections and University Archives, Marquette University Libraries, Project Equality, Incorporated Records).

by the NAACP Youth Council and Father James Groppi in 1967.[25] After her involvement in these direct-action campaigns, she worked for the Council of Urban Life until she started as deputy director of Project Equality of Wisconsin. Years later, Thompson reflected on the importance of her work—work that had been characterized as "low-key" and "slow."[26] She insisted, "It would be far worse if we were not here. . . . We have put out fires, we've been behind the scenes, we've met with youth groups, we've talked to employers."[27]

PE-W's work with the Madison Public Schools (MPS) illustrates the slow process PE-W engaged in to bring companies into compliance with equal employment opportunity laws. PE-W's work with MPS began under Helen I. Barnhill's tenure in 1971 and continued through Betty Thompson's tenure. In 1971, George Shands, a social studies teacher at East High School in Madison, along with some of his students, investigated the Madison Public School System. They focused their research on MPS's policies on hiring, purchasing, and construction contracts, concluded that MPS policies regarding affirmative action could be "strengthened," and contacted the Equal Opportunities Commission.

After learning that the office was interested but busy working with the City of Madison on its affirmative action programs, the EOC recommended Helen Barnhill and Project Equality. After months of conversations and meetings, in July 1972, the MPS School Board approved of implementing an affirmative action plan. Several months later, in February of 1973, the board selected Project Equality to develop the program.[28] After PE won the contract "because of its excellence and skilled organization," its work began in earnest.

In the process of coming to an agreement with Project Equality, the Madison Public School System had to come to terms with the structural discrimination that was exposed by Shand and his students. The agreement between MPS and Project Equality explicitly stated MPS's shortfalls. Although MPS had a generic commitment, via a written policy, to equal opportunity in employment, the policy's implementation had not resulted in "significant numbers of minority and women employees throughout all levels of the school system."[29] PE found this typically to be the case with most businesses and organizations that crafted unspecific policies to comply with the federal legislation but then put no money, resources, or procedures behind policy enforcement. As a result of MPS and PE's partnership, PE suggested policy changes and designed procedures for the implementation of equal opportunity policy. PE also agreed to train MPS employees on equal employment policy and procedure as well as lead workshops on the topic. In terms of the contracts MPS held with external suppliers, PE suggested the school system review the current contracts to determine whether the suppliers that MPS hired had equal employment practices.[30] Over the next several years, the PE office helped MPS revise its policy, write up procedure, disseminate this knowledge to its staff, and implement an affirmative action program. In 1975, the funds ran dry and MPS concluded its formal consulting relationship with PE. MPS remained a PE partner, however, and continued to be listed in the national *Buyer's Guide* because of its cooperation with its local PE office.[31]

A Blueprint for Economic Justice

In addition to working with organizations, like the Madison Public Schools, to reach equal opportunity compliance, Project Equality also expended much energy on its educational program, which consisted of workshops and training opportunities, as well as its frequent newsletter. Workshops offered by PE included topics such as human awareness, sexism, racism, assertiveness, and conflict management. Additionally, businesses could request training programs specific to their organizational needs. PE-W, including the executive director, administered these workshops in addition to carrying out the daily tasks of the office.

More than anything, however, it was the PE-W newsletter that laid out the organization's vision for economic justice. The newsletter, which PE-W published every other month or so, featured local and national PE news, guest editorials, and a "Letter from the Executive Director." At the beginning of her tenure as executive director, the tone of Betty Thompson's letters was informative in nature; however, as the years progressed and the need for equal employment opportunity became even more acute, Thompson's letters became more urgent and spelled out her blueprint for economic justice. In the tradition of black women intellectual activists, Thompson used her pen and her position to imagine a new world economic order, one in which, as she states, "[T]he right to a decent job for every citizen who wishes to work is at the very foundation of a viable, free and open society."[32] In addition to equal employment opportunity, Thompson's blueprint for economic justice included a focus on and understanding of the ways in which the past, history, affected the present. In her editorials, Thompson continually reminded her readers of the legacy of slavery and Jim Crow. Understanding history was key in creating a new economic order.

Additionally, Thompson was not afraid to call out racism and name prejudice as the stumbling blocks in creating a new, just society. She urged supporters of PE to let their higher power be a spiritual compass in directing their efforts toward economic justice. Racism and discrimination, ultimately, were sins. Thompson also expanded the idea of who should be involved in economic-justice work—she stressed that this work was not just the work of black activists but for everyday people. "Civil rights," according to Thompson, was not "just for blacks or for other minorities. Black men and women as well as white men and women need saving." Therefore, everyone, especially white Christians, should get involved. Finally, Thompson's blueprint for economic justice meant changing structures and breaking patterns of discrimination using new methods. While each of her letters varied in its structure, taken together, they laid out her vision for a world where each person had equal opportunities, not only in employment but in life.

Betty Thompson became the executive director of PE-W in 1973, during the Black Power era, and after her own involvement in Milwaukee's civil rights struggle. While civil rights activists fought for rights and equality, a crucial aspect of the freedom struggle was consciousness raising. This process included becoming aware of African American history and the effects of racism. Thompson devoted a portion of her column to this task. In one letter, she made the clear connection between the United States' racist past and its unjust present. She stated, "When one observes the American scene today, one sees, as have countless observers, that the possibility of such human development and fulfillment is not equally available to all our citizens. This is most true, of course, of those whom we call minorities, black, brown, red, yellow, etc. The barriers they face in their inspiration and striving to be fully human have long, historical and shameful roots. These roots go deep into our racist past and still flourish in our not so open but still powerful racist present."[33] For Thompson, the only way to achieve economic justice was to uncover and recognize the historical roots of racism, roots that contributed to the disease of inequality blacks experienced in her day. Thompson wanted her readers to "acknowledge some of society's mistakes" because, ultimately, she believed that "in order for us to assure that Justice no longer waits on the scaffold while Injustice sits on its throne, the voice of PE members, the prophets and the churches will have to end their silence."[34]

Four years into her tenure as executive director, Thompson attended PE's annual meeting in Indianapolis, Indiana. She returned to Milwaukee on a mission, with Acts 17:6 as her guiding principle—"these men and women have turned the world upside down." Turning the world upside down is what Thompson believed PE-W could do. In the letter she wrote that recounted her time at the annual meeting, she made clear her ideas about PE's functions. To her, PE was a catalyst. It was "an element whose presence causes a reaction or change. We are called on to make a difference in structures which affect the lives of people. PE is a catalyst for justice in employment."[35] The goal of PE, Thompson asserted, was "systemic change—to be as revolutionary as Scripture—to make a difference in people's lives, in patterns of behavior, through purchasing patterns and employment systems."[36]

Betty Thompson worked hard to encourage everyday people to "become as revolutionary as the scriptures."[37] She told her readers, "If everyday people don't demand that all members of a society are brought to share in society's benefits, then government, social agencies, the press, and the 'church' will have no social impulses either, and the suffering will continue."[38] Demanding equality for all, getting "on the right side of the world revolution," according to Thompson, meant that the "nation must undergo a radical revolution of values" and "begin to shift from a 'thing-oriented' society to a 'people-oriented' society." Making this shift meant that Christians, everyday people, had "a moral duty to refuse to cooperate with evil" and to make a commitment to "not spend our dollars where peoplehood and personhood are not respected."[39] Yes, PE-W was an economic-justice measure, but its struggle for economic justice revolved around the needs of a group of people who for so long were thought to be less than human and not worthy of being included in the human family.

In many of her letters, Thompson took care to show how the diseases of discrimination dehumanized African Americans. In one letter, Thompson invited her readers to "do a 'Turn Around' experience in awareness for change." In her letter, she told them to imagine that what they were reading was true and reasonable:

Imagine that you are reading the paper. You read that whites are unemployed at twice the rates of blacks. Whites are 75% of the prison populations. Blacks are over 95% of those enrolled in medical schools. Whites—that feeling of being in the minority! Doesn't society know that three-fourths of the world is white? You are conditioned to be inferior. You are the minority! And how often are you reminded . . . white is fright, yellow is mellow, brown is sound, Black is where it's at!

When you attempt to buy a house in a seemingly peaceful Black neighborhood, you are given the run-around by Black realtors, and the Black bank makes it difficult for you to get a loan. Your new Black neighbors first resist you, then ignore you, and notes are left in your mailbox with the word "Honky" written on them. You begin receiving obscene and

Figure 10.2. PE-W staff in 1978, *left to right*, Charlene Faiola, Betty Thompson, and Linda Peterson (image courtesy of Department of Special Collections and University Archives, Marquette University Libraries, Project Equality of Wisconsin Records).

threatening phone calls. You can't believe it! In 1980! Finally, you are left alone, but you notice, "For Sale" signs across the street and on either side of you. Your neighbors tell you they are moving because their homes are too small, or their families are too big. You begin to hurt real bad. "Why was I born a white?"

Thompson knew that for some, this "turn-around" experience would seem crazy, but that was the intent, to illustrate the irrational nature of exclusion and discrimination in an attempt to expose the everyday experiences of African Americans and other people of color. Thompson used exercises like this to continually educate white Christians and make them aware of the social, economic, and psychic toll it took being black in the United States.

Betty Thompson's vision for a new economic order started with affirmative action and fair employment, but it centered on relationship and redemption. Thompson knew that the only way to achieve the equal rights African Americans deserved was through changing hearts and minds. Her over thirty years of experience showed her that the law could not transform people. It would take, according to Thompson, "increased knowledge and personal contact with individuals different from ourselves . . . to improve many of the conditions of a racist society."[40] In her dealings with the business community, it was Thompson's personal mission to bring about a radical transformation in each of the businesspeople she encountered. This was her life's work, labor that she continued until her retirement in 2002.

Betty Thompson's work with PE-W exemplifies the nature of black women's economic-justice activism in the urban industrial North, especially after the direct-action-oriented activism of the 1960s. Black women like Thompson understood that the law could only take black people so far. While PE-W prided itself on its amicable relationships with businesses and employers, it also articulated the idea that discrimination was both bad for business and un-Christian. New research by historians is shining a spotlight on the strategic, intellectual activism of black women, showing not only how black women acted and organized but also how they shaped the circulation of ideas.[41] This is what Betty Thompson and countless other black women did, and even though the work was hard, they continued.

Conclusion

Jim Crow employment discrimination, bolstered by the everyday actions and inactions of employers and businesses, as well as slow-moving state bureaucracies, hid in plain sight in the urban North. This is why organizations like PE-W were necessary—and ultimately unsuccessful. PE-W aimed to simultaneously uncover the nature of Jim Crow employment discrimination and help move the dial forward toward employment and economic justice. This proved difficult, and by the 1980s, the country endured a recession, deindustrialization destroyed manufacturing jobs in the United States, and affirmative action and equal employment opportunity fell out of fashion. Still, Project Equality continued. While Project Equality was heralded on both the national and local levels for the success it achieved in cooperatively encouraging business to adopt affirmative action practices, in truth, its mission could and would never be realized. In Milwaukee, specifically, over two thirds of the city's industrial jobs disappeared between 1961 and 2001—PE was fighting a losing battle.[42] As the manufacturing jobs left the city, so too did its white residents. During the same period, 1960–2000s, three formerly rural counties near Milwaukee tripled in population as white residents fled the city.[43] As a result of the conservative climate of the 1980s, when funds for social services ran dry, when crack flooded the city, and when dead-end service jobs could not fill the gap, widespread poverty engulfed African Americans in Milwaukee and further divided the city. To this day, Milwaukee is one of the most segregated cities in the nation.[44]

Project Equality asserted that economic justice should be a priority. Specifically, Betty Thompson realized, "We need each other for the larger struggle that looms on the horizon. Many do not realize that jobs, health services, housing, adequate income are not just desirable things that ought to be spread to as many people as convenience permits, but are everyone's rights. And they won't be enjoyed by all until they are acknowledged as rights to which all citizens are entitled."[45] Now, more than ever, Betty Thompson's blueprint for economic justice is needed.

NOTES

1 *Watkins, Respondent v. Department of Industry, Labor, and Human Relations,* Appellant: Herzbrun and others, Defendants, No. 28 (1974), Supreme Court of Wisconsin, September 8, 1975, Argued, September 30, 1975, Decided.

2 For more on the FEPC, see: Anthony S. Chen, *The Fifth Freedom: Jobs, Politics, and Civil Rights in the United States, 1941–1972* (Princeton, NJ: Princeton University Press, 2009), pp. 32–87; Thomas Sugrue, *Sweet Land of Liberty: The Forgotten Struggle for Civil Rights in the North* (New York: Random House, 2008), pp. 90–96. Andrew Edmund Kersten argues that the FEPC was more successful in the Midwest and examines Milwaukee, arguing that the FEPC was initially successful in this city. However, this success would be short-lived, especially after World War II ended. See *Race, Jobs, and the War: The FEPC in the Midwest, 1941–1946* (Urbana: University of Illinois Press, 2000).

3 Other stories that fit this narrative include the activism of auto workers in Detroit who participated in the Dodge Revolutionary Union Movement (DRUM). See, Heather Ann Thompson, *Whose Detroit? Politics, Labor, and Race in an American City,* with a new prologue (Ithaca, NY: Cornell University Press, 2017). Also, see *Black Power at Work: Community Control, Affirmative Action, and the Construction Industry,* edited by David Goldberg and Trevor Griffey (Ithaca, NY: Cornell University Press, 2010).

4 See introduction to this volume. Also, in his work on the civil rights movement in Brooklyn, Brian Purnell examines the impact of the culture-of-poverty discourse on the social, economic, and political status of people of color in the 1950s and 1960s. See *Fighting Jim Crow in the County of Kings: The Congress of Racial Equality in Brooklyn* (Lexington: University of Kentucky Press, 2015), 25–26.

5 "Biography/History of the Wisconsin Governor's Commission on Human Rights: Records, 1934, 1945–1971," Manuscript Series 996, State Historical Society of Wisconsin.

6 Corneff Taylor, "Employment Problems on National and Local Level," *Milwaukee Defender*, June 6, 1957.

7 "Court Decision Re-Emphasizes Need for Strong FEPC Law in Wisconsin, Congressman Henry S. Reuss Says," *Milwaukee Defender*, May 2, 1957.

8 Edris Washington vs. Bernard Goldstein, January 8, 1958, Box 17, Folder 8, Milwaukee Urban League Records, State Historical Society of Wisconsin.

9 Danielle McGuire, *At the Dark End of the Street: Black Women, Rape, and Resistance—a New History of the Civil Rights Movement from Rosa Parks to the Rise of Black Power* (New York: Vintage, 2011).

10 See, Crystal Moten, "'Kept Right on Fightin . . .': African American Working Women's Activism in Civil Rights Era Milwaukee," *Journal of Civil and Human Rights* 2:1, 2016.

11 "Plan of Cooperation between the Milwaukee Urban League and the Fair Employment Practices Division of the Wisconsin Industrial Commission, July 23, 1963," Box 2 Wisconsin Equal Rights Division, General Correspondence and Subject File 1954–1970, Series 1746, State Historical Society of Wisconsin.

12 "State Criticized in Negro Jobs," *Milwaukee Journal*, April 16, 1964.

13 Milwaukee Commission on Community Relations, *The Negro in Milwaukee: Progress and Portent* (Milwaukee, WI: Milwaukee Commission on Human Relations, 1963).

14 Ibid.

15 See Patrick Jones, *Selma of the North: Civil Rights Insurgency in Milwaukee* (Cambridge, MA: Harvard University Press, 2009), 243–46.

16 "Allen-Bradley Co. Fires Black 'Model' Vietnam Veteran," *Greater Milwaukee Star*, January 17, 1970.

17 "Allen-Bradley Rehires Vet," *Greater Milwaukee Star*, January 31, 1970.

18 Lawrence Howard et al., "Barriers to Employability of Non-White Workers" (Washington, DC: Office of Education, Bureau of Research, 1969).

19 "Equal Employment Opportunity Report" (Washington, DC: Department of Industry, Labor, and Human Relations, 1968).

20 Howard et al., "Barriers to Employability."

21 "What Is a Compliance Review?" "Project Equality of Wisconsin Inc Newsletter, Volume 10, February/March 1975." Project Equality of Wisconsin Papers, Marquette University, Department of Special Collections and University Archives, p. 3.

22 "Project Equality: Low-Key Approach to Effecting Change," *Business Journal*, April 16, 1994, p. 9.

23 "Project Equality of Wisconsin Inc. Newsletter, Volume 7, August, 1974." Project Equality of Wisconsin Papers, Marquette University, Department of Special Collections and University Archives.

24 Mary Buckley, "BD Woman Honored for Efforts to Create Fairness in Workplace," n.d. Newspaper Clippings File, Project Equality Wisconsin Papers, Marquette University.

25 Jones, *Selma of the North*.

26 "Challenge from PE Director," *Milwaukee Community Journal*, June 25, 1980.

27 Ibid.

28 "Project Equality of Wisconsin Inc. Newsletter, Volume 4, April, 1973." Project Equality of Wisconsin Papers, Marquette University, Department of Special Collections and University Archives; "Firms Dealing with City Schools May Be Checked," *Wisconsin State Journal*, July 7, 1971.

29 "Madison Public School System and Project Equality of Wisconsin, INC. Agreement," March 5, 1973, Project Equality, Inc., Series 4, Employment Audit Files, Folder 5, Marquette University, Department of Special Collections and University Archives.

30 "Background on MPS PE Partnership." Project Equality, Inc., Series 4, Employment Audit Files, Folder 5, Marquette University, Department of Special Collections and University Archives.

31 Letter to Betty J. Thompson from John V. Odom, Madison Public Schools Affirmative Action Coordinator, January 18, 1975, Project Equality, Inc. Series 4, Employment Audit Files, Folder 5, Marquette University, Department of Special Collections and University Archives.

32 "Letter from the Executive Director," *Newsletter*, Project Equality of Wisconsin Inc., August 1978, Volume 28.

33 "Letter from the Executive Director," *Newsletter*, Project Equality of Wisconsin Inc., May 1975, Volume 11.

34 "Letter from the Executive Director," *Newsletter*, Project Equality of Wisconsin Inc., January 1977, Volume 20.

35 "Letter from the Executive Director," *Newsletter*, Project Equality of Wisconsin Inc., April 1977, Volume 21.

36 Ibid.

37 "Letter from the Executive Director," *Newsletter*, Project Equality of Wisconsin Inc., July–August 1979, Volume 32.

38 "Letter from the Executive Director," *Newsletter*, Project Equality of Wisconsin Inc., Spring 1980, Volume 34.

39 Ibid.

40 "Letter from the Executive Director," *Newsletter*, Project Equality of Wisconsin Inc., September 1976, Volume 18.

41 See, for example: Mia Bay, et al., *Towards an Intellectual History of Black Women* (Chapel Hill: University of North Carolina Press, 2015); Keisha Blain, *Set the World on Fire: Black Nationalist Women and the Global Struggle for Freedom* (Philadelphia: University of Pennsylvania Press, 2018).

42 Zoe Carpenter, "What's Killing America's Black Infants? Racism Is Fueling a National Health Crisis," *Nation*, February 15, 2017.

43 Alec MacGillis, "The Unelectable Whiteness of Scott Walker," *New Republic*, June 15, 2014.

44 City of Milwaukee Community Health Assessment, 2015–2016, accessed August 1, 2017, http://city.milwaukee.gov.

45 "Letter from the Executive Director," *Newsletter*, Project Equality of Wisconsin Inc., September 1976, Volume 18.

H. Rap Brown, SNCC, addresses reporters, July 27, 1967.
Library of Congress, U.S. News & World Reports Photograph
Collection.

11

The Media and H. Rap Brown

Friend or Foe of Jim Crow?

PETER B. LEVY

Traditionally, historians have portrayed Jim Crow as a southern phenomenon, while simultaneously casting the national media, headquartered in the Northeast, as a vital ally in the fight for equal rights. Or as SNCC legend John Lewis put it, "If it hadn't been for the media . . . the civil rights movement would have been like a bird without wings, a choir without a song." But what role did the national media play in the struggle against the Jim Crow North? Did it highlight stories and images that strengthened protests against racist practices and policies or paint these efforts in a negative light? By focusing on the *New York Times'* and *Washington Post's* coverage of SNCC chairperson H. Rap Brown in the late 1960s and early 1970s and contrasting it with that of the African American press, this essay will show that the national media was a friend, not a foe, of Jim Crow. From the moment he burst into the public limelight in late July 1967, these national newspapers as well as several of the nation's most widely read magazines cast Brown, and by extension Black Power, which he came to symbolize, and the struggle against Jim Crow in the North, as violent in deed as well as in words, and as an illegitimate representative of the civil rights movement. Moreover, by downplaying Brown's and his attorney's warnings about the government's worrisome attacks upon civil liberties, as well as his broader critique of the criminal justice system, the national media not only helped undermine the struggle against Jim Crow; it helped fuel the cry for "law and order" and the politics of white resentment, which in turn raises questions about the heroic role usually attributed to the national press in much of the recent literature.[1]

While this case study focuses on the press's coverage of H. Rap Brown, it dovetails with Matt Delmont's argument that the media played a seminal role in maintaining segregated schools, in particular, and Jim Crow, more broadly, in the North and the West. Deeply vested in seeing themselves and the northern metropolitan communities they represented as the polar opposite of the Jim Crow South, the reporters, editors, and publishers of the national press chose civility over civil rights when conflicts arose out of the lack of the latter in their own backyards.[2] The major exception to this came, unsurprisingly, from the black press, an institution that existed in large part because of the prevalence of Jim Crow in the North, from segregated neighborhoods to lily-white press rooms, including at the nation's most liberal newspapers, such as the *New York Times*.[3]

Prior to the summer of 1967, Hubert Geroid Brown was unknown to most Americans. Born in in the fall of 1943 in Baton Rouge, Louisiana, he earned the nickname "Rap" as a youth for his quick wit and oratorical skills—particularly as a player in the game of dozens, where he set his verbal jabs to rhyme. As a student at Southern University in the early 1960s, he was introduced to the Non-Violent Action Group (NAG) by his older brother, Ed, a veteran of SNCC's activities in the Deep South. Time spent in Mississippi during the summer of 1964, and then in rural Alabama, reinforced Brown's Black Nationalist sentiments. But his activism garnered him virtually no media attention. The only exception came in the spring of 1965 when Drew Person reported that "Hubert Brown" had declared during a group meeting with the president that he did not care if White House protesters caused LBJ's daughter to lose sleep at night because her problems paled in comparison to those faced by blacks in the South. And this sole mention of Brown's name by the national press was buried in the middle of Person's section C "Merry-Go-Round" column. (Brown later converted to Islam and changed his name to Jamil Al-Amin. For the purposes of this paper, I will use the name H. Rap Brown.)[4]

Even after he assumed the leadership of SNCC in the spring of 1967, the press paid him little heed, maintaining its gaze on Brown's predecessor, Stokely Carmichael, who had popularized the slogan "Black Power" the summer before. The press reported without question SNCC's statement that Brown would tone down the group's rhetoric and reconcentrate SNCC's efforts on grassroots organizing, with *Newsweek* assuring its readers that Brown was "far less *flammable* [my emphasis]" than his predecessor. Mid-July 1967 stories on the Newark Black Power Conference, where Brown appeared, focused on LeRoi Jones (Amiri Baraka),

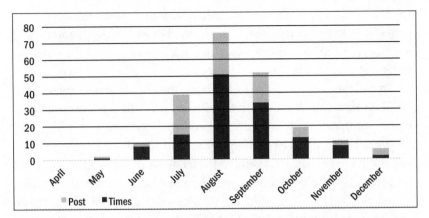

Figure 11.1. H. Rap Brown by month, April–December 1967, *New York Times* and *Washington Post*.

Stokely Carmichael, and Floyd McKissick. The article quoted McKissick and Jones extensively, Brown's name only appearing in the caption of a photograph of the gathering.[5]

This quickly changed following Brown's appearance on the night of July 24 in Cambridge, Maryland, where he declared, "[I]f this town don't come around, this town should be burned down," and where, in fact, a massive fire erupted. Over the course of the next two weeks, Brown appeared in over forty-nine stories in the *Times* and the *Post*, including thirteen in which he made the front page. The *Times'* headlines announced that Brown had "incited" a riot, was being "Hunted by [the] FBI," and was urging blacks to "Get Guns." The first full *Times* biography of Brown asserted that he "had not left much doubt among whites, whom he usually refers to as 'honkeys,' as to where he stands on race relations," noting that he had "urged 400 Negroes to 'burn this town down'" and a few days later "exhorted a group of 100 Negroes" in Jersey City to "wage guerilla warfare." In sum, America's first introduction to Brown unequivocally cast him as an advocate of violence, as an opponent of integration, and as a betrayer of the fundamental principles of the modern fight against Jim Crow.[6]

Simultaneously, the press's coverge of Brown reinforced the public's belief that radicals, not structural and institutional racism, had caused the nation's riots. Reviewing its earlier coverage of Brown, the *Times* noted that SNCC's "Angry Rights Leader" had made similar inflammatory statements in four riot-torn cities, Cincinnati, Houston, Montgomery, and Dayton. In a separate front-page story, the *Times* relayed the congressional testimony of several city police chiefs, all of whom asserted that Brown had "incited rioting." Most notably, the papers quoted chief of police Brice Kinnamon's statement that Brown was "the *sole* [my emphasis] reason" for the riot in Cambridge. An editorial in the August 8 edition of the *Times* encapsulated its framing of Brown. Entiled "Verbal Fire Setters," it noted that when Brown assumed the leadership of SNCC, Carmichael had uttered, "'People will be happy to have me back when you hear from him—he's a bad man.'" The editorial then stated that Carmichael had been right because "in three short months," Brown had "hopscotched around the nation's ghettos, preaching hate and violence and leaving ruin in his wake."[7] Likewise, stories in the *Post* led readers to believe that Brown had sparked the riots that had erupted in Detroit, because Brown, Cambridge, and Detroit often shared the same headlines, with the headline of the July 27, 1967, *Post* reading, "Daylight Sniping Worsens in Detroit: Cambridge Riot Figure Seized Here," without making clear where "here" was. The subheadlines of the story, "Troops and Police Battle Rifle Fire: Rap Brown Held on Fugitive Charge," did not offer any clarification.[8]

The nation's leading magazines echoed the *Times*' and *Post*'s coverage. *Time* magazine's headline rang out, "Cities: Man with a Match." The article below began, "Last week Firebrand H. Rap Brown applied the match." A separate *Time* magazine story on the Detroit riot contained a photograph of Brown speaking in Cambridge with the italicized caption, "'That cop they stomped. Good. He's dead.'" Why Brown's photograph appeared in a story on Detroit remained unexplained, though the caption to his photograph suggested he had instigated the "stomping" of the policeman. Similarly, in an article entitled "The Firebrand," *Newsweek* showed an angry-looking Brown, with dark sunglasses and a Band Aid above his left eye, captioned "Brown: 'Burn America down.'" The article also pictured National Guardsmen marching through the smoke-filled ruins of "[t]his sick city." The average reader easily could have missed the fact that the statement "This is a sick city" came from the mouth of Governor Agnew, not Brown. Likewise, *Life* magazine's August 4, 1967, issue on the "Negro Revolt," which included numerous horrifying photographs of Detroit aflame, displayed a photograph of H. Rap Brown getting arrested in Alexandria, Virginia, with the caption "An advocate of arson who got caught" in extra-large font, which may have led readers to believe he had incited the riot in Detroit. While some stories probed the long-term causes of the turmoil of Cambridge rather than Brown's culpability, these arguments were buried deep inside the newspapers and magazines.[9]

The photographs that accompanied these stories accentuated the public's image of Brown, in particular, and Black Power, more generally, as representing a sharp rupture from the civil rights movement of old. Brown was usually adorned in a leather jacket, with sunglasses, a bandage over his eye suggesting he had been in a gunfight, an "Afro" haircut, and a black beret. Often he was pictured waving his finger or shaking his fist. All of these images contrasted with the typical photograph of Martin Luther King Jr., which showed him wearing a preacher's blue suit, sporting shortly cropped hair, and marching hand in hand with white ministers. While SNCC's newspaper, the *Movement*, contained similar photographs, it also showed Brown in wire-rimmed glasses and posing in a bookstore next to photos of black artists and historic figures, suggesting that he had a cerebral side, something the national papers never did. Moreover, the photographs in the national papers came with captions like "Violence is 'as American as cherry pie,'" or similalry bombastic statements that the accommanying articles failed to contextualize.[10]

Following this initial flurry of stories, coverage of Brown diminished. Yet he continued to make the news, particularly through the middle months of 1968, at which point the media began to focus much more on the Black Panther Party as the embodiment of Black Power and militancy. Throughout that time, the national press portrayed Brown as a dangerous criminal, who incited riots, bore arms, and defied the courts.[11] Through a compendium of disconnected and relatively brief and nonanalytical stories, readers came to believe that the charges that Brown had incited a riot were unimpeachable and that he did not just advocate violence but practiced it as well.[12] Shortly after he was released on bail for inciting a riot in Cambridge, the national papers published stories about Brown's rearrest for illegal possession of a weapon. Notably, these stories failed to observe that Brown had never shot anyone or been convicted of committing any violence and that the illegal gun possession charge would never stand up in a court of law.[13]

At the same time as the national press cherry-picked Brown's fiery quotations, it ignored key aspects of his speeches and writings, most notably his critiques of the Vietnam War and the criminal justice system. Beginning with his speech in Cambridge, Brown repeatedly argued that the United States' actions in Southeast Asia demonstrated its hypocrisy. The United States, he observed, justified the use of violence abroad allegedly in defense of freedom. Yet, at the same time, it characterized blacks who fought for freedom at home as outlaws. To make matters worse, Brown emphasized that the war was resulting in the disproportionate loss of black lives. Brown's opposition to the war in Vietnam was part and parcel of his and SNCC's broader critique of American imperialism, which included establishing an international committee, talking about itself as a "human rights" organization, and supporting the rights of Palestinians, for which it was vilified by the national press (see below.) In terms of the criminal justice system, Brown joined other black militants, such as the Black Panther Party, in decrying police brutality. In doing so, Brown sought to place his critique of the criminal justice system within a broader theoretical framework, one that focused on the ways blacks had been and continued to be treated like subjects of colonialism.[14]

Instead of reporting on these parts of Brown's public and written presentations, the national press emphasized Brown's ostensible sympathy for communist regimes, his purported antisemitism, and his differences with the mainstream civil rights movement. The *Times* went out of its way to use the words of Jewish and black Americans to criticize Brown, perhaps because it felt this lent more legitimacy to its claims. For instance, in an August 1, 1967, piece, the *Times* quoted the relatively unknown Robert Magnum, who was black, declaring that Brown "certainly" did not "speak for members of his family or friends" who lived in Harlem. The *Times* did not follow up this assertion nor did it ever quote Magnum again.[15] Likewise, when SNCC defended the rights of Palestinians, the *Times* quoted representatives of the Jewish community declaring that SNCC, under Carmichael and H. Rap Brown, had "now irrevocably joined the anti-Semitic American Nazi party and the Ku Klux Klan as an apostle of racism in the United States." Numerous scholars have studied the relationship between blacks and Jews, including SNCC's alleged antisemitism, and we lack the space to rehash their findings. Yet it is worthwhile quoting scholar Clayborne Carson's extensive examination of this subject. Carson writes that at the time, "[F]or many Jews, there was no proper way for blacks to condemn Israel," and the national press displayed no willingness to allow Brown and SNCC to break from the liberal consensus that antisemitism and anti-Zionism were one and the same.[16]

One important exception to this general treatment of Brown came from the pen of Staughton Lynd, a colleague of Brown's. In its September 10, 1967, issue of the Sunday *New York Times Magazine*, Lynd sought to place Brown's rise within the context of the history of the New Left and the hypocrisy of the government's claim that it was fighting for freedom in Vietnam while simultaneously refusing to protect the freedom of blacks in the Deep South.[17] Yet, the *Times* made clear that Lynd's views were his alone. It did so by following up Lynd's piece with sixteen negative stories on Brown, including several that linked Brown to a riot in East St. Louis and school clashes in New York City. The *Times* also printed a series of letters to the editor that lambasted Lynd's story. This reportage culminated with a lengthy piece by veteran *Times* reporter Walter Goodman that singled out Brown for the failure of the New Politics convention to build a bridge between the New Left and liberals.[18]

This is not to argue that Brown did not have a penchant for making fiery statements. Yet, we need to recognize the difference between words and deeds. Brown may have declared at the beginning of his speech in Cambridge that the town should be burned down, but in reality he did not light a match, fire a gun, or loot stores, and he cautioned against burning up "your own stuff." As National Guard general George Gelston made clear in testimony to the Senate Judiciary Committee, both Cambridge chief of police Brice Kinnamon and the national press had distorted what had actually taken place. A fire had not erupted immediately following Brown's speech, which, as Gelston testified, was one of the reasons he had ordered his troops to stand down two hours after Brown concluded his address.[19] Consistent with its preference for the sensational, and for words over deeds, the *New York Times* did not cover Gelston's testimony, and the *Washington Post* highlighted Dorchester County's state's attorney William Yates's statement that Gelston's claims were false rather than his testimony itself.[20] The placement of the *Post*'s articles further reflected its lack of balance. Whereas stories that raised questions about Brown's guilt were buried deep in the first section or in the B or C sections, pieces on

Brown's arrest and militant pronouncements appeared on the front page and received far more column inches.[21]

Similarly, the press misrepresented Brown's statement, "Violence is as American as cherry pie," ignoring the context in which it was made. Brown made the statement at a press conference in reference to President Johnson's creation of the Kerner Commission. Brown "scoffed" at the idea of creating a commission on the grounds that "the causes of the riots were a mystery. 'Rebellions are caused by conditions,'" he asserted. "[V]iolence is as American as Cherry Pie." Put somewhat differently, Brown's pronouncement was more an observation of fact than an advocacy of violence, as the papers implied.[22] When the Kerner Commission issued its report, Brown jibed that its authors should be thrown in jail because they had said essentially the same thing he had been saying for months.

Nor did the national press contemplate the possibility that Brown's rhetoric, like Malcolm X's and many other Black Nationalists', was provocative because of the self-congratulatory veneer of liberalism, including, as noted above, the press's own underreporting on the extent of racism in its own backyard and its unsympathetic coverage of a variety of black radicals. The New York Times, he declared, is "one of the biggest pieces of white nationalism in the country." Along with the rest of the national media, it told black people that Malcolm X, Muhammad Ali, and Adam Clayton Powell were "bad" people, or "uppity niggers." Why, Brown rhetorically inquired? Because it sought to maintain the system rather than fundamentally alter it. Put somewhat differently, Brown's fiery rhetoric grew out of his distrust of the press as an accurate and sympathetic voice in the fight against Jim Crow, especially in the North. Black activists delivered what one scholar has termed modern jeremiads because they believed it was the only way they could challenge the assumption that Jim Crow was a southern rather than a national phenomenon. Along the same lines, the national press failed to consider that Brown did not seek to incite black-on-white violence but rather to empower blacks by enhancing pride and solidarity.[23]

Moreover, rather than admit that it had erred in its coverage of Brown, the press downplayed reports that he had not caused Cambridge's riot. In early March 1968, staff members of the Kerner Commission leaked an internal memo that revealed that Cambridge had not experienced a riot but only a "low level disturbance." The same memo presented a detailed timeline of the events that followed Brown's speech, which undermined the claim that rioting occurred immediately after his address. Both the *Times* and the *Post* released stories on this leaked memo. Yet, the *Times* buried its story deep in its paper, and the *Post* incorrectly stated that the "report contain[ed] little documentation of the events . . . that had not been previously published." Moreover, the *Times* highlighted the Kerner Commission's disavowal of this "draft," quoting verbatim commission spokesperson Alvin Spivak's assertion that it was only a "very preliminary" report, "kind of a trial run on a method for conducting the inquiry." Neither paper mentioned the memo again or noted that the commission's final report strangely omitted any discussion of the Cambridge's 1967 riot (not counting footnotes) even though the city was one of less than two dozen out of over one hundred that had received intense scrutiny by its investigators.[24]

Concomitantly, the media forfeited an opportunity to use Brown's story to raise public awareness about the state's efforts to silence him and other advocates of Black Power. It lent little credence to William Kunstler's assertion that "[n]o other contemporary American dissenter" faced such "vindictive and unrelenting efforts to destroy him." And it failed to print an equally powerful claim made by one of his other attorneys, Arthur Kinoy, that the government's goal was never to get a conviction. Rather, Kinoy proclaimed, it hoped to create an "atmosphere of fear and paralysis . . . so that the well-springs of social action can't move in a directed form."[25]

In 1973, Brown was sentenced to five to fifteen years for armed robbery and assaulting a police officer. William Kunstler, among others, forcefully argued that Brown's conviction was influenced by the negative press he had received all along. Ultimately, federal and state prosecutors dropped all riot-related charges against Brown. Yet, by the time these charges were dropped, Brown and much of the Black Power movement had, as Kinoy predicted, been effectively suppressed. Not surprisingly, the national press spent litle energy on the decision to drop the riot charge. The Montgomery *Sentinel*, a small suburban newspaper, not the *Times* or the *Post*, broke the story that the state never had enough evidence to prosecute Brown for inciting a riot, according to a Maryland district attorney.[26]

To further appreciate the degree to which the national press was a friend rather than a foe of Jim Crow in the North, one need look no further than the black press, which during the same time period presented a much more nuanced view of Brown. In its first issue following the "riot" in Cambridge, Baltimore *Afro-American* reporter George Collins emphasized police chief Brice Kinnamon's responsibility for the fire, not Brown's, as well as the city's racist history. Follow-up stories in the black press focused on Brown's legal travails, or what the *Chicago Defender* termed his "legal lynching" rather than his fiery words.[27] The black press also proved far more willing to contextualize Brown's rhetoric than the national media. When *Afro-American* reporters asked Gloria Richardson, the long-time leader of the civil rights movement in Cambridge, to comment upon Brown's speech, she emphasized that Brown and other militant leaders were "voicing the needs of the black community" and "if officials can't listen to the people articulating these needs, then we really are in trouble."[28] She also pointed out that when Dick Gregory and Adam Clayton Powell had delivered fiery addresses in Cambridge earlier in the decade, riots had not erupted, implying that white actions (and inaction), not radical speeches, had caused the fire that had burned down much of the all-black second ward. Likewise, the black press's coverage of the Kerner Commission's internal memos diverged significantly from the national media's. The *Afro-American*, the *Atlanta Daily World*, and the *Pittsburgh Courier* all emphasized that the commission had evidence that the police, not Brown, had started the riot and that they, not SNCC's leader, should be held responsible.[29]

Just as importantly, the black press, hardly a champion of Black Power, highlighted Kunstler's claim that the government's pursuit of Brown was part of a broader attack on blacks, in particular, and the civil liberties of all Americans, in general. In a banner story entitled "Set Rap Brown Free: Jesse; Plans for Nationwide Campaign," the *Chicago Defender* detailed Jesse Jackson's support of William Kunstler's efforts to get the government to drop all charges against Brown. "I know that you are just a scapegoat, unjustly charged with white Maryland's wrongs," Jackson declared. "I salute you (Brown), for hurling yourself as a flaming force for freedom against such engrained racism."[30]

Whereas the national media cast Brown as an illegitimate voice of the movement, the black press, by and large, did not. For instance, shortly before his death, a broad spectrum of black leaders, including Martin Luther King Jr., signed a press release that cast the government's treatment of Brown as a threat to everyone's liberty. "If there is anything that history teaches us, it is that those who sit silent while another's rights are violated inevitably come to one of two ends. . . . Either they ultimately compromise their own principles to survive in a police state, or they are eventually crushed themselves when it is too late to resist." Whereas neither the *Times* nor the *Post* mentioned this press release, the *Afro-American* quoted it in its entirety.[31] Similarly, when Brown was arrested on unrelated armed robbery charges in New York City, a number of black papers used the occasion to summarize the government's longstanding efforts to silence him. In "The U.S. vs. H. Rap Brown," the *New York Amsterdam News* delivered the "inside story of Rap Brown's five-year running battle to stay and speak his mind." Brown's most recent trial, the story explained, "has been virtually ignored by the national press." Brown had been hounded by the government from the moment he left Cambridge in July 1967 until his recent arrest in the spring of 1972 on charges that had yet to be proven in a court of law.[32] Likewise, in "How Md. 'Fraud' Led to Rap Brown's Legal Genocide," *Afro-American* reporter John Jasper detailed the "legal hell" Brown had endured since 1967. Jasper also emphasized that this "legal hell" had transformed Brown from a "militant, proud, articulate, courageous, bold and effective spokesman for America's oppressed black masses" into a "ghost" of his former self.[33]

Interviews televised on black-run shows similarly allowed viewers to see Brown in a much different and more favorable light. Most notably, in late 1968, Gil Noble interviewed Brown on his weekly ABC show "Like It Is." Wearing wire-rimmed glasses and dress clothes, rather than a leather jacket, a black beret, and sunglasses, Brown came off as a black sage rather than as a flamethrower. Via his thoughtful answers to Gil Noble's questions about the persecution he faced from prosecutors and the police, Brown displayed his deep understanding of history and demonstrated his willingness to place the needs of others above his own. Similarly, Brown's comments on the limitations of electoral politics challenged the naïve view that the ballot, alone, would or could achieve equality.[34]

Perhaps the most glaring divergence between the national media's and the African American press's treatment of Brown was their respective coverage of the March 10, 1970, near-bombing of the courthouse in Bel Air, Maryland, where H. Rap Brown was to be tried for inciting a riot. Accepting claims made by authorities, the national press reported that the bomb was meant for the courthouse but blew up inadvertently in a car driven by Ralph Featherstone and William (Che) Payne, Brown's associates. Various stories confirmed this frame, including one by Carl Bernstein, of future Watergate fame, which described Featherstone as a "bitter" militant. In a story on a slew of recent bombings, including one by the Weathermen in which white radicals blew themselves up in a Greenwhich Village apartment, the *Times* described Featherstone and Payne, as well as their better-known associate H. Rap Brown, as "frustrated radicals" who "share a rhetoric of violence" and talk of the "need to arm in self-defense if not for outright guerilla war." Alongside stories of this bombing, the national press reported that Brown had been placed on the FBI's ten most wanted list, reinforcing the claim that he was responsible for the bombing. In spite of their reputation for investigatory journalism, none of the national papers pursued Kunstler's suggestion that Featherstone and Payne had been killed by indivduals who thought Brown was in the car nor countenanced the possibility that state authorities were either directly or indirectly responsible for their deaths.[35] True, the *Times'* Ben Franklin noted that a group of unidentified blacks from Washington, D.C., had "released a statement . . . charging that Mr. Featherstone and William (Che) Payne were murdered by whites who had intended to kill Mr. Brown." But neither he nor his colleagues at the *Times* or the *Post* followed up on this charge. Instead, in the only other story published by any major papers, the *Post* reported, matter-of-factly, that the police had "concluded that two associates of black militant H. Rap Brown were killed by their own bomb,"and that the investigation into the bombing had been "closed."[36]

The black press, in contrast, presented a vastly different intepretation of the bombing. The *Philadelphia Tribune* detailed Ralph Featherstone's funeral, which, according to the paper, was attended by "10,000 Nigerians." At the funeral, the paper observed, Featherstone's widow, Charlotte Orange Featherstone, adamantly denied that her husband had carried a bomb. She also "expressed the hope that the black press would carry out its responsibility to give the true picture of what happened," more than implying that the national press had not. The *Afro-American* found the entire government theory that Featherstone and Payne had blown themselves up dubious. "The thing that left a bad taste in many people's mouths," the *Afro-American* observed, "was the way some police and certain officials started dribbling out theories about what happened . . . when they were still saying their investigation had not determined the facts."[37]

Unfortunately, lacking the resources to mount a sustained investigative report, the black press proved unable to fulfill Charlotte Featherstone's wish, leaving unsolved one of the most mysterious bombings of the era. Even in the wake of revelations about COINTELPRO, the national press did not reexamine the bombing, in spite of the documents showing that the FBI had sought to "neutralize" black radicals, including Brown. More sympathetic views of Brown did not appear in the national press until the mid-1970s, when the *Post* noted the irony that the "Brown amendment," enacted by Congress in 1968 to make it illegal to cross a state line for the purposes of inciting a riot, was probably misnamed since it was likely that Brown had done nothing wrong all along. Yet, the *Post* did not probe its own complicity in framing Brown as a riot inciter nor the way that its coverage had helped legitimize the cry for law and order.[38] Moreover, it is hardly coincidental that the most sympathetic piece on Brown published in the 1970s was penned by William Raspberry, the *Post*'s only black editorialist.[39]

To be clear, the framing of black radicals as inciters of violence and as betrayers of the principals of the civil rights movement did not originate with the press's coverage of H. Rap Brown. Brown's predecessor, Stokely Carmichael, who had popularized the term "Black Power," already had encountered similar treatment. Practically from the day he uttered the phrase, Carmichael complained that the national media had "malicously distorted" his words. On the basis of misleading press reports about "plots to get Whitey," most whites, Carmichael asserted, believed that "black power means the Mau Mau are coming to the suburbs at night." To counter this belief Carmichael penned "What We Want" and subsequently coauthored *Black Power: The Politics of Liberation*. Yet, the explanations he made in these works barely dented the overarching frame of Black Power as a philosophy of violence and reverse racism. This image was reinforced by the press's coverage of the riots of the summer of 1967, which, the Kerner Commission concluded, exaggerated the level of violence and destruction while concomitantly failing to "report on the causes and consequences of civil disorders and the underlying problems of race relations."[40]

Indeed, the *Movement*, a SNCC-affiliated newspaper, had made the same claim as the revolts of the long, hot summer were breaking out.

Describing the "events of the riot, without giving the causes," the paper exclaimed, "is to imply that black people riot for no reason." In addition, the paper continued, this frame confirmed the widely held view that blacks are "naturally violent," which in turn fueled calls for repression. Contemporaneoulsy, SNCC's long-time executive leader, James Forman, observed that the "mass media, as a pillar of the Establishment," agreed to "help supress black resistance." Along with the Johnson administration, it sought to "discredit" Black Power by associating it with violence, which in turn justified repressive measures that laid the foundation for the war on crime.[41]

In her scholarly study of the media and the Black Panther Party, Jane Rhodes confirms the validity of Forman's observations, noting that the *Oakland Tribune* introduced its readers to the birth of the Black Panther Party (BPP) with alarming photographs of the Panther's "Armed Invasion" of Sacramento, accompanied by stories that cast the BPP as "a group prone to violence and criminality . . . driven by an irrational (and) dangerous hatred of whites." This from a paper, Rhodes adds, that "had a reputation for ignoring the concerns of black residents," including protests against racist police. As with its reporting on Carmichael and Brown, this framing of the Black Panthers said little about "why the organizaton existed" or the history of the struggle against Jim Crow in the North that preceded its birth. Likewise, the press minimized those actions that undercut the image of it as a band of gangsters, such as the Panthers' free school breakfast program, while simultaneously paying little heed to the enactment of "reforms," such as the Mumford Act, that were aimed at preventing blacks from defending themselves. In sum, writes Rhodes, "instead of enabling meaningful conversations about the nation's problems, they [the national media] fanned the flames of racial discord," which in turn bolstered calls for law and order.[42]

In her insightful article "Frontlash: Race and the Development of Punitive Crime Policy," Vesla Weaver confirms Rhodes's findings, observing that in the latter half of the 1960s the black freedom struggle was criminalized. Though there was no empirical connection between rising crime rates and calls for Black Power and urban uprisings, politicians and pundits associated the two anyway. While Weaver casts conservatives as the prime movers in this development, she notes that hundreds of pieces of legislation were enacted with the support of liberals and conservatives between 1965 and 1968, including the so-called Brown amendment.[43] And though Elizabeth Hinton does not focus on the role played by the national press in her pathbreaking book *From the War on Poverty to the War on Crime*, she too notes that the media's "sensational-ized" coverage of crime and the "fear-mongering political rhetoric at the time" enabled President Johnson and others to call for and gain passage of a series of federal "war on crime" measures that ultimately resulted in the mass incarceration of millions of African Americans. Simultane-ously, by enabling those who sought to silence Brown and other radicals, the national press ceded important ground in the fight for the rights of the accused, a fight that had made steady gains in the 1950s and the 1960s but that lost ground as the call for law and order gained steam.[44]

To reiterate, the national press tended to close its ears to the voice of the black community in the latter part of the 1960s. It amplified the inflamma-tory rhetoric of Brown and other Black Power advocates, mistook words for deeds, and simultaneously minimized evidence of the government's denial of basic rights, from freedom of speech to the right to a fair trial. In contrast, the black press was more willing to follow leads that suggested that Brown was not culpable of inciting a riot in the first place and that the government's pursuit of him represented a broader effort to silence black radicals. In spite of the national press's reputation as a bastion of the fight for civil rights, not so surprisingly promoted by many veteran reporters and editors, this case study suggests that the press helped maintain Jim Crow in the North. Disinclined to look for racism in their own backyard, including its own skewed treatment of black militants and sensational coverage of racial uprisings, the "national" media, which was located in the North (and West), framed H. Rap Brown and the Black Power move-ment for which he spoke as an illegitimate offspring of the civil rights movement. Prioritizing civility over civil rights, which entailed leaving the racial status quo in place, the national media sought to delegitimize the messenger rather than grapple with his message, raising questions about its commitment to the broader freedom movement.

NOTES

1 Gene Roberts, *The Race Beat: The Press, the Civil Rights Struggle, and the Awaken-ing of the Nation* (New York: Vintage, 2007); Martin Berger, *For All the World to See: Visual Culture and the Struggle for Civil Rights* (New Haven, CT: Yale Univer-

sity Press, 2010); Sasha Torres, *Black, White, and in Color: Television, Policing, and Black Civil Rights* (Princeton, NJ: Princeton University Press, 2003); Lewis quoted in Sarah Scalet, "Confrontational Coverage: Imagery, Media Exposure, and the Civil Rights Movement," Honor's Thesis, Hamilton College, Fall 2014 (in author's possession); Jenny Walker, "A Media-Made Movement? Black Violence and Nonviolence in the Historiography of the Civil Rights Movement," in *Media, Culture, and the Modern American Freedom Struggle*, ed. Brian Ward (Gainesville: University Press of Florida, 2001), pp. 41–66. See also, Terry Ann Knopf, "Race Riots and Reporting," *Journal of Black Studies* 4, no. 3 (March 1974), pp. 303–27. This study will consider both the press's selection bias—what events get reported—and the description bias—how the events were covered. See: Robert W. Entman, "Framing: Toward Clarification of a Fractured Paradigm," *Journal of Communication* 43, no. 4 (December 1993), pp. 51–58.

2 Matt Delmont, *Why Busing Failed: Race, Media, and the National Resistance to School Desegregation* (Berkeley: University of California Press, 2016); William Chafe, *Civilities and Civil Rights: Greensboro, North Carolina, and the Black Freedom Struggle* (New York: Oxford University Press, 1981).

3 Armistead Pride and Clint C. Wilson II, *A History of the Black Press* (Washington, DC: Howard University Press, 1997); as of 1964, the *New York Times* only employed four black reporters. See: Michael Flamm, *In the Heat of the Summer: The New York Riots of 1964 and the War on Crime* (Philadelphia: University of Pennsylvania Press, 2017). See also, Jeanne Theoharis, *A More Beautiful and Terrible History: The Uses and Misuses of Civil Rights History* (Boston: Beacon, 2018).

4 Clayborne Carson, *In Struggle: SNCC and the Black Awakening* (Cambridge, MA: Harvard University Press, 1981), pp. 252–55; "H. Rap Brown 'The Lamb' Turns Erring Lion," *Afro-American*, August 19, 1967; H. Rap Brown, *Die Nigger Die!* (New York: Dial Press, 1969); Jamil Al-Amin, *Revolution by the Book: The Rap Is Live* (Beltsville, MD: Writers' Inc. International, 1993); "We Are Going to Build," *Movement*, June 1967, p. 1; "Carmichael Out as S.N.C.C Chief: Returns to Field Work and Is Replaced by Alabamian," *New York Times* [henceforth *NYT*], May 13, 1967, p. 20; "The Man from SNCC," *Newsweek*, May 22, 1967, p. 45; Drew Pearson, "The Washington Merry-Go-Round: Johnson Breaks with the South," *Washington Post*, March 20, 1965, p. C7; Ekwume Michael Thelwell, "H. Rap Brown: A Profoundly American Story," *Nation*, February 28, 2002. Thelwell incorrectly claimed that Evans and Novak reported this story.

5 "Carmichael Out as S.N.C.C Chief"; "The Man from SNCC"; "Newark Leaders Scored by Jones," *NYT*, July 22, 1967, p. 29; "Still Much to Be Done," *NYT*, July 23, 1967, p. 131; "Black Power Parley Reports Aid by 50 Concerns," *NYT*, July 25, 1967, p. 2; "SNCC Leader Warns of Possible Violence," *Washington Post*, June 23, 1967, p. 6; "Black Power Parley Opens in Newark: Farmer Calls Place and Time Proper for Such Conference," *Washington Post*, July 21, 1967, p. 1; "4 Wounded in Alabama Gun Battle Following Carmichael's Arrest," *Washington Post*, June 13, 1967, p. 3; "Absolute Equality Demanded by Negroes, McKissick Says," *Washington Post*, July 22, 1967, p. 1.

6 "Detroit Smolders in an Uneasy Calm: Guard Patrols Riot-Torn Cambridge," *NYT*,
   July 26, 1967, p. 1; "Cambridge School Fire Held Arson," *Washington Post*, July 24,
   1967, p. 3; "Brown Seen Spark to Fuel Old Discontent," *Washington Post*, July 26,
   1967, p. A3; "H. Rap Brown, SNCC Leader, Makes a Habit of Militancy," *Washington
   Post*, July 26, 1967, p. A3; "Cambridge Riot Beautiful, Brown Says," *Washington Post*,
   July 27, 1963, p. A3; "Daylight Sniping Worsens in Detroit: Cambridge Riot Figure
   Seized," *Washington Post*, July 27, 1967, p. A1; "Brown Blasts Johnson and Rights
   Chief," *Washington Post*, July 28, 1967, p. A1; "S.N.C.C. Head Advises Negroes in
   Washington to Get Guns," *NYT*, July 28, 1967, p. 14; "An Affable but Angry Rights
   Leader: Hubert Geroid Brown," *NYT*, July 28, 1967, p. 14; "Some Liberals Discern
   a Crossroads for Negroes," *NYT*, August 5, 1967, p. 9; "Brown Keeps Power Policy:
   Carmichael Said Successor Is "a Baaaad Man,"" *Baltimore Sun*, July 27, 1967, p. A5;
   "Rumor of Militant in Ghetto Attracts Extra Police Guard," *NYT*, August 3, 1967, p.
   18; "Secret House Study Says Reds Stir Hatred Linked to Rioting," *NYT*, August 3,
   1967, p. 16; "Washington Proceedings," *Washington Post*, August 3, 1967, p. 18; "The
   Race Problem: Why the Riots, What to Do? Congressional Skeptics," *NYT*, August
   6, 1967, p. 141; "Black Challenge: The Violence Spreads," *NYT*, July 30, 1967, p. 133;
   "Failure in the Movement," *Washington Post*, July 26, 1967, p. A20; "Verbal Fire
   Setters," *NYT*, August 8, 1967, p. 38; "Rap Brown Calls Riots 'Rehearsals for Revolution,'" *NYT*, August 7, 1967, p. 1; "Chief of S.N.C.C. Hunted by F.B.I.: Missing Leader
   Accused of 'Inciting to Riot,'" *NYT*, July 26, 1967, p. 1; "Police in 3 Cities Say S.N.C.C.
   Chiefs Incited Rioting," *NYT*, August 3, 1967, p. 1.
7 "An Affable but Angry Rights Leader," *NYT*, July 21, 1967, p. 14; "Police in 3 Cities
   Say S.N.C.C. Chiefs Incited Rioting," *NYT*, August 3, 1967, p. 1; "Verbal Fire Setters," *NYT*, August 8, 1967, p. 38.
8 "Detroit Smolders . . . Agnew Blames Brown," *Washington Post*, July 26, 1967, p. 1;
   "Brown Seen Spark to Fuel of Old Discontent," *Washington Post*, July 26, 1967, p.
   3; "H. Rap Brown, SNCC Leader, Makes a Habit of Militancy," *Washington Post*,
   July 26, 1967, p. 3; "Daylight Sniping Worsens in Detroit: Cambridge Riot Figure
   Seized Here . . . Rap Brown Held on Fugitive Charges," *Washington Post*, July 27,
   1967, p. 1; "Cambridge Riot Beautiful, Brown Says: 'Honky Should Be Taught They
   Shouldn't Mess with Us Any More,'" *Washington Post*, July 27, 1963, p. 3; "Brown
   Blasts Johnson and Rights Chiefs," *Washington Post*, July 28, 1967, p. 1; "Brown's
   Attorney Is Doing His Research," *Washington Post*, July 29, 1967, p. 9; "Rector
   Defends Decision to Let Brown Speak at Church," *Washington Post*, July 29, 1967,
   p. B1; "Cambridge Negro Unit Wants to Tell Its Side," *Washington Post*, August 4,
   1967, p. 5; "'Outsiders' Called Disrupters of Cambridge Race Accord: Police Chief
   Testifies on Cambridge Riot," *Washington Post*, August 3, 1967, p. A1; "Police in 3
   Cities Say S.N.C.C. Chief Incited Rioting," *NYT*, August 3, 1967, p. 1.
9 "Cities: Man with a Match," *Time*, September 22, 1967; David Boesel and Louis C.
   Goldberg, "Crisis in Cambridge," in *Cities under Siege: An Anatomy of the Ghetto Riots, 1964–1968*, David Boesel and Peter Rossi, eds. (New York: Basic Books, 1971), p.
   127; *Time*, August 4, 1967, p. 15; *Newsweek*, August 7, 1967, p. 28; *Life*, August 4, 1967.

10 "Cambridge Riot Figure Seized Here," *Washington Post*, July 27, 1967, p. 1; "Hubert Geroid Brown: An Affable but Angry Rights Leader," *NYT*, July 28, 1967, p. 4.

11 FBI Director, "Counterintelligence Program Black Nationalist–Hate Groups Internal Security," August 25, 1967, FBI FOIA, Black Extremist, 100–448006, Section 1; "Fighting Government Repression: 'Take the Offensive," Says Kinoy; Speech to SDS Convention by Rap Brown Lawyer," *Movement*, January 1968, p. 5; "Black Movement: Repression and Resistance," *Movement*, April 1968, p. 1.

12 "Rap Brown Indicted in Cambridge, Md., On 3 Riot Charges," *NYT*, August 15, 1967, p. 42.

13 "Rap Brown Seized on an Arms Charge by Federal Agents," *NYT*, August 19, 1967, p. 1; "Rap Brown Is Held in Bail of $25,000," *NYT*, August 20, 1967, p. 1.

14 Brown, *Die Nigger Die!*; H. Rap Brown, "Who Are the Real Outlaws?" July 1967, Civil Rights Union Veterans, www.crmvet.org; Gil Noble, Interview with H. Rap Brown, on "Like It Is," December 21, 1968, www.youtube.com; H. Rap Brown, "Address to the Black Panther Party," Oakland, CA, 1968, www.youtube.com; H. Rap Brown, "The Politics of Education," n.d., www.youtube.com (all accessed May 11, 2018).

15 "Magnum Pledges a 'Busy Time': As Head of Rights Panel in State," *NYT*, August 1, 1967, p. 18.

16 "Havana Interviews Brown," *NYT*, September 1, 1968, p. 18; see also: "S.N.C.C. Criticized for Israel Stand," *NYT*, August 16, 1967, p. 28; "New Carmichael Trip," *NYT*, August 19, 1967, p. 8; "Young Cites 'Freedom' to 'Die in Vietnam,'" *NYT*, August 26, 1967, p. 23; "War Foes Try to Shut Pentagon," *NYT*, August 29, 1969, p. 12. On SNCC's support for anticolonialism and its support of the Palestinians see: SNCC, "Position Paper: The Indivisible Struggle against Racism, Apartheid, and Colonialism," Civil Rights Union Veterans, www.crmvet.org; and "SNCC and the Arab-Israeli Conflict," *Movement*, September 1967, p. 2; "The Palestine Problem," *SNCC Newsletter*, June–July 1967; Clayborne Carson, "Blacks and Jews in the Civil Rights Movement: The Case of SNCC," Martin Luther King Jr. Research and Education Institute, Stanford University, https://kinginstitute. stanford.edu, quoted p. 45.

17 Staughton Lynd, "A Radical Speaks in Defense of S.N.C.C.," *NYT*, September 10, 1967, p. 271.

18 "Rap Brown Calls Nation on 'Eve' of a Negro Revolution," *NYT*, September 11, 1967, p. 76; "East St. Louis Negroes Throw Firebombs in Fresh Disorders," *NYT*, September 12, 1967, p. 25; "Negroes and Pickets Clash at School," *NYT*, September 13, 1967, p. 35; "2 East St. Louis Negroes Hurt by Firebombs as Unrest Goes On," *NYT*, September 13, 1967, p. 32; "Negro Shot in East St. Louis in 4th Night of Racial Unrest," *NYT*, September 14, 1967, p. 12; "Brown Put in Jail to Await Hearing," *NYT*, September 14, 1967, p. 35; "Volunteers Help to Run Schools," *NYT*, September 14, 1967, p. 52; "East St. Louis 'a Doomed City,'" *NYT*, September 17, 1967, p. 40; "A Hearing Is Set on Bond for Brown," *NYT*, September 17, 1967, p. 60; "A Militant Priest Kicks Up a Storm," *NYT*, September 17, 1967, p. E4; "Milwaukee

Priest Asks Whites to Help on Open Housing Project," *NYT*, September 18, 1967, p. 36; "Rap Brown Is Released on Bail," *NYT*, September 19, 1967, p. 28; "Groppi Ask Fund Cutoff," NYT, September 22, 1967, p. 38; Walter Goodman, "Yessir Boss, Said the White Radicals: When Black Power Runs the New Left," *NYT*, September 24, 1967; "Letters," *NYT*, October 1, 1967, p. 223. The *Post*'s coverage of Brown paralleled the *Times'*. See: "New Left Rejects 3d Party," *Washington Post*, September 4, 1967, p. 1; "Rap Brown Predicts Negro GI 'Rebellions,'" *Washington Post*, September 1, 1967, p. 2; "Brown Jailed in Richmond," *Washington Post*, September 14, 1967, p. 1; "New Generation of Barnburners," *Washington Post*, September 12, 1967, p. 16; "N.Y. Teacher Strike Shrinks Classes: 'Black History' Taught at IS 201 by H. Rap Brown," *Washington Post*, September 13, 1967, p. 6; "Jewish Leader Raps SNCC 'Anti-Semitism,'" *Washington Post*, September 26, 1967, p. 6.

19 Peter B. Levy, *Civil War on Race Street* (Gainesville: University Press of Florida, 2003), 146–47.

20 "Gelston on Cambridge," *Washington Post*, August 31, 1967, p. A20; "Gelston Didn't Tell Truth, Cambridge Official Says," *Washington Post*, August 27, 1967, p. D2; "Gelston Lessens Brown Riot Role: Says Early Action Was Needed in Cambridge," *Baltimore Sun*, August 27, 1967, p. A10; "Yates Requests Conduct Probe of General Gelston," *Washington Post*, August 27, 1967, p. C24; "Gelston Accused of 'Fairy Tale,'" *Washington Post*, August 28, 1967, p. C18; "Guard Leader at Cambridge Opposes Riot-Inciting Law," *Washington Post*, August 26, 1967, p. B1.

21 "Rap Brown Predicts Negro GI 'Rebellions,'"; "Brown Hails Riots in Detroit Speech," *Washington Post*, August 28, 1967, p. A4; "Detroit Mob Hears Brown," *Baltimore Sun*, August 28, 1969, p. A9; and "Carmichael's Black Power Text to Appear Next Month," *Baltimore Sun*, September 12, 1967, p. A3.

22 See: "As American as apple pie, cherry pie—and violence . . ." www.thisdayin-quotes.com (accessed March 3, 2015); Brown repeated the phrase in Brown, *Die Nigger Die!*

23 David Howard-Pitney, *The African-American Jeremiad: Appeals for Justice*, rev. ed. (Philadelphia: Temple University Press, 2005); Noble, interview with H. Rap Brown, "Like It Is."

24 Office of the Assistant Deputy Director for Research, "Staff Report No. 4: Analysis of Cambridge, Maryland, Disturbance, draft," October 29, 1967, in *Civil Rights during the Johnson Administration* [microfilm], ed. Stephan Lawson (Lanham, MD: UPA), Reel 27; "Report Says Rap Brown Didn't Cause Md. Riot," *Washington Post*, March 5, 1968, p. A1; "Riot Report Is Disavowed," *Baltimore Sun*, March 5, 1968, p. C9; "'Raw Memo' to Panel Links Cambridge Riots to Fears of Whites," *NYT*, March 6, 1968, p. 24; National Advisory Commission on Civil Disorders, *Report of the National Advisory Commission on Civil Disorders, New York Times Edition* (New York: Dutton, 1968). The text of the report only mentioned turmoil in Cambridge in 1963.

25 William Kunstler, "J. Edgar Hoover, Frank Hogan, Cambridge, Md., New Orleans Parish, New York Magazine vs. H. Rap Brown," *University Review*, March 1973,

p. 35; William Kunstler, with Sheila Isenberg, *My Life as a Radical Lawyer* (New York: Birch Lane Press, 1994); William Kunstler, "In Defense of Rap Brown," n.d., Student Nonviolent Coordinating Council Papers, Box 5: Folder 33.

26 "Maryland Ends 6-Year Rap Brown Case after Plea Bargaining," *NYT*, November 7, 1973, p. 27; "Md. Drops 3 Charges Against H. Rap Brown," *Washington Post*, November 7, 1973, p. 1; "Arson Charged against Brown Termed False," *Washington Post*, January 15, 1971, p. A1; "Rap Brown Figure Takes the Stand," *Washington Post*, January 17, 1971, p. C1; "Kinlein Statements 'Prejudicial,'" *Baltimore Sun*, October 20, 1971.

27 "Brown Faces a 'Legal Lynching' If Extradited, His Attorneys Warn," *Chicago Daily Defender*, September 7, 1967, p. 5; "Brown Is Thwarted Again in Bid to Avoid Extradition," *Chicago Daily Defender*, October 4, 1967, p. 3.

28 "Church Padlocked: B.P. Rally Moved," *Afro-American*, October 7, 1967.

29 "Lively, Moore Prod Agnew on Rap Brown, Cambridge," *Afro-American*, March 16, 1968, p. 1; "Riots Commission Accuses Cambridge Police of Helping to Start a Riot," *Atlanta Daily World*, March 5, 1968, p. 1; "Maryland Report Clears Rap Brown," *New Pittsburg Courier*, March 16, 1968, p. 1. See also: "Maryland Report Clears Brown," *Chicago Daily Defender*, March 12, 1968, p. 20.

30 "Free Rap Brown: Jesse."

31 "Statement on Behalf of H. Rap Brown," n.d; "Let Rap Rap" [leaflet], n.d.; SNCC, "Honky Harassment of H. Rap Brown," March 3, 1968, all in Ella Baker Papers, Box 6, Folder H. Rap Brown, Schomburg Center for Research in Black Culture, New York Public Library, New York, NY; "The Militant Front: Rap's Treatment Is New Pattern," *Afro-American*, April 6, 1968, p. 4.

32 "The. U.S. vs. H. Rap Brown," *New York Amsterdam News*, April 1, 1972, p. D8; "U.S. Rap Brown: A Fight for Justice," *New York Amsterdam News*, April 15, 1972, p. A5; "Angela's Free, but Rap's Held in $200,000 Ransom," *Philadelphia Tribune*, August 1, 1972, p. 7.

33 John Jasper, "How Md. 'Fraud' Led to Rap Brown's Legal Genocide," *Afro-American*, November 17, 1973, p. 1.

34 Gil Noble, Interview of H. Rap Brown, "Like It Is."

35 "Car Blast Kills 2 Near Trial of Rap Brown," *Washington Post*, March 11, 1970, A1; "Friend of Rap Brown Dies with 2nd Man in Auto Blast," *NYT*, March 11, 1970, p. 1; "Police Claim 2 Killed by Own Bomb," *Washington Post*, November 27, 1970, p. C1; "No Sign of Rap Brown on Bel Air Trial Eve," *Washington Post*, March 16, 1970, p. A1; "2nd Bel Air Car-Bomb Victim Identified as SNCC Worker," *Washington Post*, March 12, 1970, p. A12; Carl Bernstein, "Bomb Blast Victim Was a Bitter Rights Activist," *Washington Post*, March 11, 1970, p. A10.

36 "Fatal Blast Is Laid to Dynamite," *Washington Post*, March 15, 1970, p. A1; "Gov. Mandel Asks Life in Maryland Blast Law," *NYT*, March 13, 1970, p. 27; "FBI Reports Findings on Bel Air Blast," *Washington Post*, March 26, 1970, p. A4; "Featherstone Funeral Draws Crowd of 300," *Washington Post*, March 15, 1970, p. A15; "FBI Notes Similarities in Bombings," *Baltimore Sun*, March 19, 1970, p. C20;

"Police Claim 2 Killed by Own Bomb," Washington *Post*, November 27, 1970, p. C1; "U.S. 1970: The Radical Underground Surfaces with a Fang," *NYT*, March 15, 1970, p. 171.

37 "Blast Probe Caused Concern," *Afro-American*, March 28, 1970. p. 4; "Slain Friends of Rap Brown to Be Honored," *Philadelphia Tribune*, March 14, 1970, p. 1; "'Lanta Man 2nd Victim Maryland Auto Bombing," *Atlanta Daily World*, March 13, 1970, p. 1; "10,000 Nigerians at Ralph Featherstone's Burial," *Philadelphia Tribune*, March 23, 1970, p. 6; "Hunt White Woman Suspect," *Chicago Daily Defender*, March 12, 1970, p. 4; "Brothers and Sisters—The World Is in an Uproar and the Danger Zone Is Everywhere" [from Ralph Featherstone's Memorial Service], March 1970, Civil Rights Movement Veterans, www.crmvet.org (accessed December 20, 2016). Michael Newton, *Unsolved Civil Rights Murder Cases, 1934–1970* (Jefferson, NC: McFarland, 2016), pp. 253–54.

38 "Federal Conviction against Rap Brown Voided on Appeal," *Washington Post*, September 25, 1976, p. A2.

39 William Raspberry, "The 'Street Story' of H. Rap Brown," *Washington Post*, April 30, 1973, p. A23.

40 Peniel Joseph, *Waiting 'til the Midnight Hour: A Narrative History of Black Power in America* (New York: Henry Holt, 2006), pp. 146–47, 151–52, and 163; Peniel Joseph, *Stokely: A Life* (New York: Basic Civitas, 2014), pp. 226–28; Stokely Carmichael, "What We Want," *New York Review of Books*, September 12, 1966 (electronic version available at www.nybooks.com); National Advisory Commission on Civil Disorders, *Report*, p. 363.

41 "Riots, SNCC, and the Press," *Movement*, July 1967, p. 1; James Forman, "1967: High Tide of Black Resistance," Civil Rights Movement Veterans, www.crmvet.org.

42 Jenny Walker, "A Media-Made Movement? Black Violence and Nonviolence in the Historiography of the Civil Rights Movement," in *Media, Culture, and the Modern African American Freedom Struggle*, ed. Brian Ward (Gainesville: University Press of Florida, 2001); Christopher Strain, *Pure Fire: Self-Defense as Activism in the Civil Rights Era* (Athens: University of Georgia Press, 2005); Jane Rhodes, *Framing the Black Panthers: The Spectacular Rise of a Black Power Icon* (New York: New Press, 2007), chapter 3; Judson Jeffries, "Local News Coverage of the Black Panther Party: Analysis of Baltimore, Cleveland, and New Orleans Press," *Journal of African American Studies* 7 (Spring 2004), pp. 19–24.

43 Vesla Weaver, "Frontlash: Race and the Development of Punitive Crime Policy," *Studies in American Political Development* 21 (Fall 2007), pp. 230–65. See also, Elizabeth Hinton, *From the War on Poverty to the War on Crime: The Making of Mass Incarceration in America* (Cambridge, MA: Harvard University Press, 2016).

44 Hinton, *From the War on Poverty to the War on Crime*, p. 5.

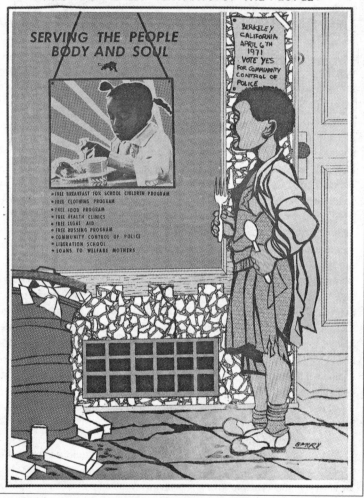

Black Panther Intercommunal News Service, March 27, 1971. Photo courtesy of Emory Douglas/Art Resource, NY.

12

Stalled in the Movement

The Black Panther Party in Night Catches Us

AYESHA K. HARDISON

He used to tell a story about George Washington going out
and fighting and then returning to Mount Vernon and living
out his days. . . . And he said, I want, I would like to have in
our race somebody who struggled against a system and went
home to Mount Vernon.
—*Negroes with Guns,* 2004

The Black Panther Party is often misrepresented in the American imagination due to abiding racism, sexism, and African Americans' maligned
relationship to history.[1] Whereas popular memory of the civil rights
movement celebrates a progressive narrative from Jim Crow segregation
to integration in the South, the dominant account of the Black Panther
Party and, more broadly, the Black Power movement, denies African
Americans' efforts to challenge racial inequality in the North. Historical
narratives frame the Black Power movement's privileging of intraracial
solidarity as an unwelcome interruption to the civil rights movement's
unifying interracial campaigns. These assessments dismiss the Black
Panther Party as gun-toting male militants initiating confrontations
with the police, and they discount the organization's community service
programs because of its stance on revolutionary violence. Myths about
northern black freedom struggles incite the culture-of-poverty rhetoric
vilifying urban centers, such as Oakland, New York, and Chicago, where
influential chapters of the Black Panther Party took root. This lore also
negates the discriminatory social structures, resurgence of conservative
politics, and missteps of liberalism that failed to differentiate the equal-

ity of opportunity from the equality of outcome, which continued to elude black communities in the late 1960s and 1970s.

The Jim Crow North's policies and procedures are amorphous in U.S. historical memory, but their repercussions for urban black communities are apparent in the independent film *Night Catches Us* (2010). Writer and director Tanya Hamilton interrogates and reimagines prevailing narratives about the Black Panther Party's ideological lapse by exploring its advocacy through free food programs and clothing drives as well as its actions of armed self-defense. Hamilton personifies the social, economic, and psychological impact of northern Jim Crowism with an African American family's suffering in the wake of a Party branch's dismantlement. Despite the disavowal of the Party's national legacy in popular memory, Hamilton demonstrates the organization's importance for local black communities even after its demise. Just as the film's narrative, visual, and aural aspects suggest that African Americans' political struggles were not over once the Black Power movement ended, its melancholic tone refuses to let viewers forget the era's psychic weight.

I argue that by engaging the nuances of the Party's rank and file, *Night Catches Us* exposes the fallibility of familiar historical narratives about the Black Panther Party (BPP), which characterize the organization as a vanguard of charismatic black male radicals without cause, ideology, or strategy. The film lays bare those unsung Panthers' difficulties in challenging distorted narratives about the Party's political history. These forgotten figures struggle, too, to preserve their version of historical events in order to sustain their personal progress.

Night Catches Us is a social drama mapped onto a family drama that unveils falsehoods about the Black Panther Party perpetuated from within and without the organization. Patricia Wilson, a widow and former BPP member played by actress Kerry Washington, raises her nine-year-old daughter, Iris, with emotional distance. As a result, Iris's detachment from her mother and lack of memories about her father are akin to her limited understanding of the Party. Meanwhile, Patricia's orphaned teenage nephew, Jimmy, who is still disenfranchised despite the accomplishments of the civil rights movement, clings to a romantic, hypermasculine idea of the BPP symbolized by guns, leather jackets, and berets. Jimmy's characterization of the Panthers omits their survival programs, the organization's most long-lasting initiatives, managed mostly by black women. Finally, Marcus Washington rounds out the film's ensemble as a formerly imprisoned ex-Panther and potential love interest for Patricia. Branded an informant for committing an act leading to the police assassination of the family's patriarch, Marcus, portrayed by actor Anthony Mackie, returns to Philadelphia to bury his estranged father. The murder hinders Marcus and Patricia's romantic relationship, as they struggle to cope with their activist past as well as their grief over her husband's death. Congruently, Jimmy and Iris falter as they come of age under misleading narratives about the BPP. Each character's relationship to the late Panther patriarch exposes the consequences of the Jim Crow North for him or her as a political subject as well as a loved one trying to reconcile this disabling trauma.

With its tight focus on four characters, the film temporally and spatially scales down African Americans' collective struggle to one household in the waning years of the Black Power movement. Hamilton employs the dynamic language, sartorial style, and political urgency of the era, but her film's muted color palette and dim intimate settings aesthetically convey a shared mourning for the BPP that goes beyond the central characters' bereavement. The film's quieting cinematographic elements reflect the way its narrative localizes the historical impact of the organization's ascent and demise to a defunct chapter, disenfranchised community, and disconnected family in 1976 Philadelphia. In this way, domestic friction stands in for the trials of the community devastated by urban blight and police brutality, the void caused by the Party branch's dissolution three years earlier, and the national organization's decline on the cusp of its formal end. In *Night Catches Us*, the movement is immobilized and the emblematic black family is in emotional discord.

By creating a melancholic narrative, Hamilton resists endorsing myths about the Black Panther Party that either nostalgically glorify it, which effectively ignores the Party's ideological debates, or solely blame the organization for its downturn, which essentially acquits conspiring local and federal law enforcement. The melancholic state of the film's four main characters is an emotional response to both their lost loved one and the Jim Crow North's physical and psychological violence. Patricia, Marcus, Jimmy, and Iris do not simply lose a partner, comrade, and father; they lose an active Party, a vibrant community, and an innocence in relation to the repressive state. Their grief is exacerbated by their systemic disenfranchisement and, thus, racialized. In *The Melancholy of Race*, Anne Anlin Cheng defines "a politics of melancholia" as "a theorization of objecthood and its entangled relations to loss and history."[2] Hamilton's characters are melancholic objects, unassimilated figures in the U.S. body politic, as well as melancholic subjects, who mourn the elusive ideal of American democracy. Their melancholia, or perpetual loss and irreconcilable mourning, is an indictment of the Jim Crow North. Although the permeating sorrow in Hamilton's narrative confirms that the BPP's objectives are unrealized, the film's melancholic tone conveys the exigency of the organization's vision for black communities' political and psychological well-being. Since the Jim Crow North's policies and procedures are not named or censured in historical memory, it is difficult for Hamilton's characters to resolve their racial trauma.

Night Catches Us addresses these melancholic silences by exploring the power relations between the state and the community, and their repercussions for the Black Panther Party and the Wilson family, through four main themes. First, the film visualizes the effects of structural inequality in the Jim Crow North with a bleak depiction of Philadelphia's deindustrialization and the family's deteriorating domestic space. Second, the film casts the BPP as more invested in survival programs, namely, social and legal aid initiatives, than in the guns for which they have been remembered. Third, the film complicates viewers' understanding of the Party's gender politics as pure misogyny, as it represents black women's contributions to the organization with its survival programs as well as the consequences they experience as a result of their involvement. Finally, the film demystifies the state's suppression of the Panthers (and the movement in the North) and its devastating ramifications for urban black communities, especially for the lives of black men and the psychic wholeness of black women. By engaging these four tropes, *Night Catches Us* deconstructs familiar narratives about the era that pit the southern movement's successes against the northern movement's failures, ignore black women's activism in urban communities, and refute the existence of the Jim Crow North.

In comparison, the commercial film *Panther* (1995) fuels some of these historical biases while capitalizing on nostalgia for the organization's larger-than-life persona. Directed by Mario Van Peebles and adopted for the screen by his father, Melvin Van Peebles, from the latter's novel of the same title, *Panther* depicts the first two years of the BPP's establishment. The plot explores Huey P. Newton's decision to solicit a double agent, Judge, to thwart FBI infiltration; a second storyline reveals the FBI's collusion with the Mafia to filter heroin into Oakland. The film has a historical and contemporary sensibility with a supporting cast that, as Tracye A. Matthews parses, "looks like a BET [Black Entertainment Television] top-forty countdown."[3] Whereas founders Newton and Bobby Seale are portrayed, respectively, by then lesser-known actors Marcus Chong and Courtney B. Vance, Kadeem Hardison leads as Judge, Bokeem Woodbine is a rank-and-file member, Chris Rock and Bobby Brown appear as men from the neighborhood, and the director makes a cameo as Stokely Carmichael. Angela Bassett also reprises her role in Spike Lee's *Malcolm X* (1992) as Betty Shabazz. The film squares this star power with black-and-white footage archiving the BPP's marches, liberation schools, and gun practice. Additionally, it recreates memorable media images, including the Panthers' face-off with Governor Ronald Reagan at the California State Capitol over gun laws and a gunshot-wounded Newton handcuffed to a hospital gurney. However, it pares down this infamous public history to Judge, a veteran and college student negotiating the tensions between the Party and the FBI.

Panther exposes Jim Crow's structural landscape, but its nostalgic lens excises the Party's ideology and female members. Black women's participation is limited to the character Alma, who is active in the plot but one-dimensional. Similarly, Judge's introductory voiceover characterizes Newton and Seale as haphazard movement architects: "No master plan. No pot to piss in. Nothing like that. Just two fed up brothers."[4] He explains that a child's hit-and-run at a neighborhood intersection with no stoplight personally motivates his BPP membership. In *Panther* (1995), the companion book to the film, Mario Van Peebles clarifies that he wanted the film to be "edutainment," to inform and captivate a young audience.[5] "If *Panther* was didactic, preachy, a history lesson, or a glorified documentary," he writes, "we'd lose."[6] Consequently, *Panther* is as oriented toward the past as it is present-minded, specifically in regard to the crack epidemic. Jane Rhodes proposes, "Just as the Black Panthers are constructed as the embodiment of black radicalism in the 1960s, the film *Panther* itself is representative of a revived expression of black rage in the 1990s."[7]

The film climaxes with the Panthers' destruction of a warehouse storing drugs, and the final scene, set in the audience's contemporary moment, shows a stoplight at the neighborhood's deadly intersection. Judge concludes, "In 1970, there were 300,000 addicts in the United States. Yesterday there were three million. The way I see it, the struggle continues." His words lament drugs' destruction of black communities, but the film's nostalgic bent also tethers the BPP's failure to this devastation. Mario Van Peebles surmises, "In the beginning the Party members persecuted drug dealers; toward the end, too many of them became their clients. It's no wonder that many Panthers say they did not leave the Party, the Party left them."[8] The drug plot incriminates the FBI and the Mafia, but in Van Peebles's understanding of this history, the Party leaders' drug use makes them abandon their constituents.

Hence the strengths of Hamilton's melancholic film hinge on the unstudied regional history it tells and the innovative way it uses the domestic space to recover this history. *Night Catches Us* confronts two major misconceptions: that the Black Power Movement was singularly tied to masculinity and that it was motivated by outside influences. To this end, the film is a local story about the Party, whose activism was catalyzed by black Philadelphians' racial and economic oppression and their subsequent efforts to ensure the betterment of their communities. To make this point, Hamilton draws on real historical events in her fictional narrative, such as the August 1970 police raid on the BPP's Philadelphia offices, when police forced Panthers to parade down the street in their underwear. Her film also details the organization's ideological transition from emphasizing armed self-defense to promoting its survival programs, which serves to foreground black female members' overlooked participation and leadership.

Unlike *Panther*, *Night Catches Us* does not heroize the BPP but uses the family's despair to reveal the consequences of state force and armed struggle for the Party's rank and file. Because the film centers the interiority of its characters and their home, it does not examine the ways Philadelphia's white liberalism (through electoral politics) and white conservatism (through white flight) engender the family's political and psychic recession.[9] Nevertheless, the police assassination of the Wilson family patriarch impresses the ways police brutality and the extralegal antagonizing of black communities asserted the city's conservative racial politics. Further, Philadelphia's structural inequalities in terms of employment, education, and housing are implicit in the film.

Hamilton signals these tensions through visual and aural markers. In effect, she constructs a vernacular history of the BPP that illustrates the strange career of Jim Crow in the North. Robert G. O'Meally defines the vernacular as *lieux de mémoire*, or sites of memory, that remain uncatalogued and undervalued, and yet, the vernacular informs historical events as well as documents their gravity. "More than any other form of human expression," he writes, "art communicates the excitement as well as the treacherous unpredictability of history's flights. Further . . . *vernacular* art and artifacts convey this fast-changing and invisible history."[10] In *Night Catches Us*, photographs and video footage from the Black Power era challenge popular notions of the Party as armed revolutionaries fighting to reclaim black manhood with evidence of black women's involvement. Additionally, Syl Johnson's Chicago soul exhibits the distinct aesthetic of northern black freedom struggles. Spirituals were the material for the freedom songs utilized during the civil rights movement, but blues-infused soul music, an adapted response to the social conditions that post–World War II migrants encountered in cities such as Detroit and Philadelphia, was the soundtrack of Black Power.[11] The gospel overtones and raw delivery of soul music's secular testifying, especially in Johnson's hard Chicago soul, resound with the decrepitude and frustration found in northern cities due to their elusive promise to hopeful southern migrants.

Soul music and its visual aesthetic register the fraught mood of the Black Power era in *Night Catches Us*. Together the aural and the ocular create the "vintage feel" film critic Betsy Sharkey notes about Hamilton's environs, in which "painterly" scenes function as "still portraits" that extend and sometimes replace the affect expressed in the film's dialogue.[12] Vernacular artifacts, including the graphic illustrations of Emory Douglas (the BPP's minister of culture), dated denim, and classic Cadillacs, along with visual aesthetics, such as melancholic camera shots containing nondiegetic music and little to no action, enrich Hamilton's film. They confirm that the Party's cultural movement, which was articulated in deferential references to "soul brothers and sisters," was vital to late-twentieth-century black freedom struggles, and its signifiers are essential to contemporary narratives of the era. The ubiquitous presence of the movement's vernacular art also deepens the film's overwhelming sense of loss.

Ultimately, *Night Catches Us* demonstrates that the unwritten histories of racial melancholia, like false narratives about the Black Panther Party, burden its legatees whether they are conscious of them or not. The film debunks censored narratives about the Party's impact, as exemplified by the free breakfast program and free sickle cell screenings later adopted by state and federal agencies. Film critic A. O. Scott perceptively describes the melancholic aesthetic distinguishing Hamilton's historiography: "That her film is so quiet, so evidently invested in contemplation rather than confrontation, gives it power as well as insight. The large dramatic gestures and sweeping implications are off-screen, between the lines."[13] With the silences of history and those of the film in mind, I outline the documented history of the BPP's Philadelphia branch before turning to a discussion of *Night Catches Us*. Hamilton's chronology reimagines the conventional narrative of the Party by engaging four main tropes: structural inequality, conflicts between revolutionary violence and survival programs, gender politics, and state suppression. These themes constitute a historical residue that lingers for the characters despite public memory's amnesiac tendencies.

A Local History of the Black Panther Party

In addition to national myths negating the Jim Crow North, misconceptions about the Black Panther Party's gender dynamics, position on revolutionary violence, and suppression distort popular memory of the organization. The Panthers' efforts to champion disempowered black communities through armed self-defense radically shifted the political landscape dominated, then, by nonviolent protest. Later scholarly preoccupations with the Jim Crow South overshadow historical studies of the era.

Newton and Seale started the organization, originally named the Black Panther Party for Self-Defense, along with four founding members in Oakland in 1966. Influenced by Malcolm X and Robert F. Williams, one of the BPP's first objectives charged outfitted members to patrol law enforcement's presence in black neighborhoods to prevent police brutality. Similar to Malcolm X's ideology for self-determination by any means necessary, Williams's philosophy of "armed self-reliance" positioned him against the nonviolent protests of Martin Luther King Jr., even though Williams believed boycotts, marches, and self-defense worked in tandem.[14] In Williams's memoir *Negroes with Guns* (1962), the one-time NAACP president of the Monroe, North Carolina, chapter affirms the need for "flexibility in the freedom struggle" when there is a breakdown in the institutions designed to protect citizens "against lawless forces that would destroy the democratic process."[15] The BPP's rhetoric on revolutionary violence took its cue from Williams's position regarding civil rights struggle and the right to bear arms.

Armed self-defense was the Party's most controversial means for setting a social revolution in motion, but the organization also established loans, schools, and health clinics to combat poverty and revitalize black communities. Revolutionary violence and social programs were both measures to achieve the Party's ten-point platform. In the October 1966 edition of the *Black Panther Black Community News Service*, which was later titled the *Black Panther Intercommunal News Service*, the organization outlines its principles, including demands for employment, military exemption, and trials by a jury of one's peers.[16] The manifesto also acutely delivers proclamations for black humanity and citizenship: "We want land, bread, housing, education, clothing, justice and peace."[17]

The *Black Panther* was a critical part of the organization's advocacy, one that epitomizes the threat the Party posed to the state. The FBI and local law enforcement harassed members selling the newspaper and sabotaged the publication by over-inking runs and watering down shipments.[18] Joshua Bloom explicates that, as an independent black publication, the *Black Panther* was "one true window into how the Panthers saw themselves."[19] A vehicle to counter hegemonic media outlets' slander of the organization, the tabloid-sized *Black Panther* included the realist illustrations of Emory Douglas to disseminate the organization's ten-point platform. His pictorial art, often serving as the newspaper's back cover, reported on the black community's economic conditions to inspirit a black revolutionary consciousness among the urban poor.

In this vein, Douglas's iconography features male and female revolutionaries holding guns as well as community members with dignity despite their dilapidated housing and limited economic opportunities.[20] As Nicholas Lampert elucidates, Douglas's images were disbursed to "recruit members, spread Panther news and ideas, and broadcast the notion that the party had mass support in the community."[21] By the end of 1968, the *Black Panther* had a circulation of 250,000, and the BPP had 5,000 members organized into forty-five chapters across the country, including branches in New York, Chicago, New Orleans, Baltimore, Cleveland, Indianapolis, Los Angeles, Milwaukee, Winston-Salem, and Philadelphia.[22]

The BPP's central committee in Oakland inaugurated the organization's platform, but its chapters initiated varied activities in response to local needs, structures, and leadership. The Philadelphia chapter appeared in 1968 before the Party's national moratorium on new members was enacted to curtail government infiltration. In *Up South*, historian Matthew J. Countryman delineates that black Philadelphia activists began to question the effectiveness of the civil rights movement's methods, especially its reliance on legislative goals and middle-class leadership, in the mid-1960s. Black freedom struggles in the city began in the 1940s, when the advent of the New Deal inspired disenfranchised citizens' expectations for federal intervention. To rectify civil rights liberalism's failed promise of equal opportunity, black Philadelphians' postwar activism first worked to secure antidiscrimination laws through the Commission of Human Relations, which was tasked with administering the city's fair practices in regard to property, facilities, services, and employment.

In the 1950s, the public sector became accessible to African American workers, which subsequently enabled more black home ownership. However, with African American workers still barred from the private sector, black Philadelphians were excluded from the suburban expansion that moved both the industry boom and coveted new housing outside the city. Discriminating housing practices, in turn, protected the de facto boundaries segregating public schools. Philadelphia's enmeshed public structures, which produced and upheld a lack of equality in outcome, was fertile ground for the rise of Black Power.

Despite the intentions of the Commission of Human Relations, there was no structural change or serious improvements in labor, housing, or schools, especially for the city's working-class black majority. Countryman notes that in the early 1960s, frustrated black Philadelphians, such as local NAACP chapter president Cecil Moore, developed "a form of civil rights activism that—despite its similarities with the southern movement—constituted a protest movement against institutions of liberal government for failing to fulfill their commitment to substantive racial equality."[23] In conjunction with entrenched structural inequality, the commission's inability to enforce policies and sanction violations propelled activists to wield intraracial solidarity to buoy and impose the liberal reform coalition's goals. Countryman explains that black Philadelphians "sought to build organizations that were accountable solely to the black community and in which leadership was based not on professional degrees or middle-class status but on one's proximity to and ability to identify with poor and working-class blacks."[24]

Following other black activists' turn from interracial coalitions to the community partnerships, control, and accountability of Black Power, the Philadelphia chapter of the Black Panther Party gained its charter in 1969. By the spring of 1970, the chapter grew from fifteen to more than one hundred members. Although the Philadelphia Panthers promoted self-defense to counteract police brutality, they rarely employed the patrolling strategies infamously used by the Oakland Panthers.[25] Led by the chapter's minister of defense, Reggie Schell, the Philadelphia branch focused on other forms of advocacy: distributing over one hundred thousand newspapers per week, organizing demonstrations, building coalitions with other organizations, and managing several survival programs, including two breakfast programs, a library, and a medical clinic. The branch earned national prominence when the Party's central leadership selected it to host the Revolutionary People's Constitutional Convention in September of 1970.[26] Thousands attended the assembly to draft a new federal document that would redistribute wealth, ban weapons of mass destruction, and represent all of "the people"—including oppressed women, gays and lesbians, and racial minorities.[27] The convention harkened back to the 1776 Declaration of Independence and 1787 U.S. Constitution, both signed in Philadelphia.

Ironically, the decline of the city's Black Panther Party chapter began with the Revolutionary People's Constitutional Convention. Chairman Huey Newton's lack of charisma and the inaccessibility of his speech dampened the event's energy and flagged the Party's weakening national allure.[28] However, a week before the assembly, police attempted to hamper the Party's planning by raiding its offices in Germantown, North Philadelphia, and West Philadelphia in search of an assailant who murdered an officer and wounded three others in West Philadelphia. At the Party's North Philadelphia headquarters, the police forced handcuffed Party members to walk down the street in their underwear, fired a .45 caliber submachine gun above their heads, and ordered them to strip naked while reporters photographed them.[29] Schell recalled, "Most of us had been in bed, and they just ripped the goddamn clothes off everybody, women and men. They had the gun, they'd just snatch your pants down and they took pictures like that."[30] Local newspapers and the associated press circulated the photographs with Philadelphia police commissioner Frank Rizzo's boast that his department had caught the "big, bad Black Panthers with their pants down."[31] In the 1950s and 1960s, Rizzo earned a reputation for racism and harassment, and his tactics to suppress the 1970 constitutional convention anticipated the demise of the Party's Oakland chapter in the 1980s due to the FBI's Counter Intelligence Program (COINTELPRO), which planted *agents provocateurs* to stir and exploit intergroup hostility, conspired against the Panthers under false pretenses, and planned sanctioned police assassinations.[32]

In 1971 the Black Panther Party underwent a transition nationally when Newton directed the organization to focus on its survival programs in order to reduce the assaults of COINTELPRO and retain its relationship with black communities. The move caused a rift between Newton and Eldridge Cleaver, head of the International Section of the Panthers, as well as dissension between the central committee and the New York and Philadelphia chapters.[33] Whereas Cleaver increasingly promoted revolutionary violence and clandestine activities to match COINTELPRO's attacks on the Party, Newton proclaimed that the Party should devote its energies to community organizing, coalition building, and electoral politics—endeavors he believed would offset the shrinking welfare state and maintain community support. The ideological divide between these factions culminated with Newton's expulsion of Cleaver and much of the New York and Philadelphia chapters' leadership from the organization. That same year Reggie Schell, Mumia Abu-Jamal, and other former members of the Philadelphia branch formed the Black United Liberation Front, which continued the Party's breakfast and prison programs as well as gang unity initiatives. By 1973, the Philadelphia chapter had less than twenty-five members and was more or less defunct.

Among other Philadelphia organizations marshaled under Black Power, the local Black Panther Party emerged in response to postwar liberalism's failure to address the inequalities affecting the city's poor black residents, but its suppression by law enforcement, as the brute arm of the city's conservative politics, facilitated its quick decline. Countryman expounds, "[T]he failure of this urban political strategy was as much the product of urban deindustrialization and of suburban antitax politics—historical developments that can be directly traced to postwar liberalism's policy making—as it was the result of white working-class backlash against the ethnic political strategies of Black Power."[34] This white backlash, often associated with "white flight," manifested before Philadelphia's 1964 race riot, which erupted after tensions between black residents and law enforcement over police brutality escalated. For example, working- and middle-class whites' stratagem to safeguard their racial privilege in battles over busing and desegregating neighborhood public schools—as well as the violence their ploys triggered—predate the Black Power movement.[35] Because of the uncompromising violence in the BPP's rhetoric, public memory obscures its unwieldy trajectory with oversimplified narratives that discredit its aims.

Set in 1976 on the eve of the Declaration of Independence's bicentennial, *Night Catches Us* demonstrates that black liberation is still out of reach. The film takes place six years after the Revolutionary People's Constitutional Convention, when the neighborhood Party branch is already gone. Local law enforcement undermined the chapter with wiretaps and extralegal threats to incite conflicts among its rank and file. The narrative opens, then, with the Wilson family fixed in debilitating cycles of mourning. The film depicts the structural inequalities that make lore about the Party's armed struggle appealing to Jimmy, who is fatherless and disenfranchised, with no prospects for employment, education, or training. It also recognizes the neighborhood's economic vulnerability with Patricia's efforts to feed children, provide legal aid, and host bail fundraising drives. *Night Catches Us* captures the Party's commonly slighted cause, ideology, and strategies as well as the battle fatigue that continues to incapacitate Patricia and Marcus. Yet, it is Iris's suppressed childhood that makes this silenced history most palpable. The film intimates that the family cannot thrive while this past remains repressed.

Imagining New Historiographies

Drawing upon archival images of the Black Panther Party, Hamilton authenticates the grim realism of *Night Catches Us* and offers viewers a melancholic portrait of the organization's purpose and goals. She initiates this grief in the film's opening credits, which recall the BPP's objectives visualized in Emory Douglas's art. His combination of illustrations and recycled photographs document the structural inequities the Party sought to address with its advocacy via grocery giveaways and editions of the *Black Panther*. The graphics also evidence the FBI's suppression of the BPP with an image exalting the martyred figure Fred Hampton, the deputy chairman of the Illinois chapter killed in his sleep during a police raid in Chicago in 1969. The opening credits establish the toll COINTELPRO takes on the Panthers and their survival programs instead of the violence for which they largely are remembered.

Douglas's most well-known graphics are of the corrupt cops who violate black communities, but a significant amount of his work depicts the Party's free breakfast programs and health clinics, which dominated covers of the newspaper after the organization's 1971 ideological shift. For example, a provocative 1967 drawing features a "pig" with its head bandaged and its hoof in a sling while it leans on a crutch surrounded by flies. The accompanying text expounds that the "pig" is "a low natured beast that has no regard for law, justice, or the rights of people . . . a foul, depraved traducer, usually masquerading as the victim of an unprovoked attack."[36] This rhetoric saturates popular memory of the organization rather than Douglas's depictions of African Americans' oppression and perseverance. Beyond profiles of Newton and Seale, Douglas's pictures call attention to the everyday agents of Black Power: the black women that catch rats in their run-down homes yet sing triumphantly; the black men who return from Vietnam to battle drug abuse; and the impoverished black children laughing despite their circumstances. The Panthers are "SERVANTS OF THE PEOPLE" comprehensively attending to the community's "BODY AND SOUL" (chapter 12 frontispiece).

Hamilton's narrative evokes Douglas's vernacular aesthetic by highlighting the Black Panther Party's rank and file, but her representation of the organization's downturn confirms that northern black freedom struggles are not resolved for "the people" it served. *Night Catches Us* implicates sardonic revolutionaries, former Panthers who become gun-runners for neighborhood gangs, as well as the pale remnants of their community programs, manifest in Patricia's extended work to feed neighborhood children. In addition to the physical and emotional damage police brutality wreaks on black men, the FBI's suppression reaps long-term emotional and economic hardships for black women and children. Making the connection between causality and casualty concrete, Hamilton creates a layered narrative, in which the present-day plot is interrupted by images from a historical archive that punctuate the drama's three acts. These series of images signal that the film's present follows the BPP's historical trajectory. Hamilton's visual historiography counterbalances the Panthers' suppression in public memory.

The narrative interruptions occur at pivotal moments in the film's melancholic portrait of the family. The first time it happens, Iris discovers photographs of Malcolm X and Fidel Castro among those of her parents and Marcus. The interruption here is not due to a personal flashback or shared anecdote, but an unwritten visual history of the BPP. Patricia initially refuses to tell a curious Iris about her father, and when she invites Marcus to move into their household she warns, "[W]e don't talk about the past, it's too painful."[37] However as Patricia and Marcus grow closer, Hamilton displays the Party's activism with video footage of rallies and photographic stills of "Free Huey" buttons. Finally, when Patricia's nephew Jimmy resuscitates the Party's rhetoric by declaring "war" on the "pigs" and throwing up the Black Power fist, Hamilton includes video footage of Party members exhibiting the same gesture at Fred Hampton's funeral. Images of Party members mourning the chapter leader foreshadow the demise of Jimmy, who suffers a slow social death until police kill him for murdering a policeman.

While *Night Catches Us* engages the national history of the Party, Hamilton represents the local branch's devastation by recreating a photograph of Philadelphia members arrested in their underwear shortly before the Revolutionary People's Constitutional Convention. She stages a scene in which white officers detain and strip Marcus and his former comrades after a bar fight. The officers demand that Marcus and DoRight, a rival played by Jamie Hector, sit shirtless and handcuffed on a street curb until a higher-ranking black officer, Detective David Gordon, played by Wendell Pierce, reminds them that such treatment is extralegal. With the scene, Hamilton reveals the gross police misconduct targeting black communities. In this moment Jim Crow is not invisible but exhibited in its ritualistic subjection, and the film's representation of police brutality after the civil rights movement's legislative accomplishments should resonate with twenty-first-century audiences who continue to witness such abuses. Nonetheless, Hamilton's cinematography stays in the historical moment by displaying vulnerable black male bodies that are realistically lean and supple instead of the hard and chiseled physiques characteristic of contemporary male actors, whom audiences might deem inviolable.[38] In this way, Hamilton visually codifies the specificity of her historiography in the context of location and period.

Notably, Hamilton's nods to historical events diverge from local events when Night Catches Us delves into the chapter's gender politics. According to Countryman's reading of Mumia Abu-Jamal's memoir, the Philadelphia chapter was "a bastion of male dominance" that had neither female founders nor female officers.[39] However, in Night Catches Us, Patricia exemplifies black women's leadership in the Party's survival programs as well as their continued community work after the organization's dissolution. In her essay "'No One Ever Asks What a Man's Role in the Revolution Is,'" Matthews complicates blanket indictments of the BPP's misogyny, as she observes that its ideology and practice in regard to gender depended on the chapter and its personnel makeup as well as the specific period in the organization's history. Thus, her work documents sexism in various BPP chapters while highlighting "the disparities between [masculinist] Party rhetoric and the concrete reality of [cooperative] daily working and living arrangements" that regularly existed between female and male members in various branches.[40] Jakobi Williams duly explains that the Oakland chapter enabled collective parenting while black women's membership in the Illinois chapter "violated their duty as mothers" because leadership expected their full-time commitment without any options for childcare.[41]

Although black women had critical positions in several BPP chapters, just as they did in the civil rights and Black Power movements' countless organizations, the metaphor of reaching manhood was often used to describe the respect and self-confidence African Americans collectively gained during the era. Such language affirmed black personhood, but literary scholar Erica R. Edwards points out that the spectacle of the charismatic black male leader enacted its own symbolic violence by subordinating black women's activism in historical fictions.[42] Countryman discloses that in Philadelphia, "[T]he more effective challenge to Frank Rizzo's violent version of law enforcement came from a network of community-based activists organized and led by [Mary Rouse,] a working-class middle-aged woman."[43] In *Night Catches Us*, Patricia's advocacy reflects the organization's uneven gender relations nationally in lieu of the Philadelphia chapter's trends.

Hamilton also maps the organization's changing position on revolutionary violence onto the family's drama along gendered battle lines—with Patricia's husband and nephew symbolizing her extreme opposition in the conflict. In addition to organizing fundraisers for defendants, Patricia's legal career echoes the *Black Panther*'s "pocket lawyer," which readers cut out of the newspaper and carried with them as a quick guide to "legal first aid."[44] Patricia's interventions have obvious benefits, but her devotion to such activism creates a gendered problematic: fostering the black community's livelihood comes at the cost of her daughter. Marcus criticizes that Patricia is so busy feeding the neighborhood that she neglects Iris. What is more, Detective Gordon opines that she has lost her way because she takes advantage of legal technicalities to free old comrades who distribute guns to black youth, a corruption of some BPP chapters' efforts to politicize street gangs.[45] The film visually reveals its ambivalence about Patricia's decisions when, in an emotional scene, Iris discovers that their home's peeling wallpaper hides the bloodstains from her father's shooting. Patricia shields Iris from the ugly truth about Neil's murder—that she, not Marcus, made decisions leading to his death—but she also raises Iris in the very home in which he was killed.

Whereas Patricia's politics echo Newton's proclamation that the Party should focus on its survival programs, Neil's stance on revolutionary violence represents the subversive actions Cleaver endorsed to respond to COINTELPRO. Neil is angry and disillusioned after the murder of two comrades, and he murders a police officer in retaliation. The police arrest and threaten Patricia with the possibility of losing custody of Iris, so she gives up her comrade and husband to save her child. Qualifying that premeditated manslaughter was never the Party's objective, Patricia leads Iris to believe that Neil was an avenging hero, and she allows Marcus to take the blame for naming him as the slain officer's shooter. Her deception blurs her mores in ways that continue to reverberate for the family and its understanding of the Party. For Patricia, Neil is collateral damage in ensuring the family's salvation, but this truth's suppression undermines the family's domestic space, as both Iris and Jimmy are kept in the dark by the custodian of this history.

Like Neil, Jimmy's character registers the Jim Crow North's oppression of black communities and its violent repercussions. With no economic prospects beyond the limited money he makes recycling refuse for "the man," Jimmy represents deindustrialized Philadelphia's structural inequality. He is disaffected further when the police arrest him, beat him, and charge him a fine because he resists capitulating to them. Syl Johnson's classic hard soul song "Is It Because I'm Black?" (1969) underscores a poignant scene in which Jimmy evades the police and practices shooting a gun. The song's titular question heightens Jimmy's desperation among abandoned buildings by critiquing institutional racism's deferment of his aggregate dreams. Johnson's song and the camera's composition of the city's postindustrial vistas lament Jimmy's frustrations. *Night Catches Us* climactically ends his struggle with his death, which implies the ineffectiveness of retaliatory violence.

The film implies that Jimmy's death is due as much to his misunderstanding of the Party's objectives as it is to the police's extralegal tactics. His knowledge of the Party's politics is based on the few, misleading facts he knows about his uncle's murder. He is aware of the Party's heated rhetoric, which often professed masculinist notions of protest, but he is ignorant of its survival programs and female leadership. Thus, Jimmy's wounded psyche, on the verge of manhood, is beguiled by a children's coloring book, a bogus copy of print media immortalizing the hypermasculine image of the Panthers deployed by *agents provocateurs*. The FBI devised and distributed such materials to alienate the organization from sponsors and parents participating in its breakfast programs. Animated in a cartoon sequence that disrupts the realism of *Night Catches Us*, the counterfeit comic portrays the Panthers as hate mongers encouraging black children to use guns and knives to initiate confrontations with police officers, who in turn are characterized in the coloring book as cartoonish pigs assaulted by black communities. Ward Churchill posits that the BPP's central committee decided such violent graphics were inappropriate for children, but *agents provocateurs* circulated copies of analogous materials in order to demonize the organization. Jimmy grapples with this concealed history about COINTELPRO and the Panthers' iconic hypermasculine image, which transcends the Party's self-construction. When Marcus informs him that the comic is an FBI conspiracy, Jimmy distrusts Marcus because he resents Marcus's patriarchal authority in Patricia's home. Deluded by the comics, the teenager dons the sartorial signifiers of the vanguard—a leather jacket, beret, and gun—and starts brushes with the police that lead him to commit murder and culminate in his death. With Jimmy's character, Hamilton stresses the importance of discerning the BPP's misrepresentation in hegemonic media and its glamorization in black cultural imaginations.

Hamilton contrasts Jimmy's susceptibility to his younger cousin's hyperawareness of the past to explore how state suppression affects the dominant narrative history of the organization. While Patricia and Marcus struggle to contend with their trauma, Jimmy pays the price for their omissions. The family's trauma, of which Iris is mostly ignorant, also hurts her emotionally. The perils of the movement are immediate for her, as there is no separation between the past and present in her childhood. She matter-of-factly informs Marcus that the FBI still taps the family's phones and that ghosts are "all around us . . . they're everywhere." When she tears down the wallpaper masking the foyer's blood-stained plaster, she struggles to come to a critical awareness of the past. Whether it is the police violence that kills her father or the secrets that preoccupy her mother, Iris's lack of knowledge is a result of the myths perpetuated within and outside of the Party. Marcus and Patricia's forlorn romance reiterates these silences' impact on the rank and file's personal lives. The archetypal black family—like the surrounding community and local chapter—is not reconstituted by the film's end.

Home after the War

In *Night Catches Us*, Hamilton employs the family's home to stage the Black Panther Party's gender politics, as the divide between violence and programs, and the breakdown between surviving and thriving, is gendered in the film. With a history that includes the trans-Atlantic slave trade and northern and western migration, African Americans' relationship to the concept of home is taxed further during late-twentieth-century black freedom struggles. In the documentary *Negroes with Guns*, Robert Williams's wife, Mabel, recalls his desire to return to the United States after eight years of exile in Cuba and China. She shares that he expressed his desire "to have in our race somebody who struggled against a system and went home to Mount Vernon."[46]

Fleeing the United States to resist being railroaded for false kidnapping charges, Williams drew on the memory of a founding father and plantation estate to convey his longing for an end to his displacement. In Hamilton's melancholic narrative, the country, city, and house are contested spaces. Marcus returns to Philadelphia after his chapter expulsion and imprisonment to settle his affairs following his father's death. His arrival forces Patricia to confront the chapter's history, but their budding romance does not liberate her from this past trauma. The family home sits at the interstices of their political goals and emotional needs, wherein the stalled social movement delays their personal liberation.

The couple's differing perspectives on the house prevent them from creating a viable domestic space together. Patricia turns down Marcus's invitation to leave Philadelphia after he accepts an out-of-town job. "We're never gonna be happy here," he tells her, but she remains rooted to the location of her family's trauma. Patricia's decision to stay in the home suggests that this history has debilitated her. Marcus assures her that she can call him "whenever she's ready," but the film's melancholic tone implies that she will never leave her house and progress their romance. Unable to embrace a future with him, Patricia survives the Philadelphia black freedom struggle's violence, but she does not thrive in its aftermath. She is active in the community, but she has not recovered from her personal loss or the chapter's demise.

On the contrary, Marcus lives, recovers, and transcends, as he balances the reclamation of history with its forfeiture. In the film's closing moments, he walks away from the house toward the Cadillac Eldorado he has inherited from his father. The extreme wide camera shot positions him in relation to the neighborhood and establishes his emotional reconnection. The closing song, "How I Got Over" (2010) by Philadelphia native sons The Roots, a contemporary hip-hop and neo-soul band that somberly scores the entire film, rousingly announces Marcus's imminent well-being. Moreover, "How I Got Over" sonically merges Marcus's soul past and the audience's hip-hop-infused present, as he presumably heads toward a more liberating future. His leaving is reminiscent of a type of mobility with which men have historically been privileged, but it also suggests that Patricia's home is irreparable. Marcus benefits from emotional growth, if not romantic coupling or social progress. His departure signals that he has coped with the past and moved beyond its melancholic preoccupations.

By contesting popular historical narratives about the Black Panther Party, *Night Catches Us* interrogates the narrow ways public memory engages the organization's history—especially in regard to its political power and emotional weight. The film's title alludes to the allegorical end, the "night," that catches up with its characters. Yet Hamilton denies her audience romanticized closure in regard to the question of the Black Power movement's legacy for its participants and successors. By visualizing blacks' systemic oppression, recounting the Party's survival programs, complicating its gender politics, attesting to its suppression, and conceding the personal costs of its struggle, *Night Catches Us* grieves the cultural, economic, and political vestiges left in the wake of the organization's passing. However, the film neither mythologizes the Black Power era nor rarefies the Black Panther Party.

The film's narrative resistance is important for post–civil rights audiences' discernment of this history given public memory's proclivity for sanitizing twentieth-century black freedom struggles. As Herman Gray reminds, film, television, documentary, advertising, and music "are the chief means by which memory, history, and experience of the past become part of the common sense understanding of the present."[47] Popular cultural texts repeatedly render the civil rights movement's fight against the Jim Crow South as a success in order to confirm today's social progress. These familiar historical narratives locate racial oppression firmly in the past and portray the movement as an ideological consensus aligned with long-held American ideals. However, public memory holds no self-congratulatory narratives about the Black Power movement's struggle against the Jim Crow North. Popular historical discourse regularly represents it as a failed campaign with a flawed ideology and untenable strategies. Public memory is uncomfortable with the movement because the conditions sparking it are not fixed in the past but still unfolding in the present, as contemporary police brutality, segregated public schools, and economically devastated black communities evidence.

The movement's most cogent historical narratives, such as *Night Catches Us*, are irreconcilably melancholic because its ambitions await realization. Such cultural texts wrestle with history to promote the utility of past experience and convene shared insight. Similarly, public memory must contend with the Jim Crow North precisely because of its unsettling history.

NOTES

1 Several studies address inaccurate, dismissive, and limited approaches to the organization: Charles E. Jones, ed., *The Black Panther Party Reconsidered* (Baltimore, MD: Black Classic Press, 1998); Jama Lazerow and Yohuru Williams, eds., *In Search of the Black Panther Party: New Perspectives on a Revolutionary Movement* (Durham, NC: Duke University Press, 2006); Joshua Bloom and Waldo E. Martin Jr., *Black against Empire: The History and Politics of the Black Panther Party* (Berkeley: University of California Press, 2013); Jakobi Williams, *From the Bullet to the Ballot: The Illinois Chapter of the Black Panther Party and Racial Coalition Politics in Chicago* (Chapel Hill: University of North Carolina Press, 2013); Bryan Shih and Yohuru Williams, eds., *The Black Panthers: Portraits from an Unfinished Revolution* (New York: Nation Books, 2016); and Robyn C. Spencer, *The Revolution Has Come: Black Power, Gender, and the Black Panther Party in Oakland* (Durham, NC: Duke University Press, 2016).

2 Anne Anlin Cheng, *The Melancholy of Race: Psychoanalysis, Assimilation, and Hidden Grief* (New York: Oxford University Press, 2001), 133.

3 Tracye A. Matthews, "'No One Ever Asks What a Man's Role in the Revolution Is': Gender Politics and Leadership in the Black Panther Party, 1966–71," in *Sisters in the Struggle: African American Women in the Civil Rights–Black Power Movement*, eds. Bettye Collier-Thomas and V. P. Franklin (New York: NYU Press, 2001), 231.

4 *Panther*, dir. Mario Van Peebles (Universal City, CA: Gramercy Pictures, 1995).

5 Mario Van Peebles, Ula Y. Taylor, and J. Tarika Lewis, *Panther: A Pictorial History of the Black Panthers and the Story behind the Film* (New York: New Market Press, 1995), 140.

6 *Ibid.*, 146.

7 Jane Rhodes, *Framing the Black Panthers: The Spectacular Rise of a Black Power Icon* (New York: New Press, 2007), 16.

8 Van Peebles, Taylor, and Lewis, *Panther*, 128.

9 The film also suggests the betrayal of the black middle class and inadequacy of electoral politics with Patricia's short-lived relationship with a local politician. This is another common way the Black Power movement is remembered.

10 Robert G. O'Meally, "On Burke and the Vernacular: Ralph Ellison's Boomerang of History," in *History and Memory in African American Culture*, eds. Geneviève Fabre and Robert G. O'Meally (New York: Oxford University Press, 1994), 245.

11 In addition to Motown, the Philly sound, and Chicago's Curtis Mayfield, Memphis's Stax Records produced memorable soul artists, including Isaac Hayes. Robert Pruter, *Chicago Soul* (Urbana: University of Illinois Press, 1991).

12 Betsy Sharkey, "Tanya Hamilton's 'Night Catches Us' Captures a Point in Time," *Los Angeles Times* (January 26, 2010), http://articles.latimes.com.

13 A. O. Scott, "Radical Actions of the '60s, Reverberating in the Reflective '70s," *New York Times,* December 2, 2010.

14 Timothy B. Tyson, "Robert F. Williams, 'Black Power,' and the Roots of the African American Freedom Struggle," *Journal of American History* 85, no. 2 (1998): 541.

15 Robert F. Williams, *Negroes with Guns* (New York: Marzani & Munsell, 1962), 40.

16 The change in the publication's title heralds the Party's efforts to tie U.S. black freedom struggles to global decolonizing projects. Elaine Brown, "The Significance of the Newspaper of the Black Panther Party," in *The Black Panther: Intercommunal News Service, 1967–1980,* ed. David Hilliard (New York: Atria Books, 2007), x–xi.

17 "Black Panther Party Platform and Program: What We Want, What We Believe," *Black Panther Community News Service,* October 1966, in *The Black Panthers Speak,* ed. Philip S. Foner (New York: Lippincott, 1970), 3.

18 David Hilliard, preface to *The Black Panther: Intercommunal News Service, 1967–1980* (New York: Atria Books, 2007), viii.

19 Joshua Bloom, "If You Can Get Your Hands on Copies of the Black Panther Newspaper," in *The Black Panther: Intercommunal News Service, 1967–1980,* ed. David Hilliard (New York: Atria Books, 2007), xxi.

20 Colette Gaiter, "What Revolution Looks Like: The Work of Black Panther Artist Emory Douglas," in *Black Panther: The Revolutionary Art of Emory Douglas,* ed. Sam Durant (New York: Rizzoli, 2014), 93–109.

21 Nicholas Lampert, "Party Artist: Emory Douglas and the Black Panther Party," in *A People's Art History of the United States: 250 Years of Activist Art and Artists Working in Social Justice Movements* (New York: New Press, 2013), 204.

22 Christopher Murray, "Black Panther Party for Self-Defense," in *Encyclopedia of Black Studies,* eds. Molefi Kete Asante and Ama Mazama (Thousand Oaks, CA: Sage, 2005), 135; Judson L. Jeffries and Ryan Nissim-Sabat, "Introduction: Painting a More Complete Portrait of the Black Panther Party," in *Comrades: A Local History of the Black Panther Party,* ed. Judson L. Jefferies (Bloomington: Indiana University Press, 2007), 7.

23 Matthew J. Countryman, *Up South: Civil Rights and Black Power in Philadelphia* (Philadelphia: University of Pennsylvania Press, 2006), 6. Cecil Moore synthesized nationalist themes to protest employment discrimination and segregated schools.

24 Countryman, *Up South,* 8.

25 *Ibid.,* 287.

26 *Ibid.,* 289.

27 Omari L. Dyson, Kevin L. Brooks, and Judson L. Jefferies, "'Brotherly Love Can Kill You': The Philadelphia Branch of the Black Panther Party," in *Comrades: A Local History of the Black Panther Party*, ed. Judson L. Jefferies (Bloomington: Indiana University Press, 2007), 223–28.

28 George Katsiaficas recalls that Newton, who was recently released from prison, was unfamiliar to audiences beyond his writings and the media coverage of his trial. George Katsiaficas, "Organization and Movement: The Case of the Black Panther Party and the Revolutionary People's Constitutional Convention of 1970," in *Liberation, Imagination, and the Black Panther Party*, eds. Kathleen Cleaver and George Katsiaficas (New York: Routledge, 2001), 147–48.

29 Dyson, Brooks, Jefferies, "'Brotherly Love Can Kill You,'" 242.

30 Countryman, *Up South*, 282–83.

31 Katsiaficas, "Organization and Movement," 145.

32 Ward Churchill documents that roughly thirty black men in their twenties were the victims of "police-induced fatalities" between 1968, the year of the Party's peak, and 1971, the year of its shift in focus. Ward Churchill, "'To Disrupt, Discredit, and Destroy': The FBI's Secret War against the Black Panther Party," in *Liberation, Imagination, and the Black Panther Party*, eds. Kathleen Cleaver and George Katsiaficas (New York: Routledge, 2001), 109.

33 Countryman, *Up South*, 289. In 1972, the BPP's central leadership called key members from local chapters to its Oakland headquarters to work on Bobby Seale's and Elaine Brown's political campaigns. Paul Alkebulan dates the BPP's national demise to the early 1980s when Newton's legal troubles contributed to the organization's negative reputation, membership dwindled to twenty-seven members, and the Party closed its last community school. Paul Alkebulan, *Survival Pending Revolution: The History of the Black Panther Party* (Tuscaloosa: University of Alabama Press, 2007).

34 Countryman, *Up South*, 9.

35 *Ibid.*, 255.

36 Emory Douglas, *Black Panther: The Revolutionary Art of Emory Douglas*, ed. Sam Durant (New York: Rizzoli, 2014), 28.

37 *Night Catches Us*, dir. Tanya Hamilton (New York: Magnolia Pictures, 2010).

38 I would like to thank Charles Swanson for mentioning this subtle detail.

39 Countryman, *Up South*, 258.

40 Matthews, "'No One Ever Asks What a Man's Role in the Revolution Is,'" 243.

41 Jakobi Williams, "'Don't No Woman Have to Do Nothing She Don't Want to Do': Gender, Activism, and the Illinois Black Panther Party," *Black Women, Gender + Families* 6, no. 2 (2012): 44.

42 Erica R. Edwards, *Charisma and the Fictions of Black Leadership* (Minneapolis: University of Minnesota Press, 2012).

43 Countryman, *Up South*, 283. Mary Rouse led the Council of Organizations on Philadelphia Police Accountability and Responsibility (COPPAR), which included the BPP among other organizations.

44 "Pocket Lawyer of Legal First Aid," *Black Panther Black Community News Service*, March 23, 1969, in *The Black Panthers Speak*, ed. Philip S. Foner (New York: Lippincott, 1970), 176.

45 Dyson, Brooks, and Jefferies, "'Brotherly Love Can Kill You,'" 228.

46 *Negroes with Guns: Rob Williams and Black Power*, dirs. Sandra Dickson and Churchill Roberts (New York: Films Media Group, 2005).

47 Herman Gray, "Remembering Civil Rights: Television, Memory, and the 1960s," in *The Revolution Wasn't Televised: Sixties Television and Social Conflict*, eds. Lynn Spigel and Michael Curtain (New York: Routledge, 1997), 350–51.

ACKNOWLEDGMENTS

This book began as a 2015 NEH Summer Faculty Seminar, "Rethinking Black Freedom Studies in the Jim Crow North," that Komozi Woodard and Jeanne Theoharis directed. Despite a growing group of researchers on segregation and black struggle outside of the South, most scholars had pushed forward on their own without sustained support from other researchers who were experts on the North. Many had told us they longed for space dedicated to bringing together researchers on the North. The NEH seminar was the culmination of those desires. It created a community where scholars working on the North could read, discuss, and workshop drafts of articles, book proposals, and chapters. Brian Purnell participated in the seminar as a guest lecturer. The synergy of ideas in those two weeks proved profound and inspirational. Out of that came the idea for an anthology. Brian offered to host a symposium at Bowdoin College to bring us together again to continue the work of honing our ideas. In September 2016, we spent a weekend in Maine doing just that.

We are very grateful to the National Endowment for the Humanities, especially Richard Pettit, for recognizing and supporting the need for a faculty seminar on the northern black freedom struggle. Deep thanks go to Sarah Lawrence College, particularly Fred Baumgarten, Rosemary Weeks, Karen Lawrence, and the indefatigable Taylor Smith, for hosting the seminar and working so hard to make the seminar such a success. It was extraordinary to get to spend two weeks delving into the Black Freedom Struggle outside of the South. Ujju Aggarwal, Stefan Bradley, Natanya Duncan, Hasan Jeffries, Verdis Robinson, and Lynnell Thomas, all members of the seminar, have left their considerable mark on this volume. Matthew Delmont, Clarence Taylor, Eric Gellman, and Karen Miller presented guest lectures that helped frame the seminar's intellectual approach and connections to contemporary political and social issues.

We are grateful for the grant from Bowdoin College's Faculty Symposia Program, administered by the office of the Dean of Academic Affairs, and the college's special events office. Jennifer Scanlon's support of this project proved crucial. In September 2016, as Bowdoin's interim dean of academic affairs, Jen funded a symposium ("The Strange Career of Jim Crow, North and West") that brought the authors in this anthology to Brunswick, Maine, for public presentations of their papers, and an all-day workshop. That two-day symposium and workshop gave us time and space to fine tune these pieces for publication and grapple with the larger ideas that animate this volume. Sherrie Randolph, Jen Scanlon, and Jeanne Theoharis kicked off that event with an energetic and memorable roundtable discussion on the lives and activism of three phenomenal Black women: Florence Kennedy, Anna Arnold Hedgemen, and Rosa Parks. Judith Casselberry, associate professor of Africana Studies at Bowdoin College, moderated their discussion and contributed her brilliance to the conversation. Michelle Morin's work in the Bowdoin events office made all the events and logistics associated with the symposium a success. We could not have done this anthology without our time at Bowdoin.

Clara Platter and Amy Klopfenstein at NYU Press shepherded the project from proposal to publication. Edited volumes like this one exist only because a press—usually a press that publishes books by scholars and academics—devotes money and labor to its production and marketing. Historical anthologies bring together different scholarly voices, showcase new research, and advance innovative interpretations. They are important ways to review, critique, and develop historiography. We are very thankful that NYU Press decided to publish the scholarship in this book, and that Clara and Amy invested their vision, labor, and creativity into its creation. Emily Wright's careful copyedits, Alexia Traganas's attentiveness during production, and Saned Diaz's diligent indexing helped complete the book.

In a profession that does not always value collaborative efforts, these years working on this book have demonstrated how much more powerful our ideas and interventions can be made when they are accomplished collectively. We are grateful for the community of scholars that created this anthology, namely, the authors who drafted and revised and rewrote and tweaked and edited their essays. Along the way, they pushed and supported each other—and us—with care and professionalism. They offer a model for how to advance scholarship through collective, communal commitment.

Finally, a deep note of thanks goes to Komozi Woodard for his political vision, intellectual intrepidness, and collective spirit. Komozi's work on Newark helped pioneer this field. He embodies an ethos of collectivity and communal solidarity, brought from his life and long-time work in Black social movements, that has informed two decades of often-unsung commitment to mentoring project after project on the North into fruition. Undergraduate and graduate students, and new and midcareer scholars galore, owe a great debt of thanks to Komozi's generosity and labor. For us, his friendship, tremendous insight, and huge heart have proved essential to sustaining our dedication to this project's completion.

ABOUT THE EDITORS

Brian Purnell is Geoffrey Canada Associate Professor of Africana Studies and History at Bowdoin College and the author of *Fighting Jim Crow in the County of Kings: The Congress of Racial Equality in Brooklyn* (2013).

Jeanne Theoharis is Distinguished Professor of Political Science at Brooklyn College of CUNY. She is author and editor of numerous books, including *The Rebellious Life of Mrs. Rosa Parks* (2013) and *A More Beautiful and Terrible History: The Uses and Misuses of Civil Rights History* (2018).

ABOUT THE CONTRIBUTORS

Mary Barr is an Assistant Professor of Sociology at Kentucky State University and the author of *Friends Disappear: The Battle for Racial Equality in Evanston* (2014).

Balthazar I. Beckett is Assistant Professor with the Department of English and Comparative Literature at the American University in Cairo. He holds a PhD from the City University of New York, Graduate Center, and his work has appeared in *Callaloo: A Journal of African Diaspora Arts and Letters* and *South Atlantic Review.*

Say Burgin is Assistant Professor of History at Dickinson College. Her articles have appeared in *Journal of American Studies, Women's History Review, Journal of International Women's Studies,* and *Critical Race and Whiteness Studies.*

Kristopher Bryan Burrell is Assistant Professor in the Behavioral and Social Sciences Department at Hostos Community College in New York. His articles have appeared in *Western Journal of Black Studies, Radical Teacher Magazine,* and *Encyclopedia of American Urban History.*

Tahir H. Butt is a PhD Candidate in Urban Education at the Graduate Center, CUNY.

Aliyah Dunn-Salahuddin is a Faculty Instructor in the Departments of African American Studies and History at the City College of San Francisco.

Ayesha K. Hardison is Associate Professor in the Departments of English and Women, Gender, and Sexuality Studies at the University of

Kansas. She is author of *Writing through Jane Crow: Race and Gender Politics in African American Literature* (2014).

Laura Warren Hill is Associate Professor of History and Africana Studies at Bloomfield College and co-editor of *The Business of Black Power: Community Development, Capitalism, and Corporate Responsibility in Postwar America* (with Julia Rabig, 2012).

Shannon King is Associate Professor of History at the College of Wooster and author of *Whose Harlem Is This, Anyway? Community Politics and Grassroots Activism during the New Negro Era* (NYU Press, 2015).

Peter B. Levy is Professor of History at York College. He is author and editor of numerous books, including *The Great Uprising: Race Riots in Urban America during the 1960s* (2018) and *The Seedtime, the Work, and the Harvest: New Perspectives on the Black Freedom Struggle* (with Jeffrey Littlejohn and Reginald Ellis, 2018).

Crystal Marie Moten is Assistant Professor in the Department of History at Macalester College. Her articles have appeared in *Icons of Black America*, *Journal of Civil and Human Rights*, and *Souls: A Critical Journal of Black Politics, Culture, and Society*.

John S. Portlock is a PhD candidate in American History at the University of Rochester. His dissertation studies black antiwar activism and the modern civil rights movement.

Komozi Woodard is Professor of History, Urban Studies, Public Policy, and Africana Studies at Sarah Lawrence College. He is author and co-editor of numerous books, including *A Nation within a Nation: Amiri Baraka (LeRoi Jones) and Black Power Politics* (1999) and *Want to Start a Revolution: Radical Women in the Black Freedom Struggle* (with Dayo Gore and Jeanne Theoharis, NYU Press, 2009).

INDEX